Movies & Mental Illness

Movies & Mental Illness

Using Films to Understand Psychopathology

Danny Wedding
Missouri Institute of Mental Health
School of Medicine
University of Missouri-Columbia

Mary Ann Boyd
School of Nursing
Southern Illinois University at Edwardsville

 **McGraw-Hill College**

Boston   Burr Ridge, IL   Dubuque, IA   Madison, WI   New York   San Francisco   St. Louis
Bangkok   Bogotá   Caracas   Lisbon   London   Madrid
Mexico City   Milan   New Delhi   Seoul   Singapore   Sydney   Taipei   Toronto

McGraw-Hill College

*A Division of The **McGraw-Hill** Companies*

MOVIES & MENTAL ILLNESS: USING FILMS TO UNDERSTAND
PSYCHOPATHOLOGY

 This book is printed on recycled, acid-free paper containing 10% postconsumer waste.

2 3 4 5 6 7 8 9 0 QPD/QPD 9 3 2 1 0 9 8

ISBN 0–07–068990–3

Editorial director: *Jane E. Vaicunas*
Senior sponsoring editor: *Joseph Terry*
Developmental editor: *Susan Kunchandy*
Senior marketing manager: *James Rozsa*
Senior project manager: *Jayne Klein*
Senior production supervisor: *Mary E. Haas*
Coordinator of freelance design: *Michelle D. Whitaker*
Typeface: *11/13 Times Roman*
Printer: *Quebecor Printing Book Group/Dubuque, IA*

Cover designer: *Nicole Dean*
Cover image: *© 1997 TriStar Pictures/The Kobal Collection*

Library of Congress Cataloging-in-Publication Data

Wedding, Danny.
    Movies & mental illness : using films to understand
psychopathology / Danny Wedding, Mary Ann Boyd. — 1ˢᵗ ed.
      p. cm.
    Includes bibliographical references and index.
    ISBN 0–07–068990–3
    1.   Psychology, Pathological —Study and teaching—Audio-visual
aids. 2. Mental illness in motion pictures. I. Boyd. M. (Mary
Ann) II. Title.
RC459.W43   1999
616.89—dc21   98–38002
                                                      CIP

www.mhhe.com

Dedication

For Lester R. Bryant, MD, ScD
Dean, School of Medicine
University of Missouri-Columbia
Mentor, model, scholar, friend.
DW

For Jim
My viewing partner.
MAB

TABLE OF CONTENTS

Foreword

John Milton, in *Paradise Lost*, tells us that we must "strike the visual nerve, for we have much to see." So, too, in this present work, do Wedding and Boyd admonish us that there is much to learn by seeing with the mind's eye what these well-chosen films, by turns sad and silly, offer us in illuminating the psychopathologies set forth in the *Diagnostic and Statistical Manual* of the American Psychiatric Association.

Ranging from such classics as the depiction of alcoholism in *Lost Weekend*, to relatively obscure films perhaps known only to the aficionado of foreign films, Wedding and Boyd have achieved a work which may itself become a classic in this genre, particularly with respect to its intended purpose of teaching how the various psychopathologies might play themselves out in an approximation of real-life, real-world situations of which these films are a simulacrum.

Wedding and Boyd provide a brief synopsis of the particular film in relation to the major category of psychopathology being covered in a chapter, and they relate the manifest and latent content of the film to the various diagnostic symptoms within a category, such as childhood disorders, and further provide an illustrative case study to assist in the process of generalizing from the film to actual diagnostic work.

As a didactic tool, the work by Wedding and Boyd should have a salutary effect in engaging the attention of the student, as well as in engaging the affective response of the student to the vicarious identification with the film characters portrayed and, hopefully, enhancing the learning process of what otherwise tends to be a rather tedious pedagogical adventure for most students.

The authors provide a lively expository style, and the use of epigraphs for each chapter is a particularly happy device for setting a tone for each chapter and for capturing a pithy bit of dialogue that may cause the reader to engage in some cognitive restructuring, as when one of the characters says, "I recall every fall, every hook, every jab" in the chapter on the dementias, a quote which instantly evokes an image of the prizefighter with organic brain damage. Other such examples abound and contribute significantly to the teaching potential of the work.

On balance, this is a work that is likely to become a classic of its type and a particularly useful teaching tool for the diagnosis and understanding of the various psychopathologies for students of the helping professions. I commend it to the reader, be the reader student or professor.

Allan Barclay, PhD
St. Louis, MO

Preface

We wrote *Movies and Mental Illness* because of our conviction that films are a powerful medium for teaching students in psychology, social work, medicine, nursing, and counseling about the fascinating world of psychopathology. Both authors love movies, and we believe we have been able to enrich the classes we teach by sharing this passion with our students.

The book is designed to supplement a core text in abnormal psychology and psychopathology, and the relevant core chapters in the primary text should be read *before* reviewing the corresponding chapter in *Movies and Mental Illness*. In addition, we recommend viewing the films selected by the class instructor after reading the relevant core chapter, but before reading the corresponding chapter in this book. (However, it will almost always be helpful to review the "Questions to Consider" section that introduces each chapter on psychopathology before seeing the recommended film.) We will occasionally present factual information about mental illness, but this information is almost incidental to the discussion of the films themselves, and we have tried to avoid redundancy with the many fine textbooks that already discuss psychopathology in considerable detail.

Both authors are therapists who have used standard clinical terminology in their description of clients and the discussion of films. We assume students will look up unfamiliar terms or discuss them in class, and we have not defined each new term. However, this is the language students will encounter in patient records and charts, and it is the language they will use if they enter clinical practice.

Each clinical chapter is introduced with a *fabricated* case history and mental status examination. We have developed composite presentations linked as closely as possible to the character being portrayed in the film being discussed. Sometimes it is quite easy to draw on clinical information presented in the film; however, when this has not been possible, we have embellished the cases with our own experience with similar patients or through our fantasy about how a film's protagonist could be treated (i.e., speculating about how we think a given character would present in one of our clinics). We hope these patient histories provide useful and meaningful clinical vignettes that expand and supplement the experience of watching films, and we anticipate spirited classroom debate over whether or not our speculations accurately capture the kind of clinical presentation likely to occur.

Each patient history also includes a fictitious mental status examination. We have consistently used the Mini-Mental Status Examination, a screening exam widely used in clinical practice. The actual examination is presented in Appendix A. We hope those students aspiring to careers as mental health professionals will find this practice useful; we like to think it will introduce students to the sort of screening examination many of them will be conducting in the future.

We have also included multiple boxed questions throughout the text. Some of these are designed to shape the students' experience and thinking as they view the films discussed; others are designed to stimulate discussion outside of class. We realize that there will not be sufficient class time to address each question in depth; however, we hope the questions will be stimuli that will trigger both thought and meaningful dialogue.

Although educated and trained in different disciplines (Clinical Psychology - DW; Nursing - MAB), we are both educators who have found that the judicious use of films dramatically increases students' understanding of abnormal behavior. For example, when lecturing about alcoholism, we supplement our lectures with a "demonstration" of delirium tremens using *The Lost Weekend*. Likewise, before a lecture on bipolar disorder, we'll ask our students to watch *A Woman Under the Influence* or *Mr. Jones*. Both films have richness and an intensity that simply can't be captured by a classroom lecture or the printed page.

We discuss a variety of films throughout the book; however, we usually use one or two films as *primary* illustrations of each disorder. These "primary" films are movies we have watched repeatedly. In many cases, they are popular movies that students are likely to have already seen on their own (e.g., *Fatal Attraction, Benny and Joon, As Good As It Gets*).

Usually the connection between the films being discussed and the chapter is immediate and direct, but we occasionally include obscure films when a small section relates in a meaningful way to the points made in the chapter. There are other classic films such as *A Clockwork Orange*, that have tremendous pedagogical value, and we take great pleasure in introducing a new generation of students to these films. In addition, films such as *Pelle the Conqueror* are occasionally included, even when there is no direct connection to psychopathology, because the films are provocative and moving and are good illustrations of psychological phenomena, even if they do not address psychopathology per se.

Films can be integrated into courses in abnormal psychology and psychopathology in a variety of ways. The particular approach selected will vary from course to course, depending on the needs of the instructor and the interests of students.

First, students can be asked to take responsibility for seeing many of these films on their own. Because we have selected popular films as the exemplars for each clinical chapter, students can easily rent them from any number of commercial sources. Costs are minimized if students choose to see the films in small groups. This promotes the intellectual camaraderie, discussion, and debate that are found at the heart of the educational process. We recommend that whenever possible students see the films *before* coming to class to discuss the corresponding topic.

Second, we have used films in classes that meet twice weekly. The first class meeting is devoted to seeing the film; the second is spent discussing the content of the related textbook chapter and determining whether or not the film accurately represents the disorder being discussed. It is often ideal when such courses can be team taught by a mental health professional and a literature/drama professor.

Most professors choose to use class time to show selected vignettes from pedagogically powerful films, and they encourage students to view the entire film and other related films on their own time. The goal with this approach is to augment lectures with relevant in-class discussion while minimizing the total amount of class time spent watching films. Using a film vignette that vividly depicts a psychiatric disorder circumvents the ethical issues (confidentiality, securing releases and permission, etc.) associated with using "real" cases and clients as illustrations in the classroom.

When films are used in the classroom, it may be necessary for the educational institution (or the members of the class) to pay a fee for public usage. Most colleges and universities have audiovisual departments well equipped to handle such administrative details.

Many readers will disagree about the ratings we have assigned films included in Appendix B. However, it is important to remember that *our ratings are based primarily on the utility of the film as a teaching tool and only secondarily on the film's artistic merit.*

We are both enthusiastic patrons of the Internet, and we are including our e-mail addresses below so we can get feedback about the book. We also hope those readers who share our enthusiasm about cinema as a teaching tool will recommend additional films that we can include in the next edition of *Movies and Mental Illness*.

Danny Wedding, PhD, MPH
weddingd@mimh.edu

Mary Ann Boyd, PhD, DNS, CS
mabdns@slue.edu

Acknowledgments

We drew from a variety of sources in preparation of our final manuscript, but six books were especially helpful: Fleming and Manvell's *Images of Madness* (1985), Gabbard and Gabbard's *Psychiatry and the Cinema* (1987), Greenberg's *Screen Memories* (1993), Hill's *Illuminating Shadows: The Mythic Power of Film* (1992), Hesley and Hesley's *Rent Two Films and Let's Talk in the Morning,* and the second edition of Kolker's *A Cinema of Loneliness* (1988). In addition, we were impressed with and influenced by the scholarship of Steve Hyler, who has written extensively about the portrayal of mental illness in movies and who consulted with us as we planned the current volume.

Many special people contributed to our efforts over the four years we spent watching movies, reading reviews, and thinking about films as we prepared this book. Many of our ideas and the selections of films to be included in *Movies and Mental Illness* grew out of discussions with our friends, especially those who were mental health professionals and interested in the fascinating ways in which psychopathology is portrayed in film. Over time, almost all of our close friends came to share our fascination with this topic.

John Waite, a psychiatrist, was instrumental in helping us plan and organize the book. We had planned on having John serve as a co-author, but the demands of a busy practice kept him from participating as a primary author. We hope (but doubt) that the book is as good as it would have been had he been able to stay with the project. Another friend, psychologist Tom Zimmerman, helped us think through what we wanted to do and the messages we wanted to get across. Tom's help was especially valuable because he has had years of experience teaching courses that use film as a vehicle for helping students understand abnormal behavior. Tom and John both contributed in many ways, but their contributions are most salient in the introductory chapter they helped write.

Ray Corsini, arguably the world's best editor, consulted on the book from its inception to its final printing. Ray has been the major mentor for Danny Wedding and has had a profound influence on his writing, thinking, and life.

Leon McGahee, our most literate friend, is also a psychiatrist. His recommendations were always timely and right on the mark. Other helpful suggestions came from literally dozens of new friends on the PSYART listserve. The participants in the Missouri Institute of Mental Health (MIMH) Film Series had wonderful ideas to share as we met once a month to explore films that shaped public opinion about mental illness, substance abuse, mental retardation, or developmental disabilities. Other ideas came from our students at Washington University and Southern Illinois University–Edwardsville and from friends in the Missouri Psychological Association. Bruce Fuchs with the National Institutes of Health also had dozens of helpful suggestions, and Danny was delighted and grateful when Bruce invited him to Bethesda to discuss the portrayal of schizophrenia in films following a showing of *Benny and Joon* during a special NIH series highlighting "Science in the Cinema."

Lisa Marty, an extraordinarily smart woman with a love of language and an editor's eye, reviewed many chapters and made numerous helpful suggestions. We genuinely appreciate Lisa's numerous contributions to this project.

Vicki Eichhorn helped with selection of the epigraphs and preparation of the manuscript. She helped us manage the myriad details associated with formatting, citations, and permissions with consistent good humor. Brian McKean, Meerha Dash, Joe Terry, and Kristen Mellitt, our four successive editors at McGraw-Hill, ensured the book was well written and relevant. Finally, we appreciate our partners and children, who were long-suffering and patient and never questioned our apparent obsession with films about depression, suicide, schizophrenia, drug abuse, and alcoholism.

Chapter 1

Films and Psychopathology[1]

For better or worse, movies and television contribute significantly to shaping the public's perception of the mentally ill and those who treat them.
Steven E. Hyler

In all of human perceptual experience, nothing conveys information or evokes emotion quite as clearly as our visual sense. Filmmakers capture the richness of this visual sense, combine it with auditory stimuli, and create the ultimate waking dream experience: the movie. In the best movie theaters, the viewer is fully enveloped in sight and sound, absorbed with the plight of the characters, and engrossed by the story. Many writers consider movies to be the most engaging form of mass communication (Kernberg, 1994).

Hollywood took the original invention of the cinematic camera and invented a new art form in which the viewer becomes enveloped in the work of art. The camera carries the spectator into each scene, and the viewer perceives events from the inside as if surrounded by the characters in the film. The actors do not have to describe their feelings, as in a play, because we experience what they see and feel.

In order to produce an emotional response to a film, the directors carefully develop both plot and character through precision camera work. Editing creates visual and acoustic **Gestalten,** to which the viewer responds. The more effective the technique, the more involved the viewer. In effect, the director *constructs* the film's (and the viewer's) reality. The selection of locations, sets, actors, costumes, and lighting contributes to the film's organization and shot-by-shot *mis-en-scene* (the physical arrangement of the visual image).

THE SOCIAL INFLUENCE OF FILMS

Film has become such an integral part of our culture that it seems to be the mirror in which we see ourselves reflected every day. The widespread popularity of videocassette recorders (VCRs) and the availability of literally thousands of films in every corner video store have greatly expanded the influence of this medium.

When someone is watching a movie, an immediate bond is set up between the spectator and the film, and all the technical apparatus involved with the projection of the film becomes invisible as the images from the film pass into the spectator's consciousness. With the best films, the viewer experiences a sort of dissociative state in which ordinary existence is temporarily suspended. No other art form pervades the consciousness of the individual experiencing it to the same extent and with such power.

We believe films have a greater influence than any other art form. Their influence is felt across cultures and across time. Films have become a pervasive and omnipresent part of our culture with little conscious awareness of the profound influence the medium may be exerting.

---

[1] We are grateful for the contributions of Tom Zimmerman and John Waite, who helped us write this chapter.

Films may be especially important in influencing the public perception of mental illness because many people are relatively uninformed about the problems of people with mental disorders, and the media tend to be especially effective in shaping opinion in those situations in which strong opinions are not already held. Although some films present sympathetic portrayals of people with mental illness and those professionals who work in the field of mental health (e.g., *The Three Faces of Eve, David and Lisa,* and *Ordinary People*), many more do not. The victims of mental illness are portrayed most often as aggressive, dangerous, and unpredictable; psychiatrists, psychologists, and other professionals who work with these patients are often portrayed as bumbling and inept (and sometimes venal and corrupt). Films such as *Psycho* (1960) perpetuate the continuing confusion about the relationship between schizophrenia and dissociative identity disorders (multiple personality disorders); *Friday the 13th* (1980) and *Nightmare on Elm Street* (1984) both perpetuate the myth that people who leave psychiatric hospitals are violent and dangerous; movies such as *The Exorcist* (1973) suggest to the public that mental illness is the equivalent of possession by the devil; and movies such as *One Flew over the Cuckoo's Nest* (1975) make the case that psychiatric hospitals are simply prisons in which there is little or no regard for patient rights or welfare. These films in part account for the continuing stigma of mental illness.

Stigma is one of the reasons that so few people with mental problems actually receive help. The National Institute of Mental Health (NIMH) estimates that only 20 percent of those with mental disorders actually reach out for help with their problems, despite the fact that many current treatments for these disorders are inexpensive and effective. In addition, there is still a strong tendency to see patients with mental disorders as the *cause* of their own disorders — for example, the National Alliance for the Mentally Ill (NAMI) has polling data that indicate that about one in three U.S. citizens still conceptualizes mental illness in terms of evil and punishment for misbehavior. (In this context it is interesting to note the historical derivation of the word *stigma*. It has its roots in the name for the scars left by hot irons placed on the faces of evildoers as warnings for others.)

THE TOOLS OF THE DIRECTOR

For the most skilled directors, virtually everything that the camera "sees" and records is meaningful. The sense of subjective experience produced by a sequence of **point-of-view shots** facilitates the audience's identification with the film's characters, their perceptions, and their circumstances. Extreme **close-up shots, high-angle shots,** and **low-angle shots** and a variety of **panning techniques** facilitate the process. The care applied to the script, the dialogue, and the sound track, coupled with skillful editing, produce the final montage of sounds and images. The use of **voice-over narration** adds emphasis to certain visual images and may provide clues to guide the viewer when a character is reflecting or experiencing flashbacks. In addition, a director can use a combination of techniques to condense or expand film time. The experience of time is also often manipulated through the use of **jump cuts.** The result is that the finished product, the film, conveys a statement that the director intends to make, explicitly or subtly, along a continuum that ranges from **realism** to **expressionism.**

Each person brings to a film certain expectations, apprehensions, and interests based upon the film's advance publicity, a critic's review, or prior exposure to the subject matter of the film. In addition, each viewer possesses unique perceptual preferences, prior knowledge about the film's content, and preconceptions about the images the film contains that mediate his or her perceptions and experience. Rarely, if ever, do any two viewers have an identical experience when viewing the same film. Each viewer subjectively selects, attends to, and translates the visual and acoustic images projected in a theater into his or her own version of the story. Often audiences are affected by or identify with the film's characters so strongly that it appears clear that the defense mechanism of *projection* is present. This process is facilitated when the audience can anticipate the story line, the plot, or the outcome. The avid moviegoer quickly realizes familiar themes, similar settings, and "formulas" for plots and endings across a variety of films. The more one views films, the easier it becomes to identify a specific film type, or **genre.**

The Close-Up
When we see an isolated face on the screen, our consciousness of space is suspended and we find ourselves focusing on physiognomy. We become vividly aware of all the nuances of emotion that can be expressed by a grimace or a glance. We form beliefs about a character's emotions, moods, intentions, and thoughts as we look directly into his or her face. Indeed, many of the most profound emotional experiences (such as grief) are expressed much more powerfully through the human face than through words.

This ability to share and comprehend subjective experiences through empathic interpretation of the language of the face is clearly evident in early silent films, and these films still have the power to evoke strong emotions. In fact, many early directors of silent films, confronted with the development of "talkies," feared that the addition of sound would place a barrier between the spectator and the film and restore the external and internal distance and dualism present in other works of art.

The principles of physiognomy and microphysiognomy can be extended from the human face to the background and surroundings in which the character moves, and a character's subjective vision can be reproduced by a film as objective reality. For example, film can show the frightened, paranoid individual, but also the distorted, menacing houses and trees which the protagonist views. This technique was used in the expressionist film *The Cabinet of Dr. Caligari* (1919). Unusual camera angles can also be used to produce unusual physiognomies, which in turn suggest unusual moods.

Even with vastly improved technology and the addition of sound and color, the essence of film still remains its visual content. Gestures and facial expressions convey inner nonrational emotions that cannot be expressed in spoken or written language. They also express emotions that lie in the deepest part of the self and which often cannot be adequately expressed by words, which are mere reflections of cognitions. What we see in a facial expression is made immediately apparent to the spectator without the intermediary of words, and a good actor can convey multiple emotions simultaneously.

All this is achieved through the skill of the actor. It has been found time and again that real people playing themselves are less convincing than actors. This is true with instructional films, advertisements, and docudramas, as well as feature films. In *Ordinary People* (1980), the director, Robert Redford, attempted to cast an actual psychiatrist in the role of the therapist, but the effect was unconvincing. Redford ended up casting actor Judd Hirsch in the role.

Identification
As a film is being projected onto a theater screen, we project ourselves into the action and identify with its protagonists. At one time it was thought that, in order for the audience to maintain the attention of viewers, a film had to have a central character and theme. At times this central figure has been an "anti-hero." However, directors such as Robert Altman and Quentin Tarantino have experimented with techniques in which they rapidly shift among short vignettes that may be only loosely linked with a story line or central character. Altman's *Short Cuts* (1994) and Tarentino's *Pulp Fiction* (1994) are two recent examples of this approach.

Filmmakers have also experimented with other means of holding the psychological continuity together, such as making an inanimate object or an animal the center of the story. Most films, however, use a single character to hold the film together as a psychological whole.

The classic question posed to students regarding films in introduction to cinema classes — "Are movies merely art imitating real life?" — is perhaps unanswerable. For some viewers, seeing movies takes on such importance that it seems as if films and film characters have supplanted their lives.

Suture

Viewers integrate separate, disjointed photographic images into coherent scenes and different scenes into the whole film experience without conscious effort or any appreciation for the complicated psychological processes involved. "**Suture**," to use a medical metaphor, occurs when cutting or editing occurs and the resulting cinematic gaps are "sewn" shut by viewers.

According to suture theory, instead of asking, "Who is watching this?" and "How could this be happening?" viewers tacitly accept what is seen on the screen as natural and "real," even when the camera's gaze shifts abruptly from one scene, location, or character to another. Suture works because cinematic coding makes each shot appear to be the object of the gaze of whoever appears in the shot that follows. The most commonly cited example of suturing is the **shot/reverse shot**, in which each of two characters is alternately viewed over the other's shoulder.

THE REPRESENTATION OF PSYCHOLOGICAL PHENOMENA IN FILM

Film is particularly well suited to depicting psychological states of mind and altered mental states. The combination of images, dialogue, sound effects, and music in a movie mimics and parallels the thoughts and feelings that occur in our stream of consciousness. Lights, colors, and sounds emanate from the screen in such a way that we readily find ourselves believing that we are actually experiencing what is happening on the screen.

In 1926 in *Geheimnisse einer Seele (Secrets of a Soul)*, German director G. Pabst dramatized psychoanalytical theory with the help of two of Freud's assistants, Abraham and Sachs, and depicted dream sequences with multilayered superimposition (achieved through rewinding and multiple exposures). Freud himself did not want his name connected with the project and had misgivings about the film's ability to convey the nuances of psychoanalytic process. In a letter to Abraham, Freud wrote, "My chief objection is still that I do not believe satisfactory plastic representation of our abstractions is at all possible." Freud himself remained skeptical about the cinema all his life.

Film has always been used to objectively portray subjective states such as dreams. Perhaps the best example of this is Hitchcock's collaboration with Salvador Dali on the dream sequence in *Spellbound* (1944). Hitchcock wanted to "turn out the first picture on psychoanalysis." He was determined to break the traditional way of handling dream sequences through a blurred and hazy screen. Hitchcock wanted dreams with great visual sharpness and clarity, and images sharper than those in the film itself. He chose Salvador Dali as a collaborator because of the architectural precision of the artist's work. Hitchcock originally wanted to shoot *Spellbound* in the open air and in natural light, but he wound up shooting the film in the studio to cut costs. *Spellbound* depicts the cathartic recovery of repressed memories, an emotional experience intense enough to eliminate the hero's amnesia. This is a psychological process that has been depicted in film since its early days.

Films can also be used to interweave fantasy and reality, and a director may intentionally set up situations in which the viewer cannot tell if the film portrays reality or the unconscious fantasies of a character. Examples of this technique include Bergman's *Persona* (1966), Fellini's *Juliet of the Spirits* (1965), Bunuel's *Belle de Jour* (1966), and Altman's *Images* (1972) (Fleming & Manvell, 1987).

Processes such as thinking, recalling, imagining, and feeling are not visible, but the language of the **montage** and camera techniques such as **slow fades** can suggest these invisible processes. Also, the film can be edited in such a way that the viewer is forced to think about psychological phenomena. The inclusion of images with symbolic meaning, such as a hearse passing by or the well-known chess game with Death in *The Seventh Seal* (1957), can evoke certain moods or prepare the viewer for events that are about to occur. Symbolic sounds, such as a baby crying, can have a similar effect.

The skilled director employs a variety of filming and editing techniques to engage the viewer, and the film-viewing public has become remarkably sophisticated in **film grammar** — the way in which the film images are joined and flow into one another. **Flashbacks, jump cuts, and parallel action** are identified with the thoughts, emotions, and behavior of the protagonists in the film to a degree unattainable in any other medium.

Films offer numerous examples of unconscious motivation and **defense mechanisms,** involuntary patterns of thinking, feeling, or acting that arise in response to the subjective experience of anxiety. For example, in *sex, lies, and videotape,* Cynthia, who is having an affair with her sister Ann's husband, inadvertently

> "I'll think about it tomorrow. Tara! Home. I'll go home, and I'll think of some way to get him back! After all, tomorrow is another day!" *Gone with the Wind* (1939)

loses a pearl earring after a sexual encounter in the home of her sister. The earring is discovered and the discovery forces Ann to confront the fact that Cynthia is sleeping with Ann's husband. **Acting out** is present in Michael Douglas' response to the stress in his life in *Falling Down* (1993), **altruism** can be seen in the character of the doctor who devotes himself to the indigent people of India in *Streets of Joy* (1994), **denial** is dramatically illustrated in Katharine Hepburn's wonderful role as the morphine addicted mother in *Long Days Journey into Night* (1962), **intellectualization** is present in *Lorenzo's Oil* (1992), and **suppression** is commonplace in *Gone with the Wind* (1939).

The Depiction of Psychopathology in Films

The depiction of mental illness in films commonly appears in two popular genres: the horror film and the suspense thriller. Often the most effective portrayals of mental illness are those that infuse surreal and expressionistic images into a montage that is basically realistic and plausible, powerfully conveying the "interior" of a character's psyche. For a skilled director, convincing perceptual aberrations such as macropsia, micropsia, and visual hallucinations are easy to construct and to project to an audience. An early film that served as a prototype for horror films, Wiene's *The Cabinet of Dr. Caligari* (1919), is highly expressionistic and established a precedent for setting macabre murders in mental institutions. Like dozens of films that followed, it linked insanity and the personal lives of psychiatrists and implied that mental health professionals are all "a little odd." Evidence of the enduring effects of these themes is found in the successful and highly acclaimed film *The Silence of the Lambs* (1991), in which Anthony Hopkins plays a mentally deranged and cannibalistic psychiatrist.

The seminal films of Alfred Hitchcock provide the best examples of the suspense genre. They are unique in the way in which they engage the viewer and pander to his or her anxieties in subtle, unrelenting, and convincing ways. The majority of Hitchcock's films, noted for their stylized realism, invariably evoke a sensation of vicariously pulling the viewer "in" to the plight of the characters as a not-so-innocent bystander, through a carefully edited montage of a variety of objective and subjective camera shots and angles. Hitchcock's filmography reflects not only a fascination with pronounced and extreme psychopathology (e.g., *Psycho,* 1960), but, more important, an appreciation of more subtle psychological phenomena such as acting out, reaction formation, idealization, repression, and undoing. These defense mechanisms are depicted in Hitchcock's films *Shadow of a Doubt* (1943), *Spellbound* (1945), and *Marnie* (1964). Hitchcock's style is immensely popular and has been imitated frequently by other directors such as Brian DePalma and Roman Polanski.

Mental illness is also depicted, although less often, in the genre of documentary films and comedies. Frederick Wiseman's *Titicut Follies* (1967) is a clear example of the former genre. It is interesting to contrast this movie with the horror film *Bedlam* (1945) or the "docudramatic" films such as *The Snake Pit* (1948), *Pressure Point* (1962), and *One Flew over the Cuckoo's Nest* (1975), all dealing with mental institutions and the treatment of people with mental illness. At least two heralded films, *The Three Faces of Eve* (1957) and *Sybil* (1976), provide viewers with full-scale case histories and the struggles between patient and psychiatrist. John Huston attempted to portray Sigmund Freud's personal struggles with and professional inquiries into the human psyche in his biographical film *Freud, the Secret Passion* (1962), the only complete cinematic work devoted to Freud and his work. Two 1991 comedies, *Drop Dead Fred* and *What About Bob?*, portray psychological aberrations with quirky humor that is used to defuse the sense of anxiety that is produced by the behavior of the lead characters in both films.

Steven Hyler (1988; Hyler, Gabbard, & Schneider, 1991) has provided the most compelling analyses of the portrayal of mental illness in films. In the 1991 article, Hyler and his colleagues describe six common stereotypes that perpetuate stigma. The first of these is that of the mental patient as **rebellious free spirit.** Examples of this portrayal can be found in films such as *Nuts* (1987), *The Dream Team* (1989), *The Couch Trip* (1989), *Francis* (1982), *An Angel At My Table* (1990), *Shine* (1996), and perhaps most clearly in *One Flew over the Cuckoo's Nest* (1975).

The stereotype of the **homicidal maniac** is present in most of the slasher/horror films described above. However, the authors point out that this stereotype can also be traced back as far as D. W. Griffith's 1909 film *The Maniac Cook,* in which a psychotic employee attempts to kill an infant by cooking the child in an oven. More recent films such as *Sling Blade* (1996), a well-intentioned and sympathetic film about a mentally retarded man who commits a second murder after leaving a psychiatric hospital 25 years after murdering his mother and her lover, perpetuate the myth that people with mental illness and mental retardation are dangerous.

The patient as **seductress** is seen in films such as *The Caretakers* (1963) and *Dressed to Kill* (1980) and, most clearly, in the 1964 film *Lilith,* which stars Warren Beatty as a hospital therapist who is seduced by a psychiatric patient, Jean Seberg. The stereotype of the **enlightened member of society** is linked to the work of writers such as R. D. Laing and Thomas Szasz and is illustrated in films such as *King of Hearts* (1968) and *A Fine Madness* (1966). The **narcissistic parasite** stereotype presents people with mental disorders as self-centered, attention-seeking, and demanding. It is reflected in films such as *What About Bob?* (1991), *Annie Hall* (1977), *High Anxiety* (1977), and *Lovesick* (1983). Finally, the stereotype of **zoo specimen** is perpetuated by films that degrade people with mental illness by treating them as objects of derision or a source of amusement or entertainment for those who are "normal." Films that exemplify this stereotype include *Bedlam* (1948) and *Marat/Sade* (1966). A variation on this theme occurs in Brian De Palma's *Dressed to Kill* (1980), in which a psychotic and homicidal psychiatrist murders a nurse in a surrealistic amphitheater-like setting, with dozens of other patients sitting in the gallery and watching in silent approval.

In the article from which the epigraph for this chapter is taken, Hyler (1988) describes three dominant themes in film that help establish stereotypes about the etiology of mental disorders. The first is the **presumption of traumatic etiology.** This theme reinforces the belief that a single traumatic event, most often occurring in childhood, can have profound ramifications on later life, often precipitating mental illness. Examples include the amnesia experienced by Gregory Peck that was eventually shown to be related to his role in the childhood death of his brother (revealed by Hitchcock in a dramatic and unforgettable flashback scene) in *Spellbound* (1945) and the dissociative identity disorder that resulted when a child was required to kiss the corpse of her dead grandmother in *The Three Faces of Eve* (1957). Other examples of this theme are found in films such as *Suddenly Last Summer* (1959), *Home of the Brave* (1949), *Nuts* (1987), and, more recently, Robin William's character in *The Fisher King* (1991).

Hyler's second theme is that of the **schizophrenogenic parent.** This is a widely held myth that holds parents (most often, the mother) accountable for serious mental illness in their children. The National Alliance for the Mentally Ill (NAMI) has worked hard to dispel this unfounded but pervasive belief, but it is deeply rooted in popular culture and commonplace in films. Examples include *Agnes of God* (1985), *Face to Face* (1976), *Sybil* (1980), *Carrie* (1976), *Frances* (1982), *Fear Strikes Out* (1957), and *Shine* (1966).

The final myth discussed by Hyler is that **harmless eccentricity is frequently labeled as mental illness and inappropriately treated.** We see this theme most vividly presented in the film *One Flew Over the Cuckoo's Nest* (1975). Jack Nicholson's character, Randle P. McMurphy, is charismatic, flamboyant, and colorful. The only diagnosis that seems at all appropriate is that of antisocial personality disorder, although it is not even clear that this is justified. However, once in the system he cannot get out, and he is eventually treated with electroconvulsive therapy and lobotomy, presumably as a way of punishing his misbehavior in the name of treatment. The same theme is found in two films released in 1996, *King of Hearts* and *A Fine Madness,* and in the more recent film *Chattahoochee* (1990). A related theme, that treatment in mental health facilities is actually a form of social control, is reflected in the work of Thomas Szasz (e.g., in books such as *The Myth of Mental Illness* and *Psychiatric Slavery*). It is also reflected in films depicting excesses in treatment such as the aversion therapies portrayed in *A Clockwork Orange* (1971).

> "Insanity runs in my family. It practically gallops." Cary Grant in *Arsenic and Old Lace* (1944)

Psychopathology and its representation in films will be discussed in some detail in the chapters that follow. In general, we will follow the nosology of the American Psychiatric Association's *Diagnostic and Statistical Manual, Fourth Edition (DSM-IV).* The *Mini Mental Status Examination* is included in Appendix A. By the end of the semester, all students using this book should be able to intelligently administer and interpret this examination. In addition, Appendix B includes a filmography broken down by diagnostic category, roughly corresponding to the chapters in the Alloy, Acocella, and Bootzin book, *Abnormal Psychology: Current Perspectives.* Students who will take time to review the films included in Appendix B will find that the experience will supplement and enhance their understanding of psychopathology.

Chapter 2

Anxiety Disorders

It wasn't your fault. . . .
They got in the goddamn way!
Advice to Ron Kovic in
Born on the Fourth of July

Questions to Consider While Watching *Born on the Fourth of July*

- To what extent do drugs and alcohol complicate Kovic's rehabilitation program?
- Is substance abuse common in people with post-traumatic stress disorder (PTSD)?
- How were the combat experiences in Vietnam different from those soldiers experienced in previous wars?
- Do you think PTSD is correctly classified as an anxiety disorder, or should it be placed in a separate category of its own in the next revision of the *Diagnostic and Statistical Manual?*
- Was heroin addiction a serious problem for returning veterans? Why or why not?
- Have you known people who have experienced similar trauma in their lives? How have they coped?
- In what ways, if any, would the trauma associated with rape or an automobile accident differ from that associated with combat experience?
- Ron Kovic dreams that he is able to run. Do people who develop disabilities in midlife typically dream of themselves *without* the disability?
- If you were treating Ron Kovic, would you have advised him to meet the Wilsons, the parents of the friend he shot in Vietnam? Why or why not?
- Is the quality of care portrayed in *Born on the Fourth of July* realistic? Are attendants who are paid minimal wages more likely to abuse patients?
- What treatments exist for post-traumatic stress disorder?

PATIENT EVALUATION

Patient's stated reason for coming: "I drink too much. I can't sleep. My stomach's always in a knot. I'm trapped in this fucking wheelchair and I'll never get out."

History of the present illness: Ron Kovic is a 23-year-old white Vietnam veteran who suffered a serious spinal cord injury in Vietnam. He is paralyzed from the midchest down. He was treated in a rehabilitation unit at the Bronx Veteran's Administration Medical Center for approximately six months. Since leaving the VA hospital, Mr. Kovic has become increasingly bitter about the war and his disability. He describes himself as "constantly nervous," and he becomes especially anxious in situations that trigger memories of Vietnam (e.g., in noisy settings or in congested areas). Flashbacks of combat occur often and are typically triggered by auditory stimuli (e.g., a car backfiring, fireworks, or the sound of a passing helicopter). There is marked sleep disturbance, and the patient rarely sleeps throughout the night (unless he has passed out from drinking). He reports frequent nightmares, usually involving combat. This patient experienced a large number of horrific experiences while in Vietnam. Although he is unwilling to fully discuss these experiences, it appears that he is especially distressed by his role in killing civilians (especially women and infants) and by the accidental shooting of one of his best friends during an especially intense and confusing firefight.

Past psychiatric illness, treatment, and outcomes: There is no individual or family history of psychiatric illness. Mr. Kovic appears to have been a healthy and well-adjusted young man prior to his combat experiences.

Medical history: Mr. Kovic was hospitalized for appendicitis in 1965, and his appendix was removed. The rest of the medical history is insignificant.

Psychosocial history: Mr. Kovic is the oldest of five children. He reports a happy childhood. He denies any history of academic difficulty, and he reports that he obtained average grades. He was preoccupied with sports in high school and achieved some fame statewide as a wrestler. He dated occasionally during his senior year, and he had intended to marry a high school girlfriend after returning from Vietnam. He was not sexually active in high school, but he had brief sexual encounters with a number of prostitutes in Vietnam. None of these relationships involved more than casual sex.

Mr. Kovic was seriously injured during combat in Vietnam. He was stabilized in a military hospital in Vietnam and then sent to Bethesda Naval Hospital for additional treatment. He was medically discharged from the Marines and transferred to a VA Medical Center for rehabilitation services. After leaving the VA hospital, Mr. Kovic returned to live with his parents; however, this transition has not gone well and he frequently becomes involved in altercations (both verbal and physical) with his parents and siblings.

Drug and alcohol history: Mr. Kovic drinks heavily, consuming approximately two six packs of beer and a half bottle of tequila each day. He often drinks until he passes out. He claims he is unable to sleep without the help of alcohol or drugs. Mr. Kovic smokes marijuana approximately once per week, usually in the company of other veterans. Mr. Kovic did not drink or use drugs until he was introduced to substance misuse while in the Marines. He drank heavily while in Vietnam, and he has continued to abuse alcohol and other drugs since his injury and discharge.

Behavioral observations: Mr. Kovic was appropriately groomed and dressed. He was quite facile in moving around the room in his wheelchair. Affect was generally angry, and Mr. Kovic seemed to be annoyed by the examiner's questions. Although generally cooperative, Mr. Kovic was hostile throughout the evaluation. He became annoyed and sarcastic when told he could not smoke until the examination was completed. He frequently "drummed" his fingers on the desktop. When asked about his religious beliefs, Kovic replied, "There is no God. God is as dead as my legs."

Mental status examination: Mr. Kovic was alert and responsive. There was no evidence of thought disorder noted during the examination. This patient denies homicidal ideation; however, he acknowledges frequent thoughts of suicide and he has a plan (use of a gun). There is no apparent intent, and the patient claims he would never commit suicide because of his religious beliefs (Mr. Kovic is a Catholic).

This patient is fully oriented to time, place, and person. He was able to repeat serial sevens without difficulty. Short- and long-term memory appear to be intact. There are no difficulties with naming or repetition. The patient can follow both verbal and written commands. He writes well, and there is no evidence of construction dyspraxia. Mr. Kovic attained a perfect score of 30 on the Mini Mental Status Examination.

Functional assessment: Mr. Kovic has a guaranteed income for life because of his service-connected injury. He is an intelligent individual who qualifies for tuition assistance under the GI Bill; however, Mr. Kovic is not currently interested in attending college or pursuing additional vocational training. His reported problems with concentration would probably limit his academic potential. He has full use of his arms, head, and neck, and he is quite adept at using his wheelchair. His family appears to be generally supportive, although the relationship with most family members has been strained by his history of substance abuse and his chronic anger. The patient appears to have good social skills, although his only friends are other Vietnam veterans, and he appears to do little with them except drink and smoke marijuana.

Strengths: This patient is obviously smart enough to perform a wide variety of vocational tasks if he had sufficient motivation. He is quite knowledgeable about Vietnam and its language, culture, and history. He has read widely. He appears to be capable of leading a group, and he is sometimes quite articulate. He currently lives with a loving family that is angry with his behavior but not yet totally alienated.

Diagnosis: 309.81 Post-traumatic Stress Disorder
                  305.90 Alcohol Abuse
                  303.9 R/O Alcohol Dependence

Treatment plan: (1) Weekly therapy aimed at establishing rapport and trust; (2) medical evaluation to assess need for detoxification; (3) participation in Alcoholics Anonymous; (4) participation in Vietnam Veterans support group unaffiliated with the VAMC; (5) consider hypnosis and eye movement desensitization and reprocessing (EMDR) as treatment modalities.

Prognosis: This patient is intelligent and motivated, and the prognosis for treatment of both his alcoholism and his PTSD appears to be moderate to good.

TYPES OF ANXIETY DISORDERS

The prevalence of anxiety disorders is higher than that of any other psychiatric condition, and up to 7.3 percent of the population of the United States will be affected at any one time. Lifetime prevalence rates are 14.6 percent. Higher rates for almost all the anxiety disorders occur in women and in lower socioeconomic groups (Bourdon et al., 1992; Regier, Narrow, & Rae, 1990).

Post-Traumatic Stress Disorder

Post-traumatic stress disorders *(PTSD)* occur after exposure to traumatic events. The individual with a post-traumatic stress disorder must have personally witnessed or experienced some event that involved actual or threatened death or serious injury and must have responded with "intense fear, helplessness, or horror" *(DSM-IV)*. The traumatic event is then reexperienced by the individual as nightmares, recurrent recollections, and flashbacks or as physiological distress. The PTSD victim works hard to avoid these recurrent experiences. In addition, the diagnosis requires that an individual experience at least two of the following: sleep disturbance, irritability, difficulty concentrating, hypervigilance, or an exaggerated startle response. The diagnosis requires that the problems persist for at least a month and result in significant distress or impairment. Ron Kovic clearly meets the *DSM-IV* criteria for PTSD.

Military combat is a common cause of post-traumatic stress disorder, but the disorder can occur in response to earthquakes, fires or floods, mugging, rape, the witnessing of violence, or any of a variety of other traumatic situations. Often, innocuous stimuli will cause an individual to relive the anxiety-producing experience; for example, hearing a car backfire may trigger a terrifying war memory for a Vietnam veteran.

Many victims of combat or natural disasters experience what is sometimes referred to as **survivor guilt.** For example, one of our patients was a infantryman in Vietnam. He reported being on patrol one evening with a small group of his friends. His best friend, walking immediately in front of him, stepped on a land mine and was literally blown to pieces. The patient reported being splattered with blood and body tissue and wiping it off his face with horror. However, he was almost instantly overcome with guilt when he realized that he was wiping away the brains of his best friend. Other people may question God's judgment when they realize that their lives were spared while those of more "worthy" individuals (e.g., children, young parents) were taken. *Kovic's guilt about the death of his buddy "Wilson" is an example of survivor guilt.*

Suicide and suicide attempts are common in patients with post-traumatic stress disorder. In addition, it is essential to assess for comorbidity (especially substance abuse) in cases of post-traumatic stress disorder. Nearly all post-traumatic stress disorder patients who are suicidal will be found to have a concomitant psychiatric condition. Kovic never appears to be suicidal in the film, but it would be highly unusual for someone in his situation not to have recurrent fantasies of suicide.

The movie *Fearless* (1993) provides an interesting picture of a somewhat unusual reaction to trauma. Jeff Bridges is one of a small group of survivors of a devastating plane crash. Bridges assists a number of other passengers and is celebrated as a hero and a saint. He becomes convinced he is invulnerable, and he grows increasingly impatient with the pedestrian concerns of his wife and child. After a near-death experience precipitated by an allergic reaction to strawberries, he returns to normal and reestablishes a loving relationship with his wife and son. The movie includes a very interesting segment in which a psychiatrist (who is employed by the airlines because he has written a best-selling book about post-traumatic stress disorder) leads a discussion group of survivors of the crash.

In *The Fisher King* (1991), Robin Williams plays a former college professor who becomes homeless and psychotic after witnessing his wife gunned down in a restaurant. However, *the sort of active, well-formed, and specific hallucinations Williams experiences (e.g., a red knight riding a horse in Central Park with flames shooting out of his head) would be very unlikely to occur as a result of a traumatic experience. The character Jeff Bridges plays in the same film, a disc jockey who withdraws from life and abuses alcohol and drugs after a traumatic event, presents a far more realistic portrayal of post-traumatic stress disorder.*

Although *The Fisher King* is imprecise and confusing in the way its plot links trauma to psychosis, post-traumatic stress disorder is common among people who are homeless. Carol North and Liz Smith studied homeless people in St. Louis and found that 18 percent of the men and 34 percent of the women met diagnostic criteria for post-traumatic stress disorder. The most common traumatic experience was rape (North & Smith, 1992). Some of the stresses experienced by homeless people are illustrated in the films *Ironweed* (1987) and *The Saint of Fort Washington* (1993).

Acute stress disorder is in many ways similar to post-traumatic stress disorder. However, acute stress disorders occur relatively quickly after the traumatic event (within no more than four weeks) and resolve fairly quickly. In contrast, the symptoms of post-traumatic stress disorder by definition have to last more than a month, and the onset of symptoms may occur months or even years after exposure to trauma. Acute stress disorder was added to the *DSM-IV* to ensure compatibility with the *International Classification of Diseases (ICD-10)*.

Ironweed (1987) is a compelling film in which Jack Nicholson plays an alcoholic whose drinking is apparently related to his guilt about dropping and killing his infant son. Many of the symptoms of PTSD have become obliterated by Nicholson's alcoholism, which has become the dominant theme in his life. Ironweed *illustrates the way in which alcohol abuse can develop as a secondary problem in response to trauma and then can become the primary psychological problem as abuse progresses to addiction.*

Generalized Anxiety Disorder

Some people are characteristically anxious: they walk around with a sense of apprehension and experience physiological arousal in many different situations. They display what is sometimes called **free-floating anxiety.** They are not phobic — i.e., their fears are not tied to any specific stimulus, such as dogs or elevators. However, they can be very unhappy, and their condition can be quite debilitating. The diagnosis requires that worry and anxiety be present more days than not.

Anxiety symptoms associated with **generalized anxiety disorder** include the same physiological, cognitive, and behavioral symptoms associated with other anxiety disorders, but they are chronic. The individual with this disorder may have multiple somatic complaints such as tachycardia, a dry mouth, and gastrointestinal distress. He or she will be constantly worrying about the multiple things that can go wrong in life and may be irritable and short-tempered because of anxiety. The lifetime prevalence of generalized anxiety disorder in the general population is about 5 percent, but relatively few of these patients actively seek out treatment. Onset of symptoms typically occurs in childhood or adolescence.

Almost any Woody Allen comedy will include at least one character with a generalized anxiety disorder, and the existential anxiety produced by the need to cope with a complex and impersonal world is the basis for much of Allen's humor. Annie Hall *(1977) and* Manhattan *(1979) are the Allen films that best illustrate generalized anxiety disorder.*

Specific Phobias

Vertigo (1958) is a classic Alfred Hitchcock film that stars Jimmy Stewart as a San Francisco police detective paralyzed by his fear of heights. The phobia has a traumatic etiology: while chasing a criminal across a rooftop, Stewart almost falls to his death. A fellow officer, trying to aid Stewart, is killed when he plunges to the street below. Stewart, overcome with guilt, develops **acrophobia,** a debilitating fear of heights. In *DSM-IV,* this would be diagnosed as a specific phobia. The term *vertigo* refers to either marked dizziness or a confused, disoriented state of mind. Both meanings apply in this complex and engrossing film.

At one point in the film, Stewart designs his own behavior modification program, stating, "I have a theory that I can work up to heights a little bit at a time." He puts a stepladder near the window, stands on the first step, waits, gets down, stands on the second step, waits, goes to the third step, becomes frightened and dizzy, and then falls to the floor.

The plot of *Vertigo* is complex and detailed. Stewart is hired as a private detective and given the job of trailing Kim Novak around San Francisco. He soon falls in love with her. Novak eventually leads him to a mission at San Juan Batista. She ascends the bell tower and inexplicably jumps to her death. Stewart, unable to assist in any way because of his paralyzing acrophobia, watches helplessly.

Stewart responds to Novak's death by becoming so anxious and confused that he has to be hospitalized. When he leaves the hospital, he becomes enamored with a woman who appears to be an identical twin to Novak. Later in the film we learn that the woman *is* Novak, and that the earlier suicide had been faked.

Trying for a second time to treat his phobia, Stewart insists that Novak accompany him as he confronts his fear and ascends the mission bell tower. However, when they are at the top, a nun dressed in black appears and startles Novak, who jumps back from the figure and falls to her death. Stewart has overcome his acrophobia, but only at tremendous personal cost.

*Jimmy Stewart's fear of heights would be classified as a **specific phobia** under* DSM-IV. In the older nomenclature, it would have been called a simple phobia, and even earlier usage would have assigned a precise label (such as acrophobia). However, the panoply of terms formerly used to describe phobias suggested a diagnostic understanding and therapeutic precision that simply did not exist. Most mental health specialists now prefer more general rubrics such as specific phobias, using one of five subtypes: animal, natural environment, blood-injection, situational, and other. Examples of these five types are, respectively, small animal phobias, fear of heights, fear of vaccinations, fear of running water, and an exaggerated fear of clowns.

Anxiety is a normal part of life, and specific fears are sometimes justified. Spiders can bite us; people do fall from high spaces; and even small cats can scratch us. Existential writers and psychologists have made the point that anxiety is an expected part of the human condition. However, when anxiety becomes socially or occupationally debilitating, a psychiatric label and treatment may be justified.

Fears are labeled as phobias only under strict conditions. Marked anxiety must be present in the presence of the phobic stimulus and must routinely occur with exposure to the stimulus. In addition, the phobic individual must be aware that the magnitude of the fear response is excessive. Most phobics will avoid the stimulus situations that leave them fearful or will experience considerable distress in these situations. Finally, there must be evidence that the reaction to the feared stimulus situation significantly interferes with the person's normal life. Jimmy Stewart's character in *Vertigo* would clearly meet *DSM-IV* criteria for the diagnosis of a specific phobia.

Approximately 13 percent of the U.S. public will experience a specific phobia at some point in their lives (Bourdon et al., 1992). This is a remarkable percentage when one remembers that those fears that do not incapacitate an individual or cause marked distress do not qualify for the diagnosis. An individual with a fear of elevators, for example, may be able to function quite adequately in a rural environment where he or she is not required to cope with the stress of confronting elevators on a regular basis. The magnitude of the fear that is experienced seems to be a function of the proximity of the stimulus and the extent to which the individual's escape options are limited.

Women are two to three times more likely than men to experience specific phobias. For example, the majority of patients diagnosed with animal, natural environment, situational, or blood-injection phobias are women. In the National Comorbidity Study, about 16 percent of the women had experienced a specific phobia and about 7 percent of the men (Kessler et al., 1994).

Many phobias are triggered by a specific traumatic event. This was clearly the situation in Vertigo. Specific phobias will occasionally remit spontaneously in the absence of treatment, but this is relatively rare.

Social Phobias

Intense and persistent fears of criticism and rejection characterize social phobias. People with social phobias experience crippling fears in response to thoughts of evaluation or scrutiny, and they avoid situations in which they are likely to be observed by others. The disorder can take many different forms and occurs in situations that require public speaking, public performance, test taking, or social skills. Some male patients with social phobias are unable to urinate in public places; other patients are unable to eat in public for fear they will make a mistake and be ridiculed. The disorder is related to common phenomena such as performance anxiety, stage fright, and shyness and is differentiated from these disorders primarily in terms of severity and the extent of impairment that results from the problem. When fears relate to almost *every* social situation, the diagnosis of generalized social phobia is appropriate.

One study (Uhde et al., 1991) rank-ordered the most common fears of patients with social phobias. These fears, in order, were speaking in public, eating in public, writing in public, using public lavatories, and being the center of attention in a group of people.

The symptoms of social phobia include tachycardia, trembling, sweating, blushing, dizziness, and hyperventilation. Even more distressing is the sensation of impending doom that frequently occurs. Finally, patients feel an overwhelming need to escape from the social situation that is causing their distress.

Anticipatory anxiety about social situations often sets up a self-fulfilling prophecy. The phobic individual ruminates excessively about the performance demands of an upcoming event, loses sleep worrying about the situation, becomes tremendously anxious just before the event, and in fact performs poorly in the actual situation because of the high levels of anxiety. This poor performance then confirms the individual's beliefs about his or her inability to perform adequately in these situations, and the fear is exacerbated.

Social fears are commonplace, and epidemiological studies suggest that the lifetime prevalence of social phobia is between 3 and 13 percent. Onset of the disorder typically occurs during the late teens. The disorder appears to be somewhat more common in women. Fear of public speaking is the most common social phobia, and surprisingly large numbers of people have dropped courses, changed jobs, or avoided promotions in order to avoid the stress of public speaking. Unfortunately, relatively few individuals with social phobias wind up seeking treatment, even though the disorder can be successfully treated. Groups such as *Toastmasters International* provide an opportunity to practice skills in a safe, structured environment and are often useful in helping social phobics with specific concerns about public speaking.

Panic Attacks

Panic attacks result in extreme fear and discomfort, and the individual experiencing the attack may believe that he or she is literally going to die. Panic attacks are one of the symptoms of many anxiety disorders, and the diagnostic criteria for panic attacks are listed in a separate section in *DSM-IV*. Essentially, a panic attack can be said to occur when an individual experiences intense fear or discomfort and four or more of the following symptoms: palpitations, pounding heart, or accelerated heart rate; sweating, trembling, or shaking; sensations of shortness of breath or smothering or a feeling of choking; chest pain or discomfort; nausea or abdominal distress; feeling dizzy, unsteady, lightheaded, or faint; derealization or depersonalization; fear of losing control or going crazy; fear of dying; numbness or tingling sensations; and chills or hot flushes.

Panic Disorder

When *panic attacks* occur on a regular and unpredictable basis, a diagnosis of **panic disorder** may be appropriate. These episodes are not associated with any particular situation or event (such as public speaking); instead, they seem to come from nowhere. The fact that they can seemingly occur anywhere and anytime is one of the reasons that panic disorder is such a debilitating condition. Many patients can vividly recall their first panic attack.

Some people will have daily panic episodes, while others may be able to go for weeks or months without experiencing panic. People experiencing panic disorder frequently believe they are having heart attacks or other undiagnosed medical problems. In fact, many people with panic disorder wind up being treated for unrelated conditions before their true problem is diagnosed. Likewise, patients with genuine medical conditions, such as **mitral valve prolapse,** are sometimes erroneously diagnosed as having panic disorder.

Agoraphobia

The term **agoraphobia** is derived from the Greek word *agora* and means "fear of the marketplace." Agoraphobics are individuals who are afraid of being vulnerable and experiencing an anxiety attack in open, insecure places. They are likely to experience the symptoms of panic whenever they venture far away from their home. Often these patients are literally housebound and cannot leave the perceived safety of their home. In extreme cases, they are unable to leave their bedrooms.

People with agoraphobia believe something awful will happen if they leave the security of their home. They may fear fainting, falling down, vomiting, or dying. Agoraphobia tends to develop in young adulthood and may persist throughout life. It is the phobia most frequently encountered in clinical practice, and it is about twice as common in women as in men. Many patients with agoraphobia will experience panic disorder as well.

The best cinematic portrayal of agoraphobia is found in Robert Taicher's 1987 movie Inside Out *(1986). In this film, Elliott Gould plays Jimmy Morgan, a New York businessman with marked agoraphobia who hasn't left his house for ten years.* He has food delivered to him, arranges for call girls to come to his apartment for anonymous sex, places bets over the phone, and almost never ventures out of his house until forced to by circumstances beyond his control.

It is important to differentiate between true agoraphobia (which results from a rational desire to avoid the overwhelming symptoms of anxiety that occur whenever one leaves a safe area) and isolation, withdrawal, and seclusion that result from thought disorders such as paranoid schizophrenia. One of the authors once ran an evening support group for a group of high-functioning agoraphobics. When an announcement of the group was made in the local paper, one person called and requested an opportunity to participate. However, a brief telephone interview disclosed that the woman was concerned about being eaten by aliens if she ventured far from her home. This was *not* agoraphobia.

Obsessive-Compulsive Disorder

People with **obsessive-compulsive disorder** are troubled by obsessions or compulsions. These thoughts and/or behaviors take up a significant amount of time, cause considerable distress to the individual, and frequently interfere with occupational or social adjustment. In severe cases, an obsessive-compulsive disorder can come to dominate virtually every minute of its victim's life. Unfortunately, obsessive-compulsive disorder remains one of the most difficult anxiety disorders to treat, although there have been encouraging findings from recent innovations in both behavior therapy and psychopharmacology. In some extreme cases, obsessive-compulsive disorder has been so debilitating that psychosurgery has been performed.

Obsessions are defined as "recurrent and persistent thoughts, impulses, or images that are experienced . . . as intrusive and inappropriate and cause marked anxiety or distress" *(DSM-IV)*. These experiences are of greater magnitude than the worry that is part of almost all our lives. Although people with obsessive-compulsive disorders try to suppress these thoughts, these attempts are usually unsuccessful. Finally, it is important to appreciate that people with obsessions experience the thoughts as disagreeable and alien to their own sense of self (i.e., ego-dystonic).

Common obsessional themes include harming others (especially children or helpless individuals), contamination with germs or feces, exposure to toxins or infectious diseases such as AIDS, blasphemous thoughts (such as calling the Virgin Mary a whore), and sexual misbehavior. Obsessions can also coexist with post-traumatic stress disorders and may sometimes have traumatic etiologies. For example, one patient who had observed his friend being stabbed to death could not stop thinking about the event and was obsessed with the image of the knife entering his friend's chest.

Compulsions are repetitive behaviors that serve to reduce anxiety. Sometimes there is a logical connection between the compulsive behavior and the event it is supposed to prevent (for example, repeated hand washing *may* help prevent contamination from germs). However, in other cases there is no logical connection between the two (e.g., the patient who feels a compulsive need to sing the first few lines of a popular commercial before pulling away from every stoplight knows there is no meaningful connection between the behavior and the likelihood of an accident).

Either compulsions or obsessions are sufficient to justify the diagnosis; however, it is common for these two problems to occur in tandem, and the vast majority of patients present with both problems. It is often evident that the compulsion addresses the individual's need to find some way to cope with his or her obsession. For example, one patient had an obsession that involved the belief that he would drive over the body of a child lying in the road. In order to cope with this distressing image, he would circle the block whenever he hit a bump in order to ensure that he had not hit a child. This patient would spend hours getting to work each day because of his compulsive need to check and recheck every bump in the road.

About 2 to 3 percent of the public will meet the criteria for a diagnosis of obsessive-compulsive disorder in their lifetimes. In addition, it is relatively common for people to experience mild obsessive or compulsive symptoms that are not severe enough to warrant a diagnosis. Almost all of us have had the experience of a catchy jingle from a commercial running through our mind when we would rather be focusing on more compelling issues.

The best recent film portrayal of a person with obsessive-compulsive disorder is found in Melvin Udall, the character Jack Nicholson plays in As Good As It Gets *(1997).* Melvin is a misogynist and a homophobe, but he is also a character with a pronounced obsession for cleanliness. He eats every day at the same restaurant, sits at the same table, insists on the same waitress (Helen Hunt) and always orders the same meal. Udall always brings his own paper-wrapped plastic wear to this restaurant, so he doesn't have to risk contamination from unclean silverware. Whenever anything disrupts this well-established routine, Udall gets anxious and belligerent. He also wipes off door handles before opening doors, and he carefully avoids stepping on cracks as he walks to his therapist's office. *Nicholson's obsessions are his repetitive thoughts about germs and disease; his compulsions are the ritualistic behaviors he engages in as a consequence of his thoughts.* Patients with OCD frequently have multiple obsessions, and the film *As Good As It Gets* presents a realistic presentation of the disorder (with the possible exception that *a patient with an obsession about cleanliness as severe as that present in Nicholson's character would be unlikely to handle a small dog*).

TREATMENT OF ANXIETY DISORDERS

There are numerous approaches to the treatment of anxiety, and all of them are at least partially efficacious. Education can be a critical first step in therapy, and it is often tremendously therapeutic for the patient with an anxiety disorder simply to realize that he or she is not going insane and that these disorders are commonplace and always respond to treatment. In addition, patients need to realize that their symptoms are not life-threatening, that they will not pass out or fall down no matter how bad they feel, and that many people experience similar symptoms but assign different labels to them (e.g., a tingling sensation in your stomach before you give a speech can be interpreted as anticipatory excitement and a signal that you're alert and going to do a good job).

It is also critical to carefully assess a patient's prior use of alcohol or drugs as ways of coping with his or her anxiety symptoms. Many of these patients have learned to use substances to modulate their anxiety levels: for example, alcoholism is common in veterans with post-traumatic stress disorders. In addition, it is necessary to assess the consumption of coffee, soft drinks, and nicotine. All three exacerbate the symptoms of anxiety.

Psychotherapy may be helpful with some patients with anxiety. In particular, behavior therapy appears to be the treatment of choice for many phobic disorders, and some patients have been helped by behavioral methods after years of insight therapy. Almost all behavior therapies will involve exposure to the feared stimulus or situation. **Systematic desensitization** requires teaching patients how to relax and then involves the careful introduction of images selected from a graduated hierarchy of arousing scenes carefully prepared by the therapist and the client. After a client is able to imagine the feared situation without experiencing arousal it is common to move to **in vivo desensitization** in which, when possible, patients are encouraged to actively participate in the feared behavior. Small animal phobics will be asked to pet dogs, and those patients with fears of enclosure will be asked to ride up and down in elevators. Of course, in vivo exercises are also graduated and the therapist carefully regulates exposure. **Flooding** and **implosion** are related techniques that involve massive exposure to the feared stimuli. There is no attempt to develop a graduated hierarchy with these techniques, and in implosion the stimuli are presented dramatically and as forcefully as possible. A person with a rodent phobia, for example, will be asked not simply to visualize rats, but will be presented with scenes like that from George Orwell's book *1984* in which a cage with rats is attached to a prisoner's head. Biofeedback, relaxation training, and hypnosis may also be used as adjunctive therapies in the treatment of anxiety.

Cognitive therapy such as that advocated by psychologist Albert Ellis or psychiatrist Aaron Beck may be helpful for many patients. Cognitive therapists practice **cognitive restructuring** — i.e., they help their patients identify and understand the internal statements and irrational thoughts that may trigger arousal in certain situations and settings (Beck & Emery, 1985).

Medication may also be used as a treatment or, more commonly, as an adjunct to therapy. **Beta-blockers** such as pro-pranolol (Inderal) are sometimes efficacious in the treatment of social phobias and seem to be especially helpful in situations in which performance is impaired by cardiovascular arousal. Beta-blockers appear to affect the somatic aspects of anxiety but have little effect on the psychological component.

Albert Ellis is a world famous clinical psychologist and the father of what is known as **Rational Emotive Behavior Therapy.** He tells the story of being painfully shy as a young man, and especially frightened by attractive girls. In fact, his fears were so extreme, he had never asked a girl out for a date. Determined to overcome these fears, and showing some promise for the good therapist he was going to become, he promised himself that he would go to Central Park and ask one hundred successive girls out for a date. He reports "97 turned me down and the other three never showed up – but I was never again afraid to ask a girl for a date." (Personal Communication, 1994)

Tricyclic antidepressants such as imipramine (Tofranil) are sometimes effective in treating panic disorder and agoraphobia. Another class of antidepressants, the **monoamine oxidase inhibitors** (MAOIs), is also used to treat phobic disorders and especially panic attacks. Unfortunately, both medications produce significant side effects and the MAOIs require fairly strict dietary regulation to avoid hypertensive crises. A new generation of antidepressants, the **selective serotonin reuptake inhibitors** (SSRIs), has fewer deleterious side effects and holds great promise in the treatment of anxiety. These drugs include medications such as clomipramine and fluoxetine, which have been shown to be effective in the treatment of some cases of obsessive-compulsive disorder.

Benzodiazepines are also widely used in the treatment of anxiety symptoms, and they have largely replaced barbiturates, which are potentially lethal (especially when combined with alcohol) and highly addictive. The benzodiazepines include well-known and common drugs such as diazepam (Valium), chlordiazepoxide (Librium), and alprazolam (Xanax). It is interesting to note that the human brain has been shown to have specific receptor sites for benzodiazepine molecules. In addition, there is growing interest in the use of over-the-counter herbal remedies such as *Kava* (available from health food stores) in the treatment of mild to moderate anxiety.

Benzodiazepines are quite effective in helping anxious patients cope with their anxiety symptoms, but their use is limited by their addictive potential and serious side effects, such as drowsiness and memory impairment. These problems are especially likely when the medication is taken with alcohol. In addition, reliance on medication in every situation in which one must confront anxiety robs one of the opportunity to learn that one *can* successfully cope without reliance on medication. I'm Dancing As Fast As I Can*, a 1982 film starring Jill Clayburgh, demonstrates some of the problems associated with overreliance on Valium as a coping mechanism.*

ANXIETY DISORDERS AND FILMS

A large number of other films portray characters with anxiety disorders. For example, *The Pawnbroker* (1965) portrays a defeated concentration camp survivor who has become numb and indifferent in response to wartime experiences that included seeing his wife raped and his children killed. The problem of urban stress is illustrated by the film *Falling Down* (1994), although Michael Douglas' break is probably too serious and too complete to be explained as simply a reaction to stress. Financial and vocational stress in the real estate business can be seen in *Glengarry Glen Ross* (1992).

Dozens of movies have been made about the Vietnam War, and many of these (as well as other war movies) illustrate either acute stress disorders or, more commonly in those that follow the hero home after the war, post-traumatic stress disorder. Some of the most powerful of these films are *Born on the Fourth of July* (1989), *Coming Home* (1978), *The Deer Hunter* (1978), *Apocalypse Now* (1979), *The Killing Fields* (1984), *Platoon* (1986), *Hamburger Hill* (1987), and *Full Metal Jacket* (1987).

Social phobias are portrayed or implied in numerous films. The painfully shy girlfriend is a common motif that is illustrated by films such as *Lonely Hearts* (1981), *Rocky* (1976), and *The Fisher King* (1991). Shy and socially unskilled men are portrayed in *Marty* (1955), *Untamed Heart* (1993), *Awakenings* (1990), *Good-bye Mr. Chips* (1939), *Howard's End* (1992), *The Remains of the Day* (1993), and all of the Charlie Chaplin films in which he played the Little Tramp. The ways in which two shy adolescents come to grips with their emerging sexuality and a racist society are portrayed in the wonderful Australian film *Flirting* (1990).

Mel Brooks' *High Anxiety* (1977) makes fun of all the films with Hitchcock-like psychological motifs. A more recent comedy, *What About Bob?* (1991), presents Bill Murray as a patient with multiple problems, including overwhelming anxiety when he can't be close to his therapist, Richard Dreyfuss.

Critical Thinking Questions

- How does post-traumatic stress disorder differ from the problems faced in previous wars that resulted in conditions such as "shell shock" and "combat fatigue"?
- Some existential therapists such as Irv Yalom and Rollo May have argued that anxiety is an essential part of the human condition, and it needs to be confronted rather than avoided (e.g., they discourage the use of benzodiazepines). Do you agree?
- Drugs like Valium can be addictive, as illustrated by the film *I'm Dancing As Fast As I Can* (1982). Have you known anyone who abused anxiolytic medications? How did you know?
- Do you believe general practitioners are too quick to prescribe anxiolytics for people having difficulty coping with the day-to-day stresses of modern life?
- Does a system that *pays* veterans who develop psychiatric disorders while in service in subtle ways actually reinforce the illness behaviors and minimize the likelihood of people overcoming these problems?
- Are there some occupations in which it might be adaptive to have an obsessive-compulsive disorder?
- What are the things you fear the most? What differentiates these fears from those experienced by someone with a phobia? Is the difference qualitative or merely quantitative?
- Some people believe you can overcome your fears by confrontation. For example, some parents help their children overcome a fear of water by tossing them in the deep end of the pool. Are these methods likely to be successful?
- Do we normally fear things themselves (e.g., spiders) or what they symbolize?
- Have you ever felt a compulsive need to behave in a certain way (e.g., checking twice or three times to ensure the door is locked before you leave for a vacation)?
- What is the influence of genetics on the likelihood of developing an anxiety disorder?
- How common is it for people to treat their own anxiety with alcohol (e.g., having a drink or two before giving a speech)?

Chapter 3

Dissociative and Somatoform Disorders

Matricide is probably the most unbearable crime of all . . .
so he had to erase the crime, at least in his own mind.
A police psychiatrist attempts to explain
Norman Bates' behavior in *Psycho*

Questions to Consider While Watching *Psycho*

- Hitchcock's *Psycho* is one of the greatest films ever made. Is it an accurate presentation of mental illness?
- Do films like *Psycho* do a disservice to people with mental disorders by perpetuating the myth of the homicidal psychopath?
- Bates' voyeurism seems almost innocuous compared with his other behaviors. How often are paraphilias (such as voyeurism) linked with violence?
- Is there any evidence linking paraphilias with dissociative disorders?
- Bates has trouble saying the word "bathroom" when he shows the hotel room to Marion (Janet Leigh). Is it common for people who commit sexual crimes to be uncomfortable with mature discussions of sexuality or elimination?.
- How often in a lifetime of clinical experience would a therapist treat a patient with a dissociative disorder? How often would a Norman Bates come along?
- Marion has stolen $40,000. How does Hitchcock manage to make her a sympathetic character with whom we can all identify?
- How can a patient with a dissociative disorder suppress the evidence presented by everyday experience (e.g., the nonresponsiveness of the dead Mrs. Bates)?
- How does Hitchcock's story line fit with the psychological *Zeitgeist* of the 1960s?
- Would you feel comfortable working with a patient like Norman Bates? Would you insist that security officers be present during your evaluation?

PATIENT EVALUATION

Patient's stated reason for coming: "I had to come. They made me. Of course, I'm eager to get any help you can offer. I truly do suspect you can be helpful."

History of the present illness: Norman Bates is a 27-year-old white male who has been referred for psychological evaluation by the Madison county court. Mr. Bates is awaiting sentencing on four counts of murder. The alleged murder of his mother and stepfather occurred more than a decade ago; the two recent killings are reported to have occurred within the past 30 days.

Past psychiatric illness, treatment, and outcomes: Mr. Bates has a long history of eccentric and odd behavior, including isolation, withdrawal, seclusiveness, and secrecy. These behaviors have been noted by local authorities; however, there has never been any evidence of danger to self or others, and Mr. Bates has never received treatment in the mental health system.

Medical history: There is a history of the usual childhood diseases, such as mumps and chicken pox. Aside from these childhood experiences, Mr. Bates has never seen a physician. He has never been hospitalized.

Psychosocial history: The patient reports that he walked and talked at about the normal times. He has a long history of self-imposed isolation. He is reported to have been lonely and withdrawn in school, and he cannot identify anyone he regarded as a friend when he was growing up. He obtained passing grades, although he dropped out of school at the age of 16 to help run a family motel. When the expressway bypassed the motel, business dwindled to almost nothing. His mother and stepfather died approximately 10 years ago; since that time, Norman has managed the motel and the family home on his own. He manages the books for the motel, and he performs routine maintenance on both the motel and the family home. He has no brothers or sisters, and there are no other living relatives. He reports devoting almost all of his leisure time to his hobby of taxidermy. Mr. Bates has never been married or involved in a significant romantic relationship. He does not date, and he has no regular or routine social activities.

Drug and alcohol history: Mr. Bates denies any history of drug or alcohol use. He believes drunkenness is a sin, and he prefers not to be tempted by social drinking. He does not smoke.

Behavioral observations: Mr. Bates arrived on time for the evaluation, accompanied by a deputy sheriff. He was appropriately groomed and dressed. He was polite to the point of being obsequious. He cooperated fully with all tasks, except for those instances in which his identity would be questioned or challenged. At these points, the patient became resentful and stopped cooperating with the evaluation.

Mental status examination: Mr. Bates was alert and oriented to place and time. He was disoriented to person, however, and steadfastly maintained that he was actually his mother. He became agitated and threatened to leave the room when I pointed out the obvious (e.g., he had male features and male genitalia, she had been buried some years ago, etc.). After I stopped challenging his assertion that he was in fact his mother, he cooperated with the evaluation and was able to answer all other questions on the Mini Mental Status Exam, obtaining an overall score of 29.

Functional assessment: The patient appears to be of average intellectual ability. He has not completed high school, and he has no significant occupational abilities other than minimal bookkeeping skills. However, he appears to have been able to manage on his own for the past 10 years. He has no living family, and there are no friends to provide social support. (Mr. Bates appears comfortable in his isolation and does not appear to be distressed by the solitary nature of his existence.) Mr. Bates' social skills are limited, and he tends to be quite awkward and uncomfortable in social situations. However, his entrenched and well-defended delusional disorder appears to be his most limiting feature, and he is unlikely to function successfully in either occupational or social settings as long as he continues to maintain he is his mother.

Strengths: Mr. Bates has very limited support systems in place, but he is of at least average intelligence and he possesses the skills necessary to manage on his own. He avoids substance misuse. He has avoided financial and legal difficulties up to the present time.

Diagnosis: 300.14 Dissociative Identity Disorder

Treatment plan: Mr. Bates was referred by the court for a forensic evaluation, and therefore no systematic treatment plan has been developed. Given his legal problems, it is likely that Mr. Bates will be imprisoned for life, and it is unlikely he will be offered the benefits of active psychological treatment in the corrections system. Even if treatment is available, it will require years of daily work before this client begins to understand himself or his problems.

Prognosis: Mr. Bates lacks insight into the nature of his problems or their causes. He resists efforts to change his belief system. He has maintained these fallacious beliefs for the entire past decade, and they are likely to prove intractable. If he is acquitted by reason of insanity, he is likely to be remanded to the state hospital for intensive treatment. However, even then his prognosis is quite bleak.

PSYCHO

In the latter half of the 1900s, films began depicting the increasing psychological complexities of the human personality. *Psycho,* Alfred Hitchcock's 1960 film, describes a young man who assumed the personality of his mother after he murdered her and her lover. This film is regarded by many as Hitchcock's finest film. It is a superb movie; unfortunately, it also contributed to the negative stereotype of persons with mental illnesses.

The film begins in a hotel room in Phoenix, with Marion Crane, played by Janet Leigh, who is scantily dressed. She is discussing her future with her lover, Sam Loomis, played by John Gavin. Marion wants to get married, but Sam is unable to make a commitment because of previous financial commitments to his ex-wife. After the afternoon rendezvous, she returns to work, where she steals $40,000. The next morning she heads toward Sam's hometown with the money.

During a rainstorm she seeks shelter at the Bates Motel, only 15 miles from Sam's home. Norman Bates, played by Anthony Perkins, invites her to dinner at his home behind the motel. Marion hears Norman's mother yelling at him for wanting to bring a girl to dinner. Norman fixes sandwiches for Marion and apologizes for his mother's behavior. They talk in a room adjacent to the office, and Norman shows off his taxidermy collection. Norman later watches her undress through a peephole separating her room from the office. That night Marion is brutally murdered by someone who appears to be Norman's mother. The murder scene occurs in a shower, and this scene (with its dramatic musical background) is one of the most famous single scenes in film history.

Norman cleans up the blood from the shower room and puts Marion's body in the trunk of her new car (and unknowingly hides the stolen $40,000 there as well). He then drives the car to an isolated area, where he is able to sink the car and its contents into a swamp.

Instead of telling the police about the stolen money, Marion's boss hires a private detective, Milton Arbogast, to track Marion and recover the money. He traces her to the Bates Motel after following Marion's sister, Lila, to Sam's. Neither Lila nor Sam knows anything about the stolen money. Mr. Arbogast is killed when he visits the Bates home to investigate his hunch that Norman Bates is somehow involved in the disappearance of Marion.

Lila and Sam then contact the local sheriff, who is willing to investigate Marion's disappearance if an official missing persons report is made. He also informs Sam and Lila that Norman's mother has been dead for 10 years and that she killed herself after poisoning her lover.

Lila and Sam return to the motel to solve the case. In a very suspenseful ending, they find that Norman Bates had exhumed his mother's grave, mummified her corpse, and kept her body with him in the house for the past 10 years. Bates had always been a disturbed child, and, after he killed his mother and her lover, he coped with his guilt by assuming her identity.

By the end of the movie, Norman has totally assumed the alter ego of his mother. Bates sits in (her) cell, smiling and thinking to herself

> I'll just sit here and be quiet, just in case they do suspect me. They're probably watching me. Well, let them. Let them see what kind of a person I am. I'm not even going to swat that fly. I hope they are watching. They'll see. They'll see and they'll know and they'll say, "Why, she wouldn't even harm a fly."

DISSOCIATIVE DISORDERS

Alteration in consciousness can occur under many different conditions. During alcohol intoxication, there is a clouding of consciousness with diminished awareness of sensory stimuli and attentiveness to the environment and self. Some drugs produce a twilight, or dream-like, state, in which the individual is conscious but fades in and out of periods of alertness. Heightened states of attention increase suggestibility, which lends itself to altered states of consciousness through hypnosis. EEG studies have shown that subjects are fully awake and conscious in a hypnotic trance. However, posthypnotic suggestion can induce individuals to carry out complex actions without realizing they are doing it because of previous hypnotic instructions.

Dissociation is often viewed as a normal defense mechanism that can be used in frightening, stressful, or painful situations to cope with stress. It allows an individual to detach from overwhelming fear, pain, and helplessness generated by trauma. It is believed that these biologically and genetically based dissociative abilities develop instinctually and initially help the infant cope with the anxiety of separation from the mother. When separation is prolonged or when a relationship is abusive, the infant survives through dissociation, in effect pushing pain or distress away and out of consciousness.

The development of extreme dissociative behavior patterns has been linked to trauma. For example, *in the movie* Sybil*, the lead character's changing identity was found to be the result of repeated physical and psychological abuse she experienced at the hands of a deranged and delusional mother.* Dissociative states include amnesia, derealization, depersonalization, identity confusion, and identity alteration.

Dissociation includes normal psychological experiences, such as daydreaming, as well as dissociative disorders. The process of dissociation is not well understood, but it is known to be an alteration in consciousness that can affect memory, identity, and perception. For a period of time, information is not associated or integrated, as it would normally be. Dissociation involves a separation of consciousness with closely connected feelings, behaviors, thoughts, or memories of events (Lowenstein, 1993; Putnam, 1991). In dissociation, events that would ordinarily be connected are divided from one another.

Dissociation has been explained from a learning theory perspective, and neurobiological theories have also been advanced. State-dependent learning occurs when behaviors or information is learned or stored in one state and is best retrieved when the person recalls information in that same state. For example, once an adult returns to his or her hometown, it is easier to remember the names of childhood friends. Conversely, when an individual changes his or her physical or psychological state, information is harder to retrieve. In a calm, safe environment, memories stored in a state of panic may not be easily retrieved because the visceral stimuli associated with the memories are different (Putnam, 1991).

There have been studies that show that in dissociative states there are sensory changes that result in alterations of perceptions of external stimuli. There is also evidence that there are differences in EEG readings in the same person when in different dissociative states (Putnam, 1991). Research is continuing to further delineate the neurobiological changes that occur in dissociative states.

Dissociation can be viewed on a continuum from minor dissociative experiences of everyday life to major forms of psychopathology, such as multiple personality disorder (Allen & Smith, 1993; Bernstein & Putnam, 1986). Most people have minor dissociative experiences, such as driving a car over a familiar route and suddenly realizing that they do not remember what happened during all or part of the trip. In some cultures, dissociative states, such as trances, are common and accepted cultural activities or a routine part of religious experience. Some people experience "out of body" experiences when facing death or extreme trauma. The most severe type of dissociation is the type experienced by Sybil, in which several different personalities develop within one person and actually alternate with each other.

Amnesia

Amnesia, the inability to recall important information, is expressed through memory gaps of personal information about events that occurred during a specific period of time. There may be loss of memory about who a person is, or a person may fail to recall personal information such as his address or workplace, but the rest of the individual's knowledge base remains intact. Somewhat paradoxically, many people who experience frequent or profound amnesic episodes do not seek help. Either these episodes are not recognized as being unusual or, if they are, the individuals attempt to hide them. The missing information either returns spontaneously or can be retrieved during hypnosis (Putnam, 1991).

Amnesia is usually present in dissociative states and plays an important role in those disturbances of identity that are characteristic of multiple personality disorder. It also is often present in other psychiatric conditions, such as post-traumatic stress disorder and schizophrenia. Head trauma, physical illnesses, brain tumors, and dementia can also cause amnesia. If there are not physical reasons for amnesia, the cause is probably psychological and related to traumatizing events.

Even though filmmakers do not typically focus on the psychological etiology of amnesia, they have often used amnesia as a central theme. One example is the 1940 Academy Award-winning satire, *The Great Dictator,* starring Charles Chaplin, Paulette Goddard, and Jack Oakie. Chaplin plays a dual role as a Jewish barber and Adenoid Hynkel, dictator of Tomania. This spoof of Adolf Hitler begins when Chaplin plays a Jewish barber in a "Tomanian" ghetto who is recovering from amnesia and wakes up to find himself living under the thumb of Hynkel (also played by Chaplin). He escapes to Austria with a Jewish laundress,

Paulette Goddard, who is in love with him. In Austria, he is mistaken for Hynkel, who had recently assumed control of the country. Chaplin then assumes the role of the dictator.

Amnesia is also portrayed in the excellent 1941 film *Sullivan's Travels,* starring Joel McCrea and Veronica Lake and directed by Preston Sturges. The main character becomes amnestic when he is hit over the head and ends up being sentenced to six years on a chain gang. An example of traumatic amnesia triggered by a murder can be found in the 1991 film *Dead Again.*

Amnesia allows a spoiled, self-centered, rich women to experience life at the other end of the social ladder in the 1987 comedy *Overboard,* directed by Garry Marshall. Joanna, played by Goldie Hawn, lives on a luxury yacht with her husband. Following an argument with Dean, a carpenter played by Kurt Russell, Joanna falls overboard, is struck by a garbage scow, and is hospitalized with amnesia. Dean sees this as an opportunity for revenge and claims her as his long-lost wife, Anna. He then takes her home and puts her to work as a domestic laborer and baby-sitter for his four children. She is properly humbled and eventually reunited with her real husband. Of course, by this time she has become attached to Dean and has changed her former values.

Derealization and Depersonalization

Derealization and depersonalization are two other dissociative states. In *derealization,* the person feels detached from familiar people or places. Familiar people or places seem unfamiliar or unreal, and close friends are not recognized. The size or shape of objects may be perceived as altered or strange, and people may seem mechanical. During the 1989 San Francisco Bay Area earthquake, 40 percent of the 101 persons interviewed afterward reported feeling as though their surroundings were unreal (Cardea & Spiegel, 1993).

In **depersonalization,** there is an alteration in the perception of self and a feeling of being detached or the sense that one is living out a dream. The person feels like an outsider looking in. Transient experiences of depersonalization are common in adolescents and decline with age in normal individuals (Putnam, 1985). During a traumatic event such rape, depersonalization is sometimes experienced by women who report they were floating above their own bodies during the assault (Classen, Koopman, & Spiegel, 1993). These experiences are also common in drug-intoxicated states. Closely related to depersonalization experiences are **out-of-body experiences,** in which the individual has the experience of leaving his or her body. Often these individuals are able to describe scenes as if viewed from above and report a sense of being isolated and detached from their bodies.

Identity Confusion and Alteration

Identity confusion and alteration are also related to each other. In **identity confusion,** the person struggles to know who he or she is. This is expressed as a battle going on inside the self to establish one's true identity. In **identity alteration,** the person actually believes that he or she is someone else and uses that person's name. These individuals are perceived by others as having a different personality. *Sybil* clearly demonstrates identity alteration — each personality had a different name and very distinct behavior. Dr. Wilbur could easily identify each of the personalities by their distinct attitudes, speech, and behaviors. Of course, Norman Bates' assumption of his mother's persona would be an example of identity alteration.

Models of Dissociation

There is controversy in the mental health community about the categorization of dissociative experiences as psychiatric disorders. Dissociation, by itself, does not necessarily lead to impairment and is not necessarily viewed as evidence of psychopathology. However, if dissociative states lead to distress and impairment in psychological, interpersonal, social, or vocational functioning, then they should be evaluated as psychiatric problems. Because dissociative symptoms such as amnesia and depersonalization can be present in other psychiatric disorders such as post-traumatic stress syndrome and schizophrenia, no other psychiatric disorders can be present if a person's symptoms are diagnosed as a dissociative disorder.

There are three different theoretical models used in explaining dissociative disorders. The first is the **autohypnotic model,** which is built on the well-known connection between dissociation and hypnosis. In this model, dissociative disorders are explained as malfunctioning self-hypnosis. Proponents of this position believe that people with dissociative disorders are highly hypnotizable, and many of the symptoms characteristic of dissociative disorders can be produced by hypnosis. The second, the **states-of-consciousness model,** is an extension of the autohypnotic explanation. In this model, the presence of hypnotizability is recognized, but symptoms are presumed to result from a traumatic event that disrupts the transmission of information from one conscious state to another (Putnam, 1991). A faulty neural network has been hypothesized to account for the failure of information retrieval in different states of consciousness (Li & Spiegel, 1992).

The third model, the **strategic role enactment model,** argues that dissociative states, such as those in dissociative identity disorders (i.e., multiple personality disorders), are produced by the social demands placed on the individual. In this model, it is assumed that having a dissociative disorder is socially desirable and that therapists and others reinforce this role. The patient and therapist know how persons with this disorder should act, and these behaviors, which are believed to be under voluntary control, are acted out by the individual and reinforced by the therapist. The research supporting this model is limited, and studies have not been able to produce the same degree of psychological or physiological manifestations in control subjects that are present in people with this disorder (Putnam, 1991).

DSM-IV Classification

The dissociative disorders officially recognized in the *DSM-IV* are a group of syndromes characterized by dissociation. They include **dissociative amnesia, dissociative fugue, dissociative identity disorder, depersonalization disorder,** and other disorders not otherwise specified. These disturbances may be sudden or gradual, transient or chronic (APA, 1994). There are no good data about the prevalence of any of the dissociative disorders. In one study of psychiatric inpatients, 15 percent met the criteria for dissociative disorder, while 4 percent met the criteria for identity alteration disorder (Saxe et al., 1993).

Dissociative amnesias are characterized by an inability to recall important personal information, usually of a traumatic or stressful nature (e.g., the death of a child). **Dissociative fugues** are characterized by sudden, unexpected travel away from home or one's customary place of work, an inability to recall one's past, confusion about personal identity, or the assumption of a new identity (e.g., a person whose business is failing may show up in a new city with a new identity and no memory of previous problems). The Wim Winders film *Paris, Texas* (1984) introduces the character of Travis Clay Henderson, an individual suffering from both a dissociative amnesia and a dissociative fugue. He has been lost for four years and is found wandering in the desert. Eventually, he (partially) puts the pieces of his shattered life back together.

Dissociative identity disorders (formerly known as multiple personality disorders) are characterized by the presence of two or more distinct identities or personality states that recurrently take control of the individual's behavior with an inability to recall important personal information, too extensive to be explained by ordinary forgetfulness. The films *Sybil* (1976) and *The Three Faces of Eve* (1957) are both fine films that illustrate dissociative identity disorders (but the film *Primal Fear* [1996] should also be seen to provide a certain degree of skeptical balance). It is interesting to note that Joanne Woodward, who received an Academy Award in 1957 for her lead role in *The Three Faces of Eve,* returned almost two decades later to play the psychiatrist treating *Sybil.* A TV movie, *Voices Within: The Lives of Truddi Chase* (1990), was devoted to an exploration of dissociative identity disorder. The film was based on the popular book *When Rabbit Howls.*

Depersonalization disorder is diagnosed when there is evidence of persistent or recurrent feelings of being detached from one's mental processes or body. Film examples of depersonalization disorder are found in the classic film *Dead of Night* (1945) and the more recent *Altered States* (1980). Of course, the classic example of depersonalization disorder is the strange case of Dr. Jekyll and Mr. Hyde, explored in at least nine films since 1920 (one of the best of which is the 1996 film *Mary Reilly*).

MIRAGE

In the 1965 film *Mirage*, David Stillwell, played by Gregory Peck, develops amnesia after witnessing the accidental death of his boss and mentor, Calvin Clark. Stillwell, a scientist, had just discovered a method for neutralizing the effects of nuclear fallout. Believing that his mentor was working for world peace, Stillwell shares the information with him. When Stillwell realizes that his formula would end up being used to *produce* nuclear weapons, he sets the formula on fire in front of an open window. In an attempt to save the piece of paper, Calvin lunges toward Stillwell and falls to his death from the 27th floor. Stillwell observes the fall, is horrified, and then calmly picks up his empty briefcase and leaves the office. He has developed amnesia. The lights in the office building go out.

The audience has none of this information until the end of the film. The film actually opens during a blackout in an office building in New York City. David Stillwell appears to be a very calm, rational individual who leads a woman, Sheila, played by Diane Baker, down the darkened 27 flights. He does not recognize Sheila, but she recognizes him. Upon returning to his apartment, he is greeted by a man who attempts to kill him. Stillwell overpowers the intruder and leaves him unconscious in the service quarters. Gradually, Stillwell begins to realize that he has lost his memory, but he becomes convinced that he has been in an amnestic state for two years instead of two days. He seeks help from a psychiatrist, who questions his amnesia and throws him out of the office.

In this Hitchcock-style thriller, Stillwell's belief that he had been a cost accountant in New York was reinforced by his enemy, the Major, who hires thugs to follow Stillwell and get the formula. Stillwell next employs Detective Ted Caselle, played by Walter Matthau, to discover his identity and figure out who is trying to kill him. Caselle attempts to fit the pieces together but is killed in the process. A romance is rekindled between Sheila and Stillwell, who had previously been lovers.

Following the detective's death, Stillwell desperately contacts the same psychiatrist, who is again skeptical of Stillwell's amnesia. By now, Stillwell's memory is beginning to return and he realizes that his memory loss has been for only two days. The psychiatrist asks some questions that provoke the retrieval of more memories. Gradually, the amnesia for his friend's death lifts, and he is able to face the horror of the event.

DISSOCIATIVE AMNESIA

Individuals with **dissociative amnesias** can usually remember events up to the time of the trauma but have memory loss for events that occur after the event. Even though significant personal information is lost with dissociative amnesias, cognitive abilities and the ability to remember new information remain intact. This memory impairment is reversible. In the classic disorder, the person is quickly brought to a mental health provider because of the overt, dramatic change in memory.

Occasionally, people will be admitted to an emergency room as Jane or John Doe because they cannot identify themselves. Persons with amnesia may have intense emotional reactions to stimuli without knowing the reasons for the reaction or the significance of it. This happens several times in *Mirage,* when a conversation relates in some way to Stillwell's past and he reacts angrily without understanding why. In order to meet the *DSM-IV* diagnostic criteria, the individual cannot have any other dissociative disorders. For example, *even though Sybil has amnesia at times, she would be considered to have a dissociative identity disorder, not dissociative amnesia.* In the film *Mirage,* Stillwell's only psychiatric problem is lack of memory related to a traumatic event.

The most common types of dissociative amnesia are **localized** (failure to recall events for a few hours following an event, such as immediate memory of an auto accident) and **selective** (some, but not all, events are remembered). The other three types are less common. In **generalized** amnesia, the individual cannot recall any part of his or her life. This is the type of amnesia Stillwell has in *Mirage;* he cannot remember any part of his life and is distressed by his lack of memory. **Continuous amnesia** is the loss of memory after a certain time through the present. **Systematized amnesia** is the loss of memory related to certain types of information, such as painful family events (APA, 1994). If these last types of amnesia are present, the individual may eventually be diagnosed with more complex dissociative disorders.

DISSOCIATIVE FUGUE

Amnesia for part or all of one's past is present in **dissociative fugue,** but in addition there is sudden, unexpected travel away from home or one's customary place of daily activities (APA, 1994). There may be confusion about personal identity or the assumption of a new identity. With the onset of fugue, a person begins a new autobiographical memory that replaces the original one. When the fugue resolves, the original memories are recovered, but the fugue memories are lost. The individual then has a permanent void in personality history (Kihlstrom, Glisky, & Angiulo, 1994).

Some patients with dissociative fugue disorders will travel short distances over brief periods; others may travel far and remain in a fugue state for months or years. These individuals appear normal and will not reveal any evidence of dissociative symptoms unless asked. Amnesia is a central theme in the 1945 film *Identity Unknown,* starring Richard Arlen and Cheryl Walker. In this film, a soldier develops amnesia during World War II and tries to recover his identity.

New identities are not usually formed during a fugue, but confusion about one's identity is common. If a new identity is formed, it is usually gregarious and uninhibited. The avoidance of responsibility may be quite evident in many of these people, and sexual indiscretions, legal difficulties, financial problems, or fear of anticipated combat is frequently part of the clinical picture. Even though the prevalence of dissociative fugue has been reported as only 0.2 percent of the general population, it may be more common in times of war, natural disaster, and dislocation (Lowenstein, 1991).

THE THREE FACES OF EVE

In *The Three Faces of Eve,* narrator Alistair Cooke prepares the audience for a documentary of a true story about a woman with multiple personality disorder. The 1957 black-and-white film takes place in 1951 in a small Georgia town. Joanne Woodward, who won an Academy Award as best actress for her performance, first introduces the viewer to Eve White, a quiet, passive, modest homemaker who begins having severe headaches, followed by "spells." She cannot remember what she did during these spells. Mrs. White is married to a rigid, dull, unimaginative man named Ralph, who is frustrated with the changes in his wife's behavior. Their unhappy marriage is even more stressed by these unexplained events.

During these spells, Eve Black, the second personality, "comes out." Eve Black is a seductive, sexually promiscuous single woman, buys flashy and provocative clothes, smokes, drinks, and frequents nightclubs. Eve White, who is unaware of Eve Black's existence, is afraid she is going crazy because of her unexplained periods of amnesia and hearing voices. Eve Black, on the other hand, knows of Eve White, dislikes her husband, and their child, Bonnie, and delights in having Eve White feel the hangover following Eve Black's night of carousing. Eve White and her husband seek psychiatric treatment from Dr. Luther, played by Lee J. Cobb, for her headaches and spells.

It is well over a year before Dr. Luther is able to identify the existence of Eve Black. Following an incident in which Eve Black attempts to strangle Bonnie, Eve White is admitted to the hospital. She vows not to be reunited with her daughter until she is well. With the help of another psychiatrist, another personality is discovered who exists outside Eve White's awareness. While Eve is in the hospital, Dr. Luther is able to establish a therapeutic relationship with both personalities and attempts to integrate them into one. The diagnosis of multiple personality disorder is explained to Eve White and her spouse, who both attempt to understand the problem. Ralph is never able to truly understand the disorder and eventually divorces Eve.

As Eve White struggles to work during the day, Eve Black parties at night. They both continue to be treated by Dr. Luther. Eventually, a third personality, Jane, emerges who is aware of both Eve White and Eve Black, even though neither is aware of her. Following a visit with her daughter, Bonnie, at her parents' home, Jane begins to have memories of playing under the porch as a child. Gradually, through the use of hypnosis*, Dr. Luther is able to help Eve recall the trauma (being forced to kiss her dead grandmother's corpse) that precipitated her personalities splitting. After reliving the memory, only Jane remained.*

SYBIL

The film *Sybil* (1976), based upon a true story, stars Emmy-Award winner Sally Field as Sybil and Joanne Woodward as Dr. Wilbur. The audience is introduced to Sybil, a distressed young woman who is working as a preschool teacher while attending art school. The setting is Central Park in New York City, where Sybil is supervising art activities of preschool children. As she is talking with the children, the creaking sound of a swing stirs traumatic childhood memories. Sybil unsuccessfully attempts to attend to her assigned task of organizing the children into a game of follow-the-leader. In the next scene, Sybil is standing in the middle of a fountain, obviously confused. Her supervisor is scolding her for leading the children the wrong way. Sybil returns to her apartment, where she curls into a fetal position, trying to escape her tormenting memories. In desperation, she breaks her apartment window, which seems to give her some psychological relief. Because of her cut wrist, she ends up in an emergency room. Due to her confusion, she is referred to a psychiatrist, Dr. Wilbur, who evaluates her and begins treatment that lasts for 11 years.

This episode represents one of many in which Sybil is initially overwhelmed with flashbacks of traumatic childhood events that lead to periods of irrational behavior followed by a climactic event, such as breaking a window and injuring herself. The audience gradually realizes that, as Sybil recalls traumatic memories, one of her 16 other personalities, or "alters," gains control and triggers the irrational behavior. Through the next few months, Sybil reveals numerous personalities to her psychiatrist.

Sybil, a withdrawn, modest art student, is unable to touch others and has never been close to anyone. She lives in a world of alter personalities and memories of her past. Each of the other alters represents a part of Sybil and serves a particular purpose. For example, Vanessa is musical and enjoys playing the music Sybil once played. Vicki is very much in charge of life and is fearless. Peggy is a child who feels the terror and anger of childhood trauma. Marsha represents her despair and is often suicidal.

Through interaction with the different personalities and the use of hypnosis, Dr. Wilbur gradually pieces together Sybil's traumatic past. The goal of therapy is to integrate the personalities by helping the alters remember the past, experience the emotions associated with the traumatic events, and develop an adult perspective on the trauma. Patiently, Dr. Wilbur develops a warm, therapeutic relationship with all of the alters who are able to share their experiences. Dr. Wilbur, in turn, is able to help Sybil remember parts of her life that were previously shut off.

In the film, Sybil develops a romantic attraction to her neighbor Richard, played by Brad Davis. She is able to hide her psychiatric problems until the Christmas holidays, which are particularly problematic for Sybil. During an attempt at closeness, when she slept with him, protected by her nightgown, she had one of her recurring nightmares. Upon recovering from the nightmare and finding herself on top of a bookcase, she realizes that it will be impossible to have a relationship with Richard. She becomes very upset and her suicidal alter, Marsha, appears. Richard contacts Dr. Wilbur, who arrives just as Richard is preventing Marsha from jumping off the roof.

Through her relationships with Dr. Wilbur and Richard, Sybil learns that she really does need people and begins to recognize her feelings of loneliness. Gradually, as the repeated abuse of her childhood is relived, Sybil is able to remember her childhood experiences and integrate them into her whole personality.

DISSOCIATIVE IDENTITY DISORDER

Dissociative identity disorder, formerly called **multiple personality disorder,** is an extremely rare condition characterized by disturbances in memory and identity. The essential feature is the presence of two or more distinct identities, or alter personality states, that assume control over behavior (APA, 1994). Amnesia is present in one or more of the personalities. Usually, the more passive the personality, the greater the amnesia. Dissociative identity disorder is usually believed to be a post-traumatic condition that emerges after overwhelming traumatic childhood experiences (Kluft, 1991).

History of Dissociative Identity Disorder

Throughout history, some people have had disturbances that, by today's standards, would be diagnosed as dissociative identity disorders. The common characteristic found in these individuals is the loss of personal identity (Kluft, 1991). The first scientifically reported multiple personality was that of Eberhardt Gmelin in 1791, but people with these symptoms were believed to be "possessed" until the end of the 18th century. The phenomenon was usually explained in terms of Judeo-Christian beliefs, and the recommended treatment was exorcism by the clergy.

Benjamin Rush described patients with dissociative identity disorders in the early 19th century, but interest in multiple personalities has waxed and waned since that time. There was renewed interest in the disorder after publication of R. Schreiber's book *Sybil* in 1973. This book (on which the movie was based) described Cornelia B. Wilbur's work with a patient with multiple personality disorder. In 1984, the first international conference on multiple personality disorder was held and a specialized journal, *Dissociation,* was initiated in 1988.

Films have often presented the duality of the human personality, usually depicting a struggle between good and evil. In 1920, *Dr. Jekyll and Mr. Hyde* was first introduced as a silent film, starring John Barrymore and Martha Robinson. The 1932 remake, directed by Rouben Mammouliam, was the first sound version of this Robert Louis Stevenson classic. In this film, Dr. Harry Jekyll (played by Fredric March, who won an Oscar for his performance) represents all that is good and kind. He is a well-respected physician who devotes endless hours to hospital charity work. His innate curiosity, as well as his own socially unacceptable feelings, has led him to speculate about good and evil within human beings. He believes that the evil of humans can be captured and isolated. As the film opens, he is engaged to Muriel, played by Miriam Hopkins, with whom he is deeply in love. According to the custom of the time, Muriel's father has set a marriage date that is too far in the future to suit Harry. The audience gets a glimpse of Dr. Jekyll's underlying impulsiveness, his impatience, and the sexuality that he is trying hard to repress.

When Muriel's father takes her away for an extended trip, Dr. Jekyll tests his theory about inherent evils. He mixes and swallows a potion that he believes can isolate the evils of human beings. He then becomes the evil Mr. Hyde, who seduces, abuses, and eventually kills a woman who is his social inferior. Eventually, he can no longer control the "coming out" of the alter personality (Mr. Hyde), and he confides his mistake to his future father-in-law. After attacking his fiancée, Dr. Jekyll is caught and killed.

Attraction to the concept of alter personalities of good and evil continued through the 1900s. *Dr. Jekyll and Mr. Hyde* was remade in 1941 and starred Spencer Tracy and Ingrid Bergman. It was filmed again in 1968, starring Jack Palance, and given a new title, *The Strange Case of Dr. Jekyll and Mr. Hyde*. A somewhat different twist on the same theme is found in the excellent Hermann Hesse novel *Steppenwolf,* and in the somewhat less excellent 1974 film adaptation of the novel.

Epidemiology of the Disorder

The prevalence of dissociative identity disorder is estimated to be 1 per 10,000 population (Kluft, 1991). For a long time, the diagnosis of dissociative identity was made only in North America, raising the suspicion that therapists somehow produce the symptoms. Now there is evidence that this disorder occurs in Europe as well (Boon & Draijer, 1993). It is believed that many cases of dissociative identity disorder are undiagnosed, and multiple personality disorder may not be as rare as these statistics would indicate. The majority of those identified are females over the age of 30. It is believed that the males with this disorder enter the legal system rather than the psychiatric system and thereby go unrecognized. Many male adolescents with dissociative identity disorder encounter difficulties with the law (Kluft, 1991).

Etiology of the Disorder

The etiology of dissociative identity disorder is unknown. Kluft (1991) has proposed a four-factor model. According to this model, dissociative identity disorder develops in persons who have (1) the capacity to dissociate as a defense and (2) experienced traumatic, overwhelming life events. However, the actual formation of the alter depends upon (3) the individual's inherent personality and its influences. Additionally, in order for multiple personalities to develop, individuals must also experience (4) inadequate protection, soothing, and nurturing from significant others.

The first factor, the **capacity to dissociate,** is biologically based. Evidence for this factor is supported by research indicating that persons with this disorder are highly hypnotizable and suggestible. The second factor, **overwhelming traumatic experiences** (usually child sexual abuse) is well illustrated in *Sybil*. Sybil's experiences with her mother were torturous. Other traumatic experiences reported to be related to dissociative disorders include death or loss of significant others, witnessing deaths or deliberate destruction of significant others, and exposure to dead bodies (and especially being forced to touch or kiss them) (Kluft, 1991). The trauma in Eve's case in *The Three Faces of Eve* resulted from her mother's insistence that she kiss her grandmother's dead body at a funeral in her family parlor.

The third factor, the existence of intrapsychic configurations such as **state-dependent learning,** or autohypnosis, is unique to each individual. The expression of the phenomena depends upon cultural and environmental experiences. For example, some persons now develop alters based upon television programs, such as a ninja or Superman, that were unheard of in the early 1900s. Support for the last factor is based on observations that individuals stop manifesting their alters when they are protected from further trauma. Kluft argues that this lack of protection, soothing, and nurturing is an integral part of the development of multiple personalities.

Course of the Disorder

The symptoms of dissociative identity disorder are associated with many other psychiatric states such as anxiety symptoms (phobia, panic attacks, obsessive-compulsive behaviors), mood symptoms (manic and depressive), other dissociative symptoms (amnesias, fugues, depersonalization), somatoform symptoms (conversion), sexual dysfunctions, suicide attempts, self-mutilations, substance abuse, eating disorders, sleep disturbance, symptoms of schizophrenia, symptoms of post-traumatic stress syndrome, and borderline personality disorder. Since many symptoms of PTSD occur in dissociative identity disorder, some argue that these two are variants of the same disorder (Kluft, 1991).

Dissociative identity disorder is believed to have a long course, beginning in childhood before the age of five. Symptoms have been observed in children as young as three. In childhood, vague dissociative features may include trance-like behaviors; fluctuations in abilities, age appropriateness, and moods; and intermittent depression, amnesia, hallucinated voices, disavowed polarized behaviors, and disavowed witnessed behaviors. These children may appear to be liars, and there may be inconsistencies in school behavior. They may also show suicidal or self-injurious behavior, have imaginary companions when over five years of age, and show fluctuating physical symptoms.

In adolescence, the alter personalities become more distinct and are used in coping with nontraumatic material as well as traumatic events. New, specialized alters are formed in new academic, social, and sexual situations. Female patterns are promiscuity and withdrawn or childlike behavior. Male adolescent patterns are usually characterized by aggression, depression, or sexual misbehavior.

By adulthood, there may be many as many as 8 to 10 alters. The personalities and their self-concepts often reflect very different aspects of the self. Alters may have different experiences and be different ages, genders, races, religions, and sexual orientations. They may also have very different value systems as was evident in Eve Black and Eve White in *The Three Faces of Eve*. Each personality may be totally aware, partially aware, or totally unaware of each of the other personalities. This was a major issue in *The Three Faces of Eve*, when Eve Black realized that she knew everything about Eve White but nothing about Jane. It is not uncommon for one alter to have physical conditions that the others do not have. Eve Black was allergic to nylon and removed her stockings; in contrast, there was no allergy in Eve White. In some people, the alters are very invested in maintaining their own separateness. Because they have different memories, they truly believe that actions affecting one alter will not affect the other. Usually there is a host personality; this is the personality that seeks help from mental health providers and bears the individual's legal name. This individual is typically depressed, anxious, compulsively good, masochistic, disoriented, and suffering from physical symptoms. This description fits both Sybil and Eve White.

There is no evidence of spontaneous remission or integration of personalities without mental health treatment. The ideal target for therapy is integration of the alters into one personality. If this is not possible, the goals of therapy become resolving problematic symptoms related to daily living and helping the individual manage on a day-to-day basis. Therapy is long-term and involves the establishment of a therapeutic relationship with the individual. Hypnosis may be used at varying stages of treatment. Through the relationship, the original traumas are accessed and examined. Through the support of the relationship, the psychological pain is soothed and viewed from an adult perspective. At this point in therapy, internal conflict can be addressed and resolved. Treatment will usually require years.

DEPERSONALIZATION DISORDER

Since depersonalization occurs as a symptom in a variety of disorders, some authorities have questioned whether depersonalization is a distinct disorder. It was first defined as a separate disorder in 1968 and described as "dominated by a feeling of unreality and estrangement from the self, body, or surroundings." In order to be considered a disorder, depersonalization must be considered the predominant psychiatric experience. It is a long-term problem, and limitations in daily functioning are thought to vary from mild to severe. Depersonalization disorder is believed to begin in adolescence, although, in some instances, it may have begun in childhood. The incidence and prevalence are unknown (Steinberg, 1991).

The cause of depersonalization is unknown. Some authorities speculate that the phenomenon is related to a neurobiological disturbance produced by temporal lobe dysfunction. Others claim that depersonalization is an adaptation to overwhelming trauma. Still other authorities argue that depersonalization is a defense against painful and conflictual stimuli, or that it is a split between the observing and participating selves that allows the person to become detached from self (Steinberg, 1991).

OTHER EXAMPLES OF DISSOCIATIVE DISORDERS IN FILMS

Dissociative disorders are among the most fascinating forms of mental illness, and it is not surprising that they are often portrayed in films. Dissociative amnesia is illustrated in films such as *Spellbound* (1945), *Suddenly, Last Summer* (1959), and *Dead Again* (1991). *Paris, Texas* (1984), a wonderful Wim Winders film, is about a man recovering from a dissociative fugue. Dissociative identity disorders have been discussed in detail in this chapter and are illustrated by *Sybil* (1976), *The Three Faces of Eve* (1957), *Raising Cain* (1992), and *Voices Within: The Lives of Truddi Chase* (1990), a made-for-television movie based on the best-seller *When Rabbit Howls*. Depersonalization disorder is represented by *Altered States* (1980) and Martin Scorsese's *The Last Temptation of Christ* (1988).

In addition to the fairly clear-cut clinical examples cited, film history is replete with examples of quasi-dissociative conditions in which one character exchanges personalities (or sometimes even bodies) with another. The classic example is Bergman's *Persona* (1966), in which Liv Ullmann is treated for a somatoform disorder (the loss of speech after a performance of *Electra*) by a nurse. Ullmann and the nurse gradually exchange personalities. A similar theme is found in the Robert Altman film *3 Women* (1977), in which two of the women appear to exchange personalities. In *Zelig* (1983), Woody Allen plays a human chameleon whose personality changes to match whatever situation he is in — if he is around black musicians, he talks and acts like black musicians; around politicians, Allen becomes a politician. Ronald Coleman finds himself merging his own personality with that of Othello in *A Double Life* (1947). The 1992 comedy *Prelude to a Kiss* is about an old man and a young bride who mysteriously exchange bodies after kissing on the bride's wedding day. The film raises interesting questions about what it is that one person loves in another: is it a physical body or a set of personality characteristics, such as wit, charm, and grace? The means through which the transformation is effected is never specified in *Prelude*. In contrast, it is very clear in *Black Friday,* a 1940 horror film in which Boris Karloff transplants the brain of a criminal into the body of a college professor.

The theme of contrasting personalities in the same person is seen in those films in which someone presumed to be dead returns to his or her old social roles, usually as a vastly improved human being. We see this in *Sommersby* (1993) and *The Return of Martin Guerre* (1982). The dramatic force of both films is heightened by the sexual excitement both women feel as they go to bed with a man who may or may not be the husband who left them years earlier.

Dissociation is also used in a plethora of films that contrast the forces of good and evil inherent in all of us. Oftentimes, the evil is inherent in a twin. For example, the personalities of good and evil twins are juxtaposed in *The Dark Mirror* (1946) and in Brian de Palma's *Sisters*

(1973). The latter film adds an interesting twist by making the two women Siamese twins who were separated as children. *Steppenwolf* (1974), an adaptation of the Hermann Hesse novel, illustrates the problem of a single individual grappling with these two competing aspects of self. Finally, nothing typifies the juxtaposition of good and evil in films as well as the series of films based (often very loosely) on Robert Louis Stevenson's novel *Dr. Jekyll and Mr. Hyde*.

Occasionally, it will be necessary for clinicians to decide if a patient is malingering and feigning a dissociative disorder. Viewing the Richard Gere film *Primal Fear* (1996) will help remind clinicians of the potential for malingering in suspected cases of multiple personality disorder.

HANNAH AND HER SISTERS

Questions to Consider While Watching *Hannah and Her Sisters*

- How can nonmedical therapists rule out organic pathology? Does *every* client have to be worked up medically to ensure that there is no medical disease present?
- How common is it for a patient who has headaches to actually have a brain tumor?
- Should patients be able to insist on expensive tests (such as CAT scans), or is this decision ultimately up to the physician? Should it matter if a patient has insurance?
- Is the percentage of clients who visit psychologists for what are eventually determined to be medical problems about equivalent to the number of patients who visit physicians for treatment of what are ultimately determined to be psychological problems?
- Do the symptoms of hypochondriacs worsen under stress?
- Is the reassurance typically offered hypochondriacal patients going to be possible in a world of managed care? Will these changes in policy exacerbate or ameliorate the patients' concerns and symptoms?

Hannah and Her Sisters (1986) is one of Woody Allen's funniest and most gratifying films. Allen plays the role of a neurotic television executive who was formerly married to Hannah (Mia Farrow). He still maintains a cordial relationship with his former wife and his two sons. Part of the reason for the separation was that Allen was unable to father children because of a low sperm count, and Hannah had been artificially inseminated with sperm from Allen's partner and best friend. Allen sees the fact that Hannah conceived twins as further evidence of his own masculine inadequacy.

The film opens at a Thanksgiving dinner celebration and follows the lives of the characters for two years, during which their lives unfold in routine ways. They devote much of their time to books, music, dating, and small talk in New York's restaurants. The strength of the movie lies not in its plot but, rather, in its wonderful character development. The viewer soon begins to care about these people very much.

Most of the action in the film revolves around an affair between Hannah's husband (Michael Caine) and her sister (Barbara Hershey). Eventually, Allen marries Hannah's third sister (Dianne Wiest), and the film ends at the third Thanksgiving dinner with some semblance of harmony between the sisters. Hannah's marriage to Michael Caine has remained intact, and Barbara Hershey has married an English literature professor from Columbia. During the final scene in the movie, Allen embraces Wiest, who has just come from a doctor's appointment. She tells Allen the good news that she is pregnant. The film concludes with an apparent commitment to the sanctity of the family and the realization that only through the family can one escape the isolation, loneliness, and existential angst that have troubled Allen so much for the past two years. Michael Caine and Dianne Wiest received Academy Awards for Best Supporting Actor and Actress; Allen got the award for Best Screenplay written for the screen.

> *This time I think I really have something. . . . It's not like that adenoidal thing, where I didn't realize I had them out.* Woody Allen discussing his hearing loss with his physician in *Hannah and Her Sisters*

For our purposes, the most important parts of the film are the long sequences that explore Allen's hypochondriasis. He is on his way to get a blood test when the film opens; and we soon realize that Allen is preoccupied with doctors, hospitals, and his own fragile mortality. He works in a high-stress job as a television program director and at one-point remarks, "Has anybody got a Tagamet? My ulcer is starting to kill me." (Allen has a remarkable sense for the prevailing concerns and habits of the American public. A decade earlier, he had gotten a laugh from his viewers with a similar line about Valium.)

Allen has experienced some hearing loss and is convinced that he has a brain tumor. He suspects that his doctors have known this all along but "they don't tell you [these things] because sometimes the weaker ones will panic." He awakens in the middle of the night, terrified, crying out "There's a tumor in my head the size of a basketball." With each new test, he grows more apprehensive. When his computerized tomography scan turns out to be completely negative, he is at first elated and then plunges into despair as he realizes that this is just a temporary reprieve and that eventually he must die. Some of the funniest scenes in the film occur when Allen tries to explain to his parents why he is rejecting Judaism for Catholicism. When he finds the Catholic church unsatisfactory, he briefly flirts with the Hare Krishna movement.

SOMATOFORM DISORDERS

Somatization Disorder

Somatization disorder is diagnosed when there is a pattern of recurrent and multiple somatic complaints that require medical treatment or that limit the effectiveness of an individual, but for which no clear organic etiology can be identified. The problems must begin before the age of 30 and persist for a period of years. In addition, multiple organ systems must be involved. Specifically, there must be at least four pain symptoms, two gastrointestinal symptoms, one sexual symptom, and one pseudoneurological symptom for the diagnosis to be made. A pseudoneurological symptom is one in which a disease or dysfunction of the central nervous system is suggested. For example, a patient might have a paralyzed arm or numbness in his or her leg, and these symptoms could be part of a larger clinical picture suggesting somatization disorder was present. Somatization disorder is sometimes referred to as **Briquet's syndrome.** It has been estimated that between 10 percent and 20 percent of the health care budget is spent on patients with either somatization disorder or hypochondriasis (Ford, 1983). This amounts to about $100–$200 million at the current rate of health care spending.

Patients with somatization disorder are poor historians, and their complaints may vary from session to session. This problem is complicated by the fact that they easily become dissatisfied with their physicians and may be constantly changing doctors, sharing different parts of their story with each new physician. In addition, since most physician visits result in a prescription of some sort, these patients will be taking multiple medications, some of which produce side effects that result in general somatic distress. This pattern sets up a vicious cycle and makes diagnosis of the patient with a somatization disorder a challenging dilemma. Diagnosis is further complicated by the fact that some genuine medical conditions, such as multiple sclerosis, hyperparathyroidism, and systematic lupus erythematosus, can have vague symptoms that affect multiple organ systems. Occasionally, patients have multiple physical complaints that appear to be somatoform-like but are not sufficiently varied or of sufficient duration to meet the full criteria for somatization disorder. In these cases, the residual diagnosis of **undifferentiated somatoform disorder** is used.

Conversion Disorder

A **conversion disorder** exists when (1) patients experience significant distress or impairment from motor or sensory symptoms that appear to be neurological but for which no adequate neurological explanation can be determined and (2) it appears that psychological factors have played a significant role in the etiology or maintenance of the disorder. In addition, the clinician must rule out malingering before the diagnosis is made.

The very name conversion disorder is linked to a psychological theory that maintains that unconscious psychological distress can be "converted" into physical manifestations. Freud himself was very interested in this phenomenon, as was his mentor, Charcot. It is still illuminating to review the 1962 film *Freud,* in which Montgomery Clift plays the famous Viennese psychiatrist. The film presents multiple examples of conversion in Freud's patients.

At the time of Freud, conversion disorders were referred to as *hysteria*. The word *hysteria* is derived from the Greek and is literally translated as "wandering uterus." Obviously, the Greeks believed only women could be hysterics. In fact, there is a marked gender difference, and the prevalence of conversion disorder is two to five times greater in women. Interestingly, symptoms are far more likely to occur on the left side of the body (presumably because most people are right-handed).

Conversion disorders are fascinating, in part because the underlying dynamics seem so transparent to an external observer. The soldier who can't fire a rifle because his arm is paralyzed has found a convenient way of avoiding battle; the woman who becomes functionally blind after witnessing a car wreck in which her son was killed can never see anything this awful happen again. In actual practice, few cases of somatization disorder are this tidy. However, some patients do receive **secondary gain** as a result of their medical problems — e.g., a woman whose illness restricts her to bed may be "forced" to cancel a wedding with a bridegroom about whom she is still ambivalent.

Patients who develop conversion disorders may show little concern about their symptoms. In addition, there are often anatomical inconsistencies that help identify symptoms as hysterical in nature. For example, patients may exhibit stocking or glove anesthesia, in which the boundaries of their numbness are sharply defined and inconsistent with the distribution of the nerves of the hand and foot. It is important to separate somatization disorder and conversion disorder from both malingering and factitious disorder. In **malingering,** a person deliberately "fakes" his or her symptoms in order to achieve a clearly understood goal. A death row inmate, for example, may feign symptoms of mental illness - for example, believing that the state cannot execute someone who is not mentally competent. Likewise, a small child may complain of stomach pain, remembering that the last time this occurred he or she was allowed to stay home from school and eat ice cream. In cases of malingering, the objective of the feigned symptoms is understandable, if not laudable. In contrast, **factitious disorders** involve feigning illness with the specific intent of assuming what Talcott Parsons called the sick role. The sick role triggers solicitous concern from others, freedom from the requirements of one's routine roles and obligations, and the assumption that one is not responsible for one's illness. When achieving these more nebulous goals results in someone's faking his or her symptoms, the diagnosis of factitious disorder is appropriate. Some patients with factitious disorders will present with predominately psychological symptoms (e.g., depression, amnesia, hallucinations, depersonalization); others will have predominately physical signs and symptoms such as nausea, vomiting, fainting, or convulsions. In rare cases, it will appear that an individual's entire life has been devoted to getting in and staying in hospitals. When this occurs, the diagnosis of *Munchausen syndrome* is sometimes made. (Baron von Münchausen lived from 1720 to 1797. He was a famed storyteller, but the eponym is probably unfortunate, for there is no evidence that he had a factitious disorder. Director Terry Gilliam made a 1989 movie titled *The Adventures of Baron Munchausen,* but the film does not address the baron's reported penchant for surgery and medical treatment.)

Pain Disorder

Patients with somatoform disorders often present with pain as a symptom; in fact, the presentation is a necessary condition for the diagnosis of somatization disorder. However, some patients will be preoccupied with the experience of pain, and their activities will be dramatically limited by the presence of pain, even when there is no lesion, history of trauma, or other objective medical data that could account for their suffering. When malingering and factitious disorder have been ruled out and it is believed that psychological factors are a part of the etiology of pain, a diagnosis of pain disorder may be assigned.

In some of these cases, there may be objective evidence of a condition that would reasonably result in the experience of pain. However, the diagnosis may still be justified if the report of pain is exaggerated and dramatically disproportionate to the magnitude of the medical condition that causes it. In short, the patient "protests too much."

A large number of associated disorders can be comorbid with pain disorder. Patients with this diagnosis often use benzodiazepines or opioids to treat their pain and may become dependent. In addition, it is common for patients with chronic pain, whether due to medical or psychological reasons or both, to become depressed in response to their pain. Anxiety disorders are also found more often in patients with pain disorder.

Psychological tests such as the **Minnesota Multiphasic Personality Inventory** (MMPI) and questionnaires such as the **McGill Pain Questionnaire** may be helpful in determining the extent to which psychological "overlay" is present in a patient's report of pain.

Pain disorders appear to occur somewhat more frequently in women than in men, and in particular cultural groups. In addition, pain is a common occurrence. For example, the *DSM-IV* estimates that "in any given year, 10–15 percent of adults in the United States have some form of work disability due to back pain alone" (APA, 1994, p. 460).

Hypochondriasis

The hypochondriac is preoccupied with thoughts of disease, infirmity, and death. This person spends the day reviewing his or her body for any sign that a serious disease may be present. Routine stomach pain is interpreted to be cancer of the bowel; every headache is assumed to be a consequence of a brain tumor; every occurrence of misplaced keys or glasses is felt to be an early indication of Alzheimer's. These beliefs persist in the face of physical exams, lab tests, X-rays, and other examinations all suggesting that there is no illness present. Eventually, worry about disease comes to dominate the individual's life, and all of his or her friends become alienated because they have little interest in the details of their friend's medical concerns.

Patients who are hypochondriacs are often labeled as "crocks" by the medical establishment and are passed from doctor to doctor. There is an initial sense of euphoria and optimism with a new physician; eventually, each doctor fails and the patient moves on in search of a solution to his or her multiple problems.

Some patients who have been labeled as hypochondriacs are later found to have bona fide medical disorders. This is especially common with disorders that have vague symptoms and a slow progression (e.g., multiple sclerosis). In addition, patients who are initially believed to have hypochondriasis are sometimes later found to have somatic concerns related to anxiety, depression, or another psychiatric disorder.

Hypochrondriasis is easy to ridicule, and there is something comical about the person who goes through an "organ recital" when describing his or her health. However, the concerns of these patients are very real and deserve sympathetic attention and concern. The *DSM-IV* estimates that the prevalence of hypochondriasis in general medical practice is between 4 and 9 percent.

Body Dysmorphic Disorder

When somebody becomes so obsessed with a perceived physical imperfection that he or she is unable to function successfully interpersonally or on the job, a diagnosis of **body dysmorphic disorder** may be appropriate. Individuals with this problem may spend hours each day looking into a mirror and brooding about their perceived inadequacy. Males may be convinced that their penis is too small; females may believe they have abnormal genitalia or that their breasts are too small or too large.

Body dysmorphic disorder can take varied forms across cultures. For example, in some Asian countries, body dysmorphic disorder is relatively rare, but many patients have an abnormal concern about the quality of their breath or public sweating.

Somatoform Disorders in Films

The 1948 film *Sorry, Wrong Number* stars Barbara Stanwick as a bedridden heiress who is partially paralyzed, although her doctors cannot determine any neurological reason she is not able to walk. One evening, she happens to overhear two men planning a murder; later she realizes that she is the intended victim. Much of the suspense of the film revolves around the realization that she must get out of bed in order to save herself.

Persona (1966), one of Ingmar Bergman's most complex films, deals with a famous actress (Liv Ullmann) who suddenly, and seemingly without reason, stops talking. Her doctor can find nothing wrong with her and is at a loss to explain her patient's symptom. However, she prescribes rest and constant attention, and Ullmann spends the summer at a house on the coast in the care of a full-time nurse, Bibi Andersson. Although Ullmann almost never speaks, we know that she retains the capacity for speech. At one point, when the nurse appears to be about to throw boiling water on Ullmann, the actress shouts, "Don't." Although the conversion disorder portrayed in the film is fascinating, the more interesting element is the merging of the personalities of the two women. There are a number of interesting dream sequences, and one scene presents a face on the screen that is a composite of Ullmann and Andersson (one-half of each woman's face is shown). In selecting the title for the film, Bergman was likely thinking both about the masks worn by Greek actors in classical theater and of Carl Gustaf Jung who used the term to refer to those parts of our personality that we show to the outer world. Perhaps

Ullmann quit speaking because she had resolved to stop acting and wear no more masks. The ending of the film is somewhat unclear, but it appears that Ullmann returned to acting and that Andersson returned to nursing and that the personalities of the two women did not remain merged.

Another complex film, albeit one of more recent vintage, is *Agnes of God* (1985), starring Meg Tilly as a young nun (Sister Agnes), Anne Bancroft as the Mother Superior of the convent, and Jane Fonda as the psychiatrist sent to investigate the apparent murder of a newborn baby who was found wrapped in bloody sheets and stuffed in a wastebasket at the convent. The film juxtaposes reason and faith and quickly convinces the viewer that, although Sister Agnes is surely one of "God's innocents," she is just as surely the mother and the murderer of the child.

Fonda uses hypnosis in treating Sister Agnes, and it turns out that she was sexually molested by her mother as a child. It also turns out that the mother was the sister of the Mother Superior. At the end of the film, the court finds Sister Agnes not guilty by reason of insanity, and she returns to the convent, where she will continue to receive psychiatric care.

Sister Agnes' confusion seems very real, and the diagnosis of insanity appears justified. It appears that a dissociative amnesia may have been present, and one believes that Sister Agnes had repressed the memories of her rape and was genuinely amnestic for the incident in which she strangled the child with his umbilical cord. For purposes of this chapter, however, the most interesting scenes are those in which **stigmata** appear. This occurs once in a convent room and once in a chapel when Agnes is praying. Stigmata is the name given to bleeding in the hands and feet, presumably from the sites where nails were driven into when Christ was crucified. It is a relatively rare but well-documented phenomenon that is found in people with deep religious convictions. In the case of *Agnes of God,* the blood of Christ, the blood of the murdered infant, and the blood of Agnes all seem to commingle.

Perhaps the best example of body dysmorphic syndrome is found in Gerard Depardieu's portrayal of *Cyrano de Bergerac* in the 1990 French film by the same name. Cyrano is deeply in love with his cousin Roxanne but cannot profess his love because he is too ashamed of his long (and to him) deformed nose. Instead, he writes long love letters for his friend Perez. The letters are successful, and Roxanne falls deeply in love with the romantic Perez. Perez is killed in battle and Roxanne enters a convent, where Cyrano continues to visit her. Fifteen years later, as he is dying, Cyrano recites one of the last letters from Perez by memory and Roxanne realizes that he has been the one whom she has really loved all this time.

In 1987 Steve Martin played the role of a modern-day Cyrano in the film *Roxanne*. However, in this film his nose is truly of grotesque proportions and he would not qualify for the diagnosis of body dysmorphic syndrome (which requires an *imagined* defect in appearance). In the French film, Depardieu's nose is elongated but not grotesque, and one suspects that his concerns are at least as much psychological as real.

Critical Thinking Questions

- How can an understanding of the phenomenon of hypnosis help us understand dissociative disorders?
- Movies such as *Primal Fear* (1996) suggest it is relatively easy to fool lawyers and therapists into believing you have a multiple personality disorder. How would you assess the likelihood of malingering if you were a clinician evaluating a patient with an alleged dissociative disorder?
- How do somatoform disorders affect the national health care budget?
- How will people with somatoform disorders be affected by the adoption of managed care practices?

Chapter 4

Psychological Stress and Physical Disorders

There's crippled, very crippled,
totally crippled, and dead.
Stephanie Anderson's pessimistic
appraisal of her future in *Duet for One* (1986)

Questions to Consider While Watching *Duet for One*

- How does the stress of Stephanie Anderson's career influence the manifestations of the symptoms of her illness, multiple sclerosis?
- Throughout the film, Stephanie handles the stress of the multiple sclerosis differently. Trace her emotional responses to her disorder in the beginning, middle, and end of the film.
- Stephanie's personality and career were important factors in maintaining the relationship with her husband, Alan Bates. When her career changed, how did her relationship with her husband change?
- What emotions are evoked in you when Alan's affair with his secretary becomes so blatant? Is that different from Stephanie's sexual relationship with the junk dealer, Totter?
- Explain how Stephanie redefines her relationships with her husband, student, accompanist, and manager as a result of her illness. Are these changes because of the physical limitations of her illness or her responses to it? Explain.
- Dr. Feldman is a fairly inadequate therapist. How have his feelings for his patient influenced the patient-therapist relationship. Speculate about whether he will be a better companion to Stephanie than he was a therapist. What purpose does he serve in the movie?

PATIENT EVALUATION

Patient's stated reason for coming: "I came because my husband thought I was getting a little upset, and seeing a psychotherapist would help . . . . I've been getting a little low lately . . . . I've got multiple sclerosis."

History of the present illness: Ms. Stephanie Anderson is a 45-year-old internationally renowned concert violinist who is self-referred at the recommendation of her husband, who is a composer/conductor. She was recently diagnosed with multiple sclerosis that will ultimately affect her ability to perform, and Ms. Anderson dreads confronting the day when she can no longer play the violin. This fear is beginning to interfere with her confidence on the stage. She describes music as being her "life." Ms. Anderson acknowledges being depressed. She has sleep onset insomnia and early morning risings. She experiences frequent nightmares in which she is onstage but unable to move her fingers or play the violin.

Past psychiatric illness, treatment, and outcomes: There is no past history of psychiatric illness.

Medical history: Ms. Anderson was diagnosed with multiple sclerosis (MS) last year, following an extensive workup for numbness. Currently her MS is in remission, but she has unpredictable episodes of finger numbness and weakness of leg muscles. She fell down the stairs at home and in her psychiatrist's office. She appears to be in denial of her physical illness, and this denial is gradually being eroded by the appearance of physical symptoms.

Psychosocial history: Ms. Anderson began playing the violin as a young child. Her grandfather had given her his violin as a gift when she was small. During one of the blitzes, her home was destroyed by fire. Her mother died in the fire, and the violin burned. Stephanie reports being most upset about the loss of the violin. Her mood improved when she realized that it was the music she wanted, not the violin. Ms. Anderson is married to conductor/composer David Cornwallis, and they reside in a comfortable, large home in a fashionable area in London. They have never had children.

   Both Ms. Anderson and Mr. Cornwallis work from their home. Ms. Anderson teaches and prepares for concerts. Mr. Cornwallis serves as administrator of the orchestra and maintains his office in the home with the help of a personal secretary. Ms. Anderson's social system consists of her husband, students, accompanist, manager, and household help.

Drug and alcohol history: Ms. Anderson is a moderate social drinker, but her husband is reported to be addicted to alcohol. Recently, Ms. Anderson has been using alcohol to relieve stressful feelings.

Behavioral observations: Ms. Anderson is a very well dressed, engaging, attractive woman who arrived for her appointment on time. She answered questions but did not elaborate upon responses. During periods of silence, she appeared depressed and angry. At several points during the interview, Ms. Anderson began crying at the injustice of having a chronic illness. This weeping alternated with a false bravado — e.g., at one point, she described her many volunteer activities and remarked, "That seems like a full life, doesn't it — especially for a cripple?" Her left hand was bandaged, apparently as a result of cuts she sustained (without her awareness) when she was slicing steak with a meat cleaver.

Mental status examination: Ms. Anderson has normal cognitive functioning, and there is no evidence of any psychosis. She earned a perfect score of 30 on the *Mini Mental Status Examination* (although she did experience mild difficulty copying the intersecting crosses). She reports episodes of crying, sad feelings, and a depressed mood most of the day. Her weight is stable, but she has difficulty sleeping and routinely wakes in the early morning hours. She expresses feelings of worthlessness because her illness is interfering, and she is unable to play the violin. Changes in her physical functioning have also led her to question her value as a partner to her husband. She often thinks about killing herself.

Functional assessment: Ms. Anderson is an accomplished concert violinist who is regularly engaged in international concert tours. She supports herself and her husband. Her relationship with her husband is strained; most marital tension relates to her illness. She has no social network outside her work relationships.

Strengths: Ms. Anderson is an accomplished artist who has had many successes in life. She is articulate and self-supporting and easily engages in interactions. She expresses her feelings and is beginning to recognize her need for support during the illness.

Diagnosis: 296.22 Major Depressive Disorder, Single Episode, Moderate.

Treatment plan: Ms. Anderson will need supportive psychotherapy as she adjusts to the limitation of her illness and her changes in lifestyle.

Prognosis: Ms. Anderson may be able to accept her illness and develop new relationships. Her depression will probably be long-term.

PSYCHOLOGICAL STRESS

Stress is a part of everyday life. Coping with stress should be viewed as a natural part of life. Usually, stress is viewed as a negative experience, but its outcomes can be positive. Stress is difficult to define, but it is one of the most complex concepts in mental health care. Stress is associated with physical illness (e.g., heart attack), mental disorders (depression), and social problems (divorce). Over time, stress can actually cause physical illnesses and emotional problems.

Stress can be understood from a variety of theoretical perspectives. The behavioral perspective views stress as a consequence of an illness. How one copes with an illness is determined by whether or not "illness behaviors" are rewarded. For example, if a person receives attention while experiencing the stress of adapting to a wheelchair, the attention is rewarding. The individual then may be more likely to seek out situations in which a wheelchair is necessary in order to receive attention.

Cognitive theorists emphasize what is going on inside a person's head, as well as his or her behavior. This approach relates stress to the meaning of the illness or the person's control over it. If the illness were serious or terminal, according to cognitive theorists, that person would more likely experience stress. An example of a cognitive approach is represented by the work of Richard Lazarus and his colleagues (1984). Lazarus argues that stress depends on the relationship between a person and the environment that is "appraised" by the person as taxing—the more threatening the environment, the greater the stress.

Psychodynamic theorists focus on interpersonal relationships and family interactions. They believe that, the greater the dysfunction of the interpersonal relationships, the greater the stress. The sociocultural perspective says that stress is a result of the society in which the person lives. Social disruption, such as a divorce or the death of a family member, precipitates stress in an individual.

The biological perspective would argue that impairment in physical functioning could result from changes in the immune system. These physiological changes follow stressful events. During stressful periods, illness symptoms can get worse in chronic diseases that are sensitive to the immune system. It is hypothesized that emotional upsets, common in interpersonal relationships, seem to be related to changes in physiological functioning.

DUET FOR ONE

In the film *Duet for One* (1986), a chronic, debilitating illness, multiple sclerosis, is the major stress in the life of Stephanie Anderson. Multiple sclerosis (MS) is a progressive disease characterized by a gradual breakdown of the tissue (myelin) surrounding the nerve fibers of the brain and spinal cord. It begins slowly, usually in young adulthood, and continues throughout life, with periods of exacerbation and remission. There is no cure for MS, and the symptoms are treated as they appear. In the early part of the illness, there are abnormal sensations in the extremities or on one side of the face. There are also symptoms of muscle weakness, dizziness, and problems with vision such as double vision and partial blindness. Later in the illness, there may be **emotional lability** (rapid shifting of moods), **ataxia** (staggering gait, poor coordination), and difficulty urinating.

Stephanie Anderson's symptoms in *Duet for One* are more characteristic of someone moving into the later stages of MS. She suffers from the lack of sensation in her hands but also has a problem of falling and has confined herself to the wheelchair. Throughout the movie, Stephanie vacillates between very good feelings (euphoric through denial) to extreme depression and suicidal thoughts. Part of her mood swings can be explained by the meaning of the devastating illness to her career and her lifestyle. *Some of her mood changes can be attributed to the MS.* If a mental health specialist were treating her today, an antidepressant would be given to help her cope with her changing moods and thoughts of suicide.

Duet for One portrays the plight of a middle-aged woman whose life changes dramatically in a few short months. She goes from being a famous concert violinist, married to a well-known, glamorous composer who is blatant about his womanizing, to living in the country with a new husband, her former psychiatrist. Her struggle with her illness becomes an identity crisis. Her self-esteem had been tied to being rich and famous. When her illness forces her to give up the stage and her concert life, she tries to find meaning in her life. Her husband, who doted on her when she was famous, rejects her in illness. His romantic attachment to his secretary leads to his eventually leaving Stephanie. In an attempt to validate her attractiveness, Stephanie takes a married lover. The relationship ends, and she is even more alone.

There are a variety of ways to understand Stephanie's responses to her physical illness and her experience of stress. From a strictly behavioral perspective, Stephanie can be viewed as a woman whose achievement as a world-class violinist reaped positive rewards throughout her life— success, money, and marriage. These rewards became reinforcing and, now that she will lose her ability to perform, she has no system of rewards. She cannot cope because the rewards are no longer there. Consequently, her stress increases and she is seeking new experiences that are rewarding.

From a cognitive perspective, Lazarus' stress model would explain Stephanie as someone who is experiencing an environmental event (loss of ability to perform), and she appraises this loss of functioning as extremely threatening. She in turn is trying to cope with the threat of the loss of functioning. Her inability to cope in turn negatively affects her health status.

The psychodynamic perspective focuses on Stephanie's feelings about herself and about being afflicted with a chronic, progressive illness. The anger that is evident throughout the film in her interactions with her husband, student, manager, and domestic housekeepers represents the anger toward the illness and the changes that are occurring. Her personality is that of a high achiever who is self-centered and ambitious. For someone with this type of personality, a chronic illness is devastating because it strikes at the very core of the personality.

> "I'm healthy and I'm normal and I'll be alive after you die!" Alan Bates confronting Julie Andrews with the reality of her illness in *Duet for One* (1986)

The sociocultural perspective becomes particularly evident as we observe an attractive woman who is losing her physical functioning to aging as well as a chronic illness. Her sexual conquest of the junk dealer represents her developmental struggle with aging and the disease process. Stephanie has surrounded herself with people like her: self-centered high achievers. People in her life also are attracted to her because of her fame and money. They are not likely to provide her with the emotional support that she needs when she is no longer a celebrity. Instead, they become alienated from her and eventually leave her at a time when she needs them the most. At the end she, like all of us, faces death alone.

PSYCHOLOGICAL STRESS AND PHYSICAL DISORDERS IN FILMS

Films dealing with post-traumatic stress disorder are reviewed in Chapter 2. Almost any film dealing with war will also address the physical and psychological consequences of prolonged exposure to combat stress. Films like *The Caine Mutiny* (1954), staring Humphrey Bogart as Captain Queeg, illustrate the stress of confronting and challenging inept leadership, while other classic films like *Twelve O'Clock High* (1949) document the stress associated with military life.

The stress associated with everyday life is convincingly portrayed by Michael Douglas in *Falling Down* (1993), while the stress of the business world is apparent in films such as *Jerry Maguire* (1996), *Glengarry Glen Ross* (1992), and *Death of a Salesman* (1951/1985).

The Waterdance (1992), starring Eric Stoltz, Wesley Snipes, and Helen Hunt, offers a convincing portrayal of what life is like for someone confined to a wheelchair after a biking accident. The film deals very convincingly and sympathetically with the sexual concerns accident victims often face after their injuries. At one point, one of the hospitalized patients clearly articulates a question the new patient, Joel Garcia (played by Eric Stoltz), has been asking himself: "How long is it going to take before that pretty little girl leaves you for someone who can tune her engine?" The patients in the hospital are divided by race, values, and social class; however, they are united in a profound way by the devastating reality of their injuries and the resulting physical limitations, and ultimately these similarities prove to be far more significant than the trivial differences that separate them. Many of the same themes had been effectively portrayed by a wheelchair-bound Marlon Brando in *The Men* (1950), a film cast with real paralyzed veterans from a California Veteran's Administration Hospital.

Jimmy Stewart is confined to a wheelchair and uses his injury as an excuse to practice voyeurism in Hitchcock's *Rear Window* (1954). The psychological adaptation required to adjust to life in a wheelchair is portrayed in *Born on the Fourth of July* (1989) and *Coming Home* (1978), and somewhat less convincingly in *Crash* (1996). Pathological adaptation to paralysis is presented in *Bitter Moon* (1992), *The People vs. Larry Flynt* (1996), and *Breaking the Waves* (1996). The stress associated with caring for someone who is wheelchair-bound is presented in *Passion Fish* (1992); the stress parents experience with a chronically ill or dying child is poignantly illustrated by the film *Lorenzo's Oil* (1992). *The Accidental Tourist* (1988) is a film in which William Hurt plays a man unable to cope with the death of his son. Samuel Goldwyn's film *The Best Years of Our Life* (1946) depicts the changes that occur in the life of a sailor who comes home from the war missing both hands.

Successful adaptation to a degenerative disease such as amyotrophic lateral sclerosis is documented in films such as *Pride of the Yankees* (1942), the life story of Lou Gehrig, and *A Brief History of Time* (1992), an examination of the life and ideas of cosmologist Stephen Hawking. The effects of Tourette's syndrome on the life of a young girl and her lover are effectively portrayed in *Niagara Niagara* (1998).

Critical Thinking Questions

- What is the best explanation for Stephanie Anderson's reaction to her illness — behavioral, cognitive, psychodynamic, or biological?
- How common is it for someone to react to a devastating diagnosis (such as multiple sclerosis) by beginning an affair?
- How would paralysis affect your life? What would you do to facilitate your adjustment to your new circumstances?
- Are films such as *Falling Down* accurate in their suggestion that contemporary American life is becoming more stressful? Support your answer with evidence.

Chapter 5

Mood Disorders

What we're looking for here is balance.
Dr. Elizabeth Bowen in *Mr. Jones*

Questions to Consider While Watching *Mr. Jones*

- Why does Dr. Elizabeth Bowen question the resident's admitting diagnosis of paranoid schizophrenia?
- At what point is the doctor/patient relationship first compromised? Are there early warning signs that should have alerted the psychiatrist to her countertransference to this patient?
- To what extent is a mental health provider required to reach out to a troubled and potentially suicidal patient? Would it have mattered if Mr. Jones had become manic in a different town, state, or country?
- Does Mr. Jones' history of a previous suicide attempt increase the likelihood of another attempt?
- Is an affair between a doctor and a patient more serious than one between an orderly and a patient? Would it have mattered if the patient had been discharged? Why?
- Is it ethical for a psychiatrist to visit a university to get historical information that may be relevant to a patient she is treating?
- Should patients with illnesses such as bipolar disorder be required by the courts to take medication, even if they dislike the effects of the medication?
- At one point, Mr. Jones angrily throws books and a lamp around his therapist's office. Would you have let him act out like this, or should security have been called?

PATIENT EVALUATION

Patient's stated reason for coming: "There's nothing wrong with me and I don't belong here." (Involuntary 72-hour admission)

History of the present illness: Mr. Richard Jones is a 40-year-old white male who was brought to the hospital emergency room by the city police after an apparent attempt to fly from the scaffolding of a building on which he was working. He was agitated and delusional, and he appeared to be having auditory hallucinations. The patient required both restraints and sedation (10 mg. Haldol IM). There is a recent history of poor judgment, expansive generosity, and inappropriate social behavior.

Past psychiatric illness, treatment, and outcome: Mr. Jones reports a 20-year history of intermittent hospitalization, most often for the treatment of manic episodes or marked depression. The modal discharge diagnosis following these hospitalizations has been bipolar disorder.

Medical history: Mr. Jones had his stomach pumped following a suicide attempt by ingesting a bottle of aspirin when he was approximately 20 years old. There is no other significant medical history.

Psychosocial history: Mr. Jones was a child prodigy who played the piano at the age of three. A promising career as a concert pianist was cut short by the development of bipolar disorder. The patient currently lives alone and has never been married. Mr. Jones states that his parents are no longer living, and there does not appear to be a well-established support network. A coworker, Howard Bevins, accompanied the patient to the emergency room.

Drug and alcohol history: This patient has a history of alcohol abuse during manic episodes. He has experimented with marijuana and cocaine, but denies recent use of either drug.

Behavioral observations: The patient was clean but disheveled. He was obviously agitated. His speech was rapid and pressured but generally coherent. He resisted restraints and actively fought with the police until he was sedated. Once restrained, Mr. Jones was able to appropriately respond to questions.

Mental status examination: The MSE could not be administered at the time of admission. However, when the patient was examined with the *Mini Mental Status Examination* 36 hours after admission, he achieved a perfect score of 30. A subsequent Wechsler Adult Intelligence Scale-Revised (WAIS-R) yielded a verbal IQ of 137, a performance IQ of 115, and an FSIQ of 131.

Functional assessment: Mr. Jones is well educated, and he has a graduate degree in music from a prestigious conservatory. He appears to have a long history of underemployment, and he has worked as a carpenter between episodes of illness. He is personable and charming, and he is able to function at a very high level – when he is well. He has never married, and he reports that his parents are deceased. Mr. Jones maintains an active interest in the piano and in music, and he reads widely.

Strengths: This patient is highly intelligent, verbal, and articulate. He has considerable interpersonal charm. He has trade skills (carpentry) that are in high demand. Mr. Jones functions at a very high level during those periods when he complies with his medication regimens.

Diagnosis: 296.43 Bipolar Disorder, Type 1, Recurrent, Most Recent Episode Manic, Severe Without Psychotic Features, in Partial Remission.

Treatment plan: This patient is to be started on a trial of Lithium.

Prognosis: The patient's prognosis would be excellent if he would comply with his medication regimen. However, given his history of failure to comply, the prognosis is believed to be poor.

MR. JONES

Alan Greisman and Debra Greenfield's 1993 film *Mr. Jones* is about a musician, Mr. Jones, played by Richard Gere, and his psychiatrist, Dr. Libbie Bowen, played by Lena Olin. The film shows Mr. Jones as elated, seductive, and euphoric. He is a charismatic man with tremendous charm. He persuades a contractor to hire him, proceeds to the roof, and prepares to fly after rhythmically pounding a few nails into the roof. Before climbing to the very front tip of the roof, he insists that Howard, his newfound friend, accept a $100 bill. After realizing that Mr. Jones really believes that he can fly, Howard persuades him to move away from the beam where he was teetering. The ambulance arrives and takes Jones to a local psychiatric emergency unit, where he is released after a few hours. At the hospital, he is misdiagnosed and given inappropriate medication.

Next, Mr. Jones goes to a bank and withdraws $12,000 and picks up the teller in the process. Jones manages to seduce her while on his spending binge. He purchases a baby grand piano, checks into an expensive hotel, and then attends a concert. He is arrested and returned to the hospital after he disrupts a symphony concert by attempting to take over for the conductor as the orchestra is playing Beethoven's "Ode to Joy," convinced that Beethoven would have wanted the piece played at a much faster tempo. Mr. Jones is once again hospitalized in a state of manic exhaustion and is this time accurately diagnosed and treated by psychiatrist Elizabeth (Libbie) Bowen.

Jones knows he has manic-depressive illness. He was first diagnosed in late adolescence and had several hospitalizations. However, he refuses to take his medication, which makes his hands shake. It is during the "highs" or the manic phases that he feels best about himself. The rest of the time Mr. Jones is lonely and depressed. His lows are life-threatening and result in suicide attempts. The viewers are able to gain some insight into the impact of a mental illness on the promising career of a classical musician. In addition, *the film illustrates the ways in which interpersonal relationships are affected by a disease such as bipolar disorder.* Mr. Jones' one important relationship ended when a woman he loved could no longer deal with his mood swings.

Unfortunately, the rest of the movie involves the romantic relationship that develops between Dr. Bowen and Mr. Jones. Even though Dr. Bowen resigns from the hospital, suggesting the unethical nature of this doctor-patient relationship, the true impact of the psychiatrist's behavior is never addressed in the movie. The questions at the end of this chapter explore the ethical implications of the doctor's decision to have an affair with her patient.

AFFECTIVE DISORDERS

Periods of depression are normal in most persons' lives. For example, failing an examination or ending an affair often precipitates a normal period of sadness. On the other hand, the feelings of high energy that accompany major events such as a graduation or marriage are also common in everyday life. However, some illnesses involve affective states that resemble these normal periods of depression or elation, but in fact they are very different. The individual experiencing a mood disorder becomes consumed by the feelings and is unable to alleviate them through normal coping mechanisms. These illnesses are characterized by emotions that are so intense they dominate a person's life. Mood disorders include many different emotional problems and behavioral manifestations, but the overriding symptoms of all mood disorders are *emotional* in nature. That is, people with mood disorders have problems because of their emotions and their reactions to these emotions, rather than problems with putting their thoughts together, as people with schizophrenia do. The *DSM-IV* categorizes types of mood disorders as **bipolar** and **depressive.**

Bipolar Disorders

Bipolar disorder, one of the most interesting of the mental illnesses, occurs less frequently than depressive disorders but affects approximately .5 to 1 percent of the population. Unlike depression, bipolar disorders occur equally often among males and females. Like most mental disorders, the prevalence is greater in the lower socioeconomic groups, in part because these illnesses interfere with a person's ability to work and in part because the cost of the illnesses quickly depletes the economic resources of all but the very wealthy. Even wealthy clients can quickly become impoverished, however, because of the poor judgment associated with manic episodes (e.g., Mr. Jones withdrew all his savings and gave away hundred dollar bills).

A **manic episode** is a distinct period of an abnormally and persistently elevated, expansive, or irritable mood, lasting at least one week, during which the mood disturbance causes marked impairment of work or functioning. The manic episode may range from mild to severe and may be accompanied by psychotic features. If delusions or hallucinations are present, typical themes involve inflated worth, power, knowledge, or identity, or a special relationship to a deity or famous person. In the film *Mr. Jones,* the title character believed that he could fly. Patients experiencing manic episodes may also believe that someone or something is putting thoughts in their heads (thought insertion) or believe that others are controlling them. A **hypomanic episode** results in a period of sustained elevated mood, lasting at least four days. This change is obvious to others and alters a person's level of functioning. However, by definition, a hypomanic episode is *not* severe enough to impair work or social functioning.

People with bipolar illnesses are often very likable, just like Mr. Jones. Their basic personality is usually outgoing, and they often work in people-intensive occupations such as sales. During a manic episode, they feel good about themselves and their moods are contagious. They are often very generous and may buy strangers expensive gifts. During a manic episode, judgment is typically very poor. Individuals may gamble away their life savings or charge all their expenses on an expensive vacation. They often have multiple sexual partners within a short period of time. They also seem to have endless physical energy, appear to function fine without sleep, usually eat very little, and may lose 30 or 40 pounds within a few weeks. The potential for physical exhaustion during a manic episode is very real. The long-term consequences of a manic episode can be devastating for families. For example, it may take years to pay back a debt or forgive infidelities. In the film, when Mr. Jones was manic, he endeared himself to others, gave away money, and attempted to seduce a number of women.

Bipolar I illnesses are diagnosed when a person has both manic and depressive episodes and cycles from one to another. The depressive episode may last three to six months before the person swings to a manic phase. The diagnosis **bipolar II** disorder is reserved for those who have primarily depressive episodes, with occasional hypomania. These patients do not have full-blown manic episodes. **Cyclothymic** disorders are found in individuals who never experience a major depressive or manic episode but who have hypomanic and depressive symptoms. Mr. Jones appears to be a clear-cut illustration of bipolar 1 disorder.

One of the best films depicting a bipolar illness is *Call Me Anna,* a 1990 made-for-TV movie starring Patty Duke, who plays herself in this adaptation of her best-selling autobiography. The film traces her career and her battle with a bipolar disorder and vividly portrays her mood swings and the accompanying personality changes. In real life, Patty Duke has become an advocate for persons with mental illness.

Additional Questions for Classroom Discussion

- Patty Duke is a well-known personality who has "come out of the closet" and openly shared the story of her mood disorder. Can you think of other celebrities who have been candid about their own struggles with mental illness? Did any of them have bipolar disorder?
- How could you distinguish between someone experiencing a manic episode and someone experiencing the elation and energy associated with amphetamine abuse?

Lithium carbonate is the treatment of choice for the bipolar disorders. This agent is a naturally occurring element that has been found to be effective in correcting the chemical imbalance associated with this illness. No one is sure how or why lithium works, but it is believed that it either alters the neurotransmitters or inhibits viruses that affect DNA. If lithium carbonate is not effective, antipsychotic drugs are sometimes used to treat bipolar disorder. However, they are often ineffectual. For example, Mr. Jones did not respond to treatment with Haldol.

Depressive Disorders

Depressive disorders, one of the most common types of mental disorders, occur in an estimated 16 million people in the United States. Most surveys show that depression is twice as common in women. This difference can be attributed to psychosocial factors (females may have more difficult lives, may be exposed to greater stress, may have more frequent negative life experiences, and may have fewer coping skills than males) or genetic factors (supported by twin and adoption studies). There is also a relationship between depressive disorders and social class, and depressive symptoms have been found to be much more prevalent in individuals with fewer economic advantages.

A **major depressive episode** is associated with depressed mood and a loss of interest or pleasure in daily activities. An episode can range from mild (few if any symptoms) to severe, and major depressive episodes can be accompanied by psychotic symptoms. Some people get so depressed that they actually develop delusions and experience hallucinations. The typical themes of a psychotic depression are personal inadequacy, guilt, disease, death, nihilism, and deserved punishment. Persecutory delusions (not directly related to depressive themes), thought insertion, thought broadcasting, or delusions of control may also be present. Some people unconsciously mask their depression and experience physical aches and pains rather than the typical psychological depression. These physical manifestations of depression are often misdiagnosed as physical illnesses and treated accordingly. If most of the symptoms of major depressive episode are present, then a diagnosis of **major depressive disorder** is made. If chronically depressed moods, low self-esteem, and feelings of pessimism, despair, or hopelessness are present for two years without suicidal thoughts or limitations in functioning, the less serious diagnosis of **dysthymic disorder** is made.

In *Scent of a Woman,* Lieutenant Colonel Frank Slade experiences many of the classic symptoms of a major depressive episode and would probably qualify for this diagnosis. He has both a depressed mood and a loss of interest and pleasure in everyday activities (anhedonia). Slade's angry comment "I have no life, I'm in the dark" clearly suggests depression, and the sentence captures the lack of meaning and purpose in his life. His daily activities, sitting alone and drinking himself into a drunken state or tormenting his four-year-old niece, are clear indications of his loss of interest in life.

Additional Questions for Class Discussion

- Are dysthymic disorders, major depressive episodes, and major depressive disorders qualitatively different phenomena, or are they simply different quantitative expressions of a single disorder?
- Are children who are described as "moody" more likely to develop mood disorders as adults?

People who are depressed are not pleasant, and they can be quite difficult to be around. They are often irritable and become angry easily. This serves to hide their underlying need for help. Colonel Slade is irritable, intimidating, and orally abusive to anyone who approaches him. Expression of this type of anger and abuse has a distancing effect on others, who naturally withdraw from unpleasant situations. Charles Simms did not want to stay with Slade after meeting him, and Simms dreaded the week-end he had to spend with the Colonel.

Additional Questions for Class Discussion *(Scent of a Woman)*
- Colonel Slade drinks heavily. Is there an association between depression and alcoholism?
- Do depressed people ever use alcohol to assuage their depression? If so, does it help?
- The Colonel decides to shoot himself while in uniform. Would his previous military experience increase the likelihood that Slade would actually kill himself?
- Does the true likelihood of suicide increase because Slade is male?
- Would the risk of suicide be higher if Slade were black?
- Would you argue that suicide could be a rational choice for someone as discouraged as the Colonel?
- Who should determine if a decision about suicide reflects an accurate appraisal of life and its likely rewards? Who is qualified to determine if the decision is the consequence of a disease such as depression?
- Should physicians and psychologists be empowered to involuntarily hospitalize people who are believed to be at risk for suicide?

Another interesting film depicting depression is the 1971 Academy Award winner, *The Hospital,* starring George C. Scott as Herbert Bock, a middle-aged, depressed, suicidal physician who is trying to cope with the mayhem of a crowded and disorganized institution, where negligence and confusion result in a series of deaths. Bock's personal life is also a mess. He is recently divorced, alienated from his children, and suffering from both personal and sexual impotence. He had been believed to be a medical genius in his early career; at the point we are introduced to him in the film, he is washed up and discouraged. At one point in the film, Bock is seen sitting in his office, preparing to inject a fatal dose of potassium.

Bock demonstrates the classical symptoms of a depressive episode. His depressed mood is expressed through his explosive angry episodes and chronic irritability. He is anhedonic and expresses no interest in his patients, his profession, or any of the activities of daily living that bring pleasure to most of us. Bock cannot sleep, he feels worthless, and he is plagued by recurrent thoughts of suicide. Dr. Bock's behavior is remarkably similar to that of Lt. Colonel Slade — both men are clinically depressed.

Additional Questions for Class Discussion *(The Hospital)*
- Do mood disorders occur more often in medical personnel than in the general population?
- Are physicians more likely than other professionals to commit suicide?
- What medical specialists are most at risk for suicide?
- Does this physician's apparent depression put his patients at risk?
- If you were a physician colleague of Dr. Bock, would you report his depression? To whom?
- Would your ethical obligations be any different if you were a nurse providing care for one of Dr. Bock's patients?

Medications are used to treat depressive disorders. Depression is treated with antidepressants that inhibit the "reuptake" of certain neurotransmitters, thereby increasing their ability to transmit impulses across the synapses. When this occurs, the patient's mood usually improves. Generally, it takes 3 to 10 days for antidepressants to produce a clinical effect.

At times, medications are not effective or they may be contraindicated, and **electroconvulsive therapy** (ECT) may be administered. ECT is also the treatment of choice when a patient is believed to be at high risk for suicide.

ECT, now viewed as one of the most successful treatments for someone who is acutely suicidal or who does not respond to antidepressants, involves a series of 6 to 10 treatments given over several weeks. ECT involves passing an electrical current through the temporal lobe of the brain, causing a seizure that lasts for 20–30 seconds. Unilateral ECT with the right temporal lobe is usually used to minimize the procedure's effects on language and memory.

Most authorities believe it is actually the seizure that triggers the release of neurotransmitters and alleviates depression. The procedure is performed under a short-acting general anesthesia, and a muscle relaxant is given in order to protect the person from injury during the actual seizure. The whole procedure from beginning to end takes approximately 10 minutes and is often done on an outpatient basis.

Films usually depict the negative effects of electroconvulsive therapy. In Jane Champion's 1991 film *An Angel at My Table,* Janet Frame is inappropriately subjected to more than eight years of ECT. In the Academy Award-winning film *One Flew over the Cuckoo's Nest,* Randle Patrick McMurphy, played by Jack Nicholson, is subjected to ECT as a form of punishment. *Both films portray ECT as a frightening procedure accompanied by the muscle vacillations of a grand mal seizure. Neither Janet Frame nor Jack Nicholson would be treated with ECT today.* In modern psychiatry, ECT is used in specific circumstances, and muscle relaxants prevent the muscle twitches and jerking movements shown in these films. Additionally, while patients may be apprehensive before a treatment, they quickly become accustomed to the short procedure, and many patients welcome the treatment, convinced it has saved their lives.

Additional Questions for Class Discussion (*One Flew over the Cuckoo's Nest*)
- *Cuckoo's Nest* presents a misleading picture of electroconvulsive therapy. Is its portrayal of lobotomy any more accurate?
- How accurate is the character of Nurse Ratched? Does the film perpetuate a stereotyped image of psychiatric nurses?
- Is the scene depicting Billy's suicide realistic? If not, how is it flawed?
- McMurphy smuggles alcohol into the hospital, and many of the patients become drunk. What are the likely consequences of combining alcohol with neuroleptic medications?

THEORIES OF MOOD DISORDERS

There are three main theoretical explanations associated with mood disorders: the *genetic,* which is useful in understanding familial tendencies; the *biologic,* which explains the physiologic changes and the rationale for pharmacotherapy and electroconvulsive therapy; and *psychological,* which give direction for understanding behavior and psychotherapy treatment for the impact of the illness. Environment is also an extremely important factor in the manifestation of mood disorders, and mood disorders can be triggered by environmental events such as a loss of a job or a recent divorce.

Genetic Theories

Research evidence supports a genetic transmission of vulnerability to mood disorders. Twin and adoption studies have shown that there is a genetic vulnerability, and family studies have shown the degree to which a disorder is actually familial. For example, a 1977 study of adoptees with a bipolar illness found that 31 percent of their biologic parents also had a mood disorder; whereas only 2 percent of the biologic parents of adoptees without mood disorder had a mood disorder.

When researchers compared the incidence of mood disorders in identical twins (who share the same genetic code) with that of fraternal twins (who have different genetic codes), the concordance rate was 67 percent for the identical twins and 15 percent for fraternal twins. The high concordance for identical twins has also been found in twins who were raised in different environments. Clearly, there is a significant genetic component in mood disorders.

Biologic Theories

The biologic approach to mood disorders focuses on the activity of the neurotransmitters in the limbic system. The neurotransmitters involved include **dopamine, serotonin, acetylcholine, and norepinephrine.** In depression, it is believed that there are fewer available neurotransmitters in the synaptic junction; in mania, there is excess.

The limbic system also regulates the pituitary hormone, a key element in the highly complex endocrine system. Changes in the endocrine system also influence mood. There have been many studies documenting the changes in the functioning of the pituitary and thyroid that occur with mood disorders. Some depressed persons have been found to secrete an excessive amount of **cortisol,** a hormone produced by the pituitary. Additionally, persistently low thyroid hormone levels have been noted in some cases of depression, and an elevated thyroid hormone is present in some rapid cycling bipolar disorders.

The hormonal system is responsible for the diurnal variations in circadian rhythms. Research is showing there is a relationship between changes in circadian rhythms and mood disorders. For example, melatonin, a hormone produced by the pineal gland through the synthesis of serotonin, has been implicated in seasonal depressions. When the relationship between light-induced changes in melatonin secretion and depression is examined, it has been noted that there is a lower nocturnal melatonin level in certain depressed patients. It is believed that this accounts for the depression experienced by some who live in areas far away from the equator, where there are long periods of darkness (e.g., winters in Alaska).

Psychological Theories

Psychological theories have always played an important role in the understanding and treatment of mood disorders. While the depressive and bipolar disorders clearly have a biological basis, the psychodynamic conceptualization of these disorders provides a different way of understanding the behavioral and emotional problems associated with these conditions. Many of the psychological features of depression are readily apparent in films.

The early psychoanalysts (Freud, Abraham) noticed that people with depression experienced **ambivalence** toward significant persons in their lives. That is, they often acted as if they loved and hated the same person. *In* Scent of a Woman, *Lt. Colonel Slade is both affectionate and antagonistic toward his niece, brother, and other family members.* He also becomes antagonistic and aggressive when Simms tries to help him.

Introjection, the unconscious "taking in" of qualities and values of another person or a group with whom emotional ties exist, was also identified as a characteristic feature of depression. *In* Scent of a Woman, *Slade had introjected the values of the military and continued to treat everyone as if he or she reported to him.* Interestingly, Slade had been discharged from the military because of his overbearing behavior. Most "nondepressed" persons would not have become so entangled with their job.

Regression, another characteristic of depression, refers to a return to an earlier pattern of behavior. During a depression, childhood behavioral patterns may appear, and a person may act less mature. For example, Slade's ongoing battle with a four-year-old is not acceptable adult behavior for a retired Colonel. However, Slade's life is so meaningless that he resorts to battling with a four-year-old.

Denial, ignoring the existence of reality, is characteristic of persons experiencing a manic episode. They often stop taking their medication because they believe that there is nothing wrong with them. They reject any advice from family members and may become belligerent at any suggestion that there is something wrong. Mr. Jones has been hospitalized multiple times after he has gone off his medication, and he is smart enough to know it will happen again. However, *each time he convinces himself that this time will be different.* This is a classic example of denial.

Ambivalence, introjection, regression, and denial are examples of some of the psychological problems that can affect the interpersonal relationships of a person with mood disorders. Psychotherapy can supplement medication and help a person deal with the personality changes that occur as a result of the illness. Through a warm, supportive, therapeutic relationship, it is possible for an individual to be able to identify those characteristics and behaviors most likely to interfere with meaningful interpersonal relationships.

COGNITIVE BEHAVIORAL CONCEPTS

Behavioral theorists have contributed significantly to the understanding of the experience of depression. Aaron Beck, who described a cognitive triad that is common in these patients, has identified the characteristic thoughts of depressed people. The triad consists of (1) perceiving oneself as defective and inadequate, (2) perceiving the world as demanding and punishing, and (3) expecting failure, defeat, and hardship. *These "automatic thoughts" are readily apparent in both* Scent of a Woman *and* The Hospital.

Beck and his colleges have developed a psychotherapeutic technique, cognitive therapy, which addresses the defective thinking process. This approach to psychotherapy forces the patient to examine the evidence for his or her negative beliefs, and the therapist encourages patients to reframe their beliefs based on the evidence presented in therapy. Once beliefs change, the patients begin to perceive the world in a more positive light and begin to make choices that result in success. This technique has been very successful and is generally believed to be as efficacious as antidepressants in the treatment of mild to moderate depression.

Additional Questions for Class Discussion

- Can you identify automatic thoughts that would be likely to occur in either Lieutenant Colonel Slade or Dr. Herbert Bock?
- Would either of these individuals be likely to cooperate in psychotherapy?
- Is there any evidence that matching personality types with treatment approaches enhances treatment outcomes?

BIPOLAR DISORDER AND CREATIVITY

There is compelling evidence that mood disorders may be related to the creative process, and numerous artists, poets, and composers have either been diagnosed as depressed or bipolar, or have biographies that suggest that these disorders were present. Examples of poets believed to have experienced mood disorders include William Blake, Lord Byron, Alfred Lord Tennyson, John Berryman, Sylvia Plath, Theodore Roethke, and Anne Sexton; examples of painters and composers with mood disorders include Vincent van Gogh, Georgia O'Keefe, and Robert Shuman (Jamison, 1993). Sylvia Plath's difficulties with depression are detailed in the 1979 film adaptation of her semi-autobiographical novel *The Bell Jar.* The troubled life of Beethoven is portrayed in the 1995 film *Immortal Beloved.* Vincent van Gogh's life, work, and mental illness (which may have been bipolar disorder) have recently been documented in the films *Vincent* (1987), *Vincent & Theo* (1990), and *Van Gogh* (1991). However, none of these match the artistic achievement established by the 1956 film *Lust for Life,* in which Kirk Douglas plays van Gogh and Anthony Quinn plays the supporting role of Paul Gauguin.

Additional Questions for Class Discussion

- What are your own views on van Gogh? What behaviors support a diagnosis of mood disorder? What evidence suggests a seizure disorder may have been present? Are there any other competing hypotheses?
- If you had the power to cure someone like van Gogh, but you knew that the treatment would destroy his creativity, would you proceed?
- Can you identify other artists and writers who have experienced mood disorders?

DEAD POETS SOCIETY

Dead Poets Society is a 1989 film starring Robin Williams as John Keating, an unconventional English teacher at a rigid boys' prep school. This film was nominated for several Academy Awards. Set in 1959, this drama contrasts institutional values and individual creativity. By fostering "critical thinking" in his classroom, Keating broadened students' educational experience and their ability to think independently. The students also discovered that, when Keating was a student at the school, he started a secret society, the Dead Poets Society, dedicated to intellectual creativity. These students reactivate the secret society.

The main conflict in the film is between Neil, a student who wants to be an actor, and his father, a domineering businessman who wants his son to be a doctor. Neil's father will not allow him to try out for a campus production of *A Midsummer Night's Dream.* Neil disregards his father's demands, auditions, and is selected for the lead role. Keating encourages Neil to explore the relationship with his father and to enlist his father's support. Neil's father is enraged when he views his son's successful performance. Neil is immediately brought home and, in an act of desperation, Neil shoots himself with his father's gun. Keating becomes the scapegoat for Neil's suicide, and the school's administration uses the suicide as an excuse to fire the unconventional teacher. The film ends with the other students protesting Keating's firing.

> **Additional Questions for Class Discussion** *(Dead Poet's Society)*
> - Would Neil qualify under *DSM-IV* for a psychiatric diagnosis? If so, which one?
> - How common is it for someone to commit suicide as a way of punishing someone else?
> - Does the presence of a handgun in a house increase the likelihood of suicide?
> - Would a daughter have been as likely to shoot herself?
> - What else could John Keating have done to reduce the conflict between Neil and his father?

SUICIDE

Suicide and Depression

Suicide is the eighth most frequent cause of death throughout the world. Suicide rates vary widely among different countries. Generally, the suicide rate is low in the less prosperous Roman Catholic countries and highest in the more affluent ones, such as Germany, Switzerland, and Sweden. However, the suicide rate is also high in all the Eastern European nations. The suicide rates in the United States and Canada are in the middle range. Based upon 1988 data, in the United States, the true suicide rate is 12.4 /100,000. However, the rate of attempted suicide is much higher. Among adolescents, suicide is the third most frequent cause of death. While men are more likely than women to commit suicide, women attempt suicide more frequently than men. Men are more successful because they are more likely to choose a more lethal means.

Mortality rates for suicide are generally higher in urban areas, and prevalence rates for suicide have been shown to be positively correlated with the size of cities. Although suicide has a low incidence in closely knit rural communities, the problem is more common among the elderly, in areas where agriculture is in decline, and among workers who are emigrating to the cities. The incidence of suicide increases with age, with the elderly population having the highest suicide rates.

The best predictor of who will attempt suicide is a history of a psychiatric disorder. People who are depressed are at especially high risk for suicide. Psychological "autopsy" studies show that two disorders, depression and alcoholism, are associated with 79–85 percent of all suicides. In research studies, more than 90 percent of the patients who succeed in committing suicide were shown to have a psychiatric illness at the time of death. In the movie *Dead Poets Society*, Neil struggles to win his father's approval for a career that is totally unacceptable to his parents. Following the realization that his father would never "allow" him to become an actor, Neil becomes depressed and kills himself. *The leading characters in* Scent of a Woman *and* The Hospital *both have definite plans for committing suicide.*

A clinical characteristic that has been found to be highly related to suicide ideation is hopelessness (Beck et al., 1993). This is well depicted in the film *Night, Mother,* starring Sissy Spacek as Jesse and Anne Bancroft as the mother, Thelma. This 1986 movie is a thought-provoking and gripping film adaptation of the Pulitzer Prize-winning stage play about suicide. The entire film takes place in the mother's home, where Jesse has lived since her divorce. As the play begins it is 6:05 P.M., and Jesse has just informed her mother that she plans to kill herself that night. The two women examine their lives as Thelma tries to protect her daughter from her decision. Ultimately, Jesse explains that she has no hope and ends her life at 7:45 P.M.

Risk Factors and Antecedents

There are many risk factors associated with suicide. The demographic risk factors include being adolescent or elderly, male, white, separated, divorced or widowed, isolated, and unemployed.

Other risk factors include depression, alcoholism, bipolar disorders, and organic brain syndrome.

Unfortunately, even though risk factors and the antecedents of suicide have been well established, accurately predicting who will commit suicide is nearly impossible. Most clinicians include a suicide assessment in their initial interaction with any client who has an emotional problem or a mental illness. An assessment for suicide focuses on three areas: intent, plan, and lethality.

Intent, or thinking about suicide, is a specific indicator of an impending suicide and probably the single most important predictor. Those people most intent on suicide have worse insomnia, are more pessimistic, and are less able to concentrate than those with less intent. In the film *Night, Mother,* the total story focuses on Jesse's intent to kill herself. Those most intent on killing themselves are more often males, older, single or separated, and living alone. However, experts also know that intent is episodic and that, even if there is no intent today, there may be tomorrow. In *Dead Poets Society,* there is no mention of Neil's intent and the viewer is led to believe that he does not intend to kill himself until he returns home, feels helpless, and convinces himself there is no way out of an untenable situation. *If someone had recognized his intent or if he had reached out for help (e.g., by calling a suicide hotline), Neil might have been able to identify creative alternatives to suicide.*

Most experts believe that, even though a person is intent on suicide, there is almost always an underlying wish to be rescued. Thus, a person who is very intent upon killing himself or herself may consciously or unconsciously emit signals of distress, evidence of helplessness, or pleas for help. Some of the verbal cues may be "I am going away" or "You won't be seeing much of me." There may also be unusual acts such as putting one's affairs in order, giving away prized possessions, engaging in unusual behavior, or becoming socially isolated. These behaviors are all present in *Scent of a Woman*. Lt. Colonel Slade puts his financial affairs in order, visits his family and says good-bye, and has his "last fling."

People who have a **plan** for committing suicide are more likely to actually kill themselves than those who have vague thoughts about not wanting to live. Clinicians determine if their patients have a plan to kill themselves and how specific the plan is. An individual who does not have a plan is considered to be at lower risk than someone who knows how he or she can commit suicide, and who has access to the planned method. In *The Hospital,* Dr. Herbert Bock plans to kill himself by injecting a lethal dose of potassium. *He demonstrates both plan and intent, and, because of his easy access to potassium, he is clearly at high risk.*

The **lethality** of the method is also an indicator of the risk of suicide. The more lethal the chosen means, the more likely the person will commit suicide, especially if there is easy access to the method selected (e.g., guns in the home). The most lethal suicide methods are using guns, jumping off buildings and bridges, and hanging. Slashing one's wrists and ingesting 15 or fewer aspirin are common methods of attempting suicide, but they are unlikely to be lethal. Other methods that carry a moderate to high risk of lethality are drowning, carbon monoxide suffocation, and deep cuts to the throat. *In both* Scent of a Woman *and* Dead Poets Society, *the lethality was high because guns were the means selected for the suicidal act.*

Prevention of Suicide

Since there are no clear predictors of suicide, there are no foolproof prevention strategies. Treatment of an acutely suicidal individual involves protecting him or her and connecting with that part in each person that wants to be rescued. Usually, a person who is suicidal is hospitalized and not allowed to be alone. Even in those instances, if a person wants to commit suicide, a hospital environment cannot prevent it, and many suicides have been completed in a protected environment. In the film *Crossover* (1983), a psychiatric nurse is plagued by self-doubt after one of the patients he works with commits suicide.

ORDINARY PEOPLE

Ordinary People, a 1980 Academy Award-winning film based on Judith Guest's novel by the same name, depicts the aftermath of a suicide attempt. Conrad Jarret, played by Timothy Hutton, is a sensitive teenager who has attempted suicide following a boating accident that killed his brother, Buck. Conrad could not overcome his feelings of guilt, attempted suicide, and was hospitalized for four months. The film begins following Conrad's return home and traces his struggle for personal redemption and his futile attempts to communicate with his parents. His father, Calvin, played by Don Sutherland, is a successful tax attorney who tries to respond to Conrad's needs. His mother, Beth, played by Mary Tyler Moore, is well intentioned but ultimately unable to meet the needs of her son. Beth is the nucleus of a family in a crisis.

Upon his return from the hospital, Conrad is inattentive in class and distant with classmates. He is also ill at ease with his parents. His father encourages Conrad to contact a psychiatrist, and eventually he begins therapy with Dr. Berger, played by Judd Hirsch. In therapy Conrad explores his relationship with his parents. When Dr. Berger suggests that the entire family meet together, Beth refuses. Throughout the movie, Beth's feelings toward her living son become obvious. Calvin begins to question his relationship with Beth and unsuccessfully attempts to reengage his wife in their relationship. Beth eventually leaves her husband and son, who come to terms with Beth's limitations and begin to rebuild their lives around their love for each other.

There are other characters who play an important role in the movie. One is Conrad's swim coach, who quizzes him about his hospitalization, asks him if he received shock treatment, and is demanding during training sessions. Conrad's brother was a championship swimmer. Conrad finally decides to quit the swim team.

The other important character is Karen, a girl Conrad met at the hospital. While hospitalized, Conrad and Karen had a completely "open and honest" relationship. When Conrad contacts her at home, she is distant but appears to be in control. She is involved in school activities and maintains she no longer thinks about the problems that resulted in her suicide attempt. She also decides not to see a therapist. Karen's newfound confidence is startling to Conrad, who begins to question his own fragile condition. When he tries to get in touch with her later, however, Conrad learns that she has committed suicide.

Karen's death forces Conrad to relive the boating accident that took Buck's life. At last he is able to explain his guilt — he lived and Buck did not. Conrad realizes that he was angry with Buck because he did not hang on to the boat. With the help of Dr. Berger, he experiences the intense pain of his loss and resolves his guilt.

Additional Questions for Class Discussion *(Ordinary People)*
- How would you describe Conrad's family in *Ordinary People*?
- If you were a therapist working with this family, how would you proceed?
- Do any of the characters in the film meet *DSM-IV* criteria for depression?

PROBLEMS OF SUICIDE ATTEMPT SURVIVORS

If a suicide attempt is survived, the meaning of the attempt should be examined. Even though the viewer is not told whether or not Conrad has symptoms of depression, it is safe to assume that they were present prior to the suicide attempt. *In the film* Ordinary People, *Conrad's suicide attempt was not only an attempt to kill himself but also a cry for help.* His family fails to appreciate or respond to his distress over his brother's death. His mother is unable to relate to anyone, and his father is withdrawn from family interaction. Through a suicide attempt, Conrad got his family and friends to acknowledge his desperate situation.

Every suicide attempt should be taken seriously. While attempting suicide is often an impulsive act, it is also an act of communication. If Conrad had possessed the necessary communication skills, he could have discussed his feelings and explored their meaning.

THE REPRESENTATION OF MOOD DISORDERS AND SUICIDE IN FILMS

Gena Rowlands plays a woman who appears to have a bipolar disorder in the John Cassavetes film *A Woman Under the Influence* (1974). She is quite convincing during a manic episode, and there is a memorable scene in which a neighbor stops by to drop off his kids and then decides that it is not safe to leave them with Rowlands. He doesn't know exactly what's wrong, but it is clear to him that *something* is not right. Unlike *Mr. Jones,* the actual diagnosis is never specified in *A Woman Under the Influence,* despite the fact that Rowlands spends six months in a psychiatric hospital.

Another example of an apparent bipolar disorder is found in the Harrison Ford character in *Mosquito Coast* (1986), although Ford's eccentric habits and obsessional style are probably adequate to support multiple diagnoses. Finally, the biographical film *Mommie Dearest* (1981) suggests that Joan Crawford had a bipolar disorder.

Examples of the type of rapid speech, quick thinking, and impulsive behavior associated with a hypomanic episode can be seen in the college president character played by Groucho Marx in *Horse Feathers* (1932) and in the more recent film *Good Morning, Vietnam* (1987), in which Robin Williams plays an Air Force disc jockey with a rapid and clever repartee that endears him to his military audience.

There are even more illustrations of depressive disorders in films (and perhaps this should be the case, since depression is a more common problem than bipolar disorder). Marlon Brando plays a depressed man trying to come to grips with the meaning of his wife's suicide in Bernado Bertolucci's powerful film *Last Tango in Paris. The character of the coach's wife in Peter Bogdanovich's* The Last Picture Show *(1971) is clearly depressed, and her affect and behavior offer good teaching examples of depressed affect for students learning how to give a mental status examination.* The despair that overcomes a man when he is abandoned by his wife is presented in the Australian film *My First Wife* (1984), and Alfred Hitchcock portrays marked depression in a couple wrongfully accused of murder in his 1956 film *The Wrong Man.* Finally, Joanne Woodward presents a memorable performance as a depressed housewife in *Summer Wishes, Winter Dreams* (1973).

Hyler (1988) has pointed out that many of the characters that appear depressed in films would meet the *DSM-IV* criteria for **adjustment disorder with depressed mood** rather than major depression. The examples Hyler cites include Jimmy Stewart's character in Frank Capra's *It's a Wonderful Life* (1946) and Henry Fonda's character in *The Wrong Man* (1957). In the latter film, Fonda develops a reactive depression after he is unjustly accused of murder.

Suicide makes for high drama, and it is a common theme in films. Some examples include the unforgettable Russian roulette death of the soldier who remained in Vietnam in *The Deer Hunter* (1978); the suicide by drowning of a young man who feels he cannot please his critical father in *The Field* (1990); the lead character in the Roman Polanski film *The Tenant* (1976), who becomes suicidal after renting the apartment of a woman who in fact had recently committed suicide; Greta Garbo's suicide by stepping in front of an oncoming train in *Anna Karenina* (1935); and the suicide staged to look like a hunting accident in *Mountains of the Moon* (1990). The film *'Night, Mother* (1986) revolves around a discussion a mother and daughter have over the daughter's decision to commit suicide. Japanese novelist Yukio Mishima, one of the most fascinating characters in contemporary literature, committed *seppuku* (ritualistic suicide), and his life and death are portrayed in the 1985 film *Mishima*. Peter Finch, playing Howard Beale, the mad prophet of the evening news, announces to the world that he will commit suicide on the air in two weeks and sees his ratings soar in the film *Network* (1976).

Often a failed suicide attempt is a means by which a director can heighten tension or set the stage for future character development. When Pu Yi, the last emperor of China, attempts to commit suicide by slashing his wrists in a railroad station restroom in Bernardo Bertolucci's *The Last Emperor* (1987), we get some insight into his character and a better sense of the despair he is experiencing. Glenn Close attempts suicide by slashing her wrists in *Fatal Attraction* (1987), and the attempt is necessary to establish the extent to which she is willing to go to manipulate and control her lover. When Gary Oldman shoots himself in the chest in the opening scenes of *Chattahoochee* (1990), we learn that he is not genuinely psychotic but is afraid to die, just as most of us would be in the same situation.

Shakespeare was fascinated by suicide, and his plays and their film adaptations provide a useful and fascinating way to approach the study of suicide. Major Shakespearean plays in which suicide figures prominently include *Romeo and Juliet, Julius Caesar, Hamlet, Anthony and Cleopatra, Macbeth, Othello,* and *King Lear.* Of course, there have been multiple film adaptations of each of these plays.

Suicide is sometimes romanticized in film, such as in the hauntingly beautiful *Elvira Madigan* (1967), in which two lovers decide on a double suicide. In a French film, *The Hairdresser's Husband* (1992), the female lead jumps to her death by drowning in order not to lose the happiness she has found with her new husband.

Finally, suicide is often treated as a humorous topic. Examples include Burt Reynolds' character in *The End* (1978), the multiple suicide attempts of Harold in the black comedy *Harold and Maude* (1972), the Italian judge who tries to get his sister to commit suicide in *Leap into the Void* (1979), the elaborate last supper for the impotent and suicidal camp dentist in *M*A*S*H* (1970), and the inadvertent death by hanging in *The Ruling Class* (1972).

Critical Thinking Questions

- If you genuinely believe a friend is suicidal, what are your ethical and moral obligations, if any?
- Do your responsibilities to that person change if you are a therapist rather than a friend?
- How often is talk of suicide a plea for help?
- The suicide rate for both men and women is much higher in Sweden, Denmark, and Austria than in the United States. What cultural factors could account for these differences?
- Have you had personal experiences in which you have had to assess suicidal risk in a friend or relative?
- Can you think of popular films in which suicide was portrayed? Was there evidence of intent, plan, and lethality?
- Is there a suicide hotline in your community? Do you know how to access it?

Critical Thinking Questions Continued

- Dr. Bowen hugs a young woman who is being discharged from the hospital and touches Mr. Jones at several points before they initiate their affair. Is touching ever appropriate in a therapeutic relationship? If so, when?
- After the confrontation with the assaultive patient, Dr. Bowen tells Mr. Jones, "I thought about buying you something for saving my life." Would this have been wise? Would it have been ethical?
- At one point in the film, a physician compares bipolar disorder to diabetes. In what way is the comparison apt? In what way is it misleading?
- When a colleague learns about the affair between Dr. Bowen and her patient, he agrees to cover for her as long as she would no longer see the patient. Does he have an ethical or a legal obligation to report her? What would you have done in this situation? Would you view the situation any differently if a male psychiatrist had become sexually involved with a female patient?
- Dr. Bowen states, "You're not a sick person; you're a person with a sickness!" What is the significance of this semantic distinction?

Chapter 6

Personality Disorders

*It's not going to stop. It's gonna go on and on
until you face up to your responsibilities . . . .
I just want to be part of your life . . . .
What am I supposed to do?
You don't answer my calls,
you change your number.
I'm not going to be ignored, Dan!*
Glenn Close lays down the law for former lover
Michael Douglas in *Fatal Attraction*

Questions to Consider While Watching *Fatal Attraction*

- Why is Alex Forrest (the Glenn Close character) so threatened by the termination of a seemingly insignificant affair?
- What advice would you give Dan Gallagher (Michael Douglas) if he were to consult with you about how to handle the situation with Alex? Should he return her phone calls and try to set limits or simply ignore her?
- Are there any characteristics of borderline personality disorder that are *not* present in Alex Forrest?
- Why is sexual acting out so common in people with borderline personality disorder?
- Is there any relationship between physical and sexual abuse in children and the subsequent development of personality disorders?
- Do you believe Alex is genuinely pregnant or is this simple manipulation?
- Are Alex's suicidal threats genuine or are they simply empty attention-seeking gestures? Would you caution Dan Gallagher to take them seriously?
- What's the prognosis for a patient with a borderline personality disorder?
- Can a person have several different personality disorders at the same time?
- Is multiple personality disorder more common in men or in women? Why?
- How is a personality disorder qualitatively different from an Axis I *DSM-IV* disorder?
- Has the therapist who evaluated this patient made a reasonable guess about her prognosis?

PATIENT EVALUATION

Patient's stated reason for coming: "I can't seem to hang on to a relationship. I need to know what's wrong with me."

History of the present illness: Alex Forrest is a 35-year-old woman who has never married. She has dated widely, and she has established romantic and sexual relationships with dozens of men over the past 18 years. However, she has not been able to sustain any of these relationships for more than a few months. Each new relationship appears to be characterized by intense, torrid sexual activity followed by a rapid diminution of interest by her partner.

Past psychiatric illness, treatment, and outcomes: Ms. Forrest has been hospitalized on two occasions following suicide attempts. She took an overdose of Valium from her mother's medicine cabinet when she was 17, following a fight with her boyfriend. She called her mother when she began feeling ill and was taken to a local hospital, where her stomach was pumped.

About five years ago, she purportedly attempted to drown herself by jumping into a public pool while fully clothed following an altercation with a former boyfriend who had just informed her of his plans to marry another woman. She was taken to a local psychiatric hospital, where she remained overnight for observation and was released the following morning. Approximately two days ago, Ms. Forrest attempted to cut her wrists with a razor blade; however, the cuts were only superficial and hospitalization was not required. She denies being suicidal at the current time but has engaged in self-injury behaviors during periods of stress.

Ms. Forrest has been treated intermittently by a large number of psychiatrists, social workers, and psychologists; however, these relationships, like her romantic liaisons, always start strong and then prove to be unrewarding in the end.

Medical history: Ms. Forrest has a long history of nonspecific pelvic pain and pelvic inflammatory disorders. She was treated for gonorrhea at the age of 20. An unplanned pregnancy at age 22 was voluntarily terminated. There is an intermittent history of bulimia, but she has never been hospitalized or treated for this problem. Ms. Forrest had her appendix removed approximately eight years ago. The rest of the medical history is unremarkable.

Psychosocial history: Ms. Forrest is an only child whose parents divorced when she was 11 years old. She reports that her parents were constantly fighting, and her childhood was quite unhappy. She has no siblings and no significant relationship with her grandparents or other relatives. Her mother moved frequently following her divorce, and Alex was often required to change schools in the middle of the school year. Ms. Forrest had relatively few friends and was somewhat reclusive until high school, when she learned that she could use sex as a way to gain popularity and status. She passed each grade on schedule, although there is a recurrent history of disciplinary problems in high school. She was reunited with her father during her college years. He died during her senior year. Ms. Forrest attended the State University at Stony Brook and graduated in 1967 with a bachelor's degree in psychology.

Drug and alcohol history: She reports the sporadic but frequent use of marijuana, dextroamphetamine, barbiturates, and LSD. After leaving college, she continued to smoke marijuana recreationally for about a decade but discontinued use of the other drugs. Over the past five years, she has intermittently used powdered cocaine at parties. She drinks heavily: almost every evening meal includes a bottle of wine and she sips bourbon all evening long, almost every night. She often becomes intoxicated at parties, and this public drinking has frequently impaired her judgment on numerous occasions. This patient smokes approximately one pack of unfiltered cigarettes each day.

Behavioral observations: Ms. Forrest was attractively if somewhat provocatively dressed. She wore an expensive pearl necklace for the interview. She proved to be verbal and articulate. She cooperated fully with the examination. Her speech was relaxed and articulate. She appeared to have good insight into the nature of her difficulties with men. She seemed genuinely eager to get help with these relationship problems.

Mental status examination: Ms. Forrest was oriented in all spheres. Both immediate and delayed memory were intact. She was able to repeat serial sevens without difficulty. There is no dysnomia, and she can easily repeat both simple and complex phrases. Judgment is intact. She can follow simple directions, read, write, and draw without difficulty. Ms. Forrest denied current suicidal or homicidal ideation. She earned a score of 30 on the *Mini Mental Status Examination*, and there was no evidence of cognitive difficulty or psychiatric disturbance on the mental status examination.

Functional assessment: Ms. Forrest has changed jobs frequently since graduating from college. However, she has consistently worked in the publishing industry for the past decade, and she is reportedly a good editor. Her on-the-job interpersonal difficulties and several affairs with co-workers have limited her ability to develop a career with a single publisher. Her father is deceased, she has not spoken to her mother in more than a decade, and there are no other significant family relationships. Ms. Forrest has few friends other than the men with whom she has been involved.

Strengths: The patient is attractive, intelligent, and well educated. She has had extensive experience in therapy, knows the language, and appears motivated to change.

Diagnosis: 309.4 Adjustment Disorder with Disturbance of Emotion and Conduct
301.83 R/O Borderline Personality Disorder

Treatment plan: See in individual therapy on a weekly basis. Establish and develop a therapeutic relationship, and track the cognitions and behaviors associated with the men she is currently dating. Encourage nonsexual friendships with both men and women. Continue to monitor for signs of depression and possible suicidal thoughts.

Prognosis: I believe Ms. Forrest has the cognitive capacity to identify and understand the reasons she has never been able to sustain a meaningful romantic relationship. However, her long history of unsuccessful therapy suggests her prognosis is guarded at best.

FATAL ATTRACTION

In *Fatal Attraction* (1987), Michael Douglas plays a happily married New York attorney who becomes sexually involved with Glenn Close, a glamorous and sexually aggressive publishing executive. What starts out as a simple, one-night affair for Douglas turns into a nightmare for him and his family as Close becomes increasingly possessive and manipulative. Douglas tries to extricate himself from the affair, but Close resorts to verbal threats, telephone calls to his wife, a suicide gesture (slashing her wrists after Douglas tells her the affair is over), and intimidation of his wife and child. *The performance by Close dramatically illustrates many characteristics of patients with a borderline personality disorder: anger, impulsivity, emotional lability, fear of rejection and abandonment, inappropriate behavior, vacillation between adulation and disgust, and self-mutilation.*

TYPES OF PERSONALITY DISORDERS

All of us have unique personalities and our own individual personality traits. On occasion, these personality traits get us in trouble. In some individuals, their personalities result in a persistent pattern of recurring interpersonal difficulties. When there is a persistent pattern of inflexible and maladaptive behavior that *continually* gets an individual in trouble (or that causes him or her considerable subjective distress), a diagnosis of personality disorder may be appropriate.

People with personality disorders do not have discrete symptoms of a mental illness (if they did, they would qualify for an Axis I diagnosis); instead, they have a maladaptive *orientation* that results in less than optimal functioning in a variety of situations. The threshold for diagnosis is subjectively determined by the clinician, but, before a person is diagnosed as having a personality disorder, there must be clear evidence that the problem developed in adolescence or early adulthood and has persisted continually and is not simply a response to situational stressors.

People with personality disorders exhibit enduring, pervasive, and inflexible patterns of behavior that deviate markedly from societal expectations. Their behavior seems odd, unusual, or peculiar to most other people. The differences between them and everyone else have usually been evident since adolescence or early adulthood. These differences tend to be stable over time and lead to distress and impairment.

There are many subtypes of personality disorders, but all are coded on Axis II of *DSM-IV*. This separate coding category indicates that the diagnosis relates to a pattern of maladaptive behavior rather than to a distinct mental illness—a personality disorder reflects who the person is; it is not something the person has.

If a personality disorder appears to be present, but the patient does not fit the criteria for any of the categories listed in Table 6-1, a diagnosis of **personality disorder not otherwise specified** is appropriate.

The ranking of personality disorders in Table 6-1 is not arbitrary but is based on a conceptual model that groups all personality disorders into one of three relatively distinct clusters. Cluster A (odd-eccentric) includes the paranoid, schizoid, and schizotypal personality disorders. Cluster B (dramatic-emotional) includes the antisocial, borderline, histrionic, and narcissistic personality disorders. Cluster C (anxious-fearful) includes the remaining personality disorders: avoidant, dependent, and obsessive-compulsive.

It is sometimes difficult to distinguish between major mental disorders coded on Axis I and personality disorders coded on Axis II. For example, the individual with a schizotypal personality exhibits behaviors and characteristics that overlap with those found in patients diagnosed with schizophrenia. The person with an avoidant personality may be difficult to distinguish from the patient with a social phobia.

Personality disorders are rarely diagnosed in children, and many of the traits of personality disorder that are common in children (e.g., problems with impulse control in adolescents) do not persist into adulthood. In addition, the diagnosis is inappropriate in any situation in which aberrant behavior results from transient situational factors (e.g., the individual who repeatedly gets his or her tax returns audited may become paranoid about the government). Finally, it is critical that cultural variables be considered when a diagnosis of personality disorder is being considered. For example, the Italian film *Down and Dirty* (1976) includes a protagonist who appears to have an antisocial personality. However, his behavior must be understood in terms of the culture of southern Italy and the debilitating and corrosive effects of poverty.

The major subtypes of personality disorder are listed in Table 6-1.

Personality Disorder	Characteristics	Film Example
Paranoid	Distrust and suspiciousness about the motives of others	Michael Douglas in *Falling Down*
Schizoid	Detachment from social relationships and a restricted range of emotional expression	James Spader as Graham, the impotent houseguest in Steven Soderbergh's *sex, lies, and videotape*
Schizotypal	Acute discomfort in close relationships, cognitive or perceptual distortions, and behavioral eccentrics	Jack Lemmon as the Christ figure in *The Ruling Class*
Antisocial	Disregard for and violation of the rights of others	Michael Rooker as a killer without a conscience in *Henry: Portrait of a Serial Killer*
Borderline	Instability in interpersonal relationships, inadequate self-image, labile affect, and marked impulsively	Glenn Close as the femme fatale in *Fatal Attraction*
Histrionic	Excessive emotionality and attention seeking	Blanche du Bois in *A Streetcar Named Desire*; Zaza in *La Cage aux Folles*
Narcissistic	Grandiosity, a need for admiration, and lack of empathy for the problems and needs of others	Gloria Swanson as an aging and self-centered actress in Billy Wilder's *Sunset Boulevard*
Avoidant	Social inhibition, feelings of inadequacy, and hypersensitivity to criticism or negative evaluation	Laura in Tennessee Williams' *The Glass Menagerie*
Dependent	Submissive and clinging behavior	Bill Murray in *What About Bob?*
Obsessive-Compulsive	Preoccupation with orderliness, perfectionism, and control	Jack Lemmon as Felix Unger in *The Odd Couple*

Table 6-1. Characteristics of personality disorders with examples from contemporary cinema.

Some personality disorders are more common in men (e.g., antisocial personality disorder). Others are found more often in women (e.g., borderline, histrionic, and dependent personality disorders).

CLUSTER A DISORDERS
Paranoid Personality Disorder

People with **paranoid personality disorder** are isolated, suspicious, and distrustful. They are convinced that others are talking about them behind their backs or plotting against them. The behaviors of others are carefully scrutinized for evidence of intent to harm, and overtures of friendship or good will by other people are rejected as manipulative gestures or parts of a plot. Ironically, because paranoid individuals behave in peculiar ways, a self-fulfilling prophecy occurs and people *do* begin to discuss the paranoid individual behind his or her back.

Paranoid people tend to have few or no friends. They become preoccupied with trivial events and brood over any interaction that can be interpreted as hostile or rejecting. They *personalize* almost everything and misinterpret casual remarks to make them fit into their belief structure. When they are married, they tend to be possessively jealous and become convinced without evidence that their spouse is engaged in multiple affairs. The paranoid individual always finds a reason to blame others for his or her misfortunes, and many become involved in complex legal disputes.

Paranoid personality disorder may be present in as much as 2 percent of the general population. It appears to be more common in men than in women, and there is some evidence that it is more common in the relatives of patients who have been diagnosed as schizophrenic.

Schizoid Personality Disorder

The individual with a **schizoid personality** disorder avoids close interpersonal relations. He or she is likely to be described as a loner who lacks meaningful ties to a family, community, or value system. These individuals are unlikely to display strong emotions and appear to be apathetic, diffident, and indifferent. There is no evidence of warmth or tenderness on their part, and they do not possess any particular need to fit into the social network. They most often have little or no interest in sexual encounters and few marry. They are often "drifters" who move from one job to another and one community to another.

Graham, the impotent houseguest in Steven Soderbergh's sex, lies, and videotape *(1989), displays several schizoid characteristics.* He is passing through the community when he stops to visit an old college roommate, although there is no evidence of genuine affection between the two men. He is a somewhat passive and bland individual, and we never see him getting angry in the film. His life appears to be totally devoid of passion, and he has never been able to establish a meaningful relationship with a woman. He is impotent and can become sexually aroused only when he masturbates while listening to taped interviews of women who have agreed to discuss their sexuality on tape. Although Graham displays features of the schizoid personality, the diagnosis of schizoid personality disorder would be contraindicated by his apparent drive to establish relationships with women (even through a medium as impersonal as the recorded voice) and by the potential for a meaningful relationship with Ann, the wife of his college roommate and one of the women whom he has taped. This film, which won the grand prize at the Cannes Film Festival, is worth seeing for its artistic merit as well as its psychological insights.

Schizotypal Personality Disorder

Some adopted children whose biological parents had schizophrenia will develop the disorder in their teen years or in early adulthood. However, in many more cases, these children develop "schizophrenia-like" personality traits. These observations led researchers to develop the concept of the **schizotypal personality disorder.** People with schizotypal personality disorder have a "schizophrenia-like" personality but do not meet the strict diagnostic criteria for schizophrenia. They hold odd beliefs and exhibit peculiar behavior, and they are often very superstitious as well as suspicious and paranoid. Their affect is described as flat, constricted, or blunted; and their behavior is described as eccentric. Some authorities have suggested the disorder reflects a mild form of schizophrenia. *The character of Maude in the film* Harold and Maude *(1972) exhibits the sort of highly eccentric behavior of the type that sometimes leads to diagnosis of a schizotypal personality disorder.* However, Maude's flamboyance and exuberance would be very unusual in someone with a schizotypal personality.

There is considerable overlap between schizotypal personality disorder and the other personality disorders. For example, a person who meets the diagnostic criteria for schizotypal personality disorder may have the same sort of suspicion and distrust found in individuals who meet the criteria for paranoid personality disorder.

CLUSTER B DISORDERS

Antisocial Personality Disorder

People with antisocial personality disorders break the law, are physically aggressive, write bad checks, manipulate others, lie, take senseless risks, and have no sense of remorse or guilt about the consequences of their behavior. These individuals violate the rights of others and appear to experience distress only when their behavior results in punishment or incarceration. They are impulsive and have a great deal of trouble planning their future behavior or anticipating its consequences. Individuals with antisocial personality disorder have a great deal of trouble learning from their mistakes and find themselves dealing with similar legal and interpersonal problems.

This personality disorder is also referred to as **sociopathy** or **psychopathy.** However, many clinicians prefer to avoid the term *psychopath* because of its popular association with mindless homicide that resulted in part from the popularity of films such as Alfred Hitchcock's *Psycho* (1960).

Abuse of alcohol and other drugs is common among antisocial personalities. Bar room fights, such as those in the film *Last Night at the Alamo* (1983), often occur. However, the loyalty to the Alamo bar displayed by the protagonist and his friends would be very uncharacteristic of anyone with a genuine antisocial personality.

People with antisocial personality disorder have multiple sexual partners and tend to use others for sexual gratification, with little concern for the needs or feelings of their sexual partners. They can be superficially warm and charming but become distant and aloof after their sexual conquest.

The diagnosis of antisocial personality disorder is not given to children or adolescents below the age of 18, and it requires evidence of the presence of a conduct disorder that existed before the age of 15 (e.g., lying, truancy, arson, theft, or delinquency). There is some evidence to suggest that the incidence of antisocial personality disorder falls off dramatically after the age of 40 or so, although the reasons for this precipitous decline are not well understood.

Antisocial personality disorder is about four times as common in men as in women, and may be found in as much as 4 percent of the male population. The incidence is much higher in selected populations (e.g., convicted felons and con artists).

Contemporary cinema is replete with examples of antisocial personality disorders. Some salient examples include Anthony Hopkins' character Hannibal Lecter in *Silence of the Lambs* (1991); the street hoodlum, Alec, in *A Clockwork Orange* (1971); *In Cold Blood* (1967);

The Boston Strangler (1968); *Henry: Portrait of a Serial Killer* (1990); and Dennis Hopper (who is often typecast in the role) as a sociopath in both *Blue Velvet* (1986) and *Speed* (1994). Charles Manson, as portrayed in the film *Helter Skelter* (1976), is another example of the indifferent disregard for social values and moral behavior that is found in people with antisocial behavior. (Manson, responsible for the death of nine people in 1969, never showed any remorse for his behavior or the deaths of his victims.)

A somewhat less dramatic illustration is found in the callous manipulation of naive home buyers vividly portrayed by Jack Lemmon, who plays a desperate and unhappy real estate salesman in *Glengarry Glen Ross* (1992). Natasha Richardson and Mia Farrow play two consummate con artists in *Widow's Peak* (1994), although the diagnosis is incompatible with the character portrayed by Farrow for most of the film. The manipulation of others for personal gain without concern for the consequences of one's behavior is a characteristic feature of antisocial personality disorders.

One of the classic examples of an antisocial personality is found in the role played by Robert Walker in Alfred Hitchcock's *Strangers on a Train* (1951). Walker meets tennis pro Farley Granger in the club car of a train and has soon proposed a double murder: Walker will murder Granger's wife, who has refused to give him a divorce; in turn, Granger will murder Walker's father. Granger is appalled by the idea and insists that Walker leave. When they get to Washington, DC, Walker persists in insisting that Granger murder the father. Granger takes detailed notes, sneaks into the father's home, and attempts to alert the sleeping man to his son's diabolical plans. In a shocking scene, the sleeping figure rises up and we realize that it is actually Walker, testing Granger's resolve. Walker winds up killing Granger's wife, but he fails in his attempt to totally corrupt Granger. The film ends with the two men on a runaway merry-go-round, and Granger partially atones for his murderous fantasies by saving the lives of several children.

Bruno Antony, Robert Walker's character, meets many of the requirements for the diagnosis of antisocial personality. He repeatedly engages in unlawful behavior (including murder); he is deceitful; he appears to be impulsive (e.g., proposing murder to a total stranger on a train); and there is never any reason to suspect he feels any remorse for the murder he commits or his plan to have his father murdered. These four criteria all support the diagnosis, and Walker is an adult, so the diagnosis is not complicated by age. The aberrant behavior is not restricted to specific periods (as might be the case with schizophrenia or bipolar disorder). We do not know if conduct disorder was present before the age of 15, but, with a character as evil as Walker, it is hard to imagine it *not* being present.

Borderline Personality Disorder

Borderline personality disorder is characterized by unstable but intense interpersonal relationships, labile mood, impulsive behavior, and erratic emotions. These individuals are easily angered, but their anger may pass as quickly as a summer storm, leaving no sign of its recent presence. They become overly attached in almost all of their relationships: when they initially become romantically involved, their partners are apt to feel smothered by the intensity of the relationship and perplexed by the wild swings between affection and anger; when they enter therapy, therapists quickly become concerned about their excessive dependence and inappropriate adulation. These are the patients most likely to call in the middle of the night, insisting on an emergency consultation or late-night office visit. This is most apt to occur when the patient feels isolated or alone (e.g., when the therapist is about to take a vacation or attend a conference out of state).

Suicide gestures and self-injury are common in people with borderline personality disorders. These gestures cannot be ignored, because completed suicide occurs in about 10 percent of borderline personality disorder cases. However, it is more common for the patient to behave in ways that are more attention seeking than life threatening, such as swallowing 20 Valium and then calling a crisis center or making superficial cuts on the upper arm before calling a suicide hotline. Self-mutilation is also a common and serious problem with borderline personalities.

Borderline personalities are sometimes viewed as spontaneous and creative. They are likely to share the most intimate details of their life with casual acquaintances. They vacillate between indiscriminate adulation and active hatred, often within the space of hours. They are easily bored and may seek stimulation from indiscriminate sexual behavior, reckless driving, or misuse of substances.

The symptoms of borderline personality disorder overlap with those of both depression and bipolar disorders, and many borderline personality patients respond to treatment with either antidepressants or lithium. It is also difficult at times to distinguish borderline personality disorder from other personality disorders (e.g., histrionic and dependent personality disorder). Women are diagnosed with borderline personality disorder about three times as often as men. The disorder occurs in about 2 percent of the general public, but the frequency of the diagnosis is much greater in a clinical setting. There is strong epidemiological evidence suggesting a genetic basis for the disorder: for example, the diagnosis is about five times more common among close relatives of individuals diagnosed with borderline personality disorder.

Histrionic Personality Disorder

The defining feature of **histrionic personality disorder** is dramatic attention-seeking behavior. These individuals are self-centered and preoccupied with their own appearance. They feel uncomfortable in any situation in which they are not "center stage." They resent attention directed at others and will often engage in excessive behavior to have the focus of attention redirected to themselves. They initially seem to be spontaneous and interesting people, not unlike Rosalind Russell's portrayal of the title character in the film *Auntie Mame* (1958). However, true histrionic personalities soon find that others quickly tire of their desperate attempts to remain at the center of attention and resent their inability to engage in equitable social interaction.

Histrionic people appear to experience deep and profound emotions; however, these seemingly deep feelings are turned on (and off) quickly and with little provocation. They often leave others feeling vaguely uncomfortable by invading their body space or touching them casually but inappropriately. In nonclinical settings, histrionic personality disorder occurs about equally in men and women. The diagnosis overlaps with borderline personality disorder and narcissistic personality disorder.

One of the best film examples of a histrionic personality is Katharine Hepburn's portrayal of the dying mother in Long Day's Journey Into Night *(1962).* Family life centers around the mother, and her two sons and her husband dote on her. She is extremely concerned with her appearance, openly fishes for compliments, and makes frequent references to her lost beauty. If she were being clinically evaluated, Hepburn's character would be diagnosed as a histrionic personality disorder on Axis II and as opioid dependent (morphine) with physiological dependence on Axis I.

Zaza, the gay transvestite performer in La Cage aux Folles *(1978) provides another wonderful example of a histrionic personality.* She is dramatic and flamboyant, and almost everything she does is exaggerated. When Renato tells her that he plans to invite his ex-wife to an important dinner with his son's future in-laws, Zaza is highly insulted and announces her intention to commit suicide. Neither Renato nor the audience thinks for a minute that she is actually serious about her threat.

Narcissistic Personality Disorder

The name of this disorder is taken from the Greek myth of Narcissus, who fell in love with his own reflection. People with **narcissistic personality disorder** are vain and self-centered, and they have an exaggerated sense of their own importance. They may spend a great deal of time fantasizing about success or power. They appear conceited and pretentious. Their preoccupation with themselves leads them to overlook or devalue the contributions of others. They display an annoying sense of entitlement and resent it when they are expected to conform to standard rules and social expectations (e.g., waiting in line to pay a bill or renew a driver's license).

Although seemingly confident and secure, people with narcissistic personality disorder often harbor unconscious feelings of insecurity and real doubts about their own worth. These feelings of inadequacy propel the narcissistic personality to constantly scan the environment for evidence of his or her unique value. Adolescents almost universally display certain features of narcissistic personality disorder (e.g., preoccupation with their appearance and concern about how they are perceived by others); however, these vanities generally pass by early adulthood. The narcissistic personality never outgrows this preoccupation with self and never develops a mature interest in the needs and concerns of others. In many ways, the obsession with self that characterizes a person with narcissistic personality disorder can be seen as the antithesis of Alfred Adler's concept of **Gemeinschaftsgefuhl.**

Contemporary cinema is replete with examples of narcissistic personality disorders. Some characters that come readily to mind include Gloria Swanson in *Sunset Boulevard* (1950) and an (initially) arrogant and self-serving Mickey Rooney in *Boy's Town* (1938). In a more contemporary film, *The Doctor* (1991), William Hurt plays a self-centered and narcissistic physician who cares little for anything except himself and his career until he develops a tumor in his throat and discovers what it feels like to be a patient. Finally, Warren Beatty plays a narcissistic and self-centered gangster in the Barry Levinson film *Bugsy* (1991). (It is difficult to watch *Bugsy* without recalling the widely reported rumor that the 1972 Carly Simon song "You're So Vain" was written for Beatty.)

CLUSTER C DISORDERS

Avoidant Personality Disorder

People with **avoidant personality disorder** have a tremendous fear of being revealed as inadequate and inferior. They are hypersensitive to criticism and shape their lives around fear of rejection and criticism. They generally avoid intimate relations, convinced that they would be revealed as inadequate or clumsy lovers. They are "wall-flowers" who neither cause trouble nor elicit interest. They conceptualize the world (and especially interpersonal relationships and interactions) as unsafe and threatening. They have diminished self-esteem and describe themselves as inept, incompetent, and inferior. They are apt to spend much of their time at home and alone, in large part because of their concern that their personal deficiencies will be revealed if they venture out in public. They may turn down job offers or opportunities for advancement because of their concerns about their own limitations. These pervasive feelings of inferiority typically originate in childhood. They may be socially appropriate in children, but they are clearly limiting and self-defeating in adults. In Adlerian terms, the person with an avoidant personality disorder lacks the *courage to be imperfect.*

It is important for clinicians to be sensitive to cultural differences that may affect a client's behavior. For example, in some Asian cultures, self-deprecation and extreme modesty about one's own achievements are normative behaviors and not indicative of a maladaptive personality trait.

This diagnosis overlaps substantially with the diagnosis of **social phobia, generalized type**. The overlap is so substantial that many clinicians find the distinction between the two diagnoses to be meaningless, and the *DSM-IV* acknowledges that the two diagnoses may be simply different ways of conceptualizing the same (or similar) conditions.

Dependent Personality Disorder

Dependent personalities have extreme difficulty making decisions for themselves. They are submissive and look to others for structure, meaning, and direction in their lives. They tend to be passive and clinging. These people lack assertion skills and submit to the will of others. They sometimes submit to verbal, physical, or sexual abuse by their spouses and others. They lack self-confidence and feel they cannot manage on their own. They feel incompetent to make even small decisions without support and direction. They fear the loss of approval that may occur if they express their own opinions or beliefs. They invest tremendous time and energy in maintaining the relationship with the person upon whom they are dependent. When a close, dependent relationship ends, they almost immediately seek out another relationship that supports their chronic need for succor. These individuals may spend a great deal of time worrying about what will happen to them if they are abandoned.

As with all personality disorders, it is important not to confuse culturally conditioned behavior with enduring and aberrant personality traits. Some cultures actively promote dependency, especially in women. In the United States, women are dependent personalities more often than men; however, in nonclinical settings, the prevalence appears to be approximately equal across genders.

An amusing illustration of a dependent personality occurs in the 1991 film *What About Bob?* Bob, played by Bill Murray, is the patient of psychiatrist Richard Dreyfuss. Bob pursues the beleaguered psychiatrist across the country when the psychiatrist tries to take a short vacation. Almost all therapists have had overly dependent patients, although they are unlikely to have encountered a case as extreme as that of Bob. The film is an interesting starting point for a discussion of transference and countertransference.

Obsessive-Compulsive Personality Disorder

The diagnosis of obsessive-compulsive personality disorder is applied when someone presents with enduring, inflexible, and maladaptive personality traits that involve perfectionism, orderliness, and an excessive need for control. Patients with obsessive-compulsive personality disorder display exacting attention to detail and worry a great deal about the most trivial issues. They devote a great deal of time to making lists and plans. They sometimes even make lists of their lists! Time is seen not as the fabric of life but, rather, as an enemy and something to be conquered. All of this psychological energy is expended in a futile attempt to achieve a sense of control over the exigencies of life and the vicissitudes of fortune.

People with obsessive-compulsive personality disorder are perfectionists who worry a great deal when anything can possibly go wrong. They are extremely concerned about their relative position and power in social groups. They tend to be deferential to the power of others and insist that even the most petty rules be obeyed to the letter. These are the individuals who patiently wait for the "Walk" sign at crosswalks, even if it is midnight and the street is completely deserted. They enjoy giving orders and are likely to insist that everything be done "by the book." People with obsessive-compulsive personality disorder are frequently happy in the military, where social rank is clearly defined and there are explicit rules governing almost every conceivable situation.

Two films come to mind immediately in any discussion of obsessive-compulsive personality disorder. The first is *The Odd Couple* (1968), with the memorable performance by Jack Lemmon as Felix Unger, Walter Matthau's neurotic roommate who roams the house with a can of air freshener, determined to ferret out any untoward smells. The second film is *M*A*S*H* (1970). Major Frank Burns spends the entire war fretting about the antics of Hawkeye Pierce and Trapper John McIntyre and the inability of the system to set limits on their exuberant behavior. He is obsessed with rank and bitterly resents any undue familiarity by enlisted men or junior officers. He works hard to ensure that the enlisted men do not fraternize with Korean women. He is self-righteous, moralistic, and rigid, despite the fact that he is having an affair with "Hot Lips" Hoolihan. He becomes furious when he doesn't get his way, but he is totally ineffectual in responding to the cavalier attitudes of his tent mates.

It is important to understand the difference between obsessive-compulsive personality disorder and obsessive-compulsive disorder. The first disorder reflects a maladaptive personality *style;* the second indicates the presence of a serious mental disorder characterized by recurrent and persistent thoughts, images, or impulses (obsessions) and repetitious behaviors or mental acts (compulsions) that the individual can't avoid or suppress. For example, an obsessive-compulsive personality may need to be constantly cleaning the house and "picking up." This is maladaptive (when excessive) but may not significantly impair the person's life, and may be mildly adaptive in some roles (e.g., that of a homemaker). However, the patient with an **obsessive-compulsive disorder** spends at least an hour a day focused on the obsession or engaged in compulsive behavior, is significantly distressed by his or her problem, and realizes that the behavior or thoughts are abnormal and out of control. In contrast, the person with **obsessive-compulsive personality disorder** is far less likely to be troubled by his or her condition.

PERSONALITY DISORDERS IN FILMS[1]

Humphrey Bogart playing Captain Queeg in The Caine Mutiny *(1954) is a wonderful illustration of the paranoid personality.* Queeg becomes preoccupied with trivial misdemeanors by sailors while he ignores the important parts of his job — such as maintaining the morale of his men. He eventually falls apart under pressure when he is called to the witness stand to testify in a court martial hearing for an insubordinate junior officer. There is a famous scene in which Queeg takes two ball bearings out of his pocket and begins to move them around nervously in his palm, and everyone in the court senses that this man is not well adjusted.

---

[1]Steven Hyler (1988) has provided a compelling analysis of the ways in which psychopathology is portrayed in the cinema. His analysis of personality disorders is especially helpful, and many of the following examples are drawn from his seminal article.

Bogart later plays another paranoid personality in *The Treasure of the Sierra Madre* (1948), when he becomes obsessed with the idea that his partners are out to steal the gold they have agreed to split up among them.

The figure of the loner is a staple in western films, and many of these characters would meet the criteria for schizoid personality disorder. They avoid close relationships, prefer solitary activities, lack close friends and confidants, and appear indifferent to the praise or criticism of others. Charlton Heston in *Will Penny* (1968) is one example; Robert Redford in *Jeremiah Johnson* (1972) is another.

In a more contemporary setting, *the figure of William Hurt in* The Accidental Tourist *(1988) appears schizoid.* Always cool and aloof, Hurt holds in all emotion when he identifies the dead body of his son and then pulls away from all social relationships. His wife (Kathleen Turner) tolerates his increasing isolation as long as she can and then eventually leaves him. Hurt does not seem upset by her loss. He is emotionally detached, spends his evenings alone with his dog, and has little or no sex drive. (The fact that a romantic relationship develops with Geena Davis suggests that these qualities are situational rather than characterological. This observation would support a diagnosis of adjustment disorder with depressed mood.)

The schizotypal personality is demonstrated in Flannery O'Conner's novel Wise Blood *and in the 1979 John Huston film adaptation.* The Southern preacher works hard to convince people to join his "Church Without Christ." He has numerous peculiar beliefs, odd speech, constricted affect, strange behavior, and few close friends. These five characteristics would be sufficient to justify the diagnosis of schizotypal personality. Hyler (1988) uses De Niro's portrayal of Travis Brickle in *Taxi Driver* (1976) to illustrate the schizotypal personality. He feels this film is such a useful tool for teaching medical students about psychopathology that he has incorporated it into a computer program that can be used to teach medical students to perform and record a complete mental status exam (Hyler & Bujold, 1994). The program analyzes student responses and provides feedback for the students.

The chapter-opening discussion of *Fatal Attraction* (1987) notes that Glenn Close displays many of the characteristics of borderline personality disorder, and we get some idea of her desperate tenacity in the chapter-opening epigraph. Other potential examples of borderline personalities include Diane Keaton in *Looking for Mr. Goodbar* (1977) and several of the female supporting characters in Martin Scorcese's *After Hours* (1985).

Film libraries abound with good examples of antisocial personalities. Often these are films that detail the lives of serial killers. Some salient examples include *The Boston Strangler* (1986), *The Executioner's Song* (1982), *Henry: Portrait of a Serial Killer* (1990), and *In Cold Blood* (1967). These four films are all based on true stories and provide some insight into the antisocial personality. (For example, one character in *In Cold Blood* describes serial killers in the following terms: "They all felt physically inferior or sexually inadequate. Their childhood was violent. . . . They couldn't distinguish between fantasy and reality. They didn't hate their victims, they didn't even know them.") Other film examples of antisocial killers include *M* (1931), *Peeping Tom* (1960), *Reservoir Dogs* (1992), *Silence of the Lambs* (1991), and *Speed* (1994).

Other films illustrating personality disorders are included in the appendix of this book. In addition, any film buff should be able to generate his or her own list with just a few minutes' thought. Discussing the various characters in films and whether or not they would qualify for *DSM-IV* diagnoses can be a fascinating and useful pedagogical exercise.

Topics for Class Discussion

- Is it useful to treat life-long personality characteristics as *diseases* (i.e., should personality disorders be included in the *DSM-IV*)?

- It is well established that it is difficult to treat personality disorders. Should insurance companies be required to cover the treatment of these conditions?

- Is the concept of *evil* meaningful when discussing people with antisocial personality disorders?

- How does a personality feature (such as suspicion) differ from a personality disorder (such as paranoid personality disorder) or a disease (such as paranoid schizophrenia)? Are the differences qualitative as well as quantitative?

- *Fatal Attraction* originally ended with a suicide by Alex Forrest, using a knife that had Dan Gallagher's fingerprints on it. However, viewers did not like this ending, and it was replaced with the memorable bathtub scene. Would the original ending have been more consistent with a diagnosis of borderline personality disorder?

- What kinds of trouble can therapists anticipate when they are treating clients with borderline personality disorder?

Chapter 7

Substance Use Disorders

You can't cut it short. When you're on that merry-go-round you have to ride it all the way, round and round 'til that blasted thing wears itself out and the music comes to a halt.
Don Birnam in *The Lost Weekend*

Questions to Consider While Watching *The Lost Weekend*
- How does the portrayal of alcoholism in *The Lost Weekend* (1945) differ from that of more contemporary films about alcoholism, such as *Leaving Las Vegas, Trees Lounge, Drunks,* and *When a Man Loves a Woman?*
- Is the film's portrayal of delirium tremens realistic?
- Is there a biological or genetic basis for alcoholism?
- Are there medications available now that would have helped Don Birnam cope with his withdrawal symptoms and his craving?

PATIENT EVALUATION

Patient's stated reason for coming: "I'm an alcoholic, a hopeless alcoholic. I need to sober up and I need to stop drinking. You can help me with the first problem but not the second."

History of the present illness: Don Birnam is a 32-year-old man who has been admitted to Bellevue for the third time. He is a professional writer who has a long history of alcoholism. Mr. Birnam has pawned his typewriter and most possessions of any value. He reports drinking since age 18.

Past psychiatric illness, treatment, and outcomes: Mr. Birnam has not been treated for any psychiatric problems other than his alcoholism. He has been arrested on numerous occasions for public intoxication, and he was recently arrested after stealing a bottle of rye from a liquor store. Once he begins drinking, he is unable to stop until he passes out. This is Mr. Birnam's third admission to this unit over the past two years. He presented with auditory and visual hallucinations and delirium tremens on both past admissions.

Medical history: This patient has a history of liver disease secondary to alcoholism. He broke his arm on one occasion after falling from a fire escape while drunk. He has multiple scars from abrasions that occurred during falls while drinking.

Psychosocial history: Mr. Birnam is the youngest of two children. His parents are dairy farmers in upstate New York. He did well in school and achieved normal developmental milestones at appropriate ages. There is no history of truancy or delinquency. The patient was a successful writer who supported himself writing for magazines until approximately two years ago. He is currently with a supportive and caring woman (Helen) who appears to tolerate and even condone his drinking. Mr. Birnam lives in a Manhattan apartment with his brother Nick. Nick and Helen comprise this patient's social support system.

Drug and alcohol history: Mr. Birnam has been drinking daily since his early twenties. His drinking has escalated to the point where he currently consumes approximately a quart of whisky and a case of beer each day. There are obvious withdrawal symptoms whenever this patient tries to quit drinking or reduce the amount he drinks.

Behavioral observations: Mr. Birnam was sweating and shaking during the interview. At times he appeared to be hallucinating, claiming at one point that bugs were crawling on him. The patient appeared anxious and agitated. He had trouble sitting still and frequently got up to pace around the examination room.

Mental status examination: Mr. Birnam was confused and disoriented on the mental status examination. He knew the month, season, and year but not the day of the week or the date. He was oriented to place. He was able to recall only two out of three objects immediately and none out of three after a brief delay. He could not complete serial sevens. He could identify simple objects and repeat phrases without difficulty. He could follow verbal and written commands. He was able to write a simple sentence, but his writing was barely legible because of his tremor. He also had great difficulty copying intersecting pentagons. His poor score of 18 and his obvious difficulties on the Mini Mental State Examination are believed to be secondary to his withdrawal from alcohol, and the test will be readministered after several days of sobriety.

Functional assessment: This patient's alcoholism has severely limited his ability to function as a writer. His memory impairment and general state of confusion make sustained concentration and effort virtually impossible. He has also alienated many of his friends because of his drinking. He is obsessed with alcohol and has few interests or activities that are not alcohol-related.

Strengths: Mr. Birnam is an intelligent individual who was once a successful writer. He maintains good verbal skills, although it is difficult for him to concentrate. He is a congenial individual with good interpersonal skills. His greatest strengths appear to be the consistent support of his brother and girlfriend.

Diagnosis: 303.90 Alcohol Dependence with Physiological Dependence

Treatment plan: (1) Detoxification; (2) 28-day inpatient treatment on the Alcohol Treatment Unit; (3) outpatient follow-up; (4) Alcoholics Anonymous

Prognosis: Given this patient's long history of alcoholism and previous treatment failures, his prognosis is guarded at best.

THE LOST WEEKEND

Billy Wilder's classic 1945 film *The Lost Weekend* is a powerful portrayal of alcoholism. The protagonist, Don Birnam (Ray Milland), is ready to sacrifice his brother's trust, his career as a writer, and the love of his girlfriend (played by Jane Wyman) for one more drink. Early in the film we see clear examples of *denial,* believed by many to be the characteristic defense mechanism of the alcoholic. Don Birnam minimizes the significance of his drinking as long as he can but eventually realizes that it is ruining his life. *A scene in which Birnam watches a bat kill and eat a mouse is an effective illustration of the type of hallucinations characteristic of delirium tremens.* Birnam eventually hocks his girlfriend's coat to get a gun and then writes a suicide note. However, Jane Wyman arrives before he pulls the trigger, and the film ends with Birnam planning the novel he is going to write and, in a heavily symbolic gesture, dropping a cigarette in a glass of rye.

Despite an ending that is somewhat too pat for contemporary viewers, the film is still a dramatic illustration of the destructive effects of alcohol. Milland won an Oscar for best actor for his portrayal of Birnam, and the film earned additional Oscars for best picture, director, and screenplay. Billy Wilder, the film's director, consulted with Alcoholics Anonymous before beginning work on the film.

ALCOHOLISM

Historical Use of Alcohol

The use of mind-altering substances appears to have existed almost from the time that humans first became aware of the potent effects plants could have on the human experience of reality. Oliver Wendell Holmes, Jr., once remarked, "There is in all men a demand for the superlative, so much so that the poor devil who has no other way of reaching it attains it by getting drunk," and the use of alcohol can be traced back at least 5,000 years. The relationship among alcohol, drugs, and mysticism has been explored in books such as William James' *Varieties of Religious Experience* and Aldous Huxley's *Doors of Perception.*

The biblical accounts of the drunkenness of Noah and Lot are well known, and anthropologists have discovered that the distillation of alcohol occurs in many if not most cultures. The use of alcohol by preliterate societies has been well documented, making it the "oldest and most widely used drug in the world" (Veitia & McGahee, 1995).

Tolerance for the use of alcohol has varied widely across historical periods and cultures. In colonial America, for example, drunkenness was commonplace and frequently condemned from the pulpit. Benjamin Rush, a physician who signed the Declaration of Independence and who is sometimes called the Father of American Psychiatry, was an early proponent of prohibition and the disease concept of alcoholism. It is interesting to note that the early temperance movement was started to sober up the clergy and was extended to parishioners later.

In the United States, attempts to restrain the use and abuse of alcohol were associated with one of our greatest social experiments, prohibition. Prohibition was enacted by ratification of the Eighteenth Amendment to the Constitution in January 1920; the experiment ended with adoption of the Twenty-first Amendment in 1933. Although a social failure, prohibition was a medical success because the incidence of death from cirrhosis was decreased. A fascinating portrayal of some of the social consequences of prohibition is available in the film *The Untouchables.*

Alcohol was widespread in the American West during the period of western expansion, and the frontier saloon was often one of the first buildings constructed when a new town was being built. Alcoholism and alcohol abuse appear to have been common and were associated with much of the violence found in frontier towns. The saloon became a staple motif in western films, as did the waterfront bar in any movie dealing with longshoremen. The western has always been a cinematic genre that reflects basic issues and conflicts in society. This is illustrated vividly in Clint Eastwood's 1993 film *The Unforgiven,* a story about a gunman who stops killing at his wife's insistence and becomes a devout Christian. Later in the film he is hired on as a killer and has to get drunk to do his job.

Alcohol and the Brain

Alcohol is quickly absorbed into the bloodstream and transported to the liver, which is capable of metabolizing about one ounce of 100-proof alcohol in an hour. If a person consumes only one drink per hour, the liver is able to keep up, and alcohol does not affect the brain. However, at consumption rates greater than one drink per hour, the brain is quickly affected, with obvious consequences. In particular, there is rapid uptake of alcohol in the cerebellum; and this results in staggering, diminished coordination, and slower reaction times. Judgment is impaired, and alcohol can trigger aggression in some individuals. Although alcohol may initially facilitate sexuality by reducing inhibitions, at higher levels of use there is clear impairment of sexual functioning. In the words of Shakespeare, "Lechery, Sir, it provokes and it unprovokes; it provokes the desire, but it takes away the performance" (*Macbeth,* Act II, Scene 3).

There are marked gender differences in the way alcohol is mobilized. Women absorb alcohol more quickly, and the effects of a given quantity of alcohol may be more pronounced in a woman than in a man of equal weight. Alcoholism itself begins at a later age in women and is more likely to be related to a precipitating event. Alcoholic women are more likely than alcoholic men to drink alone and are somewhat less likely to be binge drinkers.

Patterns of Alcohol Abuse

DSM-IV lists seven characteristic symptoms of dependence and requires that at least three occur at any time in the same 12-month period for the diagnosis of substance dependence. These symptoms are apparent in Michael Keaton's character's addiction to cocaine in *Clean and Sober*. Some of the symptoms that apply to Don Birnam's alcoholism in *The Lost Weekend* are presented in Table 7-1. It may be useful to think about the experiences of your own use of alcohol or that of your relatives and friends as you review these symptoms.[1]

Epidemiology of Alcoholism

The majority of American adults (about 65 percent) drink at least occasionally, and 1 in 10 consumes more than one ounce of alcohol per day. Males tend to tolerate alcohol more easily than females, in part because of their greater weight, and so the definition of a heavy drinker needs to be adjusted for males and females. However, it is generally accepted that individuals who average more than three drinks per day are heavy drinkers. Many individuals will consume far more than this average: 10 percent of all drinkers consume more than 50 percent of all alcohol.

---

[1]The symptoms of dependence are the same for all psychoactive substances. In this section they are applied to the particular problem of alcohol dependence.

It is estimated that more than 7 percent of the adult population in the United States — approximately 13 million people — are alcoholics. Alcoholism is one of our most serious public health problems, costing billions annually in lost productivity, increased health care costs, and accidents. Alcohol abuse contributes to about 30 percent of all motor vehicle accidents, and it is responsible for about half of all traffic fatalities. More information about the relationship between alcohol and accidental death is presented in Table 7-2.

(1) Alcohol is consumed in a larger amount or over a longer period than the individual intended.	Birnam is drinking when the film begins, and he drinks throughout the film.
(2) People know that their use of alcohol is excessive but fail in their attempts to control their drinking.	Birnam has tried repeatedly to go on the wagon and has "taken the cure" at least once without success.
(3) A great deal of time is devoted to acquiring alcohol, drinking it, or recovering from its effects. In severe cases, almost all of the individual's waking hours are devoted to the substance.	Birnam is preoccupied with rye and has hidden it throughout his apartment. He thinks about little else, and he steals a purse and robs a liquor store to support his addiction.
(4) Intoxication or withdrawal symptoms occur at work or in other inappropriate situations (e.g., while driving a car).	Birnam has quit writing altogether and has pawned his typewriter to buy rye.
(5) Important social, occupational, or recreational activities are replaced by alcohol.	Birnam's relationship with his brother is seriously damaged by his drinking, and he avoids spending a weekend in the country with his family. He also comes close to destroying his relationship with his girlfriend.
(6) Alcohol use persists, despite increasing awareness of the problems it causes.	Birnam describes himself as a "drunk," and he is acutely aware of his declining prowess as a writer.
(7) Tolerance develops, and an increased amount of alcohol is required to produce the same effect. (Tolerance is less marked for alcohol than for some other drugs.)	The film shows Birnam drinking approximately two quarts of rye per day, far more than most people could tolerate.
(8) Withdrawal symptoms develop when the individual cuts back on his or her use of alcohol.	Birnam develops delirium tremens and hallucinates in the film.
(9) After experiencing withdrawal symptoms, the individual begins to drink to *avoid* these unpleasant experiences rather than to produce the pleasant feelings initially associated with alcohol use.	When questioned by a bartender about drinking so early in the morning, Birnam remarks, "At night it's a drink; in the morning it's medicine."

Table 7-1. Symptoms of alcohol dependence.

About 10 percent of adults seeking treatment by physicians are alcoholics, and about a third of admissions to general hospitals are for alcohol-related problems. The mortality rate of alcoholics is two to three times greater than that of the general population, and their life span is 10 to 12 years shorter. In addition, the children of alcoholic parents are at increased risk for hyperactivity, low IQ, emotional problems, child abuse, and fetal alcohol syndrome (Kanas, 1988). Despite the severity of these problems, less than 10 percent of alcoholics will receive treatment for their problems.

There is tremendous variability across cultures in the consumption of alcohol. In wine-producing countries, such as France and Italy, annual adult per capita consumption exceeds 20 liters. This is more than twice the consumption rate of the United States and about five times the annual consumption rate found in

Aviation deaths	32%
Drowning	62%
Falls	48%
Fires	54%
Homicide arrests	7%
Homicide victims	64%
Suicides	37%
Fatal single-vehicle crashes	63%

Table 7-2. Alcohol as a contributing cause of death.

other countries such as Norway. However, although consumption rates may be correlated with the incidence of alcoholism in a country, the correlation is not precise because wine and beer are widely used with meals in European countries.

For reasons that are not entirely clear, men are far more likely than women to become alcoholic. For example, lifetime prevalence rates for alcoholism in the United States in one study were found to be more than 20 percent for men and about 5 percent for women. This may be related to a greater genetic propensity to alcoholism in males; however, it is also partly determined by the role expectations for women that are found in many cultures. There is also evidence that the true incidence of alcoholism is greater than previously suspected because women alcoholics are less likely to be identified and reported.

Helzer et al. (1990) compared lifetime prevalence rates across five sites (the United States, Canada, Puerto Rico, Taiwan, and Korea) and found strikingly different rates of alcoholism, and the prevalence rate for men was dramatically greater in each setting. The data from Korea were particularly striking: there was a lifetime prevalence rate of 43 percent for men in contrast to a rate of 3 percent for women.

In the United States, the percentage of drinkers is lower in the South than in other regions of the country; however, the per capita consumption by those individuals who drink is considerably greater than that found in other regions. These data are influenced by religious and ethnic differences across regions. Subcultures that encourage moderate use of alcohol (e.g., Chinese-Americans, Italian Americans, and Jewish-Americans) are likely to have both low abstinence rates and low alcoholism rates; in contrast, those subcultures with strong prohibitions against drinking produce higher rates of both abstainers and alcoholics. In addition, there is some evidence that Asians have a physiological intolerance for alcohol that may have a protective effect.

Alcohol use and alcoholism also vary widely across professions in the U.S. Sailors, railroad workers, and bartenders are all employed in occupations in which they are at high risk for alcoholism.

Goodwin (1988) has argued that writers (such as Don Birnam) are at especially high risk for alcoholism. He points out that four out of the six Americans who have won the Nobel Prize for literature were clearly alcoholics (Sinclair Lewis, Eugene O'Neill, William Faulkner, and Ernest Hemingway). Another Nobel Prize winner, John Steinbeck, is believed to be an alcoholic by some biographers. It is interesting to note that Pearl Buck, a woman, and Saul Bellow, a Jewish author, were two exceptions: the incidence of alcoholism is lower for both women and Jews. Other writers known for their excessive drinking include Edgar Allan Poe, Dorothy Parker, F. Scott Fitzgerald, Thomas Wolfe, e. e. cummings, Jack London, Truman Capote, and Jack Kerouac.

The Genetics of Alcoholism

Alcoholism runs in families, and both twin and adoption studies have shown that the children of alcoholics are far more likely to become alcoholic than are the children of nonalcoholic parents. Monozygotic twins are far more likely than dizygotic twins to be **concordant** for alcoholism (i.e., both twins have the same status: alcoholic or nonalcoholic); and the sons of alcoholics are about four times more likely to become alcoholic than are the sons of nonalcoholics, whether they are raised by their biological parents or foster parents. The genetic link appears to be sex-related, and the relationship is not as strong in daughters.

Adoption studies from Scandinavia and work by Robert Cloninger in St. Louis suggest there may be two genetically distinct forms of alcoholism. Type 1, or **milieu-limited alcoholism,** is associated with older age of onset, less sociopathy, marked guilt feelings, loss of control of drinking, and a dysphoria relieving response to alcohol. This form of alcoholism is more equally represented across both males and females and accounts for about two-thirds of all cases of alcoholism. In contrast, **male-limited alcoholism** occurs much more frequently in males, occurs earlier, and is associated with sociopathy, drinking to produce euphoria, and less guilt.

Assessment

The diagnosis of alcoholism is made in accordance with *DSM-IV* criteria. The **Michigan Alcohol Screening Test** (MAST) is the instrument that has been used most extensively for diagnosing alcoholism, and it is the standard against which all other alcoholism screening measures are judged in terms of validity and reliability. However, in general, the diagnosis is made on the basis of the "Three C's" of alcoholism: documentation of Compulsive use, loss of Control over alcohol consumption, and Continued use in spite of adverse consequences (Veitia & McGahee, 1995).

A number of specific assessment devices have been developed to help clinicians. The simplest of these—and one of the most effective—is the CAGE test. The *CAGE test* requires that the clinician ask four simple questions of every patient suspected of alcohol abuse: (1) Have you ever felt the need to Cut down on your drinking? (2) Have you ever felt Annoyed by criticism of your drinking? (3) Have you ever had Guilt feelings about your drinking? and (4) Do you ever take a morning Eye-opener? Two affirmative answers should raise the suspicion of alcoholism; three positive answers virtually confirm the diagnosis.

Treatment of Alcoholism

An interesting introduction to the treatment of alcoholism is available in the film *Clean and Sober.* This 1988 film stars Michael Keaton as Michael Poynter, a successful real estate broker who sees his professional and personal life deteriorate in response to his addiction to alcohol and cocaine. He eventually recovers with the help of a sponsor from Alcoholics Anonymous. His romantic interest, a woman he meets while in treatment, is not so lucky and is killed in an automobile accident after snorting cocaine. The film ends with Poynter speaking at an AA meeting after receiving a white poker chip, reflecting his first 30 days of sobriety.

The first stage of treatment is **detoxification,** or "drying out." This process can vary from several days to a month in duration and is almost always very aversive for the person involved. Vitamins are routinely prescribed in the treatment of addictions. At one time, tranquilizers (primarily Librium and Valium) were often administered to help an individual cope with the physiological distress that accompanies detoxification; however, this approach to treatment has always been controversial and is less common now.

Antibuse (disulfiram) blocks the metabolism of alcohol and may help some alcoholics avoid resumption of drinking after detoxification. An individual taking Antibuse will become violently ill if exposed to even a very small amount of alcohol and will experience nausea, vomiting, sweating, and accelerated respiration and heart rate. Antibuse is most useful in the first months of sobriety, when the craving for alcohol is most intense.

Alcoholics Anonymous, a self-help fellowship founded in 1935, is widely regarded as an important part of treatment for most alcoholics. More than a million people in the United States belong to this self-help group, and there are more than 1.5 million members worldwide. Almost every town of any size has a local chapter of Alcoholics Anonymous, and many large cities have meetings in different chapters every evening of the week. These meetings involve self-disclosure, social support, and a commitment to the disease model of alcoholism. The well-known 12 steps of Alcoholics Anonymous are presented in Table 7-3. Jellinek's gamma type of alcoholic is the most likely to feel comfortable participating in Alcoholics Anonymous. Other types may not feel welcome or understood in the AA setting. The founding of Alcoholics Anonymous is described in the film *My Name Is Bill W.* (1989). Most public computer bulletin boards have a discussion section titled "Friends of Bill W." This board is especially busy on New Year's Eve.

Al-anon is a related group for spouses and partners of alcoholics that focuses on the message that the alcoholic is responsible for his or her own behavior and significant others contribute nothing by assuming responsibility for the misbehavior of the alcoholic. **Al-ateen** is a similar affiliated group designed to serve teenage children of alcoholic parents.

Although most providers in the substance abuse community are quick to praise the good work done by Alcoholics Anonymous, there is little empirical evidence supporting the program. In addition, some individuals find the quasi-religious philosophy of the organization distasteful.

The Portrayal of Alcoholism in Films

Images of alcohol and drinking are ubiquitous in contemporary films, and one is hard-pressed to name adult films in which alcohol is not represented in some way. This may reflect the fact that alcohol affects everyone directly or indirectly.

The early success of *Lost Weekend* (1945) led to other films with alcoholism as a central theme, including *Harvey* (1950), *A Star Is Born* (1954), *Come Back Little Sheba* (1952), *Days of Wine and Roses* (1962), and *Key Largo* (1948). More recent films include *Who's Afraid of Virginia Woolf?* (1966), *Tender Mercies* (1983), *Arthur* (1981), *Ironweed* (1987), *The Verdict* (1987), *Paris, Texas* (1984), *Under the Volcano* (1984), *Hoosiers* (1986), *Barfly* (1981), and *Clean and Sober* (1988).

In contrast to the sobering representations of alcoholism in films such as *Clean and Sober,* some films portray the alcoholic as happy and carefree. *Harvey* (1950) and *Arthur* (1981) are the two most obvious examples. Writing about *Arthur,* Vincent Canby (1981) noted

Not since Nick and Nora Charles virtually made the dry martini into the national drink . . . has there been quite so much boozing in a movie without hidden consequences. Arthur drinks scotch the way people now drink Perrier. . . . When he goes giggling about town, sloshed to the eyeballs, he's not seen as a case history but as eccentric. (p. 10)

1.	We admitted that we were powerless over alcohol—that our lives had become unmanageable.
2.	Came to believe that a power greater than ourselves could restore us to sanity.
3.	Made a decision to turn our will and our life over to the care of God *as we understood Him.*
4.	Made a searching and fearless moral inventory of ourselves.
5.	Admitted to God, to ourselves, and to another human being the exact nature of our wrongs.
6.	Were entirely ready to have God remove all these defects of character.
7.	Humbly asked Him to remove our shortcomings.
8.	Made a list of all persons we had harmed, and became willing to make amends to them all.
9.	Made direct amends to such people whenever possible, except when to do so would injure them or others.
10.	Continued to take personal inventory and, when we were wrong, promptly admitted it.
11.	Sought through prayer and meditation to improve our conscious contact with God *as we understood Him,* praying only for knowledge of His will for us and the power to carry that out.
12.	Having had a spiritual awakening as the result of these steps, we tried to carry this message to alcoholics, and to practice these principles in all our affairs.

Table 7-3. From *The Twelve Steps and Twelve Traditions.* (The *Twelve Steps* are reprinted with permission of Alcoholics Anonymous World Services, Inc. Permission to reprint the *Twelve Steps* does not mean that AA has reviewed or approved the contents of this publication, nor that AA agrees with the views expressed herein. AA is a program of recovery from alcoholism only – use of *Twelve Steps* in connection with programs and activities which are patterned after AA, but which address other problems, or in any other non-AA context, does not imply otherwise.)

Unfortunately, the film presents an appealing model of Arthur tooling about Manhattan in his Rolls-Royce. In the film, he has the good fortune to have a chauffeur; most of the teenage audience emulating his example aren't so lucky.

Movies *reflect* social mores as interpreted by filmmakers, and this certainly applies to the use of alcohol. In turn, movies *affect* social mores in a cyclical manner. One of the most recent film presentations of the ways in which families are affected by alcoholism is found in the 1994 film *When a Man Loves a Woman.* Three additional, very powerful films about alcoholism have recently been released: *Leaving Las Vegas* (1995), *Trees Lounge* (1996), and *Drunks* (1997). This last film is an especially helpful introduction to Alcoholics Anonymous and is highly recommended to anyone who has not had an opportunity to visit an open AA meeting. In addition, anyone interested in the way in which alcoholism is portrayed in films is referred to an excellent book by Norman Denzin, *Hollywood Shot by Shot: Alcoholism in American Cinema.*

DRUG ABUSE

Clean and Sober

The 1988 film *Clean and Sober* stars Michael Keaton as a cocaine addict and Morgan Freeman as an addictions counselor. The film opens when Keaton receives a call from his real estate office about $50,000 in missing escrow funds. Keaton has spent the money on cocaine. Confident that he can talk his way out of the problem, Keaton begins the day by snorting a line of coke. He then offers a line to the nude woman lying beside him in bed and discovers that she is comatose from an overdose.

Keaton responds to his financial and personal problems by running away. He enrolls in a drug rehabilitation program, not so much for treatment but because it offers a confidential program and a place for him to hide away. Soon, however, he is going through the pain of detoxification. Despite this evidence of addiction, Keaton continues to deny the reality of his addiction. However, while in treatment he learns that his girlfriend has died from the overdose and that his juggling of the escrow account to cover his drug purchases has been discovered, and he fails in an attempt to cajole money from his mother, who realizes that he will only spend it on drugs.

> *Now it's thirty days later. I've been to a funeral, been on about nine million job interviews, I'm $52,000 in debt, and I've got this chip. Suddenly I've got this startling belief that I'm an alcoholic and a drug addict.*
>
> Michael Keaton referring to his 30-day sobriety chip from Alcoholics Anonymous in *Clean and Sober* (1988)

Morgan Freeman is very convincing as an exaddict now trying to help others overcome their addictions. Some of the most interesting scenes in the film show Keaton at AA meetings (as mentioned earlier, he is alcoholic as well as addicted to drugs) and in group therapy. While in the group, Keaton becomes romantically involved with an attractive woman named Charlie, played by Kathy Baker. Charlie is involved in a pathological and destructive relationship with her live-in boyfriend, and both continue to use drugs when Charlie is discharged from the program. Keaton tries to get her to leave the destructive relationship, and she does briefly. Eventually, she returns to her boyfriend, resumes using drugs, and is killed in a car wreck while high on cocaine. The film ends with Keaton getting his 30-day AA chip, acknowledging to the group that he is both an alcoholic and a drug addict, and realizing that each of us can be responsible only for his or her own behavior.

History of Drug Abuse

Our earliest history documents the use of substances taken not for nutritional value but, rather, for their mind-altering properties. For example, the poppy was cultivated as early as 4000 B.C. to provide opium, and marijuana dates back nearly as far. Alcohol has been around since at least the time of Noah.

Opium is mentioned in Homer's *Odyssey* and was used by English intellectuals such as Coleridge and De Quincey. It became a staple ingredient in the medical armamentarium of the nineteenth and early twentieth centuries. Many patent medicines contained opium, and addiction to *laudanum* (opium dissolved in alcohol) was commonplace.

Morphine, a derivative of opium, was developed around 1800. Named after Morpheus, the Greek god of sleep and dreams, the drug was found to be a powerful analgesic; and morphine was widely used in the Civil War for treating battlefield injuries. It was initially believed to be nonaddictive and free of side effects, and it was available at almost any drug store for little cost and without a prescription. Katharine Hepburn plays a morphine addict with an alcoholic son (Jason Robards) in the film adaptation of Eugene O'Neill's *Long Day's Journey into Night* (1962).

Heroin was first synthesized from morphine in 1874. The German drug company Bayer (of aspirin fame) initially marketed the new drug for the treatment of coughs. Both morphine and heroin were readily available in the United States until about 1915 (Abadinsky, 1993).

Cocaine, a powerful stimulant, was used at one time as a way of treating morphine addiction, but it resulted only in codependency. It also became widely used as a base for patent medicines and was used in a large number of popular cola drinks, the best known of which is *Coca-Cola*. In response to growing public and political concern about habit-forming drinks, the company stopped using coca leaf derivatives around the turn of the century and replaced them with caffeine. Cocaine did have legitimate medical value as a local anesthetic and was widely used in ophthalmology and dentistry. *Sigmund Freud's recreational and therapeutic use of cocaine is well known and is described in the film* The Seven Percent Solution *(1976), a historical fantasy in which Freud and Sherlock Holmes share their love of cocaine and pool their deductive talents to solve the puzzle of a missing patient.*

Amphetamines, barbiturates, and **tranquilizers** have a more recent history, and all three classes of drugs have legitimate medical purposes (although amphetamines have somewhat less utility than the other two, and their medical use is often questioned). In 1987, Kitty Dukakis, wife of Massachusetts governor and presidential nominee Michael Dukakis, acknowledged that she was addicted to amphetamines, which had originally been prescribed for weight control. *Some of the problems of tranquilizer (Valium) addiction are portrayed in the autobiography and film* I'm Dancing as Fast as I Can.

Marijuana, one of the most popular drugs of the 1960s, has a much longer history and has been used recreationally for centuries. The low-budget propaganda film *Reefer Madness* (1936) became a cult classic among young people who smoked marijuana, and the Cheech and Chong movies celebrated the drug's use and ridiculed its classification as a narcotic. A variety of films have promoted the use of LSD, psilocybin, mescaline, and other hallucinogens.

THE *DSM-IV* AND SUBSTANCE-RELATED DISORDERS

Substance use disorders include substance abuse and substance dependence. **Substance abuse** is defined in terms of a *pattern* of use characterized by *recurrent adverse consequences* related to the use of the substance. The diagnosis requires evidence of impairment as evidenced by one of the four following criteria: (1) failure to meet role obligations, (2) recurrent use in situations, such as driving, in which clear hazards are present, (3) recurrent legal problems, and (4) continued use, despite social or interpersonal problems related to the substance. In addition, the symptoms must never have met the criteria associated with substance dependence.

In Clean and Sober, *Michael Keaton meets each of the first four criteria for substance abuse:* he is failing in his job, he drives when he is high on both cocaine and alcohol, he is embezzling from his company, and he is an accomplice to a drug-related fatality, and he continues his drug use despite the adverse consequences that result (e.g., estrangement from his mother). However, in his case, because he meets the criteria for the more serious diagnosis of substance dependence, the substance abuse diagnosis is inappropriate and would not be used.

Substance dependence involves a more complex set of behaviors that include tolerance, withdrawal, and compulsive drug-taking behavior. The symptoms associated with dependence on different drugs are similar (but not identical) across drug categories. Dependence is diagnosed when clients present with three or more of the seven criteria listed in Table 7-4 at any time during a 12-month period.

Note that neither tolerance nor withdrawal is required for a diagnosis of substance dependence. If these features are present, it is appropriate to specify "with physiological dependence" as part of the diagnosis. In addition, other qualifiers may apply, depending on a particular individual's circumstances (such as status of remission, use of agonist therapy [e.g., pain-killing medication], and whether or not an individual is in a controlled environment, such as an inpatient treatment program).

Criteria	Examples from *Clean and Sober*
(1) Tolerance, defined by (a) a need for ever increasing amounts of the substance to achieve intoxication or (b) diminished effect with use of a set level of the substance	Michael Keaton finds that cocaine comes to dominate his life; he snorts it first thing in the morning to get going, and it is a part of almost every social encounter.
(2) Withdrawal, defined by (a) specific effects associated with the particular substance being abused or (b) use of the substance to relieve or avoid the withdrawal symptoms (e.g., use of the "hair of the dog that bit you")	Keaton experiences marked withdrawal symptoms (fatigue, insomnia, nausea, and psychomotor agitation) after he enrolls in the Causeway Program and is placed on a detoxification ward.
(3) Using the substance in larger amounts or over a longer period than was intended	Keaton's use of cocaine becomes so extensive that he begins to embezzle from his company to pay for his increased use of cocaine.
(4) A persistent desire to cut back or eliminate use of the substance	Keaton has failed in his repeated attempts to gain control over his use of cocaine and drugs.
(5) A great deal of time is devoted to acquiring the substance or recovering from its effects	When Keaton is unsuccessful in persuading a co-worker to bring him drugs, he drives to his office and demolishes it looking for an envelope in which he has stored cocaine.
(6) Important social, occupational, or recreational activities are ignored because of the preoccupation with use of the substance	Keaton is fired from his job and estranged from his family because of his drug and alcohol problems.
(7) The substance use is continued despite recurrent physical or psychological problems resulting from its use	Keaton persists in his use of cocaine, despite the fact that his girlfriend has been killed by an overdose in his company.

Table 7-4. Criteria for substance dependence. Adapted from *DSM-IV*.

TYPES OF SUBSTANCES

Opioids

The best-known opioids are opium, morphine, codeine, methadone, percodan, and heroin. These drugs are sometimes lumped together under the general rubric of narcotics. Opium is usually smoked; the other drugs are most often ingested or injected. Robert De Niro can be seen smoking opium in both the opening and the ending scenes of Sergio Leone's 1984 film *Once upon a Time in America,* and opium plays a significant role in both *Indochine* (1992) and Bernardo Bertolucci's *The Last Emperor* (1987).

Narcotics are sometimes injected just beneath the skin; more experienced users tend to inject directly into a vein. Heroin crosses the blood-brain barrier rapidly and produces an intense, pleasurable feeling with subsequent "crashing" about six hours later.

Opioids are prescribed as analgesics, anesthetics, or antidiarrheal drugs. All opioids produce significant tolerance, and withdrawal symptoms are common when drug use is discontinued. The marked tolerance that occurs with opioids is demonstrated by the fact that experienced heroin users frequently require doses in excess of 100 times the amount that was originally necessary to produce a state of euphoria.

A user's response to heroin or other opioids will vary depending on dose level and experience with the drug. During a state of opioid intoxication, the user tends to be euphoric, drowsy, apathetic, and usually indifferent to his or her surroundings. Constipation is common. The user's pupils become markedly constricted, and hallucinations may occur. Judgment is often impaired, although an experienced user may function in routine occupational and social roles. An example of this can be found in Quentin Tarantino's film *Pulp Fiction* (1994). John Travolta shoots up before going out on a date with his boss's wife (Uma Thurman). The two wind up at "Jack Rabbit Slims" and maintain a coherent—if not stimulating—conversation. They even manage to win a dance contest! Later in the evening, Thurman discovers the heroin in Travolta's coat pocket. Believing it to be cocaine, she proceeds to snort a line of the drug and goes into a coma. Travolta eventually manages to save Thurman's life by plunging a needle filled with epinephrine into her heart.

Opioid withdrawal occurs when use of opioid drugs is discontinued or when an opioid antagonist (any drug that blocks the effects of an opioid) is administered. Naloxone and naltrexone are the most widely used opioid antagonists. Complete withdrawal usually takes three to eight days.

The *DSM-IV* requires the presence of at least three of the following symptoms for the diagnosis of opioid withdrawal: dysphoric mood, nausea or vomiting, muscle aches, lacrimation (crying) or rhinorrhea (a "runny nose"), diarrhea, yawning, fever, or insomnia. In addition, it is common to find other withdrawal symptoms such as chills, sweating, and loss of appetite. Examples of opioid withdrawal can be seen in the Frank Sinatra film *The Man with the Golden Arm* (1955).

Sedative-Hypnotics

Sedative drugs produce a calm feeling of well-being in low doses and induce sleep in greater doses. These drugs include barbiturates such as amytal, nembutal, seconal, and phenobarbital, as well as **anxiolytics** (anxiety-reducing drugs) such as the **benzodiazepines** (Valium, Librium, etc.). Xanax, a more recently developed anxiolytic with a short half-life, combines the anxiety-reducing properties of other benzodiazepines with a mild antidepressant effect. It has become one of the most widely prescribed drugs in the U.S. today.

Barbiturates, first produced in 1903, were once widely prescribed to help people sleep and deal with anxiety. These drugs are muscle relaxants that induce feelings of well-being in small doses; with larger amounts, the user falls into a deep and profound sleep. Although tolerance develops extremely rapidly with the barbiturates, the dose which is lethal remains relatively constant. This puts the barbiturate abuser at high risk and is one of the reasons barbiturates are rarely prescribed today for anxiety. They remain the medication of choice in some cases of epilepsy.

The effects of barbiturates mimic the effects of alcohol and include symptoms such as slurred speech and staggering gait. These effects may be especially pronounced when barbiturates are combined with alcohol, and this combination is likely to be especially deadly. For example, Marilyn Monroe committed suicide by using a combination of alcohol and sleeping pills. In addition, barbiturate withdrawal is generally more difficult and more painful than withdrawal from narcotics, and it is more likely to be life-threatening.

CASE STUDY

John Belushi was one of America's most gifted young comedians. He is well known for his roles as Joliet Jake in *The Blues Brothers* (1980) and as Bluto in *National Lampoon's Animal House* (1978). However, he is probably best remembered for the range of wonderful characters he created on "Saturday Night Live" (e.g., the Samurai tailor).

John Belushi was 33 at the time of his death. The death and the events leading up to it are detailed in Bob Woodward's book *Wired: The Short Life and Fast Times of John Belushi* and in the film *Wired* (based on the Woodward book).

Belushi had been practicing polypharmacy for more than a decade before his death. The drugs he used included tobacco, alcohol, Valium, cocaine, mescaline, LSD, amphetamines, heroin, and barbiturates. He also smoked marijuana on almost a daily basis.

Part of Belushi's genius was that he was able to be funny even when he was intoxicated, and drug use was reported to be common among the cast of "Saturday Night Live." However, repeated and escalating use began to take its toll. Belushi's wife left him, and he began to miss performances. His work suffered.

It seems almost inevitable that Belushi's heavy use of drugs would result in premature death. Ultimately, it was the use of heroin mixed with cocaine that ended his life on March 5, 1982.

Benzodiazepines have largely replaced barbiturates for the treatment of insomnia because they are generally believed to be less addictive and are not as likely to be successfully used in suicide attempts. However, the benzodiazepines can also be abused, and some authorities believe they have the potential to be just as addictive as barbiturates (Miller & Gold, 1990).

The benzodiazepines are especially widely prescribed in the United States, and many people feel they are prescribed too frequently. It is shocking to realize that 250 million Americans have 70 million prescriptions filled and consume almost 4 *billion* sedatives every year (Shabecoff, 1987). There are marked sex differences in benzodiazepine use, and these medications are used by about 1 in 10 men and about 1 in 4 women in the United States (Miller & Gold, 1990).

There is a telling moment at one point in a Woody Allen film when an anxious character begins to hyperventilate in a crowded department store. Allen turns to the crowd and asks, "Quick, has anyone got a Valium?" and 30 people reach for their pockets. Audiences almost inevitably laugh at this pointed comment about the ubiquitous nature of these medications in our daily lives.

Stimulants

Stimulant drugs excite the central nervous system (CNS), fight fatigue, suppress one's appetite, and enhance mood. They are widely available and include relatively unregulated drugs such as caffeine and nicotine. Common amphetamines include **amphetamine** (Benzedrine), **dextroamphetamine** (Dexedrine), and **methamphetamine** (Methedrine). Other stimulants include **methylphenidate** (Ritalin), **khat,** and a variety of appetite suppressants such as Preludin. Cocaine is also best classified as a stimulant drug, although it is considered a narcotic in the current federal drug taxonomy.

Amphetamines were initially used in the 1920s for the treatment of narcolepsy, a condition that causes its victims to fall asleep abruptly and without warning. Amphetamines are sometimes used in the treatment of obesity and are occasionally used in the treatment of hyperactivity and attention deficit disorders in both adults and children. The drugs are usually taken orally but may be injected. Occasionally, amphetamines are mixed with heroin and injected intravenously. Methamphetamine crystals ("Ice") can also be smoked, producing a high that can last as long as 14 hours. Khat, a shrub grown in Africa and the Middle East, produces leaves that can be chewed to produce an amphetamine-like effect.

Amphetamines are highly addictive, and tolerance for the drugs like methamphetamine develops rapidly. There is a characteristic withdrawal syndrome that includes depression, fatigue, nightmares, insomnia or sometimes hypersomnia, increased appetite, and either psychomotor retardation or agitation. This "crashing" effect appears to be the price the user must pay for the euphoria that accompanies the initial drug use. Amphetamine-induced psychoses often produce symptoms that closely resemble those found with serious mental disorders such as schizophrenia.

Cocaine is derived from the coca plant, which is indigenous to Central and South America. Its use dates back to at least 3,000 years before Christ, and the leaves of the coca plant are stilled chewed by native people in cocaine-producing countries to give them energy to meet the harsh physical demands of their mountain existence. Coca paste is also prepared from the same plant. Smugglers sometimes bring cocaine into the United States in rubber condoms that are swallowed and later excreted. This practice can be fatal, and numerous deaths have occurred when the packets have ruptured or leaked.

In the United States, cocaine is usually snorted or, more rarely, injected intravenously. *Crack cocaine,* named after the sound made as the drug is consumed, takes the form of small "rocks" and is smoked. The effects of smoking crack cocaine occur almost immediately, but the high that is produced is relatively brief. Although relatively inexpensive, crack addicts can quickly develop addictions that require hundreds of dollars each day to support. For many people, cocaine addiction leads to prostitution, theft, or violence. Relatively few people can support their habits at the level demonstrated by Michael Keaton in *Clean and Sober*. Many casual users find their use accelerating until they, like Keaton, find themselves beginning the day with a line of coke.

A recent film illustrating the degradation associated with crack addiction is Sweet Nothing *(1996), a true story based on a set of diaries discovered in an abandoned apartment in the Bronx.* The film demonstrates the corrosive effects of the protagonist's addiction on his marriage, his relationship with his children, his friends, and his job. At one point, Angelo, the lead character, actually misses his father's funeral because he has an opportunity to get high and this need has come to supercede all others. Angelo loses the ability to become aroused by his wife, and we watch him become increasingly paranoid as the film progresses.

Cocaine has affected the lives and careers of many actors and directors. For example, Tommy Rettig (best known as Lassie's master Jeff on the TV series) was sentenced to five years in federal prison for smuggling cocaine; Richard Pryor became badly burned as a result of an explosion related to smoking crack cocaine; and *when Rainer Werner Fassbinder, considered by many to be Germany's finest director, died at the age of 37, his death was attributed to heart failure resulting from a combination of barbiturates and cocaine.*

Hallucinogens

Hallucinogens, sometimes referred to as psychedelics, are drugs that distort the perception of reality. Users report hallucinations involving all senses, **senesthesia** ("crossed" sensations, such as hearing sights and seeing sounds), and depersonalization. These drugs can also have profound effects on mood, depending in large part on set and setting.

Hallucinogens can occur in the natural environment but are more often produced synthetically. Naturally occurring hallucinogens include **mescaline,** derived from the peyote cactus, and **psilocybin,** which is present in psilocybe mushrooms. Some Native Americans use psilocybe mushrooms in religious ceremonies.

Mescaline can also be produced in a laboratory. However, the best-known and most widely used of all synthetic hallucinogens is **lysergic acid diethylamide** (LSD). The drug, first synthesized by chemist Albert Hofmann in 1938, was a staple part of the drug culture of the 1960s. It is most often swallowed as a pill, but it can also be mixed with a fluid, licked off of blotter paper, or swallowed in sugar cubes or gelatin sheets. LSD is colorless, tasteless, and extremely potent. It produces varied symptoms and can result in affective changes that range from euphoria to absolute terror. The most dramatic effects are often sensory in nature: when the drug experience is positive, it allows the user "to see a world in a grain of sand/and a heaven in a wildflower, hold infinity in the palm of your hand/and eternity in an hour" (William Blake, *Auguries of Innocence*). Unfortunately, the experience is not always this benign, and injury or death can result from bad decisions made while under the influence of the drug. Some users have also reported "flashbacks," in which they reexperience the sensory phenomenon associated with previous trips weeks or months after last using the drug. The drug is not addictive, but tolerance develops rapidly.

In the film *In the Name of the Father* (1993), prisoners cope with the monotony of prison life by licking LSD off the back of a jigsaw puzzle. The puzzle is a large world map, and the prisoners get high "one country at a time." The LSD experience is also portrayed in any number of films from the 1960s that document the youth culture of that period.

Phencyclidine (PCP), also known as angel dust, is another powerful hallucinogen that has been used since the early 1960s. It can be taken in pill form or dusted onto marijuana and smoked. The drug produces symptoms even more marked than those associated with LSD and may result in analgesia, depersonalization, paranoia, rage reactions, or schizophrenia-like psychoses.

Cannabis

Marijuana is obtained from the hemp plant *cannabis sativa*. The active ingredient in marijuana is the drug **tetrahydrocannabinol** (THC). The greater the THC content, the more potent the drug. The THC content of marijuana purchased illegally varies widely; in general, THC levels have been increasing over the past three decades, and the marijuana used today is approximately five times stronger than that widely available on street corners and on college campuses in the 1960s.

Marijuana is usually smoked, but it can also be ingested in "Alice B. Toklas brownies" or similar foods. When it is smoked, the drug is quickly absorbed. The resin of the cannabis sativa plant can be used to produce **hashish,** a stronger form of the drug.

Marijuana has legitimate medicinal value, and it can be obtained legally for the treatment of some disorders. The drug enhances appetite and is often helpful in controlling the nausea associated with chemotherapy. Other physical effects include tachycardia, sedation, and psychomotor impairment.

Like the hallucinogens, marijuana can produce markedly varied psychological effects, depending on the mood and situation of the user. Most often, the drug produces mild euphoria, giddiness, and a general sense of well-being. However, at a different time and in a different setting the same drug can produce marked apprehension or paranoia.

Examples of marijuana use can be found in literally dozens of films. One especially memorable scene involves Dennis Hopper, Peter Fonda, and Jack Nicholson sitting around a campfire and smoking marijuana in *Easy Rider* (1969).

Tobacco

The drug most often portrayed on television and in films is tobacco. Epidemiological studies suggest it is also our most lethal drug. The National Institute on Drug Abuse (NIDA) estimated in 1994 that tobacco accounts for 434,000 annual deaths in the United States (approximately one out of every six deaths). The estimated annual deaths resulting from other drugs are as follows: alcohol, 125,000; cocaine, 8,100; combinations of alcohol and drugs, 7,600; heroin and morphine, 6,500. Although fatality rates are only one index of the severity of a drug problem, it is clear that none of the drugs typically considered to be our most "serious" are ultimately as dangerous as cigarettes.

The seriousness of tobacco abuse is underscored by the inclusion of categories for "**Nicotine Use Disorder**" and "**Nicotine Withdrawal**" in the *DSM-IV*. Anyone who has watched a family member trying to stop smoking can appreciate that the withdrawal associated with smoking cessation can be every bit as distressing as that associated with withdrawal from other drugs. (In Riker's Prison in New York City, numerous inmates who had been addicted to both tobacco and heroin maintained that withdrawal from the former had been every bit as painful as withdrawal from the latter.)

In part because of the pain of withdrawal, less than 5 percent of smokers are successful in their attempts to stop smoking, although about 35 percent try to stop each year (and 80 percent express the desire to stop). Some of the symptoms associated with nicotine withdrawal include dysphoric or depressed mood, insomnia, irritability/frustration/anger, anxiety, difficulty concentrating, restlessness, decreased heart rate, and increased appetite or weight gain. Four or more of these signs must be present following smoking cessation or a significant reduction in nicotine use before the diagnosis can be justified.

The likelihood of smoking has been shown to be inversely related to educational levels. College graduates are less likely to start smoking, and if they once smoked they are far more likely to have quit.

The morbidity and mortality associated with tobacco use have been underscored by a series of reports issued since 1964 by the Office of the Surgeon General. Partially in response to the massive public education efforts spearheaded by the surgeon general, numerous Americans have stopped smoking. In addition, the American Medical Association and the American Public Health Association have been very vocal in their opposition to tobacco use.

THERAPY FOR ADDICTIONS

Before treatment can begin, **detoxification** must occur. In general, the severity of detoxification from narcotic drugs depends on the health status of the addict and the purity of the drugs he or she has been taking. Withdrawal from barbiturates tends to be more serious than withdrawal from heroin, cocaine, or alcohol. Detoxification is potentially life-threatening and should occur in a structured medical setting. Anxiolytics such as Valium, Librium, and Xanax are sometimes used to reduce the severity of the effects of detoxification.

Methadone is a synthetic narcotic that is taken orally rather than injected. It is administered on a daily basis, usually in an outpatient setting. The drug itself is addicting; however, it is longer lasting, and with daily use the addict is able to avoid the symptoms of withdrawal that typically occur a few hours after use of drugs such as heroin. In addition, the drug blocks the reinforcing effects of other narcotics. With methadone treatment, there is a reduction in intravenous drug use and a concomitant reduction in crime. In addition, the likelihood of needle sharing and AIDS is dramatically reduced. Despite these benefits, methadone maintenance programs remain controversial, and there are some clear disadvantages to methadone maintenance therapy, including the development of a large underground market for methadone, the fact that many people drop out of methadone treatment because of side effects (sweating, impotence, constipation, and insomnia), and the fact that many people are philosophically offended by the idea of giving addicts another addicting drug in the name of treatment.

Some programs have used **narcotic antagonists** such as **Naloxone** or **naltrexone** to treat opioid addiction. These drugs block the reinforcing effects of narcotics; in effect, the addict may still take drugs but they no longer produce a "high." However, because of the potential for precipitating withdrawal reactions, these programs are complex and costly and require medical supervision.

Programs such as **Narcotics Anonymous** (NA), modeled after Alcoholics Anonymous, advocate total abstinence from drugs. These programs are often associated with therapeutic communities in which a highly structured program and frequent group therapy are core components of treatment. Former addicts who serve as powerful role models for residents often staff these programs. Therapy is often confrontational and may involve spouses and significant others. The film *Clean and Sober* presents an excellent example of the kind of treatment that occurs in a *therapeutic community,* with Morgan Freeman in the role of ex-addict and counselor. Daytop Village, Odyssey House, and Phoenix House are all examples of successful urban therapeutic communities.

Antidepressant medications are sometimes used to assist in the treatment of amphetamine or cocaine addiction. However, in general all treatment programs for stimulant addiction have unimpressive success records.

The success of smoking cessation programs has been more notable. Nicotine gum and transdermal nicotine patches hold considerable promise as important aids in comprehensive treatment packages. Behavior modification and hypnosis are two other techniques that have helped many individuals overcome their addiction to nicotine.

Despite the success of some treatment programs, it is clear that the only real solution to the drug problem is prevention. Prevention will involve limiting the flow of drugs to the United States and educating the public about the deleterious effects of drug use.

DRUG ABUSE IN FILMS

The classic film about the heroin trade is William Friedkin's *The French Connection* (1971). Friedkin won an Oscar for his directing, and Gene Hackman won the Academy Award for best actor for his role as police detective Jimmy "Popeye" Doyle. Frank Sinatra and Kim Novak star in a dated but still interesting portrayal of the private life of a heroin addict, *The Man with the Golden Arm* (1955). *The Connection* is a 1961 film about a group of junkies waiting for the arrival of a pusher. A more contemporary, powerful, and realistic presentation of teenage addiction and prostitution is *Christiane F.* (German, 1981) which explores the drug culture of West Berlin. Other film examples of heroin addiction include *Who'll Stop the Rain* (1978), *Mona Lisa* (1986), *Chappaqua* (1966), and *Lady Sings the Blues* (1972).

One of the most powerful drug films ever made is Gus Van Sant's 1989 film *Drugstore Cowboy* starring Matt Dillon as the leader of a group of four addicts who rob drugstores to maintain their habit. The film is especially memorable because of a very realistic cameo of William Burroughs playing an old, burned out, defrocked priest/addict living in a seedy motel. Dillon sees in Burroughs the image of the man he (Dillon) will eventually become. Dillon's decision to go straight and the dilemmas he faces (including attempts by his girlfriend to seduce him back to the world they formerly shared) seem very realistic.

Anyone interested in the drug culture should read William Burroughs' *Naked Lunch*. The David Cronenberg film adaptation of the book (1991) is fascinating if not always tightly linked to the novel. William Lee, the protagonist, is a polydrug addict trying to go straight. Unfortunately, both he and his wife are addicted to bug spray, and Bill's job as an exterminator leaves him poorly situated to stay off drugs. The cinematic representation of visual hallucinations is especially fascinating.

Quentin Tarentino's *Pulp Fiction* (1994) is the most interesting recent examination of the urban drug culture. The film is especially powerful in linking the drug trade with the casual and almost indifferent violence that is a trademark of any Tarentino film. Three other compelling films dealing with cocaine addiction are *The Bad Lieutenant* (1992) starring Harvey Keitel, Martin Scorsese's *Goodfellas* (1990), and Brian De Palma's *Scarface* (1983).

Critical Thinking Questions

- Can a case be made for the prohibition of alcohol and tobacco, or is this simply a societal experiment that has been tried without success?
- Should the legal age for drinking be 21 in all states?
- How common is it for patients with psychiatric disorders to have concomitant problems with alcohol or other drugs?
- Are needle exchange programs effective in reducing the incidence of HIV in groups of IV drug users?
- Should intoxication from alcohol and drugs be a mitigating factor in sentencing prisoners for crimes they committed while high (e.g., murder in *Dead Man Walking*)?
- How important is it for therapists treating alcoholism and drug abuse to have been in treatment for these problems themselves? Can a nonaddict ever truly understand the needs and problems of the addict?
- What are the arguments for and against the legalization of drugs in the United States?

Chapter 8

Sexual and Gender Identity Disorders

Try to walk like John Wayne.
Advice given to Zaza
in *La Cage aux Folles*

Questions to Consider While Watching *La Cage aux Folles*

- Does it appear that Renato and Albin have a loving and stable relationship?
- Would there have been deleterious psychological effects if Renato's son was raised by Renato and Albin? What is your evidence?
- Why do audiences find the scene in which Albin is being coached to act more masculine so funny?
- The film suggests that gay men are likely to be especially creative and artistic. Is there any evidence supporting this stereotype? If not, where did it originate?
- Is there evidence of psychopathology in any of the characters in the film?
- Does Albin meet *DSM-IV* criteria for a diagnosis of histrionic personality disorder?
- Albin is a colorful and flamboyant character who flaunts the fact that he is a gay man. To what extent are effeminate characteristics such as those displayed by Albin characteristic of gay men? Can you identify homosexuality by observing someone's interpersonal style?
- If you are a male, would you personally be threatened by meeting a transvestite in a bar and later discovering you were flirting with a man?
- How does Albin illustrate the difficulty with and the overlap among the labels homosexual, transvestite, and transsexual?

PATIENT EVALUATION

Patient's stated reason for coming: "Renato asked me to come. He says I drive him crazy."

History of the present illness: Albin "Zaza" Serrault is a 45-year-old man employed as a dancer and performer in a local nightclub. Albin has been cross-dressing since the age of 15, and takes keen delight in being mistaken for a woman (as frequently happens both within and outside the club). His male lover (Renato) accompanied Albin for the interview and reports that Albin is self-centered, overly dramatic, and manipulative. He has a compulsive need to be the center of attention. He is almost totally dependent on Renato for both emotional and financial support. Renato reports that Albin is quite jealous of his (Renato's) former wife.

Past psychiatric illness, treatment, and outcomes: There is no significant history of psychiatric illness. Albin has never been hospitalized or treated by a psychologist or psychiatrist. Albin frequently talks about killing himself when he is angry or anxious, but he has never made a suicide attempt or gesture. He appears content with his role as a gay man who enjoys playing a female role, and Albin does not present any clear evidence of mental illness.

Medical history: The medical history is not significant.

Psychosocial history: Albin was an only child, and apparently his parents doted on him. His mother died when Albin was 11. His father maintains a close relationship with his son, although apparently he had some difficulty accepting his son's sexuality. Albin has been sexually active since the age of 16, but only with men. He is the feminine partner in a committed, long-term, stable gay relationship. Albin became comfortable with his identity as a homosexual male early in his teens. Although somewhat sexually indiscriminate in adolescence, he has maintained a stable and loving relationship with Renato for more than a decade.

Drug and alcohol history: Albin does not smoke. He is a social drinker who drinks wine with both lunch and dinner.

Behavioral observations: Albin came for the interview dressed as a woman. He is quite dramatic in his presentation. His mannerisms are exaggerated. He wore heavy (but not unattractive) make-up. He frequently interrupted Renato and the two often disagreed on details. Albin appeared nervous during the interview and he fidgeted frequently.

Mental status examination: Albin identified the day of the month as the 23rd rather than the 24th. There were no other errors on the Mini Mental State, and this patient earned an overall score of 29.

Functional assessment: Albin is an exotic dancer in La Cage aux Folles, the nightclub owned by his lover, Renato. He earns a comfortable living by dancing at the club in drag five evenings each week. He has a high school education. He is in good health and stays fit both by dancing and through regular exercise. His father, who has come to accept and value the relationship between Renato and his son, provides considerable emotional support. Albin reports a large number of friends, most of whom are members of the gay and transgendered community. Many of these friendships appear superficial, and it is clear that he is socially anchored through Renato, his significant other.

Strengths: The patient is intelligent and quick-witted. He has the support of his father, Renato, Renato's son, and the many friends who frequent La Cage aux Folles. The relationship between Albin and Renato seems stable and mutually rewarding, although not without travail.

Diagnosis: Axis I: Partner relationship problem; Axis II: R/O Histrionic Personality Disorder.

Treatment plan: Refer to social work for weekly therapy sessions devoted to improving communication skills and strengthening the existing relationship.

Prognosis: Excellent. This is a committed couple who should be able to resolve the problems in communication that have bedeviled the relationship for the past year. It is unlikely that Albin's core personality will change; however, Renato has apparently learned to live with (and at times even value) Albin's histrionic features, and the presumed personality disorder will not be a focus for treatment.

LA CAGE AUX FOLLES

Edouard Molinaro's *La Cage aux Folles* (1978) is a comedy that portrays the relationship between two middle-aged homosexual lovers, Renato and Albin. Renato owns and manages La Cage aux Folles, a nightclub in the south of France in which all the performers are male transvestites who perform as women. Albin, whose stage name is Zaza, is the star performer at La Cage aux Folles, as well as Renato's lover and longtime companion. The film revolves around dilemmas that occur as Renato and Albin attempt to present themselves as a straight couple in order to impress the parents of the young woman Renato's son (by an early and ill-fated marriage) plans to marry. The girl's father is a prominent politician who is running on a morality ticket, and the potential in-laws are pompous and rigidly moralistic

Albin is a interesting character. He cross-dresses both on and off stage and has adopted an exclusive feminine identity. Much of the humor in the film revolves around the distress he experiences as he attempts to be something he is not (masculine). Despite his hypochondriasis and histrionic style, Albin is an attractive figure in the film, and the audience is touched by his obvious love for Renato. Likewise, Renato, after a brief affair with his son's mother, realizes that he belongs with Albin and comes to appreciate the folly in trying to maintain a straight facade.

It is important to understand that this film is a farce and not an accurate presentation of either homosexual relationships or transvestites. Albin's role as a drag queen is as exaggerated as his feminine mannerisms, and probably served to perpetuate many of the stereotypes about homosexuality that existed when the film was released in 1978. However, despite reliance on stereotypes, the film can be credited for its presentation of an enduring, loving relationship between its two lead characters. Both men are secure in their sexual identity, even though it does not conform to conventional norms, and they know the life they have made for themselves is the right one for them. At one point Renato remarks, "Yes, I use make–up. Yes, I live with a man. Yes, I'm an old fag. But I know who I am. It's taken twenty years and that deputy isn't going to destroy it."

The film also highlights the sanctimonious hypocrisy of many of those people who are so quick to limit sexual expression in others and illustrates the perils inherent in denial of one's true sexual identity. The film is best viewed as the hilarious farce it is, and one does the film a disservice by insisting that it portray too strong a social message.

THE RANGE OF NORMAL SEXUAL BEHAVIOR

Few areas of human behavior are as complex, varied, and interesting as sexual behavior. Both social scientists and the general public are fascinated by the multitude of possibilities inherent in our sexuality, and it is perhaps in this chapter more than any other that students are likely to see a bit of themselves in the disorders described.

It is important to appreciate that the range of normal sexual behavior is exceptionally broad, and many behaviors that seem unusual or disturbing to some people do not qualify for a *DSM-IV* label. As a general rule, remember that complex or elaborate sexual fantasies are commonplace and do not suggest that any type of psychological disturbance is present. A psychological problem exists when a person acts on his or her fantasies with unwilling partners or behaves in ways that distress other people.

Filmmakers have been quick to exploit our fascination with sexual behavior, and contemporary cinema is replete with examples of sexual psychopathology. A serious student can learn a great deal about abnormal psychology from selective viewing.

GENDER IDENTITY DISORDERS

Transsexuals are uncomfortable with their anatomic sex and believe they are trapped in the wrong body. There is often a strong wish to replace their genitals with the genitalia of the opposite sex; these urges can be intense enough to lead to self-castration in males. Transsexual identity issues usually originate in childhood; however, the diagnosis is given only after an individual has reached puberty. Transsexuals often suffer from concomitant depression, and suicide attempts are common.

Interest in the phenomenon of transsexualism burgeoned in the United States and Europe after the 1951 gender modification surgery of Christine Jorgensen. *(The Christine Jorgensen Story*, a low-budget and somewhat insipid film, was released in 1970). The mid-1980s witnessed a revival of interest, after widespread publicity and a television movie *(Second Serve)* about the sexual conversion of male surgeon Richard Raskins into a female tennis star, Renee Richards. Other films that have explored transsexualism include *Myra Breckinridge* (1970) (starring film critic Rex Reed), *Dog Day Afternoon* (1975), *The World According to Garp* (1982), and *Come Back to the Five and Dime, Jimmie Dean, Jimmie Dean* (1982). More recently, in the 1993 film *The Crying Game,* a complex transsexual relationship was explored.

The surgical treatment of transsexuals remains controversial, although tens of thousands of patients have undergone the procedure. Some psychiatrists and psychologists, especially those who are psychoanalytically inclined, view surgery as a crude solution to a deep-seated emotional problem. Other mental health professionals have treated many patients whose lives have dramatically improved after their anatomical sex was aligned with their psychological gender identity. The Johns Hopkins School of Medicine, perhaps this country's most prestigious medical school, discontinued its gender modification program after controlled research failed to reveal any significant improvement in the psychological status or happiness of patients who had received gender modification surgery. In addition, there is at least one case on record of a biological male who had gender modification surgery only to discover that she was unhappy as a female. Believing she had made a serious mistake, this individual elected to have surgery again. An artificial penis was constructed and the patient resumed life as a male. Many medical centers have begun to discourage routine surgical solutions for transsexuals, and the operation is reserved for those individuals with the most deep-seated hatred for their genitals.

Transsexualism occurs more often in biological males than in biological females, and many more males apply for conversion surgery. This is due in part to the fact that the male-to-female operation is simpler, less expensive, and usually more satisfying. In addition, the greater latitude in roles available to women in Western society (e.g., dressing in traditionally male clothes, working in traditionally male occupations) may be an important factor in the different incidence data for males and females. This difference has been narrowing over the past two decades.

Transsexuals can be heterosexual, homosexual, or asexual, both prior to and after their surgery. Many professionals who have worked with these patients have been struck by the fact that sexual behavior per se is often a secondary concern. The core issue is one of sexual *identity,* not sexual behavior. Although the *DSM-IV* refers to Gender Identity Disorders, the term "transsexual" is still widely used in clinical practice.

THE PARAPHILIAS

The term *paraphilia* has been widely adopted as a substitute for antiquated and emotion-laden expressions such as sexual deviation or perversion. These older labels have strong pejorative connotations and carry a bias that is inappropriate in either research or treatment.

The paraphilias include fetishism, transvestic fetishism (transvestism), pedophilia, exhibitionism, voyeurism, sexual masochism, sexual sadism, frotteurism, coprophilia, necrophilia, and telephone scatalogia. It is important to reiterate that at some time in their lives most people have had fantasies or have engaged in a behavior that fits one or more of the categories listed above. However, *unused sexual fantasies are not a psychological problem— and do not warrant a diagnosis—unless a person has acted on his or her fantasies or is significantly distressed by them.* The male who has fantasies about peeping through a window and watching his neighbor undress, for example, is not considered to be engaging in deviant behavior. In fact, fantasies of this type are common among males. The behavior would be deviant if the man could be aroused *only* by the fantasy, or if he acted out and actually spied on his neighbor.

Transvestism

Unlike transsexuals, **transvestites** are comfortable with their anatomic sex. However, transvestites derive pleasure and satisfaction from cross-dressing and/or being identified as a female, and cross-dressing and fantasies about cross-dressing play a prominent role in the sexual lives of transvestites. The transsexual male may cross-dress, but it is not done for purposes of sexual arousal but, rather, because female clothes are important in establishing a female identity. In contrast, the transvestite is likely to be a prototypically masculine, heterosexual male who becomes sexually excited when he dresses up in women's clothes. The transvestite does not desire to *be* a woman but merely wants to be admired as one, or to experience the sexual excitement associated with wearing women's clothes. Many wives have learned to tolerate cross-dressing on the part of their husbands, and it may be incorporated into marital sex play. Arndt (1991) maintains that the majority of wives who discover their husband's cross-dressing after marriage come to accept the behavior, and there are no ill effects on children from these marriages, who engage in appropriate sex-role behavior as adults and who are unlikely to cross-dress themselves.

As with transsexualism, transvestites may be heterosexual or homosexual, although most are clearly heterosexual. Transvestites cannot be asexual, since sexual arousal is part of the definition of the syndrome.

The cross-dressing behavior of the transvestite almost always begins in childhood, although few little boys who dress up in the clothes of their mother or sister will grow up to have sexual identity problems. While transsexualism is found among both males and females, the diagnosis of transvestism is almost inevitably reserved for males, and there are very few case studies of women who become sexually aroused by wearing men's clothes.

Many transvestites cross-dress only on special occasions, and they may attempt to suppress the behavior, yielding to the impulse only when anxious, during periods of stress, or when separated from a sexual partner. The preferred objects of clothing include nightgowns, panties, bras, hose, and high heels. These garments are often the stimuli associated with fetishes, and in *DSM-IV* transvestism is referred to as transvestic fetishism. It is similar to other forms of fetishism in that sexual arousal is associated not with an individual but, rather, with inanimate objects (women's clothing).

Transvestism is surprisingly common in films, where it is generally treated with humor and almost never as a serious issue. The character of Albin in *La Cage aux Folles* is best described as a homosexual transvestite; Albin is happy as a gay male who cross-dresses and lives a female role. There is no evidence that his genitals disgust him; in fact, the strong presumption is that they provide considerable happiness for him in his relationship with Renato. Another comedy that has addressed cross-dressing is the popular film *Tootsie* (1982), in which an unemployed actor played by Dustin Hoffman pretends to be a woman in order to get an acting job. The counterpart to this film is Blake Edward's *Victor/Victoria* (1982), a wonderful movie in which Julie Andrews portrays a starving cabaret singer who gets her big break when she manages to land a job singing as a *male* female impersonator. Both films are sensitive analyses of the complex relationships linking gender and role.

Other films have explored cross-dressing. *Some Like It Hot* (1959), directed by Billy Wilder and starring Marilyn Monroe, Tony Curtis, Jack Lemmon, and George Raft, is the classic example of this genre. More recently, *Mrs. Doubtfire* (1993) starred Robin Williams as a man who passes himself off as a "nanny" in order to spend more time with his children. The movie *Yentl* stars Barbra Streisand as a woman who must dress in male clothes and pretend to be a man in order to achieve an education. *To Wong Foo, Thanks for Everything, Julie Newmar* (1995) is an entertaining film that examines the lives of three transvestites whose car breaks down in a small town filled with bigots. The film stars Wesley Snipes and Patrick Swayze.

Unfortunately, some otherwise good films, such as Brian De Palma's *Dressed to Kill* (1980), starring Michael Caine and Angie Dickinson, link transvestism with violence and sociopathy. There is no convincing evidence that transvestites are more likely than the average individual to be homicidal, although, like others whose sexuality may be viewed as deviant by the majority culture, they are somewhat more likely to be victims of crime.

Fetishism

An individual has a **fetish** when an inanimate object habitually arouses him or her. A *DSM-IV* diagnosis is justified only if the sexual arousal associated with the object or fantasies about it are intense and recurrent and last for at least six months. Sex often involves masturbation with the fetish, or the fetish may be incorporated into sexual activity with one's partner. The term *fetish* is used to refer to both the object itself and the inordinate attraction to it. The term is colloquially used to refer to one's predilection for particular body parts (e.g., "I'm a breast man"). However, the true fetish involves inanimate objects such as panties, silk stockings, garter belts, high heel shoes, or rubber items of clothing or body parts not normally associated with sexual activity (e.g., hair, feet, or the stumps of amputated limbs). Normally the link to sexuality can be surmised, but occasionally a patient will report sexual arousal to stimuli as obscure as file cabinets or baby buggies, and it is difficult to determine (a) how arousal initially could have been paired with the stimulus or (b) the potential symbolic value of the fetish. The fetish is often used for masturbation, but it may also be worn, worshipped, put in the rectum, hoarded, fondled, or sucked (Chalkey & Powell, 1983).

An advertisement was placed in the campus newspaper at a large midwestern university notifying coeds of the time and place for auditions that were ostensibly being held for models needed to promote orthopedic shoes. When college girls answered the ad, they were scheduled to go to a hotel room near the campus wearing a dress. After arriving, they were asked to put on orthopedic shoes (and occasionally a snap-on leg cast), use crutches, and "limp" back and forth behind a tall screen positioned about three feet off the ground. The man who placed the ad then masturbated on the other side of the screen. No job offers were ever made. When he was eventually arrested, the man acknowledged his long-standing shoe fetish and reported he had run the scam in several surrounding states for about six months before being discovered.

Some authorities have speculated that fetishism is related to the same psychological impulses that trigger transvestism and kleptomania (an overwhelming object to steal, usually trivial or inexpensive objects). The differences among the three conditions seem trivial in comparison with the similarities that link the disorders. The person with a sexual fetish longs to relate to the object sexually, the transvestite longs to wear it, and the kleptomaniac longs to steal it. Anxiety frequently precedes the unusual behavior, and masturbation is common.

Sexual activity with a fetish eliminates the anxiety associated with sexual activity with others, and the fetish is almost always available and "willing." In addition, there is no chance of rejection or ridicule by the fetish. It is interesting to wonder if Pygmalion, who fell in love with a beautiful statue he had created, would be diagnosed as a paraphiliac by today's diagnostic standards.

A number of films have included either leading or secondary characters with a fetish. One favorite is *Claire's Knee,* a French film directed by Eric Rohmer and released in 1971. This charming movie details the obsession of a soon-to-be-married writer for his friend's daughter—or, more exactly, for her right knee. The erotic elements in the film are handled with delicacy and good taste, and the writer's fixation on the girl's knee soon seems entirely plausible.

Another not-to-be-missed film demonstrating a sexual fetish is Steven Soderbergh's *sex, lies, and videotape.* This intelligent film, which won the Best Picture and Best Actor award at the 1989 Cannes Film Festival, was written, directed, and edited by Soderbergh. The film describes how the lives of three people (a man, his wife, and her sister, with whom he is having an affair) are changed forever by the arrival of the man's college roommate, Graham Dalton. Dalton is an impotent male who now can achieve orgasm only by masturbating while he is watching videotapes he makes of women discussing the intimate details of their sexual lives. Dalton has decided to live his life with absolute honesty, and he shares the details of his sexual life with Ann, the rejected wife. The two eventually become lovers, and there is a dramatic confrontation between Dalton and his old roommate (Ann's husband). Dalton is transformed through his relationship with Ann, and eventually he is able to move out of his isolation and into an emotionally satisfying and sexually mature relationship.

An equally powerful film is *Equus* (1977). This movie stars Richard Burton as a disillusioned psychiatrist who has lost all traces of passion in his life. The film revolves around Burton's treatment of Peter Firth, who plays a young man arrested for blinding four horses. This cruel act is linked to Firth's fascination with horses; he finds them both threatening and sexually exciting. *The film offers some insight into how an animal fetish might develop.*

Crash (1996) is a controversial NC-17 David Cronenberg film about people who have developed fetishes for cars and car wrecks. The film is based on a novel by J. G. Ballard, and the opening scene shows a woman rubbing her breasts against the wing of a plane and then licking metal while an apparently anonymous lover enters her from behind. She later relates this experience to her husband, who in turns shares his day's sexual adventures. The husband later becomes involved in a serious car accident in which the driver of the other car is killed. This man's wife, Helen, survives the accident but is hospitalized and has to walk on crutches while she recovers. Shortly after leaving the hospital, she becomes sexually involved with James, the man who had been driving the car that had killed her husband. Helen arouses James by telling him stories about all the men with whom she has had sex in cars. Both individuals find themselves sexually aroused by crashes and the accouterments of highway deaths (ambulances, flares, fire trucks, etc.). They are increasingly drawn into a deviant subculture that shares their sexual fascination with metal, cars, and crashing. This group is led by an unusual man who amuses himself and others by reenacting the 1955 death of James Dean in his sports car "Little Bastard." In addition to its main theme of fetishism, the film involves exhibitionism, voyeurism, triolism, and homosexuality. The film ends with a suggestion of necrophilia – James deliberately drives his wife's sports car off the road at high speed, and she is thrown from the car. He determines she is alive, then embraces her unconscious and injured body while muttering, "Maybe the next one, darling, maybe the next one."

Questions for Class Discussion *(Crash)*

- Are the fetishes described in *Crash* simply too far-fetched to be believed?
- Metal, leather, and plastic are all common fetishes. What is it about these particular materials that makes them sexually arousing?
- How common is it for a husband and wife to share fantasies about sex with other partners?
- How is it possible for sexual arousal (a positive experience) to so often become linked with pain (a very negative experience for most people)?

Exhibitionism

The exhibitionist's preferred form of sexual gratification is exposing the genitals to unsuspecting strangers. Masturbation often occurs during or after the exposure. The exhibitionist will almost never attempt to have intercourse with the women he intimidates and would be likely to be intimidated and frightened by an opportunity for an adult sexual encounter. Although reports of exhibitionism in a neighborhood almost always result in increased concern about the possibility of rape, rape and exhibitionism are dramatically different behaviors and are almost never linked.

Exhibitionism can occur at any age, but typically develops in males in their mid-twenties. Despite the popular image of a dirty old man in a raincoat, the incidence of exhibitionism falls off rapidly after the age of 40 and is rare in older males who are cognitively intact. Many exhibitionists have never had meaningful or satisfying adult sexual relationships; others have normal psychosexual development histories.

Reports of true exhibitionism in females are quite rare, although some women may be titillated by exposing their breasts or legs in public. Exhibitionism in females can also be used as a way of establishing dominance in a nonsexual encounter with males. *The potential for psychological manipulation through exposure was dramatically portrayed during Sharon Stone's interrogation scene in* Basic Instinct.

Situational variables also may influence decisions about exhibitionism for both men and women. For example, in New Orleans, it is acceptable behavior for women to expose their breasts during Mardi Gras in exchange for beads and other trinkets tossed from floats in the Mardi Gras parade (Forsyth, 1992).

Exhibitionism is a common problem, and indecent exposure accounts for about a third of all sexual offense cases. It is estimated that about 40 million women a year are victims of exhibitionists (Holmes, 1991), and about half of all adult women will at some point witness a male exposing himself (Arndt, 1991). The recidivism rate for the behavior is quite high, and because of this most males who expose themselves will eventually get caught. Few of those arrested for indecent exposure are actually imprisoned.

Exhibitionism may be related to obsessive-compulsive disorders in complex ways not fully understood. The possibility that the two problems are linked is supported by the fact that Fluoxetine, a medication effective in the treatment of obsessive-compulsive disorder, has also been used effectively in the treatment of some cases of exhibitionism. Bianchi (1990) used Fluoxetine to treat a 32-year-old man with schizophrenia who had attempted to hang himself because of his distress over his recurring fantasies of exposing himself to his children, and Perilstein, Lipper, and Friedman (1991) reported good success with Fluoxetine in the treatment of exhibitionism, pedophilia, and voyeurism.

The Good Mother *(1988) raises interesting questions about the boundaries between healthy sexuality and exhibitionism.* Diane Keaton plays the divorced mother of a six-year-old daughter. Keaton falls in love with an artist and starts to live a bohemian life that includes nudity in front of her daughter. Keaton's new lover at one point innocently lets the daughter touch his penis when he is getting out of the tub and she expresses natural childhood curiosity. When the ex-husband learns about this event, he sues for custody, and Keaton is forced to renounce her lover in order to maintain visitation rights with her daughter.

Questions for Class Discussion *(The Good Mother)*
- Would it be normal for a six-year-old child to be interested in an adult's genitals?
- If you were the judge in this case, would you have made the same decision?
- Did the bohemian artist make a foolish error of judgment, or was it appropriate to let himself be touched by his lover's daughter?
- How do children who grow up in households where nudity is common adjust sexually and interpersonally?
- At what age should a child no longer sleep with his or her parents?

Voyeurism

The **voyeur** is a "peeping Tom" who experiences arousal and derives sexual satisfaction from spying on unsuspecting people, usually strangers, as they are getting undressed, using the bathroom, or having sexual relations. Although it is normal to want to look at the bodies of others (e.g., at the beach), the voyeur goes to great lengths to find surreptitious hiding places from which he or she can watch others without being detected. Arousal is always associated with the clandestine aspects of the situation; voyeurs report little interest in watching pornographic films, visiting topless or nude beaches, or attending topless bars—all settings where public voyeurism is sanctioned.

As is the case with exhibitionism and obscene phone calls, it is rare for the voyeur to attempt to initiate sexual relationships with those women he victimizes. The voyeur will most often masturbate while viewing the arousing scene or later, when replaying the scene in his memory. These men are typically sexually immature and have poor relationships with their fathers. Surprisingly, they are often religious and conservative and are repelled by the behavior of people with different paraphilias. Although it is rare for voyeurs to progress to crimes of sexual violence, more than two-thirds of males who commit sex-related murders report early experiences with voyeurism (Ressler, 1986).

An interesting variation of voyeurism is **triolism,** or sexual gratification derived from watching other people have sex (or allowing others to watch oneself engage in sexual activity, behavior more logically linked to exhibitionism than voyeurism). This practice is sometimes referred to as **scoptophilia.** Variations on these themes include the **ménage à trois** ("family of three"), swinging, and couples that have monogamous sex in each other's presence. Swinging or mate swapping is probably widespread, although AIDS and other sexual diseases have presented serious obstacles to this form of sexual expression. A failed attempt at swinging is portrayed in Paul Mazursky's 1969 film *Bob and Carol and Ted and Alice,* starring Robert Culp, Eliot Gould, Dyan Cannon, and Natalie Wood. The film celebrates social permissiveness and the mores of the late sixties more than sexual freedom; in the final scene Bob, Carol, Ted, and Alice, all in bed together, reaffirm their commitment to monogamy. *Breaking the Waves* (1996) is a powerful Danish film that examines triolism in a situation in which a formerly virile man paralyzed from an industrial accident insists that his wife have intercourse with other men so he can derive vicarious satisfaction from her stories. The wife, a devout Catholic, goes along with her husband's demands because she is convinced that these voyeuristic pleasures are the only thing keeping her husband alive.

Relatively few films have portrayed either exhibitionism or voyeurism; one exception is the 1991 Canadian film *The Adjuster. Most films that have dealt explicitly with voyeurism have often been misleading presentations that perpetuate common myths.* For example, *Peeping Tom,* a 1960 film, presents the story of a voyeur who tortures his victims and then photographs them as they are dying. This is an example of sexual sadism, not voyeurism.

Sexual Masochism

The **sexual masochist** becomes sexually excited when he or she is humiliated, beaten, bound, or made to suffer. It is important to appreciate that the diagnosis of sexual masochism is made only when patients actually engage in these behaviors. As is the case with other paraphilias, masochistic fantasies are both common and harmless, and moderate sadomasochistic behavior (e.g., scratching and biting) can be a rewarding part of normal sex play.

Masochists allow themselves to be abused in a variety of ways, including bondage, whipping, handcuffing, spanking, cutting, and burning. They are often verbally abused as well as physically mistreated. Humiliation may be necessary for arousal to occur — e.g., a masochist may be forced to wear a diaper, or his partner may defecate or urinate upon the masochist. Whips, chains, leather, and rubber accouterments often play an important role in the sexual activity of the masochist, who is happiest with a (mildly) sadistic partner. Occasionally, masochism will be symbolic rather than physical. For example, Kernberg (1988) reported the case of an affluent woman who could achieve orgasm only when she had sex in unsafe neighborhoods with men who were paying for her services.

A woman who caters to the sexual preferences of masochistic men is referred to as a **dominatrix.** These women are contacted through bondage magazines and leather bars, or through the underground bondage and discipline (B & D) subculture. Masochists may be gay or straight, although the majority of sadomasochistic encounters are heterosexual. Among homosexuals, masochists appear to outnumber sadists (Innala & Ernulf, 1992).

Pedro Almodovar's *Tie Me Up! Tie Me Down!* (1990) is a provocative investigation of the relationship between a mildly masochistic woman and the man who kidnaps her and holds her hostage, hoping she will eventually come to love him. The theme is ancient, present in other movies, such as William Wyler's 1965 film *The Collector.* However, few directors have developed the concept with as much skill as Almodovar (who previously directed another complex psychological investigation of the relationships between men and women, *Woman on the Verge of a Nervous Breakdown*).

Tie Me Up! Tie Me Down! tells the story of Ricky, a young man released from a mental institution, whose only ambition is to find a woman, Marina, he had slept with once when he had escaped from the institution. Marina, an actress and a former drug addict, now stars in pornographic movies and has no memory of her former tryst with Ricky. Their interactions after the kidnapping present the viewer with an odd mix of sexual violence and comedy, and the film constantly jumps between the themes of love and control. Love eventually wins out, and Ricky and Marina develop a healthy, satisfying relationship. *The movie sounds misogynistic, but Almodovar very skillfully demonstrates the power Marina maintains throughout her captivity.*

Sexual Sadism

Sexual sadism presents the mirror image of sexual masochism. The sadist derives sexual pleasure from the suffering and humiliation of his or her victims. Partners may be consenting or nonconsenting. If the partner is consenting, the diagnosis requires that sexual sadism be "repeatedly preferred or exclusive" and that "bodily injury that is extensive, permanent, or possibly mortal is inflicted in order to achieve sexual excitement."

The terms *sadism* and *masochism* were first used by a German sexologist, Krafft-Ebing, in the nineteenth century. Krafft-Ebing, who wrote *Psychopathia Sexualis,* the first medical school textbook on sexuality, took the term sadism from the name of French author Marquis de Sade. De Sade's novels and short stories are replete with abuse, torture, and murder, all of which are linked with sexual gratification. One of his works, *The 120 Days of Sodom,* was made into a movie *(Salo or the 120 Days of Sodom)* directed by Pier Pasolini.

Sadomasochistic sex often involves elaborate sex toys such as chains, whips, rubber and leather garments, and spike heels. Flagellation and bondage are common practices.

Although some sadists are also rapists, it is important to understand that rapists do not derive sexual pleasure from the rape itself. Rape is an act of violence in which sexual arousal may play virtually no role. In contrast, the sexual sadist derives intense sexual pleasure from the suffering of the victim.

Ten to 20 percent of pornographic magazines are devoted to themes of submission and dominance (Dietz & Evans, 1982), suggesting that the prevalence of sexual sadism and masochism is fairly high in the United States. However, it is important to distinguish between *minor* sadism and masochism (sex play involving bondage and discipline or dominance and submission) and *major* sadism and masochism involving torture and the risk of death and bodily injury (Arndt, 1991). There is some evidence that at the minor level there are more women who dominate males; at the extreme level, men are more likely to abuse women.

Films depicting sexual sadism are common in the United States, and they play for large audiences in Europe and Asia as well. Many of these films are heavy-handed and crude and have little social value. A salient exception is David Lynch's *Blue Velvet* (1986). This remarkable film employs many of the dramatic visual techniques and effects developed by Lynch in his first film, *Eraserhead,* about a deformed and retarded child.

Blue Velvet opens with Bobby Vinton's song of the same name and scenes of a bucolic Midwest neighborhood. This idyllic scene is soon interrupted, and the viewer is never really allowed to relax again until the film concludes.

The plot of the story involves a student, Jeffrey Beaumont, who is home from college to care for his father who has just had a stroke. While walking in a field near his house, Jeffrey discovers a severed ear. It turns out to be the ear of the husband of a cabaret singer (Dorothy). Dorothy's husband is being held hostage to force her to comply with the sexual demands of a local gangster, Frank Booth (Dennis Hopper). Dorothy, one of the most complex characters in the film, discovers Jeffrey in her apartment after he goes there in a foolish attempt to solve the crime. Dorothy, in a controversial scene that disturbs many feminists, discovers Jeffrey and uses a knife to force him to have sex with her. Dorothy displays many of the features of masochism previously discussed; these become more prominent later, when Frank arrives and proceeds to savagely abuse her. Frank, both obsessed with Dorothy and fixated on the song "Blue Velvet," has cut off a piece of Dorothy's blue velvet bathrobe. It is a fetish that Frank carries with him and uses during other sexual encounters. Hopper is unforgettable as Frank Booth, who is addicted to inhalants as well as sadistic sex. The film also toys with gender identity issues, and one is never certain if Booth is a heterosexual or bisexual sadist.

One troubling aspect of the film is that *both Dorothy and Jeffrey seem attracted to sadomasochistic sex after they have been exposed to it.* A subplot involves Jeffrey's involvement with Sandy, the daughter of a corrupt local detective. The relationship with Sandy seems pale and insipid after the intensity of a sexual encounter with Dorothy.

The film won the National Society of Film Critics award for best film of 1986, and Lynch was selected as best director of the year by the same group. It is a brutally honest film, and not one that will appeal to all viewers. However, it is a film rich in psychopathology and one worth seeing by anyone interested in the complex world of the sexual psychopath (discussed more fully in Chapter 13).

Pedophilia

The **pedophile** is someone who is sexually aroused by children and who has acted on these desires or who is markedly distressed by them. The pedophile can be attracted to girls, boys, or both, although heterosexual pedophilia appears to be somewhat more common than homosexual pedophilia. The *DSM-IV* stipulates that the child be prepubescent (generally age 13 or younger) for a diagnosis of pedophilia to be appropriate; attraction to children who have achieved puberty is biologically if not socially appropriate. In addition, the diagnosis is not used unless the perpetrator is at least 16 years old and at least five years older than the child involved.

Many people have questioned the late and seemingly arbitrary age of consent, age 18 in most states, and have pointed out that young people usually become sexually active long before this age. In 1985, the Dutch government actually proposed to lower the age for sexual consent from 16 to 12; however, the proposal was withdrawn due to strong and negative public opinion.

Many pedophiles report being sexually abused as children (Freund, Watson, & Dickey, 1990). Pedophiles who have been attracted to children since adolescence are identified as

fixated pedophiles. In contrast, if an individual has satisfying adult sexual experiences, then reverts to a sexual preoccupation with children, the person is classified as a situational or **regressed pedophile.**

There are between 100,000 and 500,000 cases of child sexual abuse in the United States each year, and the number of cases is probably rising (Barnard et al., 1989).

Most people consider the practice of pedophilia reprehensible, perhaps because children are among the most vulnerable members of the human family. However, the widespread availability of "kiddie porn," despite the social opprobrium associated with the practice, suggests that sexual interest in children is as common as most of the other paraphilias. Empirical data document the extent of sexual attraction to children by adults. For example, Briere (1989) surveyed undergraduate males and found that 21 percent acknowledged being sexually attracted to children, 9 percent had sexual fantasies involving children, and 7 percent would consider having sex with a child if certain they could avoid being detected or punished.

Incest

Incest is treated as a subclass of pedophilia in *DSM-IV*. The term refers to sexual relations between persons too closely related to marry. Russell (1983, 1984) has reported that the incidence of incest for stepdaughters is as high as 16 percent, and stepfathers are seven times more likely to abuse their children than biological fathers. Barnard et al. (1989) report that one out of six women who have stepfathers experienced sexual abuse at some point during childhood.

The prevalence of the various paraphilias can be estimated by surveying pornography and looking at what topics are the most popular. For example, Lebegue (1991) reviewed 3,050 magazine and book titles collected by the 1986 Attorney General's Commission on Pornography. He found that sadomasochism was by far the most common paraphilia; however, incest titles (e.g., *Suzie Loves Her Daddy*) comprised more than 21 percent of 746 titles judged to relate to *DSM-IV* paraphilic diagnoses.

Stanley Kubrick's Lolita *(1962) is the classic example of incest in a contemporary movie.* The film takes liberties with Vladimir Nabokov's novel, but the changes were made with the permission of the great writer, who served as screenwriter for the movie. A psychoanalyst has argued that Nabokov himself was a pedophile as a result of childhood sexual abuse by an uncle (Centerwall, 1992). Considered quite daring when it was released more than three decades ago, the film portrays the love of Humbert (James Mason) for Lolita (played by Sue Lyon). Shelly Winters plays Lolita's mother and Peter Sellers has a major role in the film. *Like many actual incestuous stepfathers, Mason's downfall comes from the restrictions he places on his daughter's emerging sexuality and his paranoia about her sexual experience with anyone but him.*

Coprophilia

The close proximity of the organs of excretion and the organs of reproduction lead to confusion for many children, and it is not surprising that urine or feces sexually arouses some adults. The personal ads in underground papers frequently solicit "golden showers," and some authors estimate that 1 in 25 adults has experimented with this form of sexual expression (Haas and Haas, 1990).

The Marquis de Sade wrote about coprophilia as well as sadism, as illustrated by the following selection.

> Having then adopted the most comfortable position, he glued his mouth to the object of his worship, and in less time than it takes to tell, I delivered a globlet the size of a pigeon's egg. He sucked it, turned it a thousand times about in his mouth, chewed it, savored it, and at the end of three or four minutes I distinctly saw him swallow it; push again, the same ceremony is repeated . . . . (de Sade, 1957, pp. 90–91)

Frotteurism

The **frotteur** is someone who derives sexual pleasure from brushing or rubbing against others in a seemingly inadvertent but clearly sexual manner. Frotteurs frequent crowded stores, escalators, buses, and subways, where their behavior can be attributed to crowding. *DSM-IV* lists frotteurism as an independent paraphilia, although many authors view it as a variation of exhibitionism.

Klismaphilia

Some people derive intense sexual pleasure, sometimes leading to orgasm, from enemas. It is likely that sexual arousal was paired with the experience of receiving an enema early in childhood, and this association was later reinforced with enema fantasies during masturbation. The frequency of reference to enemas in pornographic literature and the underground press suggest it is a common paraphilia. Few individuals with klismaphilia request treatment for the disorder, so the true incidence is probably underestimated.

Necrophilia

Necrophilia, or sexual arousal in response to corpses, is perhaps the most bizarre of the paraphilias. The term is used to describe a wide range of behaviors, including sex with corpses, sexual excitement from the act of murder, the mutilation of corpses, and the eating of body parts from corpses **(necrophagia)** (Rebal, Faguet, & Woods, 1982).

Necrophilia is believed to be extremely rare, although estimating the prevalence of the disorder is difficult for obvious reasons. Public interest in the disorder was heightened by the arrest of Jeffrey Dahmer, who murdered his victims, had sex with their corpses, mutilated their bodies, and ate various body parts. Dahmer was tested with the **Minnesota Multiphasic Personality Inventory** (MMPI), a psychological test widely used to assess psychopathology. A computerized assessment of Dahmer's test results reported, "[This patient] is likely to have significant psychological problems. . . . He typically deals with frustration by acting out in an extrapunitive way. . . . [He is] quite conflicted over sexual issues."

Necrophilia is commonly portrayed in vampire movies. One of the best of these is *Bram Stoker's Dracula,* directed by Francis Ford Coppola. There are a number of case studies of people who are aroused by the sight of blood, and this phenomenon is referred to as vampirism.

Telephone Scatologia

Most American women and a considerable number of men have experienced obscene phone calls. *DSM-IV* identifies the practice of making obscene calls for sexual gratification as **telephone scatologia.** Sixty-one percent of the women in one survey had received obscene phone calls, and 75 percent of these had had two or more calls (Herold, Mantle, & Zemitis, 1979).

People who engage in telephone scatalogia are generally males with low self-esteem. They often feel sexually inadequate, and the outrage of their victims gives them a feeling of power. These feelings of power are similar to those that accompany exhibitionism; however, the man making obscene phone calls is far less likely to be apprehended, and the practice provides similar thrills with far fewer risks. Obscene phone callers seldom seek out contact with the individuals they call.

Anyone who receives an obscene phone call should simply hang up without saying a word. It is the victim's shock and anger that rewards the behavior; if this outrage is not forthcoming, the behavior will extinguish. Caller ID, a device that records the number of every incoming call, is a technological innovation that may reduce the incidence of telephone scatalogia by increasing its risk.

One form of telephone scatalogia involves calling suicide hot lines or crisis counseling lines. The caller tries until he contacts a female with a pleasant voice. Initially the caller presents a plausible situation, possibly one involving a troubled relationship with a girlfriend. The description becomes increasingly graphic while the caller masturbates, attempting to get the crisis counselor to remain on the line as long as possible.

Still another variation of telephone scatalogia involves "Dial-a-Porn" services. These "900" numbers allow one to engage in paraphilic behavior without risk and with a seemingly enthusiastic partner; however, the costs of calling can quickly escalate.

Robert Altman's film *Short Cuts* (1994) includes some very funny scenes in which a woman helps support her family by working a 900 line. She moans, groans, and sighs at the same time she is changing the diapers on her baby and cooking her family's supper. Her husband appreciates the extra income but resents his wife's verbal infidelities; later in the film, he and a male friend entice two young women to go with them to a deserted spot, where he initially seduces and then later kills one of the girls.

Another increasingly common practice is computer scatalogia using bulletin boards. Some large computer bulletin boards specialize in acquainting people who desire to "type dirty" to one another. Even large, family-oriented bulletin board services such as Prodigy and CompuServe have singles bulletin boards that are often surprisingly graphic.

Zoophilia

Zoophilia, also known as **bestiality,** has fascinated writers and artists throughout history. Well-known examples include Leda and the Swan, the beauty and the beast, and the princess forced to sleep with a frog (who later is transformed into a handsome prince). In addition, the practice was apparently common enough in biblical times to warrant a specific injunction in Leviticus 19:15: "If a man lies with a beast, he shall be put to death and you shall kill the beast." There are similar injunctions and a similar punishment is proscribed for women who engage in bestiality. Alfred Kinsey investigated zoophilia and found that in some rural areas up to 65 percent of boys had experienced sexual contact with animals.

The clinical literature is replete with case studies of zoophilia. For example, Holden and Sherline (1973) described a case in which a woman experienced anaphylactic shock as a result of an allergic reaction to the seminal fluid of her German shepherd. She acknowledged having intercourse with the dog, and had done so on other occasions without experiencing any distress. This woman was lonely, and she desired but did not have a meaningful human relationship. Psychiatric examination failed to reveal any other evidence of disturbance.

In another case study, reminiscent of Peter Firth's character in *Equus,* Rappaport (1968) described the zoophilic practices of a 20-year-old college student:

[He] could get sexually excited merely from the smell of horses. . . . [He] would try to squeeze the neck of the horse between his legs, at the same time masturbating the horse's penis. Drawing forcefully on the horse's bridle, to pull its neck backward, he wanted the horse to get on its hind legs, or, best of all, to make it roll on its back, in either case for the purpose of making the penis point upward. Often, after he had sneaked into a stable, he tied up a stallion's legs, made it go on its knees, and then pushed the horse down, jumped on top of it and had "an emission." . . . At times he managed to insert his own erect penis into the foreskin of the stallion. . . . However, what he wanted most of all was to have the stallion mount the mare and then to jump on top of the stallion and then to ejaculate simultaneously with the stallion.

Autoerotic Asphyxia

Using self-strangulation to produce excitement, erections, and ejaculation is an unusual but not uncommon paraphilia, and one that results in more than 50 deaths in the United States each year (Rebal, Faguet, & Woods, 1982). Blanchard and Hucker (1991) were able to review the cases of 117 males who died during autoerotic asphyxial activity. **Autoerotic asphyxia** is especially significant because all of the deaths that result from this practice are assumed to be accidents.

Most of what we know about the practice of autoerotic asphyxia is derived from police reports following death investigations. The victims tend to be young white males. Bondage accouterments are often employed, along with mirrors and cameras. Transvestism is a common practice in these cases. There is often evidence that ejaculation occurred before death.

Paraphilias in Films

Film examples have been included in each section in this chapter. However, numerous other examples can be cited, and the reader can probably generate a long list of film examples in which various paraphilias are portrayed.

There is a fascinating portrayal of autoerotic asphyxia in Nigisa Oshima's film *In the Realm of the Senses* (1976). This film documents the sexual obsessions of two Japanese lovers who are preoccupied with sexual pleasure. The woman increasingly resorts to strangulation to prolong the erections of her lover; eventually and predictably, he dies during one of these episodes. The film is based on the true story of a woman who accidentally strangled her lover and then wandered around in a daze, carrying her lover's severed penis with her. Oshima was tried for obscenity in Japan when the film was released but was eventually acquitted. His stature as a filmmaker was vindicated by the critical and commercial success of the film in Europe and the United States.

There are vivid scenes of bathroom seduction by a stepfather (Karl Malden) in Barbra Streisand's film *Nuts* (1987). The classic example of the combination of pedophilia and sociopathy is found in the Fritz Lang 1931 film *M,* in which Peter Lorre played a child molester stalking the streets of Berlin. A riveting presentation of the fate of child molesters when they are caught and incarcerated is found in the 1977 prison drama *Short Eyes.*

The lives and misadventures of film stars and directors also offer some insight into the study of sexual psychopathology. For example, the career of "Fatty" Arbuckle was ruined when the 320-pound actor was accused of manslaughter after a starlet died of a ruptured bladder (after supposedly having been sexually assaulted by Arbuckle). He was finally acquitted, but his career never recovered. (The 1975 film *The Wild Party* recreates the Arbuckle debacle.)

Roman Polanski was arrested in 1979 for having sexual relations with a 13-year-old girl. Polanski served a brief sentence for observation and then fled the country. Since leaving the United States, Polanski has continued to make films in France and Poland.

More recently, the career of Woody Allen was marred by controversy after he was accused of sexually molesting the adopted children of his lover, actress Mia Farrow. Many of the children have bit parts in the film *Hannah and Her Sisters* (1986). Allen's problems seem to be reflected in one of his recent films, *Husbands and Wives* (1992), in which an aging English professor becomes romantically and sexually involved with a 20-year-old college student. The same theme was found in the 1979 film *Manhattan,* in which Allen's character is living with a high school student (Mariel Hemingway).

Critical Thinking Questions

- Do the *DSM-IV* transgender categories transvestic fetishism and gender identity disorder perpetuate social stereotypes and discrimination against gays and lesbians?
- Homosexuality was deleted from the *Diagnostic and Statistical Manual* of the American Psychiatric Association in 1973. Do you agree with this decision?
- Body piercing of the genitals and nipples has become common in the 1990s, whereas it was quite rare in the 1950s. Would these behaviors have been viewed as sexual deviance in the 1950s? How do culture and context influence the process of labeling pathology?
- Why is it that women's clothes (e.g., dresses and slips) are distinctly feminine, while men's clothes (e.g., pants and belts) are far less likely to be regarded as exclusively male?
- Is it ethical for therapists to work with gays and lesbians to modify their sexual orientation? If so, under what conditions would it be appropriate?
- What psychological theories have been put forward to explain the development of fetishes?

Chapter 9

Schizophrenia and Delusional Disorders

*They put a receiver in the back of my head
and a transmitter in my finger.*
Peter Winter, *Clean, Shaven*

Questions to Consider While Watching *Clean, Shaven*

- What is tardive dyskinesia? Do you see any evidence of the disorder in this patient?
- Are auditory hallucinations more or less common than visual hallucinations in people with schizophrenia? Is there evidence of either in Mr. Winter?
- What is the role of this patient's parents in the etiology of his illness?
- If this patient's thought disorder could be effectively treated with medication, and you estimate that there was 5 percent likelihood that he would not be compliant with his medication regimen, would you release him?
- This is an indigent client. Does the public have a moral responsibility to provide treatment for people like Peter Winter?
- Can psychologists and other mental health providers make accurate diagnoses about the likelihood of violence in people with mental illness?
- Mr. Winter uses six to eight packets of sugar to sweeten each cup of coffee. Is there any relationship between diet and schizophrenia?
- At one point the patient remarks, "They're killing people out there." What defense mechanism does this suggest?
- Peter is visibly anxious during much of the film. Is anxiety a symptom of schizophrenia?
- If Mr. Winter were to be hospitalized, would he be at risk for suicide?

PATIENT EVALUATION

Patient's stated reason for coming: "There's a lot of people out there who want to hurt you."

History of the present illness: Mr. Peter Winter is a 28-year-old white male who presents with a complex history of confusion, paranoia, and disorganized thinking. He experiences frequent auditory hallucinations, most commonly the voice of an angry black man who shouts out commands and criticizes the patient. Mr. Winter believes power lines transmit these messages, which are subsequently picked up from a transmitter in his fingertip and then relayed to a receiver implanted in his head. There is a history of self-mutilation involving both the finger and the scalp. Mr. Winter avoids looking at himself in mirrors and goes to great lengths to cover or avoid any mirrors that may be present in a room. He is reported to have been living in his car for the past month. The patient is believed to be dangerous, and he may have been responsible for the recent bludgeoning death of an eight-year-old schoolgirl in a neighboring town.

Past psychiatric illness, treatment, and outcomes: Mr. Winter has received episodic psychiatric treatment, both inpatient and outpatient, since the age of 20. The patient reports a history of three previous hospitalizations and a past diagnosis of "schizophrenia." There are no available records of these hospitalizations. He reports previous treatment with Haldol and other medications; however, he cannot remember the names of the medications and he is not currently taking medication of any sort.

Medical history: There is a large laceration in Mr. Winter's scalp, and the fingernail from the index finger of the left hand has recently been removed. The patient has shaved off all the hair from his chest, arms, and genitals. There is no other significant medical history.

Psychosocial history: Mr. Winter has been married, but he reports that his wife died approximately six years ago. He is the father of Nicole, a 10-year-old girl who currently lives with her adoptive mother. Nicole is quiet, withdrawn, and reluctant to talk, but she maintains a relationship with her grandmother, Gladys Winter, the patient's mother. Mrs. Winter appears to be somewhat aloof, withdrawn, hostile, and distant. She has dominated the patient since his childhood and continues to make many decisions for him. Her husband abandoned her and her son when Peter was quite young. Peter has recently been living with his mother, paying $10 per day for rent. Mr. Winter has been picked up by the police for vagrancy, but there is no other criminal history.

Drug and alcohol history: Mr. Winter reports drinking "a beer now and then." He denies any other history of drug use.

Behavioral observations: Mr. Winter is disheveled, unshaven, and unkempt. His fingernails are dirty, and one is bandaged. He frequently paces rapidly and talks to himself. When he is not pacing, his affect appears flat and he looks mildly depressed. There is a marked tremor present, possibly a symptom of tardive dyskinesia. At times he appeared to be talking to himself during the interview. Mr. Winter appears to have little insight into the nature or the severity of his condition.

Mental status examination: Mr. Winter achieved a score of 22 on the Folstein Mini Mental Status Examination. He knows the year, season, and month but is unable to identify the date or day of the week. He is fully oriented to place but can recall only two out of three objects. He makes two errors out of five attempts when counting backward by seven. Immediate recall is good, and there is no dysnomia. He is able to repeat simple phrases but is able to follow only one out of three verbal commands. He is able to respond appropriately to written commands and is able to write simple sentences. However, some construction dyspraxia is present and the patient is unable to copy intersecting pentagons.

Functional assessment: Mr. Winter has a high school education and he achieved good grades and a stellar record as a high school student. He has a poor work history and has not been able to hold a job for more than a few weeks at any time in the past five years. He maintains a social if strained relationship with his mother, and he remains committed to his 10-year-old daughter (now adopted), although he has not seen her in several years. He is quite withdrawn, has limited social skills, and appears to have no social network outside of his relationship with his mother.

Strengths: This patient has performed well academically in high school, and he responded to previous treatment with neuroleptic medications.

Diagnosis: Schizophrenia, paranoid type. There is clear evidence of auditory hallucinations and paranoid delusions. There is no evidence of medical conditions or any history of substance abuse that could account for these symptoms. There is no history of mood swings or depression.

Treatment plan: This patient is potentially dangerous. He requires inpatient treatment and constant monitoring until his condition improves. He is to be started on Haldol 10 mg. bid. and Cogentin 1 mg. bid. Constant nursing supervision will be necessary, with at least hourly bed checks.

Prognosis: Guarded.

THE DIAGNOSIS OF SCHIZOPHRENIA

Schizophrenia usually first occurs during late adolescence or early adulthood, but it can begin in childhood or middle/late adulthood. Even though the frequency of the illness occurs equally in both genders, symptoms in males often occur earlier than females. It appears that Mr. Winter first began experiencing his symptoms in early adulthood, after he had married. This is a common presentation.

In order for a person to be diagnosed with schizophrenia, certain symptoms must be present. According to the *DSM-IV*, there must be continuous signs of the disturbance for at least six months and, during one month (the active phase), two or more of the following must be present: delusions, hallucinations, disorganized speech, grossly disorganized or catatonic behavior, or negative symptoms (i.e., affective flattening, alogia, or avolition). If delusions either are bizarre or are an ongoing commentary, only one of these symptoms needs to be present. The individual's ability to function in work, social relations, and self-care decreases during the active phase and rarely returns to the individual's premorbid level of achievement. There was clear evidence of delusions and hallucinations in Mr. Winter, and his affect appeared "flat." It appears clear that he qualifies for a *DSM-IV* diagnosis of schizophrenia, paranoid type.

Following the active phase of the illness, at least two of the following must be present in order to meet diagnostic criteria: marked social isolation or withdrawal; marked impairment of role functioning as a wage-earner, student, or homemaker; peculiar behavior; impairment in personal hygiene and grooming; blunted or inappropriate affect (expression of feeling); unusual speech patterns (the person is vague or overelaborate or does not make sense); odd beliefs or magical thinking; unusual perceptual experiences; or lack of initiative, interests, or energy. These symptoms must be present for six months before a diagnosis is made. *It is clear that Mr. Winter meets the majority of these criteria.*

Schizophrenia is categorized into five types. The most salient symptom of the **catatonic** type is psychomotor disturbance. For example, catatonic persons may appear to be in a stupor, completely unaware of their environment. They may maintain one posture for a long time, crawl into a fetal position, hold an arm in a bizarre position, or sit stiffly in a chair; it may be difficult to move the individual because of the muscle rigidity. At times these individuals may become very excited or agitated but then slip into the previous mannerisms. At times they are mute. This type of schizophrenia, although very dramatic, is less common than other types.

> "Life is cruel . . . but music will always be your friend. Everything else will let you down in the end." David Helfgott's father on the importance of music to life, in *Shine* (1996)

Disorganized schizophrenia presents with a picture of incoherent speech and disorganized behavior. These patients rapidly shift from one idea to another; often the ideas are unrelated. They may also express inappropriate emotion, such as laughing at a sad occasion. They usually have very strange mannerisms and are extremely socially impaired. The **paranoid** type (a diagnosis that appears appropriate for Mr. Winter) is characterized by systematized delusions or frequent hallucinations related to a single theme (e.g., hearing denigrating voices). These individuals are often extremely anxious, angry, or argumentative, and they may become violent. Although there is not the strong relationship between violence and schizophrenia that many people expect (and which movies suggest is common), among people diagnosed with schizophrenia, paranoid patients are the most likely to commit acts of violence.

The **undifferentiated** type is characterized by psychotic symptoms (delusions, hallucinations, etc.) but lacks the salient characteristics of the other types. The undifferentiated type of the illness is frequently found in inpatient settings. **Residual schizophrenia** is a category for persons who do not exhibit any of the symptoms of the active phase (hallucinations, delusions, etc.) but do have other symptoms such as social withdrawal or eccentric behavior (APA, 1994).

FAMILY DYNAMICS

In the 1960s and 1970s, a popular theory implicated ineffective family communication patterns in the etiology of schizophrenia. Communication within the family of a person with schizophrenia was believed to be indirect, unclear, incongruent, and growth impeding. Communication within families was thought of as distorted and based on "double messages," so that the child received two opposing messages from the parent and, thus, was in a **double bind.** For example, a parent might say, "Come here and give me a hug" and, when the child responded, the parent pushed the child away. The child then would feel that pleasing the parent was an impossible "no win" situation and would develop schizophrenic behavior in response to this psychological bind. The **schizophrenogenic** family was characterized as being severely **fused.** Members of these families never adequately separated or developed into individuals;, and, thus, the family had no boundaries.

This view of distorted family communication has been largely discounted as a cause of schizophrenia. Even though these characteristics were found in families with a schizophrenic member, they were also found in nonschizophrenic families. The research was conducted with families with an ill family member, but these dysfunctional patterns of communication may be thought to be present in many families, regardless of mental illness. Many families were alienated by this approach because the very people who could help and support the schizophrenic person were treated with disdain and were seen as the source of that person's problem. The National Alliance for the Mentally Ill (NAMI) has worked hard to discredit this antiquated theory about the origins of schizophrenia.

Despite the fact that no one seriously believes that parents "cause" their children's schizophrenia, this myth persists in both popular mythology and contemporary cinema. Peter Winter's mother is portrayed as cold, aloof, and withdrawn; there is a clear implication that she is at least in part responsible for her son's illness. Likewise, the movie *Shine,* Scott Hick's fascinating film about the life of child prodigy and pianist David Helfgott, clearly implicates David's father as the root of his son's subsequent mental illness. The father is alternately loving and hateful, telling his son, "No one can love you like me!" while at the same time actively working to limit his future and his potential. In a particularly memorable scene, David responds to his father's criticism by defecating in his bath water, and he is severely punished for his insolence.

A similar theme can be found in the 1962 film *David and Lisa.* David's mother and father epitomized the parental stereotype. The movie is about David, who is a highly intelligent but mentally disturbed boy who suffers from a variety of obsessive fears, and Lisa, who shows many symptoms of schizophrenia. The setting is a residential treatment facility run by a psychiatrist. The movie is based on a book by Dr. Theodore Isaac Rubin, which explores the need that human beings have for one another, the strength and healing power of love, and the discomfort that the outside world experiences in confronting mental illness. David's mother is portrayed as a cold, unresponsive social climber who was totally insensitive to her son's abilities and problems. The father is depicted as a passive, distant father who was unavailable to David in his younger years. Both parents were ineffective in dealing with David's problems, and the film suggests there is a link between the dysfunctional parental communication and David's mental illness. Interestingly, the psychiatrist is portrayed as a warm and loving parental surrogate who saves David from the throes of mental illness.

Family interaction theories have focused on the individual as a family member and have emphasized the importance of family relationships. Even though a family interaction etiology for schizophrenia has not been supported by research, the impact of a schizophrenic member on the family is very real. A powerful illustration of the effect of an illness such as schizophrenia on the family can be seen in Jane Campion's 1989 film *Sweetie.*

THE PORTRAYAL OF SCHIZOPHRENIA AND DELUSIONAL DISORDERS IN CONTEMPORARY FILMS

THE FISHER KING

Terry Gilliam's 1991 film *The Fisher King* is about the life of Jack Lucas, played by Jeff Bridges, a depressed former disc jockey, who meets Parry, played by Robin Williams, an obsessed yet benign street person. A listener who was sarcastically told by Jack to wipe out the yuppies before they multiply killed Parry's fiancée several years earlier during a shooting spree. Jack's sense of guilt sends him to the depth of depression, and he eventually attempts suicide. Before jumping into the river, he is doused with gasoline by thugs. At the last minute, Parry saves him.

Parry believes himself to be a knight whose mission is to save the Holy Grail. He enlists Jack's aid in his quest, which is motivated by guilt. Throughout the film, Parry has several hallucinations, including seeing friendly "little people" who communicate with him regularly and give him guidance. The Red Knight is a frightening hallucination that appears at times of extreme stress or when he is reminded of the tragedy.

Additional Questions for Class Discussion *(The Fisher King)*

- How common is it for a traumatic event (such as the murder of Parry's fiancée) to trigger mental illness?
- Is there any relationship between schizophrenia and trauma?
- Is schizophrenia related to post-traumatic stress disorder (PTSD)?
- The hallucinations of the "Red Knight" are vivid and detailed. Is this an accurate depiction of the hallucinations most commonly experienced by people with schizophrenia?

Sophie's Choice

Sophie's Choice, a 1982 Alan Pakula film based on William Styron's novel by the same name, stars Meryl Streep, Kevin Kline, and Peter MacNicol and takes place shortly after World War II. The movie received rave reviews from the critics and was acclaimed as one of the best films of the year. Meryl Streep won a Golden Globe citation and an Academy Award for her performance.

Three people are faced with a series of choices and their consequences. Sophie, played by Meryl Streep, is a Polish-Catholic woman who spent much of WWII in concentration camps after being caught by the Nazis with a contraband ham. Her father and husband, both Nazi sympathizers, were also incarcerated in camps and were never seen again. Sophie's two children were separated and lost while she was in Auschwitz; her life was somehow spared, and she migrated to Brooklyn, where she becomes romantically involved with Nathan, played by Kevin Kline. Sophie and Nathan move into an old boardinghouse and live in a room above a fledgling writer, Southern-born Stingo, played by Peter MacNicol. The three become inseparable friends, with Sophie and Nathan maintaining their turbulent romantic/sexual relationship and Stingo eventually falling deeply in love with Sophie.

The story is told from the point of view of two narrators: *Stingo,* who remembers the summer in Brooklyn, and *Sophie,* who remembers what happened to her during World War II. Throughout the movie, both Sophie and Stingo struggle to understand Nathan's eccentric, erratic behavior, which at different times involves intense love, suspiciousness, anger, hostility, and paranoia. Initially, Nathan merely appears to be an unstable, "moody" person who claims to be a Harvard graduate and an overworked research biologist. He manages to convince everyone that he is on the brink of discovering the cure for polio. As the story unfolds, the audience learns that Nathan has been diagnosed with paranoid schizophrenia and he is only marginally coping with life. In fact, he spends his days at a menial job in a pharmaceutical library. His symptoms are exacerbated with the use of speed (amphetamines) and cocaine, and his psychotic thinking leads to vicious accusations and unpredictable behavior. His bizarre behavior becomes more pronounced as his interpersonal stress increases and his denial is challenged.

As Nathan becomes more psychotic, he accuses Sophie of infidelity and threatens to kill her. Sophie seeks protection from Stingo, who confesses his love for her and explains that he will take her back to Virginia with him. He then talks of marriage and children. She tells her heartbreaking story of how she had to select one of her children to be executed (i.e., Sophie's first "choice") and concludes that she could never think of marriage and children again. Sophie and Stingo make love. The following morning, Sophie returns to Nathan and leaves a note for the sleeping Stingo. When Stingo returns to the boarding house, he finds Sophie and Nathan lying on the bed after a successful suicide (Sophie's second choice).

Additional Questions for Class Discussion *(Sophie's Choice)*

- Nathan is identified in the novel and the film as a "paranoid schizophrenic." What are the arguments for and against this diagnosis?
- Can you make a case for a diagnosis of bipolar disorder? Why or why not?
- How is accurate diagnosis in this case complicated by Nathan's history of amphetamine abuse?
- How was this novel influenced by William Styron's own experience with depression (vividly described in his book *Darkness Visible*)?

Misery

Misery, a 1990 Academy Award-winning film directed by Rob Reiner and starring James Caan as Paul Sheldon and Kathy Bates as Annie Wilkes, is based on a Stephen King novel. The film is about a writer, Paul Sheldon, who has been prostituting his talent for years with a popular mystery series about a character named Misery. In order to be free of the series, in the last novel he arranges for the heroine's death. While this novel is in production, Paul secludes himself in a cabin in Colorado and writes a serious novel.

Upon finishing his novel, Paul leaves the lodge to take his manuscript to his publisher, but he is caught in a blizzard. His car slides off the road and down a mountainside, and Paul is seriously injured with a broken arm and compound fractures to both legs. Annie Wilkes, a nurse who carries him to her isolated home to care for him, saves him. Annie tells Paul that the telephone lines are down and there is no way to take him to the hospital. She tells him that she is his "number one" fan and proceeds to care for him. In gratitude, Paul lets Annie read his latest novel.

The movie then becomes a thriller. Annie is outraged that the novel is not a Misery novel and that it contains swearing and foul language. She throws a tantrum and then regains her composure and responds, "I love you, Paul. You're mine." She gradually becomes more demanding, petulant, and possessive with Paul, who begins to realize that he is her prisoner. She forces him to burn his latest manuscript and to begin writing a Misery sequel that brings the heroine back to life. When he becomes well enough to escape, she hobbles him by smashing his ankles with a sledgehammer. In the meantime, Paul's disappearance has been reported to the Colorado authorities, who are on the lookout for him. Buster, a local sheriff, played by Richard Farnsworth, suspects Annie is involved after finding out that she lost her nursing license after a series of mysterious hospital deaths. When the sheriff visits Annie and hears Paul in the basement, she kills Buster with a shotgun. Annie then becomes depressed and decides that a double-suicide would bring her and Paul's relationship to a dramatic closure. Paul has other ideas, and the two of them engage in a life and death struggle at the end.

Additional Questions for Class Discussion (*Misery*)

- Is Annie Wilkes mentally ill or just eccentric?
- If you believe she is mentally ill, what *DSM-IV* diagnosis seems most appropriate?
- Annie Wilkes is sexually attracted to Paul. How often is sexuality a feature of delusional disorders?

Taxi Driver

The 1976 film *Taxi Driver* depicts the life of Travis Bickle, an ex-Marine, Vietnam veteran, and taxi driver. This film was nominated for several Academy Awards and starred Robert De Niro as Travis. The film was directed by Martin Scorsese, based on a screenplay by Paul Schrader.

The film begins at night in the sleazy streets of Manhattan around 42nd Street and Times Square. Travis takes a night job as a taxi driver because he suffers from insomnia. He works 12 to 14 hours a night. Even though Travis could take customers anywhere in Manhattan, he chooses to work in the worst part of New York—the world of drifters, child prostitutes, and all-night porno films. Even though he professes disgust ("all the animals come out at night"), he is attracted to this life and spends most of his free time in cheap theaters, watching pornographic films.

Travis encounters and later meets Betsy (played by Cybill Shepherd), a worker in the Palantine for President Campaign. Tall, blonde, and dressed in white, she looks like an angel to him. For a while, he is content to watch her. One day, he marches into the office and convinces her to go out with him. The first date goes well. Over coffee, Travis demonstrates sensitivity and psychological insight into her life. He also implies the men with whom she works are less than perfect. For the second date, he takes her to a pornographic film on 42nd Street and she leaves in a rage. After this incident, she refuses to have anything to do with him.

From this point on, the movie becomes a nightmare. Stung by Betsy's rejection, and rationalizing it by saying that she is like all the other animals, Travis begins to stalk her boss, Palantine. He has two altercations with Palatine's bodyguards, who are suspicious of him. The audience is led to believe that Travis will eventually attempt to kill the presidential candidate. The exmarine diligently prepares himself for an assault by arming himself, improving his physical fitness, and practicing at the firing range. His mental deterioration becomes increasingly apparent. He confides to another taxi driver that he is having "really bad ideas" and that he imagines that he has cancer of the stomach. At one point, Travis practices his spring-loaded gun in front of a mirror and says over and over again, "You talking to me?"

Travis is also attracted to a child prostitute, Iris, played by Jodie Foster. One evening, she leaps into his cab, only to be dragged out by an older man who appears to be her pimp. Later, when Travis runs into her on the street, she says she does not remember the first encounter. Trying to maintain contact with her, Travis bargains with Sport, her pimp, for 15 minutes of her time. When she realizes that he does not want to have sex with her, she is touched and agrees to have coffee with him the next day. He tries to convince her to return to her parents and gives her money for the ticket home. She considers leaving, but her pimp, Sport, persuades her to stay and continue working for him.

The last part of the movie is chilling as we watch Travis prepare for an assassination. In military fatigues and with a shaved head except for a Mohawk strip, Travis focuses on his target. His attempt to kill Palantine is aborted by the Secret Service, and Travis flees into the crowd. Once again, he is drawn to 42nd Street. He finds Sport, picks a fight with him, and then shoots him. He heads for Iris' hotel room and kills both a customer and the hotel manager. Travis is wounded and, by the time the police arrive, a bloody mess. He raises his finger to his head, mimics pulling a trigger, and then loses consciousness.

Ironically, Travis ends up a hero for rescuing Iris, who returns to her parents. Travis recovers from his wounds and resumes his work as a taxi driver. The film ends when Betsy is his passenger and obviously awed by his new hero status. When she attempts to pay her fare, Travis declines money and drives off into the night.

Travis' behavior indicates an underlying delusional disorder. His delusions that Betsy and Iris are innocent victims of unscrupulous men are consistent with the ideas of persecution that accompany a delusional disorder. Even though he discounts his feelings toward Betsy, he continues to stalk her boss, whom she obviously admires. Since Iris is only 14, Travis blames Sport for the adolescent's fallen lifestyle. At the end of the movie, he wants to kill someone. When his attempts to kill Palantine are aborted, he turns to Sport and anyone who has participated in Iris' prostitution.

Additional Questions for Class Discussion *(Taxi Driver)*

- What challenges for differential diagnosis are presented by the case of Travis Bickle?
- How are the delusions found in someone with a delusional disorder different from those found in a disorder such as paranoid schizophrenia?
- Can someone with a serious mental illness, such as a delusional disorder, actually function on the job on a day-to-day basis?

Other Examples of Schizophrenia and Delusional Disorders in Films

Psychotic disorders such as schizophrenia and delusional disorders have a long history in film but are rarely depicted accurately. There are literally hundreds of suspense and horror movies about "psychotic killers" who are on a rampage, usually attacking females. While entertaining for some, these films typically have nothing to do with any particular mental disorder, and they perpetuate the stigma associated with mental illness. The term *psychotic* is used to induce fear and suggest unpredictability. Pictures such as *Alone in the Dark* (1982), *Angel in Red* (1991), *Cape Fear* (1991), *The Caretaker* (1964), and *The Silent Partner* (1979) have all helped shape the stigma experienced by people with mental illness. Also, and in part because of films like these, the diagnosis of schizophrenia is often used as a general term that is applied to anyone who has a mental disorder. For example, in the *Psycho* series (1960, 1983, 1986) and in *The Three Faces of Eve* (1957), the protagonists suffer from dissociative disorders, not schizophrenia.

A realistic and fairly accurate portrayal of schizophrenia can be found in the recent film *Benny and Joon* (1993). In two of the other films discussed in this chapter, *Sophie's Choice* (1982) and *The Fisher King* (1991), schizophrenic symptoms are evident, but there are other behaviors that do not clearly fit the diagnosis. For example, in *Sophie's Choice,* it is unclear how much Nathan's drug usage influences his symptoms. In *The Fisher King,* Parry's cognitive ability is much greater than typical of those with schizophrenia, and it is very unusual for a traumatic experience to precipitate a schizophrenic episode, especially in someone functioning at a professional level, as Parry was (as a college professor). However, all of these films are convincing portrayals of symptomatology.

An Angel at My Table, Jane Campion's film autobiography of New Zealand writer Janet Frame, is a compelling story of misdiagnosis and malpractice. Frame, an awkward, anxious, and socially inept adolescent, is misdiagnosed as schizophrenic after an apparent panic attack and winds up receiving shock treatment and being hospitalized for eight years. She narrowly avoids receiving a frontal lobotomy, a popular treatment at the time.

One of the most vivid cinematic portrayals of psychiatric decompensation occurs in *The Caine Mutiny* (1954). Humphrey Bogart plays Captain Philip Francis Queeg, the obsessive-compulsive skipper of a World War II destroyer. The ship's crew silently watches the deterioration that occurs as Queeg is put under increasing pressure, and eventually a junior officer, Lieutenant Barney Greenwald, takes command. Greenwald is later court martialed, and the film's most dramatic moment comes when Queeg cracks under the stress of the courtroom examination while playing with steel ball bearings, as he always does when anxious.

> "Ah, but the strawberries! That's, that's where I had them. They laughed at me and made jokes, but I proved beyond the shadow of a doubt, and with, with geometric logic, that, that a duplicate key to the wardroom icebox did exist." Captain Queeg in *The Caine Mutiny* (1954)

The portrayal of delusional disorders tends to be more realistic than most film presentations of schizophrenia. In films such as *Sleeping with the Enemy* (1991), *The Fan* (1981), *Scissors* (1991), *Delusions of Grandeur* (1973), and *The Entertainer* (1960), delusions are clearly involved. None of these films, however, deal with treatment. In contrast, *Benny and Joon* depicts Joon's struggle with her need for independence, as well as with her symptoms. *David and Lisa* (1963) takes place in a treatment setting and reflects the treatment of the time. *I Never Promised You a Rose Garden* (1977) also takes place in a state mental institution and accurately depicts treatment during the 1960s.

Critical Thinking Questions

- Can a parent play a role in the development of mental illness in a child?
- Do films such as *Clean, Shaven*; *Shine*; and *David and Lisa* do a disservice to parents by blaming them for what is essentially a biological disorder over which they have no control?
- Films such as *Shine*, *David and Lisa*, and *Benny and Joon* all suggest that love can at least partially offset the deleterious effects of a disease such as schizophrenia. Is there any evidence suggesting this is true?
- Mr. Winter's daughter is described as "a quiet child who plays by herself." Does the father's history of schizophrenia increase the daughter's likelihood of developing the same disorder? If so, what are the odds that she will develop a similar illness?
- Mr. Winter murders a young girl in the film without cause or provocation. Is this a realistic portrayal of schizophrenia? Are people with this illness more likely to be the perpetrators or the victims of violent crime?
- If Mr. Winter had survived, what evidence would you require as a clinician before you authorized off-site visitation rights with his 10-year-old daughter? How would you know when it was safe to discharge this patient?
- In one memorable scene in the film *Clean, Shaven*, Peter Winter is in the library, hitting his head against the stacks. If you had been present, would you have ignored the behavior or tried to intervene and help in some way?
- This patient graduated "in the top 5 percent of his high school class." Is there any relationship between schizophrenia and intelligence? Are extremely bright people more or less likely to develop the disorder?
- The logic for involuntary commitment of Mr. Winter seems clear because he murders a child. If there were no history of violence, would you be justified in hospitalizing this patient against his will?
- People with schizophrenia can have both positive and negative symptoms. Which are most obvious in this patient? Can you give examples of each?
- What other films can you think of that present good and bad examples of schizophrenia or delusional disorder?

Chapter 10

Neuropsychological Disorders

That's frantastic!
Norman Thayer, *On Golden Pond*

Questions to Consider While Watching *On Golden Pond*

- How does Norman Thayer's personality interact with his illness?
- This patient displays some moderate hearing loss. How would this influence your evaluation?
- Norman is approaching his 80th birthday. What is the statistical risk for Alzheimer's disease in an 80-year-old man?
- At one point in the film, Norman becomes convinced he has been overcharged for gas. Are paranoia and suspicion characteristic of dementia?
- Norman retains his wit and his sense of humor throughout the film. Is this a realistic portrayal of early dementia?
- At one point in the film, Norman forgets to put the screen in front of the fireplace, and the house almost catches on fire. If someone like Norman didn't have a wife, would you recommend that he be placed in a nursing home, or does he retain sufficient cognitive ability to manage on his own?
- If Norman Thayer had written a will shortly before this 80th birthday disinheriting his daughter, would you testify that he had sufficient cognitive ability to make decisions of this sort?
- What is a scientific name for a verbal slip such as "that's frantastic?"
- How can you explain how Norman can forget what he is doing in the middle of a phone call and yet still recall lectures he used to give at the University of Pennsylvania?
- Norman has a nonspecific family history of what appears to be dementia. How does this affect his risk for the disease?
- What features in Norman Thayer's presentation and history help you rule out a diagnosis of clinical depression?

PATIENT EVALUATION

Patient's stated reason for coming: This patient reports, "There is absolutely nothing wrong with me, and I don't need to be here." The patient was brought in for the examination by his wife, who reports a progressive history of memory loss, confusion, and personality change in her husband.

History of the present illness: Mr. Norman Thayer is a 79-year-old retired college professor who spends each summer in his vacation home on the east side of Golden Pond. On his most recent visit, he has become disoriented, and he became lost once while walking to the mailbox. His wife reports that her husband exhibits marked short-term memory loss, episodic periods of confusion, and heightened irritability. These changes have become progressively worse over the past two years.

Past psychiatric illness, treatment, and outcomes: There is no history of psychiatric illness or head injury.

Medical history: There is mild hearing loss bilaterally. The patient has a history of mild to moderate hypertension, which he treats with diuretics. He takes no other medications. Mr. Thayer reports that he has an aunt who was hospitalized for 10 years at a state institution after "a nervous breakdown." Mr. Thayer's father suffered marked cognitive deterioration and died at the age of 68 from "hardening of the arteries."

Psychosocial history: Mr. Thayer retired at the age of 65, after spending 35 years as a professor of economics at the University of Pennsylvania. He was a popular and successful teacher. He has been married to the same woman, Ethel Thayer, for 40 years. He is the father of an apparently estranged daughter, Chelsea Thayer Wayne, who currently lives on the West Coast.

Drug and alcohol history: Mr. Thayer is a moderate social drinker who has a single glass of wine with dinner each evening on the recommendation of his physician. There is no significant history of drug or alcohol abuse.

Behavioral observations: The patient seemed hostile and guarded. It was clear he resented his wife's concerns and he feels they are unjustified. He minimizes her concerns and denies any change in his cognitive ability, personality, or behavior.

Mental status examination: Mr. Thayer was on time for the examination and appeared well groomed. One button on his shirt was unbuttoned. He was suspicious and guarded during the evaluation. He frequently mumbled phrases such as "I don't see what this has to do with anything." His affect was frequently angry, and he was agitated at various points in the examination. There was no evidence of loose associations or flight of ideas. There was no evidence of hallucinations or delusions. There was no significant suicidal or homicidal ideation present, although Mr. Thayer did remark at one point, "When you get old you're not good for anybody or anything and you might as well be dead."

Mr. Thayer was oriented to place and person, but he identified the day as Wednesday instead of Thursday. He could identify the month and year but not the date, saying, "I guess it is around the 13th," when in fact it was the 27th. He appears to lack insight into the nature of his memory problems, and he consistently denies any cognitive loss (reporting, "I could still teach macroeconomics, but they won't let me because I'm too damn old").

The patient is able to recall three out of three objects immediately but only one out of the three after a brief interruption. Despite his extensive education, he became confused when completing serial sevens and refused to continue the series, claiming "this is stupid." There is no dysnomia, and he is able to repeat both simple and complex phrases. He is able to follow both verbal and written commands. He is able to write simple sentences, but he became confused when reproducing intersecting pentagons, and he was unable to copy a Greek cross. Mr. Thayer scored 21 on the *Mini Mental Status Examination*, and this score suggests an early dementia may be present.

Functional Assessment: Mr. Thayer is intelligent, highly educated, and very verbal. He has a good (albeit often sardonic) sense of humor. He enjoys fishing and reading. He is committed to his wife, and they appear to have a warm and loving relationship. Mr. Thayer is estranged from his daughter, his only child, and he claims that he has not seen her for several years. He has no other children or grandchildren.

Strengths: Mr. Thayer's good verbal intelligence will serve him well. His wife reports that their daughter is planning to visit them this summer at the lake. His wife appears to be competent and capable. She sets appropriate limits for her husband and ignores his ill temper.

Diagnosis: R/O 290.0 Dementia of the Alzheimer's type with late onset, uncomplicated.

Treatment plan: Refer for a complete neuropsychological evaluation. Follow-up in three months after the results of the neuropsychological evaluation become available. Instruct Mrs. Thayer to come back to the clinic if her husband's behavior becomes markedly erratic, irrational, or seemingly dangerous to her or himself.

Prognosis: Guarded.

DEMENTIA

The term **dementia** refers to a collection of brain disorders characterized by memory disturbance, impaired judgment, and personality change. Insidious onset and gradual deterioration of cognitive abilities characterize the dementias. Although some authorities believe the term should be applied only to those conditions that are nonreversible, the more common practice (and that followed by *DSM-IV*) is to use the term descriptively, without any implications for prognosis. Hence, brain dysfunctions relating from causes as diverse as nutritional deficiencies and Cushing's syndrome can be diagnosed as dementias. After the age of 65, about one person in six will be sufficiently symptomatic to justify the diagnosis of dementia.

Some of the more common forms of dementia result from multiple infarctions in the brain (strokes), infections (e.g., meningitis, encephalitis, and syphilis), and exposure to toxins (alcohol, drugs, or heavy metals). However, the single leading cause is **Alzheimer's disease,** responsible for about half of all cases of dementia. Alzheimer's is a public health problem of enormous dimensions, and one that is becoming an ever-bigger problem as the average life span across the world steadily increases.

The brains of patients with Alzheimer's disease are demonstrably different from those of age-matched controls, and they contain **senile plaques** and **neurofibrillary tangles.** Although some neuronal loss is universal with aging, the brain of the Alzheimer's patient shrinks at a more rapid rate.

Psychological tests are often the best indicators of the presence of Alzheimer's disease, especially in the early stages, as these patients will often maintain excellent social skills and use these skills to disguise the marked problems they develop with their memory. Other early signs of developing Alzheimer's disease include diffuse generalized anxiety and inappropriate social behavior.

Recent studies have demonstrated that people who carry two copies of a gene called **apo E-4** are at high risk for Alzheimer's, but not everyone who has the gene develops Alzheimer's. Those carriers who do develop the disease have excessive production of free radicals. When carriers of the apo E-4 gene who had no symptoms of Alzheimer's were given PET scans, these scans revealed abnormally low energy levels in the areas of the brain affected by Alzheimer's. Some scientists have suggested that taking very high doses of vitamin E can delay the progression of Alzheimer's disease.

Pick's disease is an illness that is somewhat less common than Alzheimer's. Alzheimer's tends to differentially affect the parietal lobes, while Pick's disease is more likely to affect the frontal and anterior temporal lobes. The defining characteristic of Pick's disease is loss of inhibition and social skill. These patients are less likely than Alzheimer's patients to have impaired visuospatial abilities, but they are more prone to become argumentative and sexually inappropriate, presumably because of the involvement of the frontal lobes.

Some patients with Pick's disease will develop a rare disorder called **Kluver-Bucy syndrome.** This syndrome, first demonstrated in monkeys with portions of their brain removed, involves peculiar behaviors such as putting random objects in the mouth, swallowing things indiscriminately, and openly masturbating or attempting to have sex with inappropriate objects.

One of the most important tasks confronting clinicians working with older patients is the often-difficult discrimination between dementia and **clinical depression.** Appropriate diagnosis is critical in these cases, so that a depressed patient will not go untreated because he or she is inappropriately believed to be suffering from Alzheimer's disease. In the majority of cases, the two disorders will present in ways that are different enough for the alert clinician to distinguish between them. For example, Alzheimer's has a more insidious onset, whereas depression may come on more rapidly. The patient with Alzheimer's will have genuine cognitive deficits and experience difficulty with learning new tasks; the depressed patient will lack motivation and may have trouble concentrating but should be able to learn adequately, although slowly. The depressed patient is also more likely to experience loss of appetite and a fluctuating course, and he or she is far more likely to have a history of affective illness. In addition, depressed patients tend to acknowledge and sometimes even exaggerate their problems. In contrast, patients with Alzheimer's are far more likely to cover up their difficulties, deny that they are having problems, and may have euphoria. Finally, in the later stages of the illness, patients with true dementias will often have abnormal CAT scans and EEGs.

Current research into the genetics of Alzheimer's disease is focusing on the special role of the 21st chromosome. At the present time, there is no clear treatment available, but exciting advances in our understanding of the genetic basis of the disorder holds some promise for the future.

DEMENTIAS, DELIRIUM, AMNESIA, AND OTHER COGNITIVE DISORDERS

All psychological disorders ultimately involve the brain. However, when the connection between brain dysfunction and abnormal behavior is especially obvious, the behavior is often referred to as an organic mental disorder, or **organic brain syndrome** (OBS). Because the term *organic mental disorder,* used in *DSM-III,* falsely implies that other mental disorders are not organically based (i.e., the direct result of brain dysfunction, no matter how poorly understood), the *DSM-IV* has dropped the use of the term *organic* and simply classifies what used to be called organic mental disorders into three categories: (1) delirium, dementia, amnestic, and other cognitive disorders, (2) mental disorders due to a general medical condition, and (3) substance-related disorders.

Dementia Due to Head Trauma

Although not given a separate rubric in the *DSM-IV* nomenclature, it is common to see references to **dementia pugilistica** (punch-drunk syndrome) in the professional literature and in the medical charts of aging boxers. These patients, after a lifetime of repeated blows to the head (with concomitant brain injuries), often develop difficulty with movement and a tremor similar to that found in **Parkinson's disease.** They develop slurred speech and diminished mental agility, and they become especially sensitive to the effects of alcohol. Dramatic mood swings (referred to as **emotional lability**) are common, and these individuals are quick to become angry, engage in fights, and become paranoid. *Many of these symptoms can be seen in De Niro's portrayal of Jake LaMotta in* Raging Bull *(1980).*

A study reported in the *Journal of the American Medical Association* (Casson et al., 1984) found that 87 percent of the professional boxers exhibited definite signs of brain damage when they were assessed with sophisticated evaluation techniques. Neuropsychological tests proved to be more sensitive than imaging techniques or electroencephalography, and short-term memory was the cognitive ability most dramatically affected.

The American Medical Association and other professional organizations have called for the elimination of professional boxing as an organized sport. Indeed, it is hard to find redeeming social value in a sport in which the express purpose is to damage the brain of an opponent. However, boxing remains a popular American pastime, and this popularity is reflected in films *such as The Great White Hope* (1970), *The Harder They Fall* (1956), *The Joe Louis Story* (1953), *Kid Galahad* (1937/1962), *On the Waterfront* (1954), *Requiem for a Heavyweight* (1962), the ever popular *Rocky* films (1976, 1979, 1982, 1985, 1990), and many others.

> "You don't understand! I could've had class. I could've been a contender. I could've been somebody, instead of a bum, which is what I am." *On the Waterfront* (1954)

Other Head Injuries

When visualizing brain injuries, it is useful to remember that the cranium is a closed, solid container and the brain is soft and consists of a jelly-like substance that moves inside the skull when the head is struck. The brain is actually quite fragile, albeit well protected by the skull and meninges (the three layers of protective covering that are found between the skull and brain).

Head injuries are usually classified as **concussions, contusions,** or **open-head injuries.** Concussions occur when the brain is jarred, and amnesia and loss of consciousness are common consequences. Impaired memory and concentration, headaches, fatigue, anxiety, dizziness, and irritability characterize the postconcussion syndrome.

Contusions occur when the brain is actually bruised, most often as a result of an impact between the brain and the skull. Contusions produce more serious neurological consequences than concussions and can result in death. Contusions are characterized as **coup injuries** if the damage is at the site of impact (e.g., at the point where a baseball bat hits the skull). **Contrecoup injuries** occur opposite the point of impact. They most often result from acceleration injuries (such as occur when a moving head hits a stationary steering wheel).

Open-head injuries occur when the skull is hit with sufficient force to open it and expose the underlying neural tissue. Open-head injuries from missile wounds are common in wartime, and much of what we know about the organization of the brain is the result of examination of soldiers injured in battle.

Raging Bull

Raging Bull is a Martin Scorsese film that was released in 1980. It stars Robert De Niro, Cathy Moriarty, and Joe Pesci (who later went on to star in *My Cousin Vinny*). Many critics have included *Raging Bull* in their lists of the top films of the 1980s, and De Niro won an Academy Award for Best Actor for his portrayal of prizefighter Jake LaMotta.

This engrossing drama portrays the life of LaMotta, a prizefighter confronted with the need to find purpose and meaning in life once he leaves the ring. LaMotta's marriage fails, his wife takes their children with her, sexual jealousy drives a wedge between him and his brother, and he is forced to mutilate and then hock the jewels in the belt he received for winning the world middleweight championship. The viewer is never certain whether LaMotta is a pathetic or a heroic figure, but the film ends with a reconciliation between the two brothers and with the protagonist successfully performing a Broadway reading of the works of several notable authors. The recitation of one of Marlon Brando's monologues from *On the Waterfront* (a 1954 Elia Kazan film about the life of a down and out prizefighter) is Scorsese's way of paying homage to another great filmmaker and provides a dramatic conclusion for the film.

Raging Bull is replete with examples of LaMotta's poor judgment. Two especially vivid examples are his failure to defend himself in the final round of a fight with Sugar Ray Robinson and his decision to let two 14-year-old girls into his nightclub after each girl kisses him. Impaired judgment is common in aging prizefighters. *It also is likely that LaMotta's history of repeated blows to the head (concussions) contributed to his sexual jealousy and paranoia and was responsible for the slurred speech he exhibits in the film as he ages.*

Additional Questions for Class Discussion *(Raging Bull)*

- What actually happens to the brain of a fighter when he is "knocked out"?
- The American Academy of Neurology has supported a ban on professional boxing since 1983. Do you agree with this position?
- What are the characteristic features of chronic traumatic encephalopathy? What features of De Niro's presentation of Jake LaMotta suggest the disorder is present?
- Is the protective headgear used by amateur boxers effective in protecting against head injuries?
- In the film, LaMotta as an old man becomes sexually involved with two young girls. Is this an example of impaired judgment?
- LaMotta is insanely jealous of his second wife, and he becomes convinced she is having multiple affairs. Is this paranoia the result of personality or cerebral impairment?
- What is the "Whore - Madonna" complex? How is it illustrated in the life of Jake LaMotta?

Brain Tumors

Aberrant behavior and abnormal sensations and perception can result from brain tumors **(neoplasms)**. The specific behaviors that result will vary across individuals as a function of lesion site, size, type, and rate of growth. In addition, an individual's premorbid personality will in part determine how he or she reacts to a brain tumor. Huge lesions in the "silent" areas of the neocortex (e.g., the right frontal lobe) may produce minimal symptoms, whereas very small lesions can have devastating or deadly consequences if they are located in strategic areas in the brain.

Brain tumors often, but not always, result in headaches and seizures. However, less than one out of a thousand people who have headaches will be found to also have a brain tumor. Headaches associated with cerebral lesions tend to be worse in the early morning and are sometimes associated with projectile vomiting.

Although imaging techniques such as **computerized tomography** and **nuclear magnetic resonance** (NMR) can rule out the presence of tumors in patients with headaches or other nonspecific symptoms, there is little medical justification for obtaining these high-priced tests as a substitute for the clinical judgment of the physician. One of the critical questions facing society is whether or not we can continue to pay for new technologies that provide exquisite diagnostic information, but at an ever increasing cost.

About half of all patients with brain tumors first complain of psychiatric or behavioral symptoms, especially when the tumor involves the frontal or temporal lobes. Hallucinations, depression, apathy, euphoria, social impropriety, and personality change can all result from brain lesions. When hallucinations occur, they are more likely to be visual or olfactory; they are not typically as specific or as concrete as those present in schizophrenia.

Tumors that arise in the brain itself (or in the meninges) are called primary tumors. Tumors that originate in different parts of the body, most commonly the breast or lungs, and spread to the brain and other organs are called secondary, or **metastatic, tumors**. About one in five cancer patients will develop cerebral lesions as a result of metastasis.

Meningiomas, tumors that develop in the meningial layer between the brain and spinal cord, are found primarily in adults, and they tend to be slow growing. **Gliomas** are tumors that develop from rapid proliferation of cells that initially originate in the glia cells of the brain. Glia means glue, and glia cells form a supportive network for the neurons of the brain. About half of all brain tumors are gliomas, and the prognosis for these patients is quite poor. **Astrocytomas,** another form of brain tumor that arises from a particular type of brain cell, occur in children as well as adults and are often benign.

Patients who have **frontal lobe lesions** are likely to display personality changes. They may be passive, apathetic, depressed, and slow to respond. In contrast, frontal lobe lesions can result in irritability and problems with anger control. Patients with lesions affecting the motor strip (along the rear external border of the frontal lobe) will have motor functions affected.

Temporal lobe tumors are often misdiagnosed as psychiatric disorders, and this is especially likely to occur in those cases that result in **psychomotor seizures** (more properly referred to by the technical term "partial seizures with complex symptomatology"). These tumors can produce hallucinations, stereotyped movements, feelings of unreality, and intense fear. Reports of **déjà vu** (feeling you are reexperiencing a former experience) and **jamais vu** (feeling that familiar settings and situations are now very strange) are common with temporal lobe tumors.

Parietal lobe lesions are less likely to produce symptoms that mimic schizophrenia or depression, but patients with partial lobe disorders often report abnormal sensory experiences (e.g., smelling burning rubber), and they may have difficulty with simple copying tasks. **Anosognosia** (denial of illness) is most likely to result when the parietal lobes are affected. **Occipital lobe tumors** produce relatively few psychological symptoms, but these lesions may result in visual field defects.

Brain tumors can sometimes cause inexplicable violence or aberrant behavior that is totally inconsistent with an individual's history. For example, in 1966, a University of Texas college student, Charles Whitman, killed his wife, his mother, and 14 innocent people with a high-powered rifle from a tower on the university campus. An autopsy subsequently revealed that Whitman had a malignant brain tumor. In a note written the night before his death, Whitman wrote

> I don't really understand myself these days. . . . It requires a tremendous mental effort to concentrate. . . . I have had some tremendous headaches in the past and have consumed two large bottles of Excedrin in the past three months.

Whitman had been to the University Health Center several months earlier, but the possibility of neurological disease had not been seriously considered. Most therapists can relate stories of patients seeking psychological help who later turned out to have neurological disorders. (Likewise, internists and family practice physicians see patients daily who complain of physical symptoms that have their roots in psychological distress.)

Cerebrovascular Disease

A **cerebrovascular accident** (CVA), more commonly known as a stroke, occurs when there is an inadequate supply of blood and oxygen for the brain. Strokes are characterized by sudden onset and are often fatal. Cerebrovascular disease is currently the third leading cause of death in the United States, following heart disease and cancer. Twenty individuals will experience cerebrovascular accidents for every one who develops a brain tumor.

Infarctions occur when arterial blood flow is blocked. This can occur when a piece of fat or cholesterol becomes lodged in a vessel. This sudden blockage of blood flow is called an **embolus.** Blood flow can also be impeded by the gradual buildup of **atherosclerotic plaque** along the inside of a vessel, resulting in a **thrombus.**

Vessels sometimes burst, and the resulting cerebral hemorrhage can be life-threatening. Only about 20 percent of patients survive a cerebral hemorrhage.

The behavioral effects of a cerebrovascular accident will depend on the vessels affected. The majority of strokes affect the middle cerebral artery, which supplies blood to the lateral portions of the brain. Strokes involving the middle cerebral artery result in motor and sensory impairment on the **contralateral** (opposite) side of the body, with the arm and face more affected than the leg. In contrast, strokes that affect the anterior cerebral artery often produce contralateral weakness in the leg while sparing the arm and face. Urinary incontinence and impaired cognition are other common symptoms of strokes involving the anterior cerebral artery.

The posterior cerebral artery supplies the medial portions of the back of the brain. Strokes involving this vessel result in visual field disturbances, problems with reading, and, in some cases, memory disturbance (when there is damage to one or both of the temporal lobes). Bilateral infarctions in the occipital lobes can result in a fascinating clinical syndrome referred to as **Anton's syndrome.** Patients with Anton's syndrome are blind but do not realize they have lost their sight. When questioned, they will supply reasonable (but wrong) answers to questions such as "What color is the tie I am wearing today?"

An **aneurysm** occurs when part of a vessel "balloons" and threatens to burst. Signs of a ruptured aneurysm include painful headaches, nausea, and vomiting.

Multi-infarct dementia results from successive strokes that may individually be of little consequence but which, in toto, result in significant cerebral impairment. Multi-infarct dementia must be ruled out whenever the clinician is evaluating a patient suspected of having Alzheimer's disease. This disorder, which is more common in women, is especially likely when a patient has a history of hypertension.

Transient ischemic attacks (TIAs) are "ministrokes" that last for less than 24 hours. Many patients who experience TIAs will go on to have actual strokes. Other risk factors for cerebrovascular accidents include diabetes, heart disease, and the use of oral contraceptives in women who also smoke. The patient experiencing a TIA will become disoriented, confused, and sometimes amnestic.

Epilepsy

People with **epilepsy** experience uncontrollable attacks of abnormal neuronal activity. These brain "storms" can result from a variety of causes, and it is critical for the student to remember that epilepsy is a *symptom* of a variety of brain disorders, not a disease in itself.

Head trauma is the most common cause of epilepsy; and about half of all penetrating head wounds will result in seizures. If the cause of seizures is not established, an individual is said to have **idiopathic epilepsy.**

About 1 person in 200 hundred in the United States has epilepsy, and the prevalence of epilepsy is somewhat higher for men than for women, possibly due to the more frequent occurrence of head trauma in boys and men.

Prodromal symptoms and auras often precede seizures. **Prodromal symptoms** are "feelings" that a seizure is about to occur and usually appear several days before the seizure itself. In contrast, an **aura** signals the imminent arrival of a seizure and occurs only minutes before the seizure itself. Auras are often auditory or gustatory sensations.

Jacksonian seizures occur when there is a motoric response, such as twitching or jerking, that is confined to one side of the body. A "Jacksonian march" results when minor motor movements in a finger or toe become more exaggerated and spread to other parts of the body on the affected side. If the initially isolated abnormal brain activity spreads to the other hemisphere, the entire body may stiffen or jerk; this attack is referred to as a *grand mal* seizure. Grand mal seizures typically last from two to five minutes and are sometimes referred to as **tonic-clonic** seizures because of their alternating periods of rigidity and jerking.

In contrast, **petit mal seizures** (absence seizures), which are relatively common in young children, do not result in falling, jerking, or loss of muscle tone. The child experiencing a petit mal seizure will be, for a very brief period (usually two to ten seconds), totally unresponsive to the external environment. Although these seizures only last for a few seconds, often there will be multiple occurrences in a short period of time. There are characteristic **electroencephalographic** (EEG) changes that help the pediatric neurologist diagnose petit mal epilepsy.

Complex partial seizures (also referred to by the older terms *psychomotor* or *temporal lobe seizures*) are of considerable interest to anyone working in the field of mental health, because these disorders often mimic psychiatric diseases. The patient with complex partial seizures may hallucinate, engage in stereotyped motor behavior, experience feelings of unreality, or become extremely anxious. The sensations of déjà vu and jamais vu are often reported. (Déjà vu refers to the feeling that one is reliving a past experience; jamais vu refers to the sensation that ordinary, everyday events and settings are unreal or peculiar.) The EEG is typically found to be normal in these patients, and about one in five will experience auditory or visual hallucinations. Unlike the hallucinations of the schizophrenic patient, however, auditory hallucinations in the patient with a complex partial seizure will be localized within the head (rather than from an external source); and they will rarely contain bizarre, threatening, or accusatory material.

Defense attorneys have sometimes argued that their client's misbehavior resulted from a complex partial seizure. For example, Jack Ruby's attorneys argued that Ruby was experiencing a seizure when he killed Lee Harvey Oswald. Likewise, one young man presented with an uncontrollable urge to wander from his home each evening. The likelihood of this being a manifestation of complex partial seizures would have been dramatically greater if the behavior had not been sequential, timed, and goal-directed. The teenage boy somehow managed to target and time his "aimless behavior" so that it would take him to the window of the widow who lived next door about the time she was undressing for bed each evening.

Patients who have multiple grand mal seizures sometimes will not not be able to regain consciousness between seizure episodes. This phenomenon, called **status epilepticus,** is a serious medical condition that will be experienced by as many as 1 in 20 patients with epilepsy.

> One of the world's leading experts on epilepsy was fond of relating a story about a patient who had a genuine seizure disorder that could be documented with electroencephalography. However, she only seized when she heard Mahalia Jackson singing "My Heart Has a Life of Its Own." The song could be sung by anyone else, and the patient wouldn't seize. Likewise, she could listen to Mahalia Jackson sing anything else, and she wouldn't experience seizures.
>
> After several weeks in the hospital, someone asked the patient what was so special about Mahalia Jackson singing "My Heart Has a Life of Its Own."
>
> "Didn't you know?" she replied. "That was the song they played at my mother's funeral as her casket was being lowered into her grave."

Epilepsy is referred to as a "seizure disorder" because it was once believed that people with epilepsy had in fact been "seized" by the devil. There is convincing evidence that at least some of the so-called witches burned at the stake by religious zealots were in fact women with uncontrolled epilepsy. (The phenomenon of labeling and burning witches is explored in the 1943 Danish film *Days of Wrath*.)

Delirium

Delirium refers to the rapid onset of confusion and disorganized thinking and is often characterized by rambling, incoherent, or inappropriate speech. Emotions are often inappropriate as well; for example, the delirious individual may be extremely anxious or euphoric in situations in which these reactions would be inappropriate. Delirium can also cause illusions, hallucinations, or misinterpretations of sensory stimuli; for example, a doctor's look of concern may be perceived as extreme anger by the delirious patient.

Delirium most often (but not always) results from a disturbance of the metabolism of the brain, and causes can include infections, insufficient oxygen levels, ionic imbalances, vitamin deficiencies, and kidney disease. One of the most common causes of delirium is either acute intoxication with — or withdrawal from

> There was Pap looking wild, and skipping around every which way and yelling about snakes. He said they was crawling up his legs, and then he would give a jump and scream, and say one had bit him on the cheek — but I couldn't see no snakes. He started running round and round the cabin, hollering, "Take him off, take him off; he's biting me on the neck." I never seen a man look so wild in the eyes. . . . Then he went down on all fours and crawled off, begging them to let him alone, and he rolled up in his blanket and wallowed in under the old pine table, still a-begging; and then he went to crying.
> Mark Twain, *Huckleberry Finn*

— drugs. *Delirium tremens* is a common problem for alcoholics with a history of problem drinking. Patients experiencing the **"DTs"** become disoriented, hallucinate, and display marked tremors. Other symptoms may include intense fear, fevers, and sweating. *The intensity of delirium tremens is vividly portrayed in Billy Wilder's 1945 film* The Lost Weekend.

Amnesia

Patients with amnesia display marked impairment of short-term memory with relatively intact long-term memory and preserved intellectual functioning. In its most extreme form, the disorder results in the total inability to learn new information. A patient with an amnestic syndrome will be unable to recall the doctor's name, no matter how many times it is presented; simple learning tasks such as recalling the names of four objects become virtually impossible. The patient will be able to *repeat* the four items, suggesting intact understanding of the task and good receptive and expressive language skills; however, after dozens of trials the patient will still be unable to recall the four items from memory.

Patients with amnestic syndromes will sometimes **confabulate** and present detailed and plausible explanations for their obvious inability to acquire new information. The patient who can't remember four numbers for more than a few seconds will explain that he was never any good at math, and the patient in a psychiatric hospital may say he is there because of problems with his kidneys. One of our patients with an amnestic syndrome was asked four times during a one-hour, taped interview what he had had for breakfast that morning. The patient responded by supplying four different "menus" during the interview, each equally plausible. Each time, he had absolutely no recollection of being asked this question earlier in the interview.

One of the most commonly encountered amnestic syndromes is **Wernicke-Korsakoff syndrome.** Patients with this disorder have great difficulty with new learning, fail to recall recent experiences, exhibit gait disturbances secondary to cerebellar dysfunction, and display a variety of ocular disturbances, including impaired conjugate gaze. This condition is found in older alcoholics after many years of substituting the nutritionally empty calories of alcohol for the protein, carbohydrates, vitamins, and fat found in a normal diet. The disorder is particularly related to deficiencies in thiamin (B_1), and some public health experts have recommended "enriching" spirits with vitamins in the same way we enrich bread. Although this could be done with minimal cost, the distillers have not been enthusiastic about this procedure, despite its potential benefit to alcoholics.

Examinations of the brains of alcoholics who develop Wernicke-Korsakoff's syndrome typically reveal damage to the hypothalamus, mamillary bodies, pons, and cerebellum. Aggressive treatment of the disorder with intravenous thiamin will produce improvement in some patients, but many others have sustained permanent damage and never recover.

THE PORTRAYAL OF COGNITIVE DISORDERS IN FILMS

Regarding Henry (1991) is a Mike Nichols film staring Harrison Ford as a high-powered attorney who suffers a major traumatic head injury. After coming out of a coma, he discovers that his life can never be the same. There are interesting scenes in a rehabilitation hospital, and the viewer gets some sense for the sequelae of a head injury. However, *the film is flawed by an unrealistic presentation of the deficits following head injury and by the simplistic assumption that someone's personality could be improved by a head injury.*

Surprisingly few films have focused on Alzheimer's disease. One of the best of these is a made-for-TV movie *Do You Remember Love?* (1985), in which Joanne Woodward plays a college professor who develops the devastating disease. Woodward's portrayal is sensitive and moving. There is also a memorable scene between Jane Fonda's character and her mother in *Agnes of God* (1985). Fonda plays a psychiatrist who goes to visit her mother in a nursing home. The scene opens with the mother watching a children's cartoon program. The disoriented mother gets Fonda confused with her younger sister, who had died years earlier in a convent. Finally, Jessica Tandy very convincingly portrays an old woman who eventually develops Alzheimer's disease and is placed in a nursing home in *Driving Miss Daisy* (1989). Tandy won an Academy Award for her performance in this film. Actress Rita Hayworth actually died from Alzheimer's disease in 1986; she displayed symptoms of the disease the last six years of her life.

In John Steinbeck's novel *The Grapes of Wrath,* Grandpa Joad dies from a stroke. We do not actually see the old man die in John Ford's 1940 film adaptation, but there is a memorable scene in which his relatives bury him alongside the road because they are too poor to do anything else. Henry Fonda writes a short, poignant note to leave at the grave: "This here is William James Joad, died of a stroke, old, old man. His folks buried him because they got no money to pay for funerals. Nobody kilt him. Just a stroke and he died."

David Lynch's *Blue Velvet* (1986) opens with a man watering his yard. As we watch, he has a stroke and falls to the ground. His dog comes over and proceeds to drink out of the hose, and at this point the viewer becomes aware that this will not be an ordinary movie.

A number of films have portrayed characters with amnesia, including *Anastasia* (1956), *Mirage* (1955), *Spellbound* (1945), and *Desperately Seeking Susan* (1985). The 1983 film *The Return of Martin Guerre* (and the more contemporary film *Shenandoah*) are two movies that creatively explore the limits of memory and the extent to which it can be influenced by motivation and need.

In *Awakenings* (1990) we see a nice example of what would now be diagnosed as a catatonic disorder due to a general medical condition (Parkinson's disease). The film is based on the experience of neurologist Oliver Sacks, best known as the author of *The Man Who Mistook His Wife for a Hat*. Narcolepsy, a devastating sleep disorder in which the victim cannot resist falling asleep and experiencing a deep cataplexy, is seen in the character River Phoenix plays in *My Own Private Idaho* (1991).

Critical Thinking Questions

- How could a psychologist distinguish between genuine amnesia and malingering?
- Do the characters in *The Return of Martin Guerre* and *Shenandoah* display genuine amnesia?
- Should people who have seizure disorders that are controlled by medication be allowed to drive?
- Is society obligated to provide care for old people who have dementias that dramatically limit the quality of their lives? What is the alternative?
- How will the aging of the baby boomers affect society? Is it possible to estimate how many people will develop Alzheimer's disease as the baby boom generation ages?
- Are you familiar with the advocacy efforts of Christopher Reeve? What was the cause of Reeve's own injury?
- Should helmets be mandatory for bicycle riders and motorcyclists?
- Would you want to know if you carried the apo E-4 gene?
- Would it be ethical for a health insurance company to test for the apo E-4 gene and refuse coverage to people who had it?

Chapter 11

Disorders of Childhood and Adolescence

> *Alexander, why have you told your teacher that I*
> *sold you to a traveling circus . . . to be a trained acrobat*
> *with a gypsy called Tamara?*
> Alexander's mother responds to a query in *Fanny and Alexander*

Questions to Consider While Watching *Fanny and Alexander*

- Alexander's stepfather uses spanking to punish the boy for lying. Is spanking justified in this case? Is it ever an appropriate way to punish a child?
- At various points, Alexander sees and talks to his deceased father. Does the film present these as hallucinations or merely as an example of an overactive imagination?
- Fanny and Alexander share a bedroom. At what point should opposite-sex children stop sharing a room?
- Alexander responds to the stress in his life by fabricating "tall tales." At what point would this behavior be considered pathological?

PATIENT EVALUATION

Alexander Ekdahl is a 10-year-old boy who is referred by his stepfather for an evaluation for "pathological lying."

History of the present illness: Alexander's father died of a heart attack approximately one year ago. His mother has recently remarried an Episcopal bishop. Bishop Vergerus reports that his stepson has been lying to his mother and his school teachers. For example, Alexander is reported to have recently told a teacher that his parents had sold him to a travelling circus.

Past psychiatric illness, treatment, and outcomes: There is no significant psychiatric history.

Medical history: Insignificant.

Psychosocial history: This 10-year-old boy appears to have a normal developmental history. He reports being quite happy prior to his father's death. He acknowledges hating his stepfather, a man he claims abuses his mother. Alexander has a close and significant relationship with his younger sister, Fanny. He has few friends other than his sister. He reports being frequently spanked by his stepfather.

Drug and alcohol history: Not applicable.

Behavioral observations: Alexander was appropriately groomed and dressed for the evaluation. He is a quiet child who volunteered little information. At one point during the interview, he wept as he described his relationship with his stepfather. Referring to his stepfather, he reported "He's a bastard." Alexander is quite unhappy living in the bishop's home and deeply resents the bishop's dominating sister and mother. Alexander fidgeted throughout much of the evaluation.

Mental status examination: A formal mental status exam was not conducted. However, Alexander appears to be a very bright child. He is articulate and verbal. His vocabulary is quite impressive for a 10-year-old boy. Alexander reports that he gets good grades in school, and he is obviously a very intelligent child.

Functional assessment: This 10-year-old boy is quiet, withdrawn, and reclusive. However, he appears to have adequate interpersonal skills. He appears to be supported by a loving relationship with his sister and his mother. All of his problems appear to be related to his difficulty with his stepfather and his new environment.

Strengths: Alexander is an intelligent and well-developed child with an active imagination. There is no evidence of significant psychopathology in this child.

Diagnosis: V61.20 Parent Child Relational Problem.

Treatment plan: Despite Bishop Vergerus' concerns, there is no evidence of oppositional defiant disorder. I intend to see this family for approximately five sessions, which will be devoted to developing more effective means of communication between the father and son. I will also discourage the father from continuing to spank the child and will work with the father to respond in more appropriate ways to the relatively minor transgressions of his son.

Prognosis: Good.

FANNY AND ALEXANDER

Fanny and Alexander, an Academy Award winner for Best Foreign Film, is an excellent 1982 Swedish movie starring Permilla Allwin as Fanny and Bertil Guve as Alexander. Touted as one of Ingmar Bergman's finest, the film takes place in a Swedish provincial town in the early 1900s and centers on the experiences of two children, Fanny and Alexander, who are growing up within a large, happy extended family. The adult family members own and operate a local theater. Fanny and Alexander are included in the theater activities and festivities and very much enjoy their family roles. Their father dies and their mother, Emilie, remarries. Their new stepfather is a stern, authoritarian clergyman, Bishop Vergerus, who is absolutely incapable of understanding the feelings of others.

Fanny and Alexander move from a relaxed, expensive, comfortable environment to their stepfather's austere, aesthetic, drab home, which has bars on the windows and is like a prison to its new inhabitants. Within their new home, the children are physically and mentally abused. Punishment for minor infractions is severe and unrelenting. Food is withheld, the children are savagely beaten, and there is gradual erosion of self-esteem.

Within a short period, the children's mother realizes that she has made a mistake. Unfortunately, she is pregnant. Fanny and Alexander manage to escape to the home of an old

Jewish antique dealer (a friend of their grandmother), whose life still has room for mysticism and magic of an earlier time. The antique dealer's strange nephew is secluded within his home.

Throughout the movie, Alexander has unusual experiences. He periodically has visits from his father's ghost. The viewer is given the impression that his father is watching over him throughout the movie. Alexander's imagination causes a statue to take on a lifelike image and move. He also believes that he has magical powers, and, at the end of the movie, Alexander believes that he willed the house fire that caused his stepfather's death.

CHILD MENTAL HEALTH

The psychiatric problems of children are not as easily diagnosed as those of adults. The symptoms of the illnesses are difficult to distinguish from normal growth and development experiences. For example, an imaginary friend of a 4-year-old is normal, but, for an adolescent, an invisible friend would be considered a psychotic hallucination. In the film *Fanny and Alexander,* the "unusual" experiences of Alexander could easily be interpreted as either the beginning of a psychotic process or an overactive imagination of a child under stress. It is not unusual for people to report visits from the dead. Children often believe that they have caused tragic events because they were wishing them to happen.

Children who receive mental health treatment usually fall in one of the following categories:

1. Children whose behavior does not conform to social norms and is troublesome to others (disruptive behaviors or conduct disorders)
2. Children who experience repeated and excessive depression, anxiety, or states of personal distress
3. Children whose cognitive or neuromotor development is not proceeding normally (developmental disorders) (Shaffer, 1989)

In the film, behavior that is acceptable in Fanny and Alexander's parents' home becomes troublesome in their new stepfather's home. The children's behavior does not change, but the definition of "normal child behavior" does. Once they move into a restrictive environment, they adapt their behavior to the new situation. They become secretive, rebellious, and belligerent. Within the context of their new environment, these behaviors are adaptive, not symptoms of mental illnesses. Their successful plan to escape is not a typical "runaway" situation that brings a child to the attention of mental health providers. Again, this behavior makes sense within the context of their new home. As a matter of fact, the viewer is soon "rooting" for the children's escape. Once they are out of the oppressive home environment, their normal behavior returns.

If the children had been unable to escape from their new home, they may have become anxious or depressed to the point of it interfering in their daily activities. The viewer gets a glimpse of a beginning of a possible depressive and anxiety disorder when Alexander gets in trouble at school. His school problems revolve around not telling the truth. His stepfather severely disciplines him for making up the story about the bishop causing the deaths of his first wife and their two daughters as if he were a "bad" child rather than investigating the meaning of Alexander's remarks.

THE REPRESENTATION OF CHILDHOOD DISORDERS IN FILM

Some of the most powerful and poignant films in the history of the cinema have been based on the problems of children. Three films that come immediately to mind are *Fanny and Alexander* (1983), *Forbidden Games* (1951), and *The Four Hundred Blows* (1959).

Occasionally, children in films present clear evidence of mental illness. Films such as *The Best Little Girl in the World* (1981) explore specific illnesses such as anorexia nervosa, while *Rain Man* (1993) introduced thousands of people to the problems of people with autism. Truffaut's *The Wild Child* (1969) explores the life of a feral child, and Werner Herzog's *Every Man for Himself and God Against All* (1975) addresses a similar theme in its exploration of the effects of a childhood filled with almost complete isolation, deprivation, and torture.

The exact nature of the illness that causes a teenage boy to blind six horses is never made clear in *Equus* (1977), despite the best efforts of a psychiatrist played by Richard Burton, but it is clear the boy is deeply troubled and that his problems relate to his emerging sexuality and one instance in which he was impotent when confronted with his first sexual opportunity. Likewise, there is no clear diagnosis for the child in *The Tin Drum* (1979), who decides on his third birthday to stop growing, but it is clear that the child is responding to the madness of the world around him and events over which he has no control (such as the suicide of his mother).

Films sometimes portray normal children living in abnormal circumstances. Three examples of this genre include *El Norte* (1983), a film about two children escaping poverty in Guatemala and exchanging it for poverty in Los Angeles; *Pixote* (1981), a film that describes the ways in which street children in Brazil are almost inevitably drawn into a squalid life of crime, drugs, and prostitution; and *Salaam Bombay* (1988), a movie that follows the lives and misfortunes of children living on the streets of Bombay.

Critical Thinking Questions

- Many children have imaginary playmates. At what age level is this behavior appropriate? When does it become inappropriate?
- Have you known anyone who was anorexic, or who has suffered from bulimia nervosa?
- How do TV, films, and other media encourage eating disorders in young people?
- Should adolescents who commit serious crimes such as rape and murder be tried as adults?
- The spanking Alexander receives for lying in *Fanny and Alexander* appears excessive and inappropriate. Is spanking ever justified? What alternative means of punishment would be appropriate?
- The film *Kids* deals with sex, drugs, violence, and AIDS. Is the film accurate in its suggestion that these issues are becoming increasingly salient for very young children?
- The film and the novel *Lord of the Flies* suggest that without adult supervision young children quickly become savages. Do you find this position plausible?
- Films often portray stepparents as cold and sadistic. Is there any empirical evidence for this, or is it a simple and misguided stereotype?

Chapter 12

Mental Retardation and Autism

He's not crazy,
and he's not retarded.
Raymond's autism is explained
to his brother, Charlie Babbitt
in *Rain Man*

Questions to Consider While Watching *Rain Man*

- What is the symbolic value of the Buick Roadmaster in the film?
- Is the scene in which Raymond calculates complex square roots but can't make change for a dollar realistic?
- Why is Raymond unable to appreciate the humor in Abbott and Costello's "Who's on First" routine?
- Would Raymond realistically be "a voluntary admission free to leave at any time," as Dr. Bruner maintains?
- Would it have been an example of sexual exploitation if Charlie Babbitt's girlfriend, Susanna, had initiated an affair with Raymond?
- Can you identify examples of repetitive behavior in the film? Are these behaviors more likely to occur when Raymond is stressed?
- Why is Raymond's favorite word *definitely?*
- Raymond smiles at one point and appears to appreciate the ironic humor involved in asking for maple syrup when it is already on the table. Is the appreciation of subtle humor like this characteristic for someone with autism?
- How would you rate the quality of care provided for Raymond at Wallbrook?
- Raymond's knowledge of trivia serves him well when watching the quiz show "Jeopardy." What sorts of games would Raymond find the most difficult?

PATIENT EVALUATION

Patient's stated reason for coming: "My brother brought me here. It's definitely required."

History of the present illness: Raymond Babbitt is a 33-year-old man who was diagnosed as autistic at the age of 10. He has been a fulltime resident at Wallbrook ever since his diagnosis. He appreciates the routine and the stability of life at Wallbrook and appears to have been happy there. The recent death of his father and his brother's request for guardianship precipitated the current evaluation.

Past psychiatric illness, treatment, and outcomes: Mr. Babbitt is an autistic savant. He experiences marked difficulty with communication, and he does not appear to experience emotion in customary ways. He has been receiving custodial care since the age of 10. He is high functioning and can express most of his needs without difficulty. However, Mr. Babbitt becomes very agitated whenever the routine of his life is varied in any way. He also becomes upset whenever exposed to noise or atypical sounds of any sort.

Medical history: This patient experienced the usual childhood diseases. His development was delayed, and he was late in meeting many developmental milestones (e.g., he did not speak until the age of three and never reached the point of initiating spontaneous play with other children). His parents and doctors realized something was wrong with Raymond long before he was formally diagnosed with autism. The rest of the medical history is insignificant.

Psychosocial history: Raymond was separated from his brother following his mother's death in 1965. He was sent to live in an institution at that time and had little or no contact with his brother until his father's death in 1988. He developed few friends at Wallbrook, and his closest relationships appear to have been with aides and orderlies. His father kept Raymond's condition — and even his existence — a secret from Charlie, the younger brother.

Drug and alcohol history: Mr. Babbitt has not experimented with either alcohol or drugs.

Behavioral observations: The patient was appropriately groomed and dressed. He obviously felt uncomfortable during the evaluation and never initiated conversation. Mr. Babbitt avoided eye contact, and his facial expressions often seemed incongruous and inappropriate. There was little spontaneity during the exam, and Mr. Babbitt displayed few emotions. He did not respond in customary ways to simple social amenities, and he did not understand or relate to the examiner's attempts to use humor to establish rapport. He fidgeted throughout the one-hour assessment and stood up to pace the room several times during the hour (always pacing in the same area of the room in a somewhat ritualistic manner). Mr. Babbit also repeated the examiner's questions and often repeated his responses two or three times. There are also stereotyped hand movements that were repeated regularly throughout the evaluation. However, Raymond was cooperative and tried hard to do well on all tasks; the results of the assessment are believed to be valid and meaningful.

Mental status examination: Mr. Babbitt was fully oriented to time, place and person. He did well on the Mini Mental Status Examination, earning a perfect score of 30. However, some of his responses were unusual. For example, Mr. Babbitt insisted on completing serial sevens all the way back past zero to -1006, at which point I insisted that he stop. He performed the calculations quickly and flawlessly. When asked to repeat "no ifs, ands, or buts," he repeated the phrase approximately 10 times. He had difficulty composing a sentence, and prompting was required to get him to write "Lunch is always served at 11:30."

Functional assessment: Mr. Babbitt has never held a full-time job, although he has participated in sheltered workshop experiences. He is not currently employed, and his extreme rigidity and interpersonal eccentricities would make it difficult for him to perform adequately in the workplace. His father recently passed away, and Raymond's support system now consists of a single brother and his friends and caregivers at Wallbrook. He has never dated or been married. He has very circumscribed interests and activities and is reluctant to take on new projects or engage in new activities.

Strengths: Mr. Babbitt is an autistic savant with tremendous abilities in calculation and memory. He knows thousands of baseball statistics and has a seemingly limitless ability to memorize trivia.

Diagnosis: 299.00 Autistic Disorder

Treatment plan: Mr. Babbitt has responded well to custodial care at Wallbrook, and it is recommended that this program be continued.

Prognosis: Good. Mr. Babbitt clearly has an autistic disorder; however, he functions at a high level, has significant strengths, and should be able to manage well in a highly structured environment.

RAIN MAN

Rain Main, a 1988 film winner of several Academy Awards, stars Dustin Hoffman as Raymond Babbitt and Tom Cruise as Raymond's brother Charlie. The drama opens with Charlie, a cynical hustler in his mid-twenties who imports expensive sports cars to Los Angeles and is always close to bankruptcy, unemotionally learning of his father's death. Charlie and his father had been estranged for several years. Charlie's father left only a 1949 Buick to his son, leaving $3 million in a trust fund for a secret beneficiary.

Charlie traces the beneficiary and discovers that he has an older brother, Raymond, who has autism. Raymond's world is bound by the rituals of watching television programs and eating certain foods on certain days. The books and baseball memorabilia in his room must be in order, or Raymond becomes agitated and begins reciting the Abbot and Costello routine "Who's on First." When the sanitarium administrator refuses to give Charlie half of the inheritance, Charlie removes his brother.

Charlie wants to return to the coast, but Raymond refuses to fly. The story unfolds as Charlie and Raymond cross the country in the old Buick. Their adventures include viewing an accident, after which Raymond refuses to travel on interstate highways and a day in a motel because Raymond refuses to go out in the rain. Raymond has many idiosyncrasies, such as having maple syrup on the table before the pancakes, insisting upon snacks of apple juice and cheese balls, imitating any noise he hears, and being preoccupied with television.

Raymond has unusual mathematical skills that Charlie plans to use to recoup his business losses through gambling at Los Vegas. When Raymond inadvertently makes a date with a prostitute, Charlie teaches his brother how to dance. When the woman fails to show up, Raymond dances with Charlie's girlfriend, Susan, who gives Raymond his first kiss.

Charlie develops an appreciation for the complexity of the illness when Raymond goes berserk when frightened by the noise of a smoke detector. The movie ends when Charlie, who has developed a sensitivity and love for his brother, turns down a $250,000 settlement and lets his brother return to Wallbrook.

AUTISTIC DISORDER

Problems in social interaction and communication are the primary symptoms of autistic disorder. Children with this illness are not able to maintain eye-to-eye gaze, respond with facial expressions, and use normal body posture and gestures. This disorder is obvious in infancy, and an experienced mother will notice a difference in the ability of her child to relate immediately after birth. A child with autism does not cuddle or seem to like to be held. While nursing, the infant may stiffen and avoid any eye contact. As children with autism grow older, they do not develop peer relationships that are appropriate to their developmental level. In *Rain Man,* Raymond had not had age-appropriate social experiences until his brother provided him with an opportunity for a date. Even then, his responses, while entertaining, were not what would be expected of a man his age. They do not seem to be able to express pleasure in other people's happiness and are unable to "give or take" emotionally. These children are very frustrating to their parents because of their lack of emotional warmth.

Children with autism have major problems in communication. There is a delay or sometimes a complete lack of development of spoken language. If there is speech, there is an impairment in the ability to initiate or sustain a conversation with others. Their use of language is repetitive or idiosyncratic. For example, they may use words, but they are not meaningful. In *Rain Man,* Raymond's repetitive language is one of his most significant symptoms. He is continually repeating himself. As children, they may not be able to engage in make-believe play or social imitative play appropriate to their developmental level. These children will not play "house," be a firefighter, or catch a thief.

The other symptoms of autism are repetitive and stereotyped patterns of behavior, interests, and activities. There is often an encompassing preoccupation with one or more stereotyped and restricted patterns of interest that is abnormal in either intensity or focus. In the film, Raymond is preoccupied with baseball and television. In children, preoccupation with moving, circulating objects is typical. Many children with autism focus for hours on a circulating fan. When the fan is removed, they experience anxiety and frustration. Stereotyped, repetitive motor mannerisms may also be present. For example, children may rock for hours, twist their fingers, rub their hands on their legs, spin, or repeat complex body movements.

People with autism compulsively adhere to specific, often nonfunctional, routines or rituals. *In* Rain Man, *Raymond's need for rituals is evident throughout the film.* He needs specific foods and television programs. When his daily rituals are disturbed, he becomes very upset and frustrated. Typically, people with autism do not use socially acceptable skills in expressing their frustration and resort to primitive behaviors of throwing or tearing things up, as Raymond does when the smoke detector goes off. The children are also often preoccupied with parts of objects rather than people. A child with autism may be fascinated with a motor, a piece of equipment, or a model automobile. The child may literally spend hours taking the object apart and putting it together again.

An **autistic disorder** is usually diagnosed before the age of three. It occurs four to five times more frequently in males than in females and is prevalent in four to five per 10,000 in children under 15 years of age. Approximately 75 percent of persons with autistic disorder are also mentally retarded. Autism is a complex problem and requires special treatment and family support.

There are multiple causes of autism. The twin studies show a clear genetic component, with a 95.7 percent concordance rate with identical twins and a 23.5 percent with fraternal twins. Some males with autism have been determined to be positive for the Fragile X syndrome (a folic acid deficiency that is a mutation found on the X chromosome). A single gene defect, which results in an inborn error of metabolism (PKU, neurofibromatosis), has also been associated with autism (Young et al. 1984).

In autistic disorder, imaging studies show that there is significantly lower gray matter blood flow in both right and left hemispheres of the brain. There are also some studies that suggest there are changes in the actual brain structures. For example, in some studies, the ventricles of the brain are enlarged (indicating less brain tissue) and, in others, lobules in the cerebellum are smaller.

Changes in neurotransmitters have also been observed. It is estimated that one-third of the children with autism have elevated blood serotonin levels; however, excess serotonin also occurs in other medical and neurophysiologic disorders. Thus, the significance of the excessive serotonin is not really clear. Altered dopamine has also been suggested as a component of the behavioral impairments in autism. Increased dopamine is associated with reduced social responsiveness and attention and amplification of motor stereotypes in autism. Additionally, a decrease in norepinephrine has been found in boys with autism when compared with that of normal boys. There are also changes in hormonal activity in the endocrine system.

Clearly, autism is a complex neurobiological disorder with many behavioral manifestations. Treatment is also complex and multifaceted. Medications play an important role, but no one medication has been found to be ideal. Usually, antipsychotics (the same medication given for psychosis in schizophrenia) are given. These drugs are used to achieve improved behavioral control without sedation. Stimulants (amphetamines, Ritalin, antidepressants) are sometimes given to stimulate development.

Behavior modification is an essential component of treatment for most children with autism. Usually these children are in special schools or education programs that are tailored to children with pervasive development disorders. Many children can live at home until physically mature. Then many are placed in residential settings, which are safer and have staff trained to protect the children from an occasional outburst.

There are a variety of educational programs that can be successful. Children with autism who are enrolled in very structured educational programs do better in formal scholastic achievement, speech, and on-task behavior and are better behaved than those children raised in permissive environments. However, after three or four years, there are no differences. Apparently, the children in the structured school settings do well while in school but are unable to generalize behavior to other settings. The best predictor of success is IQ. Children with higher intelligent scores are more successful than those with lower ones.

Most families need help in order to deal with special children. There are treatment programs conducted within the home in order to help the child generalize from an academic setting to the home. Parents learn how to teach their children appropriate social and communication skills, as well as behavior modification techniques. Family therapy is recommended in order to help the family cope with problems associated with raising a disabled child.

The prognosis for children with autism is mixed. If they begin to acquire language, are socially responsive, and improve their cognitive skills by the ages of five to seven, they have a better prognosis than those who do not. Approximately 25 percent of children with autism develop seizures, usually in early adolescence. During puberty, they may experience behavioral changes, including a negativism that sometimes leads to aggression. Most do not develop hallucinations or delusions. However, their behavior and thinking may continue to be peculiar and concrete and their affect flat.

Adults with autism continue to be inattentive to social convention, lack social understanding, have few or no friends, and do not marry. They may also be troubled by chronic anxiety. Their repetitive behavior and movements usually continue (Young, Newcorn, & Leven, 1989).

In Rain Man, *Raymond has a specific type of problem, called **savant disorder,** which occurs with high frequency among the autistic population.* With this problem, the individual usually scores low on standardized IQ tests but has one or two outstanding talents, such as calculating dates, drawing, or musical performance. Savant disorder occurs mostly in males (O'Connor, 1989).

Rett's Disorder

In 1966, Dr. Andreas Rett from Vienna reported on 22 girls with serious neurological disabilities who had a characteristic pattern that suggested a discrete abnormality. More than 200 patients have now been identified with this problem. *Rett's Disorder* appears exclusively in girls, is generally sporadic, and is without special geographical or ethnic predilection.

In this disorder, there is normal development for at least the first six months. There is apparently normal prenatal and perinatal development and normal psychomotor development through the first six months. The head circumference size at birth is normal. Between the ages of 5 and 48 months, there is a deceleration of head growth and loss of previously acquired purposeful hand movements, with the development of stereotyped hand movements (hand wringing or hand washing) and a loss of social engagement. Poorly coordinated gait or trunk movements are present. Developmental delay and impaired expressive and receptive language with severe psychomotor retardation develops. Rett's Disorder also involves autistic-like symptoms, as well as ataxia, facial grimacing, and teeth grinding. There is also a progressive spasticity, scoliosis, and onset of seizures.

The etiology of Rett's Disorder is unknown. A Mendelian inheritance has not been found, and the expression of the disorder only in females is puzzling. There have been no discrete or consistent biochemical or cell changes identified. Pathological studies have shown a progressive decrease in the neuronal population, with brain atrophy, but no remarkable configurations have been identified. Treatment consists of developmental supportive therapies and anticonvulsant medication.

Other Pervasive Developmental Disorders

There are other disorders that can be categorized as pervasive developmental disorders. In **Childhood Disintegrative Disorder,** there is normal development for at least the first two years, then language, social, motor, or play skills are lost. There may also be a loss of bowel or bladder control. In **Asperger's Disorder,** there is an impairment in social interaction; restricted, repetitive, and stereotyped patterns of behavior, interests, and activities are present, but there is a lack of any general delay in language. Cognitive development is not delayed.

BEST BOY

Ira Wohl's 1979 film *Best Boy* is a documentary that examines the life of Wohl's cousin, Philly, a mentally retarded man who has spent his entire life living with, and being protected by, his parents. The film beautifully documents the concerns of Philly's parents about who will take care of him after their death. Philly's father dies while the film is being made, and his mother reluctantly allows Philly to become involved in a day-care program. The film is deeply moving and very effective in its examination of mental retardation as a social problem. In addition, the film does a beautiful job portraying the emotional richness of Philly's life and the strong bonds that have been formed between this man and his family.

MENTAL RETARDATION

According to the *DSM-IV,* mental retardation is identified as a mental disorder and is prevalent in one percent of the population. The distinguishing factor in this disorder is intellectual functioning or IQ measured by standard intelligence tests. Children who are mentally retarded score below 70 on standardized tests of intellectual ability. The range of mental retardation is from mild to profound. (See Table 12-1.) Before a child is diagnosed as being mentally retarded, other deficits or impairments in functioning must be present in addition to low scores on an intelligence test. That is, the child does not meet the expected standards for his or her age or cultural group in communication, use of community resources, self-direction, academic skills, leisure, health, and safety.

Category	IQ Level	Approximate % of Persons Retarded
Mild	50–55 to 70	85%
Moderate	35–40 to 50–55	10%
Severe	20–25 to 35–40	3–4%
Profound	below 20–25	1–2%

Table 12-1. Levels of mental retardation by IQ range. (Szymanski, L., & Crocker, A. (1989). Mental retardation. In H. Kaplan & B. Sadock *Comprehensive Textbook of Psychiatry/IV*. Baltimore, MD: Williams & Wilkins.)

Even though mental retardation is classified by the *DSM-IV* as a disorder, it is not a disease. The term *mental retardation* denotes the degree to which a person functions below cultural and social norms at a particular time and place. Persons who are retarded form a heterogeneous group. There are many different causes of mental retardation, such as drug or alcohol abuse in the mother, chromosomal or genetic disorders, and lack of oxygen during a difficult delivery (Szymanski & Crocker, 1989).

One of the most common syndromes of mental retardation, *Down syndrome,* a disorder caused by changes to chromosome 21, has an incidence of 1 per 1,000 live births. Twenty years ago, 50 percent of mothers of children with Down syndrome were over 35 years old; now, because of a variety of demographic and cultural changes, this figure is 20 percent. These children have distinctive physical characteristics that include hypotonia, hyperflexibility, midface depression, and shortness of ear length. Persistent epicanthic folds, single four-finger lines in the palms, and incurved fifth fingers occur over 50 to 75 percent of the time.

People with this disorder have been victims of stereotyping and prejudice. In the early 1960s about 10 percent of all residents who were institutionalized had Down syndrome. They were institutionalized because it was thought that anyone with Down syndrome needed to live apart from the rest of society. This is not true. Because of the discrimination in the past, families of children with Down syndrome have become pioneers in the understanding of developmental disabilities.

Today a child who is mentally retarded is usually kept within the family environment. Only those who are profoundly retarded reside in residential care centers. If a child is mentally retarded, his or her education receives special attention; the child is taught in a slower learning environment that focuses on discrete skills. The ultimate goal is to help the individual function as independently as possible. With the appropriate training, many adults who are mentally retarded live productive, independent lives.

Best Boy illustrates one of the dilemmas confronting Western society as we grow older. As the population ages, the number of aging retarded individuals is also increasing rapidly, although the life expectancy for people who are mentally retarded is somewhat lower than that for the population at large. This problem is compounded by the fact that mentally retarded individuals are at greater risk for developing dementia. In the case of Philly, he is forced to leave his parents' home — the only home he has ever known — and learn to cope with the outside world. Older patients who are **deinstitutionalized** face similar difficulties when they leave the security of large state hospitals, where they have lived for years, and begin to adjust to life in small group homes in community settings.

Forrest Gump

The film *Forrest Gump* (1994) portrays 40 years in the life of a man who has a marginal IQ of 75 but whose innocence and pure common sense make him seem wise. Forrest's condition would be classified as **borderline retardation** today, and he would probably be tested for a learning disability.

This superb film begins with Forrest, played by Tom Hanks, telling his life story. When Forrest was a child, his mother, played by Sally Fields, believed in his normality and was determined that he would have a full, complete life. Forrest had a weak spine and needed to wear leg-braces. He was forced to run from other children to protect himself, so that even with the leg-braces he became an outstanding runner. Eventually, a local football coach spots Forrest and signs him to play college football. He begins a brilliant career that eventually leads him to the army and Vietnam. He wins a medal and becomes a table-tennis star. After being discharged from the army, Forrest goes into the shrimp business and becomes a millionaire. Forrest has a life-long friend, Jenny Curran, who often came to his aid as a child. As an adult, he is able to help her as she and her son cope with disability and death resulting from AIDS.

Even with a limited intelligence and modest academic ability, Forrest is able to feel good about himself and who he is, a simple man who makes his mark on the world. The development of his self-esteem has its roots in his childhood and his mother's belief in him. The friendship with Jenny encourages him. As a result of the support of these two women, he never realizes that he could not succeed.

THE REPRESENTATION OF MENTAL RETARDATION AND AUTISM IN FILMS

A number of films have poignantly illustrated the difficulties — and sometimes the beauty — in the lives of people who are mentally retarded. Three especially memorable films are *Charly, A Day in the Death of Joe Egg,* and *Of Mice and Men*. Another film in which an adult with mental retardation is portrayed sympathetically is the 1962 film *To Kill a Mockingbird,* in which Robert Duvall makes his film debut as a neighbor with retardation who kills a man to protect two young children.

Anyone interested in the relationship between psychopathology and contemporary cinema will be intrigued by David Lynch's first feature-length film, *Eraserhead*. This is not a film that every viewer will appreciate; however, it has achieved cult status, perhaps because it manages to be simultaneously fascinating and bizarre.

Critical Thinking Questions

- Howard Gardner, in his book *Frames of Mind,* describes seven kinds of intelligence (verbal, visual, physical, musical, mathematical and logical, introspective, and interpersonal). How does this model help you understand figures such as Raymond Babbitt and Forrest Gump?

- How have the parents of autistic children been stigmatized in the past? Are there comparable examples of inappropriate stigma today for the parents of children with different conditions?

- Are people who are mentally retarded able to experience sexual feelings like people who are not? If so, how can institutions and health professionals support natural sexual expression while at the same time avoiding exploitation and abuse?

- Which labels are more useful: specific terms such as *autism* or more generic labels such as *Pervasive Developmental Disorder?*

- Do people who are at greater genetic risk for having children with severe developmental disorders have a moral obligation not to have children?

Chapter 13

Violence, Abuse, and Antisocial Behavior

*She's a whore. The last time I saw her
she was doing a live sex show.*
A bystander describes Jodi Foster's
character in *The Accused*

Questions to Consider While Watching *The Accused*

- How common is rape in the United States?
- What percentage of rapes involves two or more assailants?
- Are rapists usually strangers or men known to the woman involved?
- Why didn't Sarah Tobias call for help when she was being raped?
- Should a woman's dress or provocative behavior be treated as extenuating circumstances in a rape case?
- Is a woman's sexual history relevant in a rape case?
- What conformity studies in social psychology can be used to understand the behavior of the bystanders in The Mill who did nothing to help Sarah Tobias?
- What steps could police officers and hospitals take to ensure rape victims are treated humanely and compassionately?

PATIENT EVALUATION

Patient's stated reason for coming: "The judge ordered me to come. There's nothing wrong with my head. I've been raped . . . why is that so fuckin' hard to understand?"

History of the present illness: Ms. Sarah Tobias was referred for psychological evaluation by Judge Leonard Rosen. She is the plaintiff in a well-publicized gang rape case.

Past psychiatric illness, treatment, and outcomes: This patient has one arrest for cocaine possession. She claims the cocaine belonged to a friend of hers and that she was merely helping her friend move to a new apartment when they were busted. There is no history of individual or family psychiatric or psychological treatment.

Medical history: Ms. Tobias is a healthy 21-year-old woman. She has never been hospitalized, and she denies any significant medical history. Ms. Tobias does not have a personal physician, and she states that her only contact with a physician in the past decade occurred approximately three years ago, when she visited a family planning clinic to obtain a prescription for birth control pills.

Psychosocial history: Ms. Tobias is an only child who dropped out of high school in the 11th grade to move in with a boyfriend. Her parents divorced when she was six years old, and her mother proceeded to cycle through a number of live-in boyfriends. Some of these men were physically or sexually abusive; almost all of them were verbally abusive to Sarah. She reports that she was more interested in getting away from home than in actually living with the boyfriend whom she moved in with after dropping out of school. This relationship fell apart, and Sarah has been involved in several significant relationships since. She currently lives with Pete, an unemployed musician. Sarah has held a wide variety of jobs, and most of the time she has been employed as a waitress.

Drug and alcohol history: Ms. Tobias has an extensive drug history. She uses cocaine at parties but denies dependence or daily use. She smokes marijuana almost daily "to take the edge off." She is a heavy drinker, consuming an average of one six pack of beer each day and a bottle of tequila each week. She has been known to pass out at parties while intoxicated, and she has experienced alcohol-related blackouts about a dozen times. She smokes approximately a half pack of filtered cigarettes each day.

Behavioral observations: Ms. Tobias arrived approximately 10 minutes late for the evaluation. She is a petite and attractive woman who was casually but appropriately dressed in jeans and a sweater. Ms. Tobias made it clear that she resented the court-ordered evaluation and the implicit but clearly present assumption that her sexual behavior at The Mill could have been the consequence of mental illness or character flaws. She appeared to be defensive and guarded throughout the evaluation, but she cooperated fully, and the results of the examination are believed to be valid.

Mental status examination: Ms. Tobias was oriented to place, person, and circumstance. She missed the current date by one day. She was able to name three objects immediately and after a brief interruption. She made one mistake when subtracting serial sevens. There is no dysnomia, and this patient has no difficulty with repetition. She is able to follow both verbal and written commands. She can write a simple sentence ("I wish I knew why the hell I was doing this."), and she has no difficulty copying interlocking pentagons.

Ms. Tobias appeared slightly agitated, and she drummed her fingers impatiently during much of the evaluation. Her affect was appropriate to the situation. Her speech was appropriate and delivered at a normal rate. Thought processes appear to be intact, and there was no evidence of loosening of associations or flights of ideation. There is no history of hallucinations or delusions. There is no suicidal or homicidal ideation ("Sure, I'd like to kill the bastards that did it, but I'll settle for sending them to jail."). She appears to be of average or above average intelligence. Her judgment is good, and she appears to have adequate insight into her situation.

Functional assessment: Ms. Tobias has few specific job skills and she never completed high school. However, she is intelligent and articulate, and she is a good candidate for GED classes. She has held down jobs for as long as a year at a time, and she has a good work ethic. The relationship with her current boyfriend is strained, and it is unlikely she will let him continue to live in her house. He has been generally indifferent to her rape and its consequences, and he provides neither financial nor emotional support. She is gregarious and friendly and has a support system of women friends who will be important to her in the months ahead.

Strengths: This woman is bright and articulate. She presents as someone with a lot of "spunk." She is assertive, and she is resolute once she has settled on a particular course of action. Her sense of humor is an important asset. She has good common sense, and she is very unpretentious.

Diagnosis: 309.0 Adjustment Disorder with Depressed Mood.

Treatment plan: (1) Request psychological testing to provide a more complete evaluation for the court (e.g., MMPI, Rorschach); (2) offer the option of referral to a local mental health center for follow-up counseling focusing on coping; (3) refer to the local rape crisis center for follow-up and the opportunity to participate in a rape survivors' support group.

Prognosis: Excellent

THE ACCUSED

The Accused is a 1988 film based on a true story of gang rape on a pool table in a blue-collar bar. The crime was especially despicable insofar as more than a dozen spectators stood by clapping and cheering while a woman was repeatedly raped. No one made any attempt to stop the rape or to assist the victim. The complacency of the bystanders in the film based on this story, *The Accused,* is in part attributed to the fact that Foster's character, Sarah Tobias, had been drinking heavily and smoking pot earlier in the evening, had openly flirted with one of the men involved, was provocatively dressed, and had engaged in a sensuous dance immediately before being raped. Her defense is weakened by the fact that she had jokingly referred to one of the men earlier in the evening, telling her girlfriend, "I should take him home and fuck his brains out." The attorneys for the defense argue that Tobias is simply "trailer park trash" who was an enthusiastic and willing participant in everything that occurred.

Some of the most vivid scenes in the film occur during an insensitive gynecological examination by a woman doctor who asks detailed questions about Sarah's sexual history ("Have you ever made love to more than one man at a time?") and recent experiences. The insensitivity is compounded by the questions of the assistant district attorney, who wants to know how Sarah was dressed and when was the last time she experienced intercourse before the rape.

Tobias loses the first legal round, when the three rapists are convicted but have their sentences reduced from rape to "reckless endangerment." However, she is eventually successful in convicting several of the men who witnessed the rape and did nothing. *The film concludes with two sobering facts: (1) in the United States, a rape is reported every six minutes, and (2) one out of every four rape victims is attacked by two or more assailants.*

RAPE

Rape is included in this section rather than in the chapter on sexual and gender identity disorders because rape is an act of violence, *not* an act of sexual passion. The victims of rapists may be elderly women or young children.

The statistics on rape are sobering. The United States has one of the highest rates of rape in the world — four times higher than Germany, 13 times higher than England, and 20 times higher than Japan. It is estimated that one out of three women will be sexually assaulted in her lifetime, and one out of seven will be raped by her husband. Sixty-one percent of rape victims are under the age of 18, and 78 percent of rape victims know their attacker. One in four college women have either experienced rape or have been exposed to attempted rape, and the majority of both men and women involved in acquaintance rape had been drinking or using drugs at the time. About a third of the victims of rape develop a rape-related post-traumatic stress disorder sometime in their lifetime. It is estimated that only about 16 percent of rapes are reported to the police in this country, usually because women feel that nothing can be done or because they feel it is a private matter between them and their assailant. When compared with women who have not experienced rape, rape victims are found to be more than nine times more likely to attempt suicide.

There has been a great deal of recent concern about flunitrazepam, better know as *Rohypnol*. Rohypnol is a powerful benzodiazepine, about 10 times more powerful than diazepam (Valium). It is used to treat insomnia but has become popular among high school students as a "date rape drug." Rohypnol is also used to take the edge off the crash that accompanies withdrawal from binge use of other drugs. Women who have passed out after unwittingly taking Rohypnol have found that the profound sedation and memory impairment that accompany its use have made it very difficult for them to prosecute their assailants. The ways in which defense attorneys can challenge the memories of rape victims are illustrated in *The Accused*. Sarah Tobias would have had an even more difficult time making her case if a drug such as Rohypnol had impaired her memory.

RAPE IN FILMS

Rape has been a recurrent theme in contemporary American films. There were significant rape scenes in *A Clockwork Orange* (1971), Ken Russell's *The Devils* (1971), and *My Old Man's Place* (1972). Marlon Brando rapes a passive and indifferent Maria Schneider in *Last Tango in Paris* (1973). There is a vicious and unforgettable rape scene in *Blue Velvet* (1986). Farrah Fawcett takes control of the situation and exacts revenge on a rapist in *Extremities* (1986); Dustin Hoffman gets revenge following his wife's graphic rape in Sam Peckinpah's violent film *Straw Dogs* (1971); and two independent women inadvertently kill a man who tries to rape one of them in *Thelma and Louise* (1991). Vietnamese women are raped in several of the Vietnam War films, most notably in *Casualties of War* (1989). Harrison Ford is wrongly accused of rape in *Presumed Innocent* (1990). Date rape occurs in the 1995 film *Higher Learning;* gang rape is portrayed in *Last Exit to Brooklyn* (1989); and there is a homosexual rape in *Deliverance* (1972). A nun is raped in *Bad Lieutenant* (1992), but the nun forgives her assailant and refuses to press charges against him. Two children play at a game of rape in *Welcome to the Dollhouse* (1996). Ingmar Bergman takes up the theme of the rape of innocence in *The Virgin Spring* (1959), and two rapes occur in the remarkable Dutch film *Antonia's Line* (1995). (One of these episodes involves a man who rapes his retarded sister.) *Dead Man Walking* (1995) presents the viewer with difficult choices about the appropriateness of capital punishment in a case of rape and murder, and we are forced to think about whether or not drug intoxication is a mitigating circumstance in this case and others like it.

Attempted rape of a man by a woman is portrayed in the film adaptation of Michael Crichton's novel *Disclosure* (1994). When Michael Douglas rebuffs Demi Moore, the new female boss, she accuses her former lover and new subordinate of sexual harassment.

Perhaps the most troubling portrayals of rape occur in those films in which rape is shown to be a woman's fantasy, or in those films in which a woman who is being raped becomes aroused by the experience or attracted to the rapist. There are elements of these themes in two otherwise remarkable movies, Pedro Almodovar's *Tie Me Up! Tie Me Down!* (1990) and Lina Wertmuller's *Swept Away* (1975).

ONCE WERE WARRIORS

This remarkable film documents the life of a New Zealand Maori family and the devastating effects of alcoholism and domestic violence on every member of the family, including the husband/father/perpetrator. The film is especially effective in portraying the effects of domestic violence on the children in the family: one son responds by returning to his Maori roots, while a sensitive, poetry-writing daughter responds by committing suicide.

Additional Questions for Classroom Discussion *(Once Were Warriors)*
- What role does alcoholism play in the violence we witness in this family?
- To what extent is violence an important part of Maori culture?
- Should a therapist be sensitive to the fact that family violence may be judged to be appropriate and justified in some cultures?
- If you were Beth's therapist, would you actively encourage her to leave Jake, or would you leave this decision to Beth (knowing full well she has always decided to stay with him in the past)?

DOMESTIC VIOLENCE

Domestic violence is a serious, ubiquitous, and under-reported problem in our society. Violence sufficient to cause death or serious injury will occur in about 1 in 25 families, and hitting, slapping, or punching will occur in approximately one in four families. It is unfortunate that some men feel that marriage gives them special license to hit, hurt, or rape their spouse. (Whether or not a man can be charged with raping his wife is one of the themes explored in the 1959 film *Anatomy of a Murder*.) Two out of three female victims of violence know their attackers; however, they frequently will not report their abuse because they desire to protect their assailants or because they fear reprisals (Bachman, 1993).

Men who abuse their wives are also at high risk of abusing their children. *Alcohol or other drugs are commonly involved in cases of domestic violence, and this relationship is clearly present in* Once Were Warriors *(1994).*

HENRY: PORTRAIT OF A SERIAL KILLER

Henry: Portrait of a Serial Killer (1990) is loosely based on the life and confessions (since called into question) of Henry Lee Lucas. Henry shares a cheap room with Otis, a man he had met in prison in Vandalia. The film is controversial because it presents graphic details of several murders, including one in which Henry and his roommate, Otis, pretend their car isn't running and then kill a man who stops to help. In a subsequent scene, Henry and Otis videotape the murder of an entire family. The film develops a triangular sexual tension between Henry, the murder of an entire family. The film develops a triangular sexual tension between Henry, Otis, and Becky, Otis' sister, a woman down on her luck who has come to live with her brother. In the final scene of the movie, Henry decapitates Otis. The movie is especially powerful insofar as it seems to trivialize murder, as in the scene in which Henry and Otis murder two prostitutes, then go out and casually share an order of french fries.

SERIAL KILLERS

We have been fascinated with the topic of serial killers since Jack the Ripper strangled and cut the throats of five London prostitutes in 1888. More recent serial killers include Albert De Salvo (the Boston Strangler), David Berkowitz (the Son of Sam killer), Henry Lee Lucas, John Wayne Gacy, Ted Bundy ("the Preppie killer"), Wayne Williams, Charles Manson, and Jeffrey Dahmer, a harmless-looking young man who killed dozens of other young men, ate their body parts, and kept other parts in his refrigerator. The FBI defines a serial killer as anyone who has committed three or more separate murders.

Contrary to media presentations and popular opinion, few if any serial killers are psychotic. (David Berkowitz may have been a salient exception.) In contrast, many are sexual sadists who derive sexual excitement from the murders they commit; most are sociopaths who experience little remorse or regret for their crimes. Both John Wayne Gacy and Jeffrey Dahmer were homosexual pedophiles.

Some serial killers commit multiple murders for utilitarian reasons — i.e., they are "hit men" who kill for money. This is the kind of serial killer portrayed by Jack Nicholson in *Prizzi's Honor* (1985). The best film documentaries of sociopathic serial killers have been *In Cold Blood* (1967) and *Henry: Portrait of a Serial Killer* (1990).

VIOLENCE AND FILMS

Contemporary films and television programs are replete with violence, and it is difficult to avoid violence in the media or to briefly catalogue the most egregious examples of violence in recent films. According to the American Academy of Pediatrics, the typical American youngster will have witnessed about 200,000 acts of violence on television by the age of 18, and is likely will have witnessed several thousand additional acts of violence in films such as *Rambo III* (1988) or any of the *Halloween* films.

Topics for Class Discussion

- Do therapists have an obligation to respect cultural values and practices that may be harmful or degrading (e.g., slapping children for misbehaving or female genital mutilation)?
- What is the relationship between pornography and violence against women?
- Did your views of pornography change after watching *The People vs. Larry Flynt*?
- How harmful is it for children to be exposed to pornography on the Internet?
- How could two major studies (the Majority Report of the *1970 Presidential Commission on Obscenity and Pornography* and the *1986 Attorney General's Commission on Pornography*) come to exactly opposite conclusions about the effects of pornography?
- Should alcohol or drugs be considered mitigating circumstances in cases of rape or murder (e.g., in *Dead Man Walking*)?

Topics for Class Discussion Continued

- Is it possible to develop accurate "psychological profiles" that can help identify serial killers?
- Are there common factors that characterize the childhood experiences of those individuals who grow up to become serial killers?
- How do the media perpetuate violence in American society?

Chapter 14

Treatment

*They uh, was givin' me ten thousand watts a day,
you know, and I'm hot to trot. The next woman takes me out
is gonna light up like a pinball machine, and pay off in silver dollars.*
Randle P. McMurphy responds to a clinical
interview in *One Flew over the Cuckoo's Nest.*

Questions to Consider While Watching *One Flew over the Cuckoo's Nest*

- Is the stereotype of psychiatric treatment presented in *Cuckoo's Nest* still accurate? Was it at the time?
- Can you identify the theoretical position that links Billy's suicide with an intrusive, overly protective mother?
- How common is it for prisoners to evade punishment in the criminal justice system by entering the mental health system?
- The orderlies and aides in *Cuckoo's Nest* appear indifferent and apathetic. What are the entry-level wages for similar positions in your state?
- How would Paul Newman's character in *Cool Hand Luke* have fared if he had been transferred to the mental health system?
- Chief Broom chooses to murder McMurphy rather than have him beaten by the system. Is this a true mercy killing? Is it justified?
- How is it likely that McMurphy's lobotomy would have altered his personality? What is the neurological basis for the personality changes that accompany lobotomy?
- If you were an attendant working at the hospital when the ward psychiatrist recommended a lobotomy, would you have tried to stop it? What political and social tools could you have used?

PATIENT EVALUATION

Patient's stated reason for coming: "I figured the funny farm couldn't be any worse than a chain gang."

History of the present illness: Randle Patrick McMurphy is a 38-year-old white male who presents with a long history of minor legal problems dating back to his adolescence. He recently was arrested for statutory rape and sentenced to two years of hard labor in the Rivermead Correctional Facility. While at Rivermead, his behavior became increasingly erratic and "goofy," and he was sent to the state hospital for observation, evaluation, and treatment.

Past psychiatric illness, treatment, and outcomes: Mr. McMurphy has been arrested on several occasions for public drunkenness and disturbing the peace. He typically has been allowed to "sleep off" these episodes in the county jail; however, because of a conviction of statutory rape of a fifteen-year-old girl, he was sentenced to two years of prison time. He denies any history of psychiatric or psychological treatment, although he was seen sporadically by high school counselors for truancy and problems relating to authority figures, and he has received some counseling by parole officers over the years.

Medical history: Mr. McMurphy had the usual childhood illnesses and met development milestones at the expected times. He broke his arm in a school yard altercation at age 15. He states (proudly) that he has had gonorrhea at least five times. He denies any history of hospitalization or other significant medical treatment.

Psychosocial history: Mr. McMurphy's parents separated shortly after his birth, and he was raised by a widowed aunt (his mother's sister). There were no other children in the home, and the elderly aunt was an ineffectual disciplinarian. Mr. McMurphy made good grades in high school, apparently with little effort; he left high school in the middle of the 11th grade after a high school girlfriend became pregnant. "It was time for Randle Patrick to hit the road." He joined the Navy at age 18 and served for three years; however, he received a dishonorable discharge before completing his last tour of duty due to a history of frequently being absent without leave (AWOL). Since being discharged from the Navy, he has traveled widely and has worked at a series of jobs, including gardener, handyman, bouncer, massage parlor manager, car salesman, apple picker, state fair carney, and mechanic. He has never married, and his relationships with women tend to be short-term and relatively inconsequential.

Drug and alcohol history: Mr. McMurphy is candid about his history of drug use: "I've tried them all at least once." He has experimented with LSD and peyote, has snorted cocaine, and frequently uses amphetamines and barbiturates. However, alcohol remains his drug of choice, and beer and whiskey have been responsible for most of the legal problems Mr. McMurphy has experienced over the past decade. He smokes approximately a pack of unfiltered cigarettes each day.

Behavioral observations: Mr. McMurphy arrived on time for the examination. He was casually dressed. He was cheerful and talkative and seemed proud and happy to have been taken off the prison work detail. He cooperated fully with all tasks and seemed to take pride in his good performance on cognitive tasks.

Mental status examination: Mr. McMurphy's speech was rapid but not pressured. He appears to be quick-witted and mentally agile. Mood was within normal limits. There were no indications of thought disorder present. There is no evidence of suicidal ideation. Mr. McMurphy reports there were several sadistic guards at the prison: "I'll nail their balls to the wall if I ever get the chance." However, this appears to be braggadocio, and McMurphy is not believed to be a danger to self or others.

This patient was fully oriented to time, place ('the looney bin"), and person. He performed all tasks on the Mini Mental Status quickly and without difficulty, earning a perfect score of 30. When asked to write a sentence, the patient surprised the examiner by writing a line from Shakespeare: "A man can die but once, and let it go which way it will, he that dies this year is quit for the next." When asked to explain the significance of the line, McMurphy simply remarked, "I read it somewhere and liked it." This does *not* appear to be evidence of suicidal thinking.

Functional assessment: Although he never finished high school, this patient is believed to have superior intelligence. He is a group leader, and he has quickly become the dominant figure on the ward and the center of most ward activity. He has an exuberant charisma that most of the other patients find very attractive. He has worked in a wide variety of jobs and appears to be a "quick study." There are no significant work limitations, although his history of alcohol abuse may make him a high risk for some jobs (e.g., he would not be a good security guard); he may function best in a highly structured environment. He has limited social support; he is unmarried and is not aware of any living relatives. He has few hobbies and formerly spent most of his leisure time in bars. He is not well regarded by the ward staff, who tend to view him as a trouble maker and the instigator of most of the recent disciplinary problems that have occurred on the ward.

Strengths: Mr. McMurphy's engaging personality is his greatest asset. He appears to be a natural leader; both men and women are attracted to his high energy, quick wit, and ebullience.

Diagnosis: 301.7 R/O Antisocial Personality Disorder
302.2 R/O Pedophilia
305.00 R/O Alcohol Abuse

Treatment plan: There is no clear evidence of psychopathology in this individual, and I am unable to ascertain why he was transferred from the state prison to the state hospital. He does not appear to be appropriately placed, and I will investigate other treatment alternatives.

Prognosis: Good.

PATIENT ISSUES AND RIGHTS FOR HUMANE TREATMENT

Films such as *One Flew over the Cuckoo's Nest* attempt to show the human injustices that existed and occasionally are still found in the mental health system. In this film, once McMurphy moved from the prison system into the mental health system, he lost almost all civil rights, such as his right to refuse treatment. The issues addressed by the film are not the usual problems of large institutions such as lack of facilities, cleanliness, staff, or organizational communication. Instead, the film addresses fundamental issues of autonomy and paternalism. The treatment team has ultimate control over McMurphy's treatment and discharge. A rigid, overly controlled nurse engages in an ongoing power struggle with a patient whom she perceives as a threat to her control of the unit. She uses her position and knowledge of the system to gain control over McMurphy. *McMurphy's lobotomy is the ultimate abuse of psychiatric power.*

Cuckoo's Nest was not the first movie to portray patients' lack of control over treatment. One of the first movies to seriously tackle mental illness, *Snake Pit,* a 1948 movie starring Olivia de Havilland and directed by Anatole Litvak, is about a woman trying to overcome her illness in a crowded mental institution. The horrifying conditions portrayed in the film actually mobilized state legislators to improve the level of care provided in institutions. This movie further portrays the lack of power females have had in their care. In the *Snake Pit*, Virginia truly has a mental illness and is taken for treatment by a caring husband. However, many women who did not have a mental illnesses were placed in hospitals and kept in systems as a convenience for husbands who had tired of them (Geller & Harris, 1994).

A more recent film, Chattahoochee *(1990), not only depicts the horrible conditions in a Florida state hospital during the 1950s but also one patient's campaign to change these conditions.* In this film, Korean War veteran Gary Oldham (played by Emmett Foley) loses many of his rights because of his protest against authority. This film, based on a true story, begins when Gary Oldham becomes depressed by unemployment and hopes to provoke the police into killing him after he shoots up the neighborhood. He wants his wife to receive the insurance. Instead, he is sent to Chattahoochee, a prison for those with mental illness. The conditions in Chattahoochee are deplorable. With the support of a friend (played by Dennis Hopper), he begins a letter-writing campaign to protest the conditions. His writing privileges are taken away, and he starts writing in a Bible and surreptitiously slipping pages to his sister. A state commission is formed, hearings are held, and conditions improve as a result.

Movies illustrate the ongoing struggles for civil and human rights that have occurred in the mental health system. They also reflect the prevailing stigma toward persons with mental illness. Our language characterizes individuals with these illnesses as crazy, nuts, or wacky. The people who treat them are called shrinks, do-gooders, or bleeding hearts (Trachtenberg, 1986). The media portray patients as clowns, buffoons, or harmless eccentrics (Hyler, Gabbard, & Schneider, 1991). In *The Dream Team* (1989) and *The Couch Trip* (1988), a little bit of freedom proves adequate to cure mental illness. Other films, such as the *Psycho* series, depict individuals with mental illnesses as homicidal maniacs. In John Carpenter's *Halloween* series (1978–1998), an escaped psychiatric patient serially kills teenagers who have engaged in sexual relations. When Tommy Lee Wallace directed *Halloween III* (1982), the central villain was portrayed as a madman toy maker who made wicked Halloween masks programmed to harm children. However, the original madman on the loose from the mental hospital returned in *Halloween IV* and *V* (1988, 1989). These films and others have profoundly shaped public attitudes about the dangerousness of mental patients.

In spite of societal stigma and the traditionally poor treatment of persons with mental illness, the courts have established legal and regulatory safeguards. In 1986, Title II of Public Law 99-319, **Protection and Advocacy for Mentally Ill Individuals Act,** reaffirmed the Bill of Rights for people with mental illness originally recommended in *Action for Mental Health* in 1961 and part of the **Mental Health Systems Act** of 1980. (See Box 14-1.) These rights are guaranteed to each person admitted to a program or facility for the purpose of receiving mental health services. This act also requires each state mental health system to establish and operate a system that protects and advocates the rights of individuals with mental illnesses and investigates any incidents of abuse and neglect. Each state mental health department now has a separate department or agency with "rights staff" that functions as a protection and advocacy division. The rights and responsibility of these divisions are defined by law and are relatively independent of the rest of the mental health system. The protection staff is not involved in providing direct care but have easy access to the direct care settings and patient records. In 1991 the United Nations addressed the rights of persons with mental disorders by approving Resolution 119, the **Principles for the Protection of Persons with Mental Illness and for the Improvement of Mental Health Care.** This resolution includes statements on fundamental freedoms and basic rights, protection of minors, life in the community, acceptable determination of mental illness, rights regarding medical examination, confidentiality, the role of community and culture, standards of care, and treatment.

In addition to the changes in mental health system, the **Patient Self-Determination Act** (PSDA) was implemented December 1, 1991, as a part of the **Omnibus Budget Reconciliation Act of 1990.** This legislation requires hospitals, health maintenance organizations, skilled nursing facilities, home health agencies, and hospices receiving Medicare and Medicaid reimbursement to inform patients at the time of admission of their right to play a central role in health care decisions (Omnibus Budget Reconciliation Act, 1990). This bill was an outgrowth of a 1990 U.S. Supreme Court decision in the case of *Cruzan v. Harmon.* This ruling affirmed an individual's right to refuse or terminate life-sustaining treatment. The goal of the bill was to enhance an individual's control over treatment decisions and to support personal autonomy (Sabatino, 1993). This act is based on the belief that individuals have the right to privacy, autonomy, and self-determination. Inherent in the act is the standard that individuals have the right to accept or refuse treatment.

The practice of placing relatives in the hospital and leaving them there indefinitely is no longer legal. However, there may be times when an individual can be involuntarily committed through state civil laws. **Involuntary commitment** is the confined hospitalization of a person without his or her consent, but with a court order. Since state laws define the limits of involuntary civil commitment to mental hospitals, there are 51 separate commitment statutes in the United States (the 50 states and the District of Columbia). There are, however, three common elements found in most of these statutes. The individual must be (1) mentally disordered, (2) dangerous to self or others, or (3) unable to provide for his or her basic needs (i.e., "gravely disabled") (Monahan & Shah, 1989).

A person who is involuntarily committed has the right to receive treatment but may also have the right to refuse treatment. Arguments over the rights of civilly committed patients to refuse treatment first surfaced in 1975, when a federal district court judge issued a temporary restraining order prohibiting the use of psychotropic medication with an unwilling patient at a State Hospital in Boston. About half of the states have recognized the right of involuntary patients to refuse medication (Hermann, 1990). In addition, an increasing number of states are enacting legislation that enables patients to refuse treatment.

A **forensic commitment** is a special type of involuntary commitment of persons with a mental disorder who are charged with a crime and criminally committed to a mental hospital. There are five groups who may be committed in this way: (1) persons charged with a crime who are found incompetent to stand trial because of a mental disorder, (2) persons acquitted of crime by reason of insanity, (3) mentally disordered sex offenders, (4) persons adjudicated as "guilty but mentally ill," and (5) prisoners transferred to a mental hospital while under criminal sentence. Persons who are found incompetent to stand trial are treated in a mental hospital until their competency is restored. Persons who are acquitted of a crime by reason of insanity are treated in a hospital and then released. States usually have special statutes for the hospitalization of persons who are sexually dangerous. Prisoners who have a mental illness are treated for their illness and then returned to prison to complete their sentence.

The film *Nuts* (1987), starring and produced by Barbra Streisand and directed by Martin Ritt, tells the story of a prostitute, Claudia Draper, charged with murdering one of her clients. In the opening scenes, the viewer is convinced that Streisand has a mental illness. Her character, Claudia, a product of an upper-middle-class family, claims that she is innocent and killed in self-defense. Her parents, psychiatrist, and lawyer want her to claim insanity. Claudia believes that she would spend more time in a mental hospital than she would for a specified sentence of manslaughter. The key is a sanity hearing in a closed court room, where her competence to stand trial is determined. Ultimately, the family secret is exposed, and the similarity of the sexual molestation of her childhood to the events surrounding the murder is revealed.

PUBLIC LAW 99-319, RESTATEMENT OF BILL OF RIGHTS FOR MENTAL HEALTH PATIENTS

1. The right to appropriate treatment and related services in a setting and under conditions that are the most supportive of such person's personal liberty, and restrict such liberty only to the extent necessary consistent with such person's treatment needs, applicable requirement of law, and applicable judicial orders.
2. The right to an individualized, written, treatment or service plan (such plan to be developed promptly after admission of such person), the right to treatment based on such plan, the right to periodic review and reassessment of treatment and related service needs, and the right to appropriate revision of such plan, including any revision necessary to provide a description of mental health services that may be needed after such person is discharged from such program or facility.
3. The right to ongoing participation, in a manner appropriate to a person's capabilities, in the planning of mental health services to be provided (including the right to participate in the development and periodic revision of the plan).
4. The right to be provided with a reasonable explanation, in terms and language appropriate to a person's condition and ability to understand the person's general mental and physical (if appropriate) condition the objectives of treatment, the nature and significant possible adverse effects of recommended treatment, the reasons why a particular treatment is considered, the reasons why access to certain visitors may not be appropriate, and any appropriate and available alternative treatments, services, and types of providers of mental health services.
5. The right not to receive a mode or course of treatment in the absence of informed, voluntary, written consent to treatment except during an emergency situation.
6. The right not to participate in experimentation in the absence of informed, voluntary, written consent (includes human subject protection).
7. The right to freedom from restraint or seclusion, other than as a mode or course of treatment or restraint or seclusion during an emergency situation with a written order by a responsible mental health professional.
8. The right to a humane treatment environment that affords reasonable protection from harm and appropriate privacy with regard to personal needs.
9. The right to access, upon request, to such person's mental health care records.
10. The right, in the case of a person admitted on a residential or inpatient care basis, to converse with others privately, to have convenient and reasonable access to the telephone and mails, and to see visitors during regularly scheduled hours. (For treatment purposes, specific individuals may be excluded.)
11. The right to be informed promptly and in writing at the time of admission of these rights.
12. The right to assert grievances with respect to infringement of these rights.
13. The right to exercise these rights without reprisal.
14. The right of referral to other providers.

Box 14-1. Bill of rights for mental health patients.

APPROACHES TO TREATMENT

Treatment approaches can be categorized into biological, psychotherapeutic, and socioenvironmental modalities. Each approach has been depicted in many films, and often a combination of all three is presented in a single film.

Medications

The use of contemporary medications began in 1952 with the introduction of **chlorpromazine** (Thorazine), first used as an antihistamine. Several compounds with similar properties were also synthesized. Thorazine was believed to be the miracle drug and would be responsible for emptying all of the mental hospitals. These medications did enable many patients to live once again in the community; unfortunately, they were often indiscriminately prescribed, and dosages were usually excessive. Because of a lack of knowledge about the drug and its consequences, excessive sedation and **extrapyramidal side effects** (muscle cramps of the head and neck, restless pacing or fidgeting, and stiffening of muscular activity in the face, body, arms, and legs) were common. In *One Flew over the Cuckoo's Nest,* the patients were receiving very high dosages of medications that sedated them and put them at high risk for side effects.

Today there are several different classifications of pharmacological agents. **Antipsychotic medications** are given to treat thought disorders, such as schizophrenia, and some mood disorders. Antidepressants are given for the mood disorders, and **lithium carbonate** is usually the medication of choice for bipolar disorders. **Anxiolytic** (antianxiety) medications are carefully prescribed for patients with anxiety disorders. Some of these drugs, such as Xanax, Valium, and Librium, can be addictive. These drugs are also the ones most often used in combination with alcohol and recreational drugs. The 1982 movie *I'm Dancing as Fast as I Can* stars Jill Clayburgh as the award-winning TV producer Barbara Gordon, who becomes addicted to Valium, and portrays her struggle to recover.

Electroconvulsive Therapy (ECT)

In the early part of this century, many psychiatrists believed persons with epilepsy were somehow immune from mental illnesses, particularly schizophrenia. This was later found to be untrue. It was widely believed that seizures protected these patients from mental illness. It followed that, if persons with mental disorders had seizures, their mental illnesses could be cured. With some animal studies to support that approach, a long search began to discover the best way to safely simulate a seizure. In the 1950s, both electroshock and insulin shock became accepted treatment methods to induce seizures. By the 1960s, electrical stimulation, called **electroconvulsive therapy** (ECT), was considered the safest method.

Originally, ECT was used for most psychiatric illnesses, including schizophrenia. However, more effective pharmacological approaches were ultimately developed for most of these disorders. Today, severe depression, mania, and some types of thought disorders are treated with ECT, but only when other approaches have failed. The procedure is accompanied by the administration of short-acting general anesthesia and muscle paralytic agents that prevent the muscle contractions of typical seizures. Then a very mild electrical stimulus is passed through the brain, causing seizure activity. A series of 8–10 treatments is usually administered before significant results are obtained.

In the past, ECT was used frequently and indiscriminately, often with excessive voltage. In films such as *One Flew over the Cuckoo's Nest* and *An Angel at My Table,* ECT is usually pictured as a tortuous, lengthy process, with a screaming victim strapped to a table by sadistic attendants. In reality, contemporary use of ECT takes about 5–10 minutes from start to finish and rarely results in a visible seizure. There are also very clear practice guidelines regulating when ECT is appropriate and when it is not. In *One Flew over the Cuckoo's Nest,* ECT was used as punishment for expressing unwelcome opinions. Its use was just as inappropriate in *An Angel at My Table.*

Psychosurgery

Psychosurgery had a short-lived history as a biological intervention. Egas Moniz of Lisbon, Portugal, introduced **prefrontal lobotomy,** or **leukotomy** (severing all nerves to the prefrontal cortex) in 1936. This procedure was brought to the United States, and by 1944 lobotomies had been performed on 5,000 people. In 1949 Moniz received the Nobel Prize for the development of the prefrontal lobotomy.

The operation was initially received with great enthusiasm, and many genuinely believed the procedure would cure or alleviate the most severe symptoms of psychosis. However, the irreversible brain damage and personality impairment associated with lobotomies (loss of initiative and judgment) quickly made this form of treatment obsolete. There has been a recent, renewed interest in psychosurgery as more sophisticated surgical procedures have become available.

In the film, One Flew over the Cuckoo's Nest, *McMurphy receives a lobotomy.* In *Angel at My Table,* Janet escapes psychosurgery only after she wins a literary award. A controversial film biography, *Frances* (1982), portrayed the 1930s Hollywood actress Frances Farmer and her confinement in mental institutions for rebellious behavior. Frances, played by Jessica Lange, received both shock treatment and a lobotomy.

Psychotherapies

Psychotherapy can be practiced with either individuals or groups. These therapies can be of short or long duration. Individual therapy allows for a more intense relationship with the therapist and is usually used when the client has a problem requiring self-examination and disclosure. In group therapy, the individuals may have already had some individual therapy and progress to a group situation in order to learn how others handle similar problems, as well as receive support for new ways of interacting with others. Some problems are more appropriately dealt with in group situations, especially those problems associated with personality disorders.

Family therapy focuses on problems within the context of the family. Families are viewed as a system with a set of interrelated subsystems, linked in such a way that changing any one part affects the total functioning of the overall system. The family is viewed organizationally as an open system in which one member's actions influence the functioning of the total system. There are many family theorists such as Gregory Bateson, Don Jackson, Jay Haley, and Virginia Satir. Murray Bowen is associated with multigenerational family therapy that focuses on unresolved conflicts and losses. Most family therapists emphasize problems in family communication.

Psychotherapy had its beginning with Sigmund Freud, who developed **psychoanalysis,** a therapeutic process for accessing the unconscious and resolving conflicts that originate in childhood. Freud conceptualized the human mind in terms of **conscious** and **unconscious** mental processes. The material in the unconscious either has never been conscious or has been repressed. Freud introduced the concept of **defense mechanisms:** ways through which people cope with anxiety. In psychoanalysis, the personality is studied through **free associations** (spontaneous, uncensored verbalizations of whatever comes to mind) and the **interpretation of dreams. Transference** (relating to the therapist as though he or she were some other significant person in the patient's life) and **countertransference** (the therapist's feelings about his or her patient) are important components of psychoanalysis. Unfortunately, psychoanalysis has not been found to be helpful for many persons with mental disorders, but it is helpful to those individuals who want to pursue personal growth. Even for these people, analysis is a long, arduous process requiring several years of treatment. However, many psychoanalytic concepts serve as a basis for shorter, less intense psychotherapy applicable to a wider range of problems.

One of the most important outcomes of Freud's work was the recognition of the importance of the therapeutic relationship and its utility in helping patients change their behavior and attitudes. Defense mechanisms, anxiety, transference, and countertransference continue to be important concepts in many therapeutic systems.

Individual therapy is often depicted in films. *One of the best examples of the impact of a positive therapeutic relationship is found in* Sybil, *when Dr. Wilbur spends endless hours treating Sybil's multiple personality disorder.* In *Ordinary People,* Conrad, the surviving son, begins therapy with a psychiatrist (played by Judd Hirsch) who demonstrates warmth and caring and allows his young patient to examine painful family relationships within the safety of individual therapy. In *Equus* (1977), Richard Burton plays a psychiatrist who treats a very disturbed young man played by Peter Firth. During psychotherapy, the true depth of the psychological disturbance is revealed.

Behavioral and Cognitive Therapies

The behavioral therapies have their theoretical roots in learning theory. The basic idea underlying these approaches is that behavior is learned and that it is possible to teach new ways of viewing the world and changing behavior. These approaches emphasize the strong connections between the mind and body. Ivan Pavlov noticed that other triggers besides food stimulated stomach secretions of dogs. In a series of experiments, he was able to stimulate secretions with nonphysiological (conditional) stimuli such as sounds. B. F. Skinner conducted seminal experiments in **operant conditioning** that demonstrated the ways in which behavior is shaped by its consequences. **Behavior modification** methods are clearly associated with Skinner's work. Behavior modification techniques are often used for changing specific behaviors, such as smoking and overeating. They are also used in **token economy systems** in psychiatric hospitals. For these programs, individuals are rewarded with tokens for engaging in positive behaviors, which can be exchanged for rewards of their choice. Behavior modification programs are also widely used in child and adolescent treatment programs.

Cognitive therapies focus on changing thought processes in order to influence human behavior. Two leading cognitive approaches include Albert Bandura's **social learning theory** and Aaron Beck's **cognitive behavior therapy.** Bandura proposed that learning often occurs when one observes the behaviors of others and internalizes them through the process of modeling. In Bandura's model, there is an emphasis on the development of **self-efficacy,** a person's sense of his or her ability to deal with the environment. Beck focuses on cognitions that lead to errors in judgment and become habitual errors in thinking. For example, a young man believed that he had no friends because no one liked him. Because of this belief, he had not talked to any of his neighbors and stayed only in his apartment, resulting in a **self-fulfilling prophecy.** Beck's approach is very helpful in the treatment of depression.

Stanley Kubrick's A Clockwork Orange *(1971) is the best cinematic exploration of the ethical issues associated with behavioral methods.* In the film, Malcolm McDowell plays Alex, the leader of a gang. Alex and his friends are antisocial personalities: they thrive on violence and commit both rape and murder without any evidence of remorse. However, at the same time that audiences are repulsed by Alex's violence, they find themselves attracted by his high-spirited personality and his love of classical music.

Alex is captured after being set up by his friends, who resent his authority. He is convicted of murder and sentenced to 14 years in prison; however, he is given the option of early release if he is willing to participate in a conditioning experiment. In scenes almost as horrifying as the earlier rape scenes, Alex is injected with a nausea-inducing drug and is forced to watch scenes depicting rape and violence while Beethoven is played in the background.

The conditioning proves to be highly successful, and Alex cannot even imagine a violent episode without becoming ill. He is released from prison but finds himself totally unable to cope with life on the streets. He eventually attempts suicide. While he is recovering in the hospital, a reform movement occurs in the government, and Alex is portrayed as a guinea pig who was abused by the previous administration. The treatment is reversed, and Alex is once again able to happily fantasize about rape and murder. *The film dramatically presents the conundrum faced by society as it contemplates treatments that improve society by limiting personal freedom* (e.g., mandatory injections of drugs such as **Depo-Provera** to diminish sex drive in men convicted of sexual crimes).

Additional Questions for Class Discussion *(A Clockwork Orange)*

- Can Alex accurately be described as evil? Is the concept of evil meaningful for mental health professionals?
- How accurate are the behavior modification practices portrayed in the film? What behavioral treatments most resemble those applied to Alex?
- Are fantasies about rape or murder significant mental health problems? Under what conditions does their presence warrant intervention?
- What diagnostic label in *DSM-IV* would be most appropriate for Alex?
- Can you think of real-life examples of situations in which health professionals have exploited prisoners?

Socioenvironmental Approaches

When *One Flew over the Cuckoo's Nest* was released in 1975, the deinstitutionalization movement of the 1960s had gained momentum; and thousands of patients had been released from mental institutions. However, many people continue to be hospitalized or treated in residential care centers because they require the protection and level of service available in the more restrictive environment. For example, persons who are suicidal, actively psychotic, or a danger to society are often stabilized within a hospital environment. In the past, hospitalization usually lasted for months or years. Today, in part because of the escalating cost of inpatient care, relatively few people are hospitalized for more than a few days. Residential treatment centers provide most services for those requiring long-term care.

In the 1962 film *David and Lisa,* the treatment center is a large, expensive, but homelike facility where the staff actually lives. Most residential centers for children and adolescents have an institutional quality, with staff working shifts. In *Ordinary People,* most treatment occurs in individual outpatient sessions designed to supplement the earlier hospitalization.

Many persons with mental disorders are involved in rehabilitation programs. In this form of treatment, individuals live with their family or independently in an apartment or a group home and attend a rehabilitation program during the day. These programs vary according to the needs of the clients who are served. The film *Best Boy* documents the training of Phil, a 52-year-old man, in a training center for people with mental retardation. In the film *Benny & Joon,* part of Joon's rehabilitation involves living in her own apartment. The goal of all of these programs is to increase independence and level of functioning through supporting the individual strengths of the patient.

ETHICS, THE LAW, AND MENTAL HEALTH PROVIDERS

Mental health providers have traditionally been portrayed as either sadistic or emotionally cold, such as in *One Flew over the Cuckoo's Nest,* or as bumbling and inept, as in *The Dream Team,* the 1989 comedy starring Michael Keaton. In this film, four institutionalized patients are set loose on the streets of Manhattan after their doctor is knocked unconscious. In reality, mental health professionals are people confronted with complex decisions about patient care.

Privacy and confidentiality are important concepts for mental health professionals. **Privacy** involves the ability to maintain private information that is free from government and outside intrusion. Protecting an individual's privacy is an important responsibility of mental health care providers. **Confidentiality** is different from privacy and is defined by an ethical duty of nondisclosure. The provider who receives confidential information must protect that information from being accessed by others and must resist pressure to disclose. Confidentiality involves two people: the individual who discloses and the person with whom information is shared. A person's privacy can be violated at the same time confidentiality is maintained. However, if confidentiality is broken, a person's privacy is also violated (Beauchamp & Childress, 1989).

Maintaining a person's privacy and protecting confidentiality involve both legal and ethical considerations. A breach of confidentiality occurs when patient information is released in the absence of legal compulsion (e.g., a court order) or authorization to release information (Wettstein, 1994). For example, discussing a patient's problem with a relative without the patient's consent is breaching confidentiality. Sharing patient information with another professional who is not involved in the patient's care is also a breach of confidentiality, because the individual has not given permission for the information to be shared. Confidentiality is clearly breached in the film *Equus,* when the psychiatrist discusses the details of his case with his girlfriend, who happens to be the boy's judge.

There are times when professionals are legally mandated to breach confidentiality. If a client either threatens to harm or has injured another person, the professional is mandated by law to report it to authorities. For example, if there is evidence of child abuse, professionals are mandated to notify the appropriate authority. The legal "duty to warn" was a result of the 1976 decision of *Tarasoff v Regents of the University of California.* In this case, Prosenjit Poddar, a 26-year-old graduate student at the University of California, killed Tatiana Tarasoff, a 19-year-old student. Poddar had revealed his obsessions about her murder during therapy. Even though the authorities were notified, Ms. Tarasoff was not warned of his intent. Her parents initiated a separate civil action and said the therapists should have warned their daughter of the danger she would confront. The California Supreme Court agreed that psychotherapists have a duty to exercise reasonable care in protecting the foreseeable victims of their patients' violent actions.

This case has had far reaching consequences and has influenced numerous judicial rulings (Pettis, 1992). For example, the **duty to warn** has been extended to instances of intentions to abuse others, alcohol abuse and driver safety, and intent to damage property (Felthous, 1993; Helminski, 1993; Pettis, 1992; Pettis & Gutheil, 1993; Zellman, 1992). While each case is determined on its own merit, therapists usually have some latitude in exercising judgment. There have been many lawsuits based on the Tarasoff case, but most have failed.

Films rarely deal with the mandate to warn issue. In the film *Sybil,* the general practitioner, who had clear indication that Sybil was being abused, would have had an ethical and a legal obligation to notify authorities, according to the Tarasoff ruling.

The fundamental ethical principles of **autonomy** and **beneficence** guide the ethical conduct of mental health professionals. According to the principle of autonomy, each person has the fundamental right of self-determination and should be able to make decisions that shape his or her future. The principle of beneficence applies to the mental health care professional who is responsible for providing treatment to help patients maximize their potential. Ethical conflicts occur when the client is being guided by the principle of autonomy and the provider by the principle of beneficence. Additionally, the moral responsibilities of honesty and justice are important considerations in making treatment decisions, as well as the basic mandate that providers "do no harm" (Dormire, 1993; Lazarus, 1994).

In many films, professional ethical standards are compromised for the sake of the plot. In *Prince of Tides* (1991), an excellent examination of the impact of childhood trauma on the adult life, the romantic relationship between Barbra Streisand (a psychiatrist) and Nick Nolte (the brother of her client) distracts from the main story. The same is true with the film *Mr. Jones,* in which a bipolar patient becomes sexually involved with his psychiatrist. It is interesting that, in both pictures, the psychiatrist is female. In real life, it is more common for male therapists to become involved with female clients (Wedding, 1995).

Even with legal safeguards, the potential for the abuse of power by mental health professionals is always present. A patient is always in a dependent position, and any therapeutic relationship always holds the potential for exploitation. It is never acceptable for a mental health provider to become personally involved with his or her clients. Clients seek out help in a state of vulnerability and disclose information to a stranger because of the expectation that professional help will be received. If a therapist uses any personal information about the client in order to meet the therapist's personal needs, both the professional relationship and the client's confidence are destroyed.

THE PORTRAYAL OF TREATMENT AND MENTAL HEALTH PROVIDERS IN FILM

One Flew over the Cuckoo's Nest is the classic film that depicts the violation of human rights in mental institutions, but it was certainly not the first. *The Snake Pit* was one of the earliest films to raise consciousness about the treatment of persons with mental illness. One important difference between the two films is that the character of Virginia in *The Snake Pit* is truly mentally ill, whereas Randle McMurphy is not. *Chattahoochee* also describes the plight of those who disagree with institutional authority and power, and *Nuts* portrays a woman's struggle not to be committed to an institution.

Even though each of these movies reflects the deplorable treatment of persons with mental illness, their underlying messages may perpetuate fear and misunderstanding of serious disorders. The stigma of mental illness is also perpetuated in such films as the *Psycho* and *Halloween* series.

Successful treatment is usually not portrayed in films. Exceptions include films such as *Sybil, David and Lisa,* and *Ordinary People.* The treatment most often used is individual psychotherapy. In some instances, such as in *Best Boy,* a rehabilitation program is portrayed. The ethics of sound professional treatment are often compromised in films. Breaches in confidentiality are evident in *Equus,* and sexual relationships between clients and psychiatrists are depicted in both *Mr. Jones* and *Prince of Tides.*

Critical Thinking Questions

- It has been suggested that, on a college campus, the only thing separating harmless eccentricity from mental illness is tenure. How does one's environment shape expectations about what is or is not appropriate behavior?
- Vincent van Gogh was a genius, but he was also mentally ill, and his life was tragically cut short by suicide. Would the world be better off if this illness had been diagnosed and treated? Would you take the same position if you knew psychotropic medication would rob van Gogh of his creative spirit and his passion for art?
- Is it ever ethical to treat someone who refuses treatment? If so, who should be empowered to make these decisions?
- There is a clear asymmetry of power and knowledge when doctors meet with family members to discuss treatment options. How does this fact influence the principles of informed consent and patient autonomy?
- Do you think it is ethical to offer early release to prisoners who have committed sexual offenses if they allow themselves to be castrated? What if they simply agree to take medications that eliminate all sexual drive? Are the courts ever justified in mandating treatments of this sort?

APPENDIX A

Folstein Mini Mental Status Examination

Task	Instructions	Scoring	
Date Orientation	"Tell me the date." Ask for omitted items.	One point each for year, season, date, day of week, and month	5
Place Orientation	"Where are you?" Ask for omitted items.	One point each for state, county, town, building, and floor or room	5
Register 3 Objects	Name three objects slowly and clearly. Ask the patient to repeat them.	One point for each item correctly repeated	3
Serial Sevens	Ask the patient to count backward from 100 by 7. (Stop after five answers or ask the patient to spell "world" backward.)	One point for each correct answer (or letter)	5
Recall 3 Objects	Ask the patient to recall the objects mentioned above.	One point for each item correctly remembered	3
Naming	Point to your watch and ask the patient, "What is this?" Repeat with a pencil.	One point for each correct answer	2
Repeating a Phrase	Ask the patient to say, "No ifs, ands, or buts."	One point if successful on first try	1
Verbal Commands	Give the patient a plain piece of paper and say, "Take this paper in your right hand, fold it in half, and put it on the floor."	One point for each correct action	3
Written Commands	Show the patient a piece of paper with "CLOSE YOUR EYES" printed on it.	One point if the patient's eyes close	1
Writing	Ask the patient to write a sentence.	One point if sentence has a subject and a verb and makes sense	1
Drawing	Ask the patient to copy a pair of intersecting pentagons onto a piece of paper.	One point if the figure has 10 corners and two intersecting lines	1
Scoring	A score of 24 or above is considered normal.		30

Adapted from Folstein, Folstein, & McHugh, Mini Mental State,
Journal of Psychiatric Research, 12, 196-198 (1975).

APPENDIX B

Films Illustrating Psychopathology

	Key to Ratings
Ψ	Description provided for your information only; don't bother with the film
ΨΨ	Mildly interesting and somewhat educational; probably worth your time
ΨΨΨ	A good film relevant to your education as a mental health professional
ΨΨΨΨ	Highly recommended both as art and as professional education
ΨΨΨΨΨ	A must-see film that combines artistry with psychological relevance

ANXIETY DISORDERS

Arachnophobia (1990) Comedy/Horror ΨΨ
A story about a doctor with a paralyzing fear of spiders. (Actually, the spiders in this film are pretty intimidating, and fear appears to be a perfectly reasonable response.)

As Good As It Gets (1997) Romance ΨΨΨ
Jack Nicholson won his third Academy Award as Best Actor for this film, in which he portrays a homophobic, racist novelist with an obsessive-compulsive disorder.

Big Parade, The (1925) Romance/War ΨΨΨΨ
Epic film about World War I gives the viewer a sense of the stress of combat and the trauma of returning to civilian life minus a leg or an arm.

Black Rain (1989) Drama ΨΨΨ
Black-and-white film by Japanese filmmaker Shohei Imamura about the aftermath of the bombing of Hiroshima and its long-term psychological effects.

Born on the Fourth of July (1989) Drama/War/Biography ΨΨΨΨ
Oliver Stone film about the anger, frustration, rage, and coping of paralyzed Vietnam veteran Ron Kovic (Tom Cruise). Kovic was thrown out of the 1972 Republican convention but went on to address the Democratic convention in 1976. The film has especially memorable VA hospital scenes.

> "Who's gonna love me, Dad? Whoever's going to love me?"
> Ron Kovic in *Born on the Fourth of July* (1989)

Casualties of War (1989) War ΨΨΨ
Brian De Palma film about five GIs who kidnap, rape, and murder a young Vietnamese girl. The film deals with themes of guilt, stress, violence, and, most of all, the dehumanizing aspects of war.

ANXIETY DISORDERS

Coming Home (1978) Drama/War ΨΨΨ
Jon Voigt plays a paraplegic veteran who becomes Jane Fonda's lover in this sensitive antiwar film. Fonda's Marine Corps husband winds up committing suicide. Interesting analysis of the ways different people respond to the stress of war.

Creepshow (1982) Horror ΨΨ
A man with an insect phobia winds up being eaten alive by cockroaches. Directed by George Romero, who also directed the classic film *Night of the Living Dead*. Stephen King wrote the screenplay, and the film is actually better than one would expect.

Deer Hunter, The (1978) War ΨΨΨΨ
Robert De Niro in an unforgettable film about how Vietnam affects the lives of three high school buddies. The Russian roulette sequences are among the most powerful scenes in film history. Psychopathology themes include drug abuse, PTSD, and depression. The movie won five Academy Awards, including one for best picture, and De Niro has described it as his finest film.

Fearless (1993) Drama ΨΨ
Jeff Bridges in an interesting film that portrays some of the symptoms of anxiety in airline crash survivors. Interesting vignettes showing group therapy for PTSD victims.

Fisher King, The (1991) Drama/Fantasy/Comedy ΨΨΨ
Jeff Bridges plays a former talk show personality who unwittingly encourages a listener to go on a shooting spree. Bridges' withdrawal, cynicism, and substance use can all be interpreted and understood in the context of a post-traumatic stress disorder.

Full Metal Jacket (1987) War ΨΨΨ
Stanley Kubrick's Vietnam film. The first half of the film is devoted to life in a Marine boot camp, and it is a good illustration of the stress associated with military indoctrination. One of the recruits kills his drill instructor and then commits suicide in response to the pressure.

> "If you ladies leave my island, if you survive recruit training . . . you will be a weapon, you will be a minister of death, praying for war. But until that day you are pukes."
> Drill instructor Hartman in *Full Metal Jacket* (1978)

Hamburger Hill (1987) War ΨΨ
A graphic presentation of the stress and horror of war.

High Anxiety (1977) Comedy ΨΨ
Mel Brook's spoof of Hitchcock classics about a psychiatrist who works at the Institute for the Very, Very Nervous. The film is better if you've seen the Hitchcock films on which the parody builds.

House of Games (1987) Crime ΨΨ
Lindsay Crouse in the lead role plays a psychiatrist who has just written an important book on obsessive-compulsive disorders. She becomes obsessed with confidence games and is slowly drawn into the criminal life.

In Country (1989) Drama ΨΨ
Bruce Willis plays a Vietnam veteran with post-traumatic stress disorder who is unable to relate meaningfully to the world around him until he visits the Vietnam memorial.

Inside Out (1986) Drama Ψ
A little known but interesting film in which Elliott Gould plays a man with agoraphobia. He sends out for food, sex, and haircuts but finds that he cannot meet *all* his needs without leaving home.

Jacob's Ladder (1990) Drama ΨΨ
Complex film about a Vietnam veteran who has dramatic hallucinations of indeterminate etiology (possibly the result of military exposure to experimental drugs).

M*A*S*H (1970) Comedy/War ΨΨΨ
Wonderfully funny Robert Altman film about military surgeons and nurses using alcohol, sex, and humor to cope with the stress of war. The portrayal of Hawkeye Pierce, half-drunk but always ready for surgery, is troubling.

Obsession (1976) Thriller Ψ
Brian De Palma version of Hitchcock's *Vertigo*. The De Palma film doesn't live up to the original.

Paths of Glory (1957) War ΨΨΨΨ
Kirk Douglas in an early Stanley Kubrick film about the horrors and stupidity of WWI. There is a memorable scene in which a general repeatedly slaps a soldier, trying without success to bring him out of his shell-shocked state. The scene was repeated in the 1970 film *Patton.*

> "Sergeant, I want you to arrange for the immediate transfer of this baby out of my regiment. I won't have any of our brave men contaminated by him."
> *Paths of Glory* (1957)

Pawnbroker, The (1965) Drama ΨΨΨ
Concentration camp survivor who watched his wife being raped and his children being murdered copes by becoming numb. Interesting flashback scenes. Rod Steiger lost the 1965 Academy Award for best actor to Lee Marvin in *Cat Ballou.*

Patton (1970) War/Biography ΨΨΨΨ
George C. Scott is perfect in the role of the controversial general who was relieved of his command after slapping a crying soldier who had been hospitalized for combat fatigue, or what we would probably now call post-traumatic stress

> "I want you to remember that no bastard ever won a war by dying for his country. He won it by making the other poor dumb bastard die for *his* country."
> George C. Scott in *Patton* (1970)

disorder. The film won an Academy Award as best picture, and George C. Scott won the Oscar for best actor.

Phobia (1980) Horror/Mystery Ψ
Canadian film about the systematic murders of phobic psychiatric patients.

DISSOCIATIVE AND SOMATOFORM DISORDERS

Raiders of the Lost Ark (1981) Adventure ΨΨ
Steven Spielberg film with Harrison Ford as anthropologist Indiana Jones, who is forced by the situational demands of heroism to overcome his snake phobia.

San Francisco (1936) Romance/Disaster ΨΨΨ
This is one of the greatest disaster films ever made, and the special effects give the viewer some appreciation for the acute stress one would experience in a real earthquake. Clark Gable and Spencer Tracy are both marvelous in this film.

Shoah (1985) Documentary ΨΨΨΨ
Widely praised nine-hour documentary about the Holocaust. The film offers some insight into the behavior of both the German officials and their victims and illustrates antisocial personalities and post-traumatic stress disorders.

Twelve O'Clock High (1949) War ΨΨΨ
Gregory Peck in an interesting presentation of the stress of combat and the ways in which leaders can influence the behavior of those they lead.

Unmarried Woman, An (1978) Drama/Comedy ΨΨΨ
Tender, sensitive, and funny film about Jill Clayburgh learning to cope with the stress of being a single parent after her husband abandons her. Her friends, a psychiatrist, and an affair with Alan Bates all help.

Vertigo (1958) Thriller ΨΨΨΨ
Wonderful Hitchcock film in which Jimmy Stewart plays a character whose life is dominated by his fear of heights. He attempts a self-styled behavior modification program early in the film without success.

> "I have this acrophobia. I wake up at night and I see that man falling . . . ."
> Jimmy Stewart describing his symptoms in *Vertigo* (1958)

What About Bob? (1991) Comedy ΨΨ
Bill Murray plays an anxious patient who cannot function without his psychiatrist, played by Richard Dreyfuss. Not a great film, but a fun movie that explores the doctor-patient relationship and the obsessive-compulsive personality.

DISSOCIATIVE AND SOMATOFORM DISORDERS
3 Women (1977) Drama ΨΨΨΨ
Strange but engaging Robert Altman film about two California women who seem to exchange personalities.

DISSOCIATIVE AND SOMATOFORM DISORDERS

Agnes of God (1985)
Mystery ΨΨΨ
Good performances by Anne Bancroft, Meg Tilly, and Jane Fonda. Fonda plays a court-appointed psychiatrist who must make sense out of pregnancy and apparent infanticide in a local convent. Good examples of *stigmata,* an example of conversion.

Altered States (1980) Science Fiction ΨΨ
Not entirely satisfying film based in part on the sensory deprivation experiments of Dr. John Lilly. The scientist (William Hurt) combines isolation tanks with psychedelic mushrooms to induce altered states of consciousness. Good special effects.

Amateur (1994) Drama/Comedy ΨΨ
Hal Hartley film in which a man who is amnestic as a result of a traumatic head injury takes up with a nun who has left the convent to write pornographic novels. Almost every character in the film has a complex double identity and is uncertain about who he or she *really* is.

> "This is poetry, and don't you deny it. Come back tȯ me when you've written something really perverse, really depraved."
> An editor reviews Isabelle's work in *Amateur* (1994)

Anastasia (1956) Drama ΨΨΨ
Yul Brynner, Helen Hayes, and Ingrid Bergman star in this film about an amnestic woman who is believed to be the lost princess Anastasia, daughter of the last czar of Russia.

Black Friday (1940) Horror ΨΨ
Boris Karloff and Bela Lugosi star in this film about transplanting a gangster's brain in a college professor's cranium.

Cyrano de Bergerac (1990) Romance ΨΨΨ
Gerard Depardieu stars as the inimitable Cyrano, a man obsessed with the size of his nose and convinced it makes him forever unlovable.

Dark Mirror, The (1946) Thriller Ψ
Olivia De Havilland plays both parts in a story of twin sisters, one of whom is a deranged killer.

Dead Again (1991) Mystery/Romance ΨΨΨ
Emma Thompson costars with her husband, Kenneth Branagh (who also directed the film). The movie illustrates traumatic amnesia and its treatment through hypnosis. The hypnotist, an antique dealer, is not the most professional of therapists!

Despair (1979) Drama ΨΨΨ
Fassbinder film based on a novel by Vladimir Nabokov. A Russian Jew émigré in Germany runs a chocolate factory, kills another man who looks like him, and tries to pass it off as his own suicide. When his plan fails, he becomes psychotic.

DISSOCIATIVE AND SOMATOFORM DISORDERS

Devils, The (1971) Drama/Historical ΨΨΨ
Ken Russell film adapted from Aldous Huxley's book *The Devils of Loundun*. The film traces the lives of seventeenth-century French nuns who experienced highly erotic dissociative states attributed to possession by the devil.

Double Life of Veronique, The (1991) Fantasy/Drama ΨΨ
The lives of two women turn out to be linked in complex ways the viewer never fully understands.

Double Life, A (1947) Crime ΨΨ
Ronald Coleman plays an actor who is unable to sort out his theatrical life (in which he plays Othello) and his personal life.

Dr. Jekyll and Mr. Hyde (1932) Horror ΨΨΨΨ
Fredric March in the best adaptation of Robert Louis Stevenson's classic story about the ultimate dissociative disorder. Stevenson was an alcoholic, and alcohol may be the model for the mysterious liquid that dramatically transforms Jekyll's personality.

Exorcist, The (1973) Horror ΨΨ
Linda Blair stars as a 12-year-old girl possessed by the devil in William Friedkin's film based on the William Peter Blatty novel. One of the most suspenseful films ever made.

Freud (1962) Biography ΨΨΨ
Montgomery Clift in an interesting account of the early year's of Freud's life. The film illustrates paralysis, false blindness, and a false pregnancy, all examples of somatization disorders.

Great Dictator, The (1940) Comedy ΨΨ
A satire of Adolph Hitler, with Charlie Chaplin in the role of a Jewish barber who suffers amnesia and eventually finds himself assuming the personality of Adenoid Hynkel, the dictator of Tomania.

Hannah and Her Sisters (1986) Comedy/Drama ΨΨΨ
Mickey (Woody Allen) is a hopeless hypochondriac who was formerly married to Hannah (Mia Farrow). Mickey spends his days worrying about brain tumors, cancer, and cardiovascular disease.

Home of the Brave (1949) Drama/War ΨΨ
A black soldier develops a conversion disorder following his return from combat.

Last Temptation of Christ, The (1988) Religious ΨΨΨ
Challenging and controversial Martin Scorsese film in which Jesus, while on the cross and in great pain, has a dissociative episode in which he imagines himself as an ordinary man who married Mary Magdalene and lived a normal life.

DISSOCIATIVE AND SOMATOFORM DISORDERS

Lizzie (1957) Drama ΨΨ
Eleanor Parker, a woman with dissociative identity disorder (i.e., multiple personality disorder), is treated by psychiatrist Richard Boone.

Mirage (1965) Drama ΨΨ
A scientist who makes an important discovery develops amnesia after viewing the death of a friend.

My Girl (1991) Drama/Comedy ΨΨ
The film centers around an 11-year-old girl whose mother has just died and whose grandmother has Alzheimer's disease. The child responds by developing a series of imaginary disorders. Strong performances by Dan Aykroyd and Jamie Lee Curtis.

Overboard (1987) Comedy ΨΨ
Goldie Hawn plays a snooty millionairess who develops amnesia and is claimed by an Oregon carpenter as his wife and forced to care for his children.

Paris, Texas (1984) Drama ΨΨΨ
Wem Winders film about a man found wandering in the desert with no personal memory.

Persona (1966) Drama ΨΨΨΨ
Complex, demanding, and absolutely fascinating Bergman film starring Liv Ullmann as an actress who suddenly stops talking after one of her performances. Ullmann is treated by a nurse, and the two women appear to exchange "personas." Highly erotic description of a beach memory.

Piano, The (1993) Drama ΨΨΨΨ
Jane Campion film about a woman who had voluntarily stopped speaking as a child. She communicates with written notes and through playing the piano, a pleasure forbidden to her by her New Zealand husband. There are scenes of extraordinary sensuality between Harvey Keitel and Holly Hunter and a dramatic suicide attempt.

> "I have not spoken since I was six years old. Nobody knows why, least of all myself." Ada's thoughts at the beginning of *The Piano* (1993)

Poison Ivy (1992) Drama Ψ
Newcomer into a pathological family plans to take over the role of wife and mother. The father is alcoholic, the mother a hypochondriac.

Prelude to a Kiss (1992) Comedy/Romance ΨΨ
The ultimate example of a dissociative disorder. A beautiful young woman and a sad old man kiss on her wedding day and exchange bodies. The film makes this extraordinary event seem almost plausible.

Primal Fear (1996) Drama ΨΨΨ
Richard Gere stars in this suspenseful drama about a man who commits heinous crimes, ostensibly as a result of a dissociative disorder. The film raises useful questions about the problem of malingering and differential diagnosis.

DISSOCIATIVE AND SOMATOFORM DISORDERS

Psycho (1960) Horror/Thriller ΨΨΨΨ
Wonderful Hitchcock film starring Anthony
Perkins as Norman Bates, who vacillates between
his passive, morbid personality and his dead

> "Mother, my mother, uh, what is the phrase?
> — she isn't qu-quite herself today."
> Norman Bates in *Psycho* (1960)

mother's alter ego. In the final minutes of the film, a psychiatrist offers a somewhat confused explanation for Bates' behavior. The shower scene is one of the most famous shots in film history.

Raising Cain (1992) Thriller/Drama Ψ
Confusing De Palma film about a child psychologist with multiple personalities who begins to kill women and steal their children for experiments.

Return of Martin Guerre, The (1982) Historical ΨΨΨ
Gerard Depardieu as a sixteenth-century peasant who returns to his wife after a seven-year absence. His true identity is never made clear. This film, the basis for the American movie *Sommersby,* is based on a true story.

Secret of Dr. Kildare, The (1939) Drama Ψ
The good Dr. Kildare works hard to cure a patient's conversion disorder (blindness) in this dated but still interesting film.

Send Me No Flowers (1964) Romance/Comedy Ψ
Rock Hudson plays a hypochondriac convinced he will be dying soon. Hudson sets out to find a suitable replacement so his wife will be able to get along without him.

Seventh Veil, The (1945) Drama ΨΨΨ
Psychological drama about a pianist who loses the ability to play. Hypnotherapy makes it possible for Ann Todd to play the piano again and sort out her complex interpersonal relationships.

Sisters (1973) Thriller/Horror ΨΨ
De Palma film about Siamese twins separated as children; one is good, the other quite evil. The use of Siamese twins is a Hitchcock-like twist on the theme of multiple personality.

Sommersby (1993) Drama ΨΨ
Richard Gere returns to wife Jodie Foster after a six-year absence during the Civil War. Gere is remarkably changed, so much so that it appears he is a different man altogether.

Sorry, Wrong Number (1948) Thriller ΨΨ
Barbara Stanwyck and Burt Lancaster in a murder film. Stanwyck is a rich heiress who is bedridden with psychosomatic heart disease and paralysis.

Spellbound (1945) Thriller ΨΨΨΨ
Ingrid Bergman and Gregory Peck star in this Hitchcock thriller. Peck is an amnestic patient who believes he has committed a murder; Bergman is the psychiatrist who falls in love with him and helps him recall the childhood trauma responsible for his dissociative state.

DISSOCIATIVE AND SOMATOFORM DISORDERS

Steppenwolf (1974) Drama ΨΨ
Film adaptation of Herman Hesse's remarkable novel about Harry Haller (played by Max von Sydow), a misanthropic protagonist who wrestles with the competing forces of good and evil within himself.

Suddenly, Last Summer (1959) Drama ΨΨΨ
Adaptation of a Tennessee Williams story about an enmeshed and pathological relationship between a mother (Katharine Hepburn) and her homosexual son and a dissociative amnesia in a cousin who witnessed the son's death. Among its other virtues, the film includes a fascinating discussion of the benefits of lobotomy.

> "He-he was lying naked on the broken stones . . . . It looked as if-as if they had devoured him! . . .As if they'd torn or cut parts of him away with their hands, or with knives, or those jagged tin cans they made music with. As if they'd torn bits of him away in strips!"
> *Suddenly, Last Summer* (1959)

Sullivan's Travels (1941) Comedy/Drama ΨΨΨΨ
Joel McCrea plays a movie director who goes out to experience life as it is lived outside a Hollywood studio. He winds up getting a head injury, becoming amnestic, and being sentenced to six years on a chain gang.

Sybil (1976) Drama ΨΨΨ
Made-for-TV movie in which Joanne Woodward, the patient in *The Three Faces of Eve*, plays the psychiatrist treating a woman with 16 different personalities.

Three Faces of Eve, The (1957) Drama ΨΨΨΨ
Joanne Woodward won an Academy Award for her portrayal of a woman with three personalities (Eve White, Eve Black, and Jane); based on the book by Thigpin and Cleckley.

Twelve O'Clock High (1949) War ΨΨΨΨΨ
Gregory Peck plays the role of General Frank Savage, an effective leader who develops a conversion disorder (psychosomatic paralysis) in response to his role in the death of several of his subordinates. The film is based on a true story.

Up in Arms (1944) Musical/Comedy/War Ψ
Danny Kaye plays a hypochondriac in the Army.

Voices Within: The Lives of Truddi Chase (1990) Drama ΨΨ
Made-for-TV movie about a woman with multiple personality disorder; based on the best selling-book *When Rabbit Howls*.

Whatever Happened to Baby Jane? (1962) Drama ΨΨΨ
Bette Davis and Joan Crawford star as two elderly sisters who were formerly movie stars. Jane (Bette Davis) had been a child star, but her fame was eclipsed by the renown of her talented sister, now confined to a wheelchair. Jane torments her sister and experiences a dramatic dissociative episode in the final scene in the movie.

PSYCHOLOGICAL STRESS AND PHYSICAL DISORDERS

Zelig (1983) Comedy ΨΨ
Quasi-documentary about Woody Allen as Zelig, a human chameleon whose personality changes to match that of whomever he is around. He is treated by psychiatrist Mia Farrow, whom Zelig eventually marries. Watch for Susan Sontag, Saul Bellow, and Bruno Bettelheim.

PSYCHOLOGICAL STRESS AND PHYSICAL DISORDERS

12 Angry Men (1957) Drama ΨΨΨΨ
Henry Fonda stars in this fascinating courtroom drama that illustrates social pressure, the tendency toward conformity in social settings, and the stress associated with noncompliance with societal norms.

Alive (1993) Action/Adventure/Drama ΨΨ
The survivors of a plane crash in the Andes survive for more than 70 days by eating the passengers who died. The film is a vivid portrayal of traumatic stress and its consequences.

All Quiet on the Western Front (1930) Drama ΨΨΨΨ
This remarkable film illustrates the horror of war and celebrates pacifism as its only solution. The film poignantly documents that it is young men who fight our wars and shows the folly of jingoism and blind patriotism.

> "Oh, God! why did they do this to us? We only wanted to live, you and I. Why should they send us out to fight each other? If they threw away these rifles and these uniforms, you could be my brother, just like Kat and Albert. You'll have to forgive me, comrade. I'll do all I can. I'll write to your parents."
> Paul attempts to comfort a man he has killed in *All Quiet on the Western Front* (1930)

Best Years of Our Lives (1946) Drama ΨΨ
Sam Goldwyn film about servicemen adjusting to civilian life after the war. One of the sailors has lost both hands.

Blue (1993) Drama ΨΨΨ
British filmmaker Derek Jarman's last film; he died from AIDS shortly after the movie was completed. Jarman reviews his life and analyzes the ways in which his life has been affected by his disease.

Brief History of Time, A (1992) Biography ΨΨΨ
A documentary about the life of Stephen Hawking, a theoretical physicist coping with amyotrophic lateral sclerosis.

Cactus (1986) Romance ΨΨΨ
Australian film about a woman who loses one eye and considers the option of giving up sight in the other in order to more fully understand the world of her blind lover.

PSYCHOLOGICAL STRESS AND PHYSICAL DISORDERS

Children of a Lesser God (1986) Romance ΨΨΨ
The film examines the complications involved in a love relationship between William Hurt, a teacher in a school for the deaf, and Marlee Matlin, a young deaf woman who works at the school. Much of the conflict in the film revolves around Matlin's refusal to learn to lip-read. Matlin won an Academy Award as Best Supporting Actress for her role in this film.

Chinese Roulette (1976) Drama ΨΨ
Fassbinder film about a disabled girl and the ways in which he dominates and manipulates her family.

Common Threads: Stories from the Quilt (1989) Documentary ΨΨΨ
This HBO film examines the lives of five individuals linked by a single common denominator – AIDS. The movie won the Academy Award for Best Documentary Feature in 1989.

Crash of Silence (1953) Drama ΨΨ
Mother agonizes over whether to keep a hearing impaired daughter at home or send her to a special school.

Cure, The (1995) Drama ΨΨ
Two adolescent boys become best friends. One has AIDS from a blood transfusion, leading the boys to set off in search of a miracle cure.

Deaf Smith and Johnnie Ears (1973) Western ΨΨ
A deaf Anthony Quinn teams up with Franco Nero to cope with the challenges of life in rural Texas.

Doctor, The (1991) Drama ΨΨΨΨ
William Hurt plays a cold and indifferent physician whose approach to treatment changes dramatically after he is diagnosed with throat cancer.

Duet for One (1986) Drama ΨΨ
Julie Andrews plays a world class violinist who learns to cope with multiple sclerosis. Good illustration of the effects of chronic illness on psychological health. Max von Sydow plays the role of Andrews' therapist.

> "Why don't you ask me probing questions about my childhood?"
> Julie Andrews queries her therapist in *Duet for One* (1986)

Dummy (1979) Drama ΨΨ
Made-for-TV movie about a hearing impaired and mute teenager who is charged with murder and defended by a deaf attorney.

Early Frost, An (1985) Drama ΨΨΨ
Excellent made-for-TV movie (available on videocassette) that explores the pain and anguish involved as a young man explains to his family and friends that he is gay and has AIDS.

PSYCHOLOGICAL STRESS AND PHYSICAL DISORDERS

Eating (1990) Comedy ΨΨΨ
An extended conversation that examines the relationship among life, love, and food.

Elephant Man, The (1980) Drama ΨΨΨ
David Lynch film about the life of John Merrick, a hideously deformed man who is befriended by a London physician. The film is effective in forcing the viewer to examine his or her prejudices about appearance.

> "I am NOT an animal! I am a human being!"
> John Merrick in *The Elephant Man* (1980)

Falling Down (1994) Drama ΨΨ
Good presentation by Michael Douglas of the cumulative effects of stress on a marginal personality. The film does not give us enough information to clearly diagnose the character played by Douglas, but he probably displays enough symptoms to justify an Axis II diagnosis of paranoid personality disorder.

Gabby — a True Story (1987) Biography ΨΨΨ
A true story about a woman with cerebral palsy who goes on to become a respected author. Contrast this story with the life of Christy Brown told in *My Left Foot*.

Glengarry Glen Ross (1992) Drama ΨΨΨ
A hard-hitting and powerful presentation of job-related stress and interpersonal conflict in the real estate business. Wonderful cast, with Jack Lemmon playing a figure whose despair with his job is reminiscent of Willy Lomax in Arthur Miller's *Death of a Salesman*.

Heart Is a Lonely Hunter, The (1968) Drama ΨΨ
Alan Arkin stars in this adaptation of Carson McCuller's sad, poignant novel about a simple friendship between two men. One of the men is deaf; the other is mentally retarded. If you have to choose between the film and the novel, go for the novel.

Honkytonk Man (1982) Drama Ψ
Clint Eastwood produced, directed, and starred in this film about a country and western singer with leukemia who hopes to make it to Nashville before he dies.

Hunchback of Notre Dame, The (1939) Horror ΨΨΨΨ
Charles Laughton plays Quasimodo in this film adaptation of the Victor Hugo novel. The film is a classic in the genre examining the relationship between body image and self-concept.

I Sent a Letter to My Love (1981) Drama ΨΨΨ
French film about a sister caring for her paralyzed brother. They each seek romance by writing to a newspaper personals column; without realizing what is happening, each winds up corresponding with the other.

Ikiru (1952) Drama ΨΨΨΨ
Existential Akira Kurosawa film about a man dying from cancer who finds meaning in the last days of his life by helping a group of mothers build a playground for their children.

PSYCHOLOGICAL STRESS AND PHYSICAL DISORDERS

In for Treatment (1979) Drama ΨΨΨ
Dutch film about the indignities suffered by a cancer patient who has to deal with an impersonal health care system.

It's My Party (1996) Drama ΨΨΨΨ
Sensitive film about a man with AIDS who throws one last party before killing himself. Much of the film centers on the issue of voluntary suicide and the ethics of euthanasia.

Jacquot (1993) Biography ΨΨ
Moving film about the life of French director Jacques Demy, who died from a brain tumor shortly after the film was released.

Johnnie Belinda (1948) Drama ΨΨ
Jane Wyman (who was Ronald Reagan's wife at the time) earned an Academy Award for her performance as a deaf-mute woman who is stigmatized and raped. The film is dated but still offers insights into the ways in which people who are hearing impaired are perceived.

La Symphonie Pastorale (1946) Drama ΨΨΨΨ
French adaptation of André Gide novel about a Swiss minister who falls in love with his blind protégée and abandons his wife to be with her. When the blind girl later regains her sight, she is tormented by the decisions he has made because of her.

Leap of Faith (1992) Drama ΨΨ
Steve Martin plays itinerant evangelist Jonas Nightengale, whose faith healing stunts require technological support from backstage assistant Debra Winger. Contrast with Burt Lancaster in *Elmer Gantry* (1960) and the documentary *Marjoe* (1972).

Life on a String (1991) Drama ΨΨΨ
Lyrical movie about a blind Chinese musician who believes his sight will be restored when he breaks his thousandth banjo string. He grows old and wise while he waits.

Light That Failed, The (1939) Drama ΨΨ
Adaptation of Kipling novel about a great artist who goes blind as a result of an injury while in Africa.

Living End, The (1992) Comedy ΨΨ
Two HIV positive men hit the road and explore what it means to live purposively with their disease.

Longtime Companion (1990) Drama ΨΨΨ
This film explores the ways in which AIDS has affected a group of gay friends and traces the love and loss that is shared between two men as one of them dies from the disease.

> "Let go. It's all right. You can let go now."
> Bruce Davison comforts his dying lover in *Longtime Companion* (1990)

PSYCHOLOGICAL STRESS AND PHYSICAL DISORDERS

Man Without a Face, The (1993) Drama ΨΨ
Mel Gibson directs and stars in this film about a man whose face becomes terribly disfigured after an automobile accident. He becomes reclusive but finds redemption in his relationship with a 12-year-old boy he tutors.

Marvin's Room (1996) Drama ΨΨΨΨ
A compelling examination of the way in which chronic illness affects caregivers and families.

Mask (1985) Drama ΨΨΨ
Cher stars in this film about her character's son, Rocky Dennis, a spunky teenager whose life has been dramatically affected by craniodiaphyseal dysplasia, a disorder that distorts the shape of his skull and face. This is a feel good movie that succeeds. A thwarted love relationship between Rocky and a blind girlfriend underscores our tendency to judge people by their appearance.

Men, The (1950) Drama ΨΨΨ
Marlon Brando in his first film role plays a paralyzed WWII veteran full of rage about his injury and his limitations.

Miracle Worker, The (1962) Biography ΨΨΨ
Patty Duke and Anne Bancroft star in this well-known film about the childhood of Helen Keller and the influence of a gifted teacher.

My Left Foot (1989) Biography ΨΨΨΨ
The inspiring life story of Christy Brown, an Irish writer who triumphs over cerebral palsy. Daniel Day-Lewis received a Best Actor Academy Award for his role as Brown.

My Life (1993) Drama ΨΨ
Michael Keaton learns he is dying from cancer and makes a series of videotapes for his still-unborn son, including one in which he teaches his son how to shave.

Niagara, Niagara (1998) Drama ΨΨ
Two teenagers on the lam encounter multiple problems en route. Reminiscent of *Bonnie and Clyde*, the film is chiefly memorable because it is one of the few films in which Tourette's syndrome is sympathetically and realistically portrayed.

Passion Fish (1992) Drama ΨΨΨΨ
The stress of disability and the demands the disabled can make on caregivers are nicely chronicled in this film about a querulous paraplegic actress and her caretaker/companion.

Phantom of the Opera (1925) Horror ΨΨΨ
A disfigured music lover, played by Lon Chaney, lives in the bowels of the Paris opera house, unable to achieve romantic love because of his hideous face. He is eventually hunted down and killed by an angry mob.

PSYCHOLOGICAL STRESS AND PHYSICAL DISORDERS

Philadelphia (1993) Drama ΨΨΨ
Tom Hanks won an Academy Award for his portrayal of an AIDS-afflicted attorney who is fired from a prestigious law firm once illness becomes known to the partners. There is a particularly moving scene in which Hanks plays an opera and explains to Denzel Washington why he loves the music so passionately.

Places in the Heart (1984) Drama ΨΨ
Sally Field won an Academy Award for Best Actress for her role in this film about a widowed woman struggling to keep her farm and her family in a small Texas town during the Depression. The film is memorable for bringing together John Malkovich as a blind World War I veteran and Danny Glover as a hapless drifter. The standoff between a blind Malkovich and the local chapter of the Ku Klux Klan is especially memorable.

Promises in the Dark (1979) Drama ΨΨ
Melodrama about a young woman dying from cancer.

Proof (1992) Drama ΨΨΨΨ
Australian drama about a blind man who takes photographs to document his life and its meaning.

Savage Nights (1993) French Drama/Biography ΨΨΨΨ
This controversial film was directed by French filmmaker Cyril Collard, who died from AIDS three days before *Savage Nights* was selected as the Best French Film of the Year. The movie deals with the existential decisions made by a bisexual antihero who continues to have unprotected sex even after learning he has AIDS.

Shadowlands (1993) Biography ΨΨΨ
Wonderful Richard Attenborough film about the late-life romance of C. S. Lewis (Anthony Hopkins) and Joy Gresham (Debra Winger). Lewis must come to grips with the meaning of pain, suffering, and loss when Joy develops cancer.

Shootist, The (1976) Western ΨΨ
John Wayne's last film, about an aging gunfighter dying from cancer. Also stars Ron Howard and Jimmy Stewart.

> "You aim to do to me what they did with John Wesley Hardin. Lay me out and parade every damn fool in the state past me at a dollar a head, half price for children, and then stuff me in a gunny sack and shovel me under."
> John Wayne confronts the undertaker in *The Shootist* (1976)

Shop on Main Street, The (1965) Drama ΨΨΨΨ
Czechoslovakian film about a man appointed as the "Aryan controller" of a button shop in World War II. He befriends and hides the Jewish owner of the shop, who does not understand the situation because she is deaf. She assumes the new arrival has been sent as her assistant; when he later hides her in a cupboard to avoid deportation to the death camps, she smothers. Overcome with remorse, he kills himself. Selected as the Best Foreign Film of 1965.

PSYCHOLOGICAL STRESS AND PHYSICAL DISORDERS

Tell Me That You Love Me, Junie Moon (1970) Comedy ΨΨ
Otto Preminger film in which three unusual roommates come together as a family. Liza Minnelli is disfigured; another has epilepsy; the third is a wheelchair bound homosexual.

Terms of Endearment (1983) Comedy ΨΨΨ
Shirley MacLaine, Debra Winger, and Jack Nicholson star in this poignant but funny movie about relationships, caring, and cancer.

Test of Love, A (1984) Drama ΨΨ
An Australian film based on a true story of a teacher's successful attempt to reach out to a disabled girl.

Waterdance, The (1992) Drama ΨΨΨΨ
Realistic film about the way spinal cord injuries have changed the lives of three men who meet in a rehabilitation hospital.

> "Got you in a halo, huh. I call that thing a crown of thorns. I thought they was gonna screw it into my brain."
> A paralyzed patient describes his rehabilitation in *The Waterdance* (1992)

Whales of August, The (1987) Drama ΨΨΨ
Vincent Price and Ann Sothern support Lillian Gish and Bette Davis in a remarkable film about what it means to grow old. Davis plays the blind and embittered sister who is still loved by Gish.

Whatever Happened to Baby Jane? (1962) Drama ΨΨ
Bette Davis and Joan Crawford portray two elderly sisters. Crawford is wheelchair-bound as a result of an automobile accident possibly caused by her sister. Davis is obviously demented and terrorizes her younger sister. Surprise ending.

White Heat (1949) Crime ΨΨΨΨ
James Cagney plays a ruthless gangster who has debilitating migraine headaches that only his mother can cure. The film ties into the psychoanalytic ideas of the day and features a famous ending in which Cagney blows up an oil tank.

> "Cody Jarrett. He finally made it to the top of the world. And it blew up in his face."
> *White Heat (1949)*

Whose Life Is It Anyway? (1981) Drama ΨΨΨΨ
Richard Dreyfuss plays a sculptor paralyzed from the neck down after a car crash. He argues convincingly for the right to die.

Woman's Tale, A (1991) Drama ΨΨΨΨ
An Australian film directed by Paul Cox about the final days in the life of a 78-year-old woman dying of cancer.

MOOD DISORDERS AND SUICIDE

Anna Karenina (1935) Drama ΨΨΨΨ
Greta Garbo leaves her husband (Basil Rathbone) and son to follow new love (Fredric March); when she sees him kissing another woman, she commits suicide by stepping into the path of an oncoming train. Based on a Tolstoy novel.

Bell Jar, The (1979) Biography Ψ
An unsuccessful attempt to capture the spirit of Sylvia Plath's autobiographical novel *The Bell Jar*. Plath eventually committed suicide by putting her head into an oven and turning on the gas.

Crossover (1983) Drama Ψ
A male nurse is plagued by self-doubts after one of the psychiatric patients commits suicide.

Field, The (1990) Drama Ψ
Dramatic presentation of the suicide by drowning of a young man who finds he cannot live up to his father's expectations.

Fox and His Friends (1975) Drama ΨΨΨΨ
Werner Fassbinder's scathing indictment of capitalism revolves around the life of a poor gay circus performer who wins money, only to lose it through the exploitation of those he assumes are his friends. He responds by committing suicide.

Good Morning, Vietnam (1987) Comedy/Drama/War ΨΨ
Robin Williams as an Air Force radio announcer in Vietnam. Williams has a funny, frenetic style that could be described as hypomanic.

Hairdresser's Husband, The (1992) Comedy/Drama ΨΨΨ
A woman chooses to commit suicide rather than face the incremental loss of love that she believes will accompany aging. This is a beautiful movie, despite the somewhat grim ending.

Horse Feathers (1932) Comedy ΨΨ
Groucho Marx plays a very manic college president who displays flight of ideation and pressured speech.

Hospital, The (1971) Comedy/Drama ΨΨΨ
George C. Scott is first rate as a disillusioned and suicidal physician despondent in part because of the ineptitude he sees everywhere about him. There is an especially memorable scene in which Scott is interrupted as he's about to commit suicide by injecting potassium into a vein.

Inside Moves (1980) Drama ΨΨ
Man who has failed at suicide attempt makes new friends in a bar and regains the will to live. Mainly notable as the comeback film for Harold Russell, the double amputee in *The Best Years of Our Lives* (1946).

MOOD DISORDERS AND SUICIDE

It's a Wonderful Life (1946) Drama ΨΨΨ
A Christmas tradition. The film actually presents Jimmy Stewart as a fairly complex character who responds to the stress of life in Bedford Falls by attempting suicide.

> "You see, George, you've really had a wonderful life. Don't you see what a mistake it would be to throw it away?"
> Clarence in *It's A Wonderful Life* (1946)

Juliet of the Spirits (1965) Drama ΨΨΨ
Frederico Fellini film about a bored, lonely, depressed, and menopausal housewife who hallucinates about the life of the exotic woman next door.

Last Picture Show, The (1971) Drama ΨΨΨΨ
Peter Bogdanovich adaptation of Larry McMurtry's novel describing the events—and personalities—involved in the closing of the town's only movie theater. There is a striking presentation of the symptoms of depression in the coach's wife.

Life Upside Down (1965) Drama ΨΨΨ
French film about an ordinary young man who becomes increasingly detached from the world. He is eventually hospitalized and treated, but with little success.

Mishima (1985) Biography ΨΨΨ
A fascinating film about one of the most interesting figures in contemporary literature, Yukio Mishima. Mishima, a homosexual, traditionalist, and militarist, committed ritual suicide *(seppuku)* before being beheaded by a companion.

Mommie Dearest (1981) Biography ΨΨ
Biographical film based on the book by Joan Crawford's adopted daughter. Faye Dunaway plays Crawford. The film suggests the great star was tyrannical, narcissistic, and probably bipolar.

Mosquito Coast, The (1986) Adventure ΨΨΨ
Harrison Ford is an eccentric American inventor who flees the U.S. for Central America because of his paranoia. His diagnosis is never clearly stated, but Ford appears to be bipolar (although almost continually manic in the film).

My First Wife (1984) Drama ΨΨ
A moving and well-directed Australian film about a man who falls to pieces after his wife decides to leave him.

Network (1976) Drama ΨΨΨ
A veteran anchorman who has just been told he is being fired announces on national TV that he will commit suicide on the air in two weeks. Ratings soar. He eventually reneges on his promise but becomes the leader of a national protest movement.

> "... I'm as mad as hell, and I'm not going to take this anymore!"
> Newscaster Howard Beale in *Network* (1976)

MOOD DISORDERS AND SUICIDE

Nightmare Alley (1947) Crime ΨΨ
Tyrone Power's favorite film. Powers plays a carnival huckster who teams up with an unethical psychologist to dupe the public. Memorable carnival "geek" scenes include biting the heads off chickens.

Ordinary People (1980) Drama ΨΨΨΨ
This film was Robert Redford's debut as a director. It deals with depression, suicide, and family pathology and presents a sympathetic portrayal of a psychiatrist, played by Judd Hirsch. Conrad, the protagonist, would probably meet *DSM-IV* criteria for PTSD as well as depression.

Outcry, The (1957) Drama ΨΨΨ
Antonioni film about a man who becomes depressed and confused when he is rejected by his lover.

Seventh Veil, The (1945) Drama ΨΨ
Psychological drama about a gifted musician who loses the ability to play the piano and becomes depressed and suicidal. Hypnotherapy makes it possible for Ann Todd to play again, as well as to sort out her complex interpersonal relationships.

Summer Wishes, Winter Dreams (1973) Drama Ψ
Joanne Woodward as a bored, depressed housewife searching for meaning and purpose in her life. The film includes dreams that may be hallucinations, and a possible somatoform disorder.

Tenant, The (1976) Horror ΨΨΨΨ
Roman Polanski film in which a man rents an apartment previously owned by a woman who committed suicide. The man begins to assume the personality of the woman and becomes suicidal himself.

Umberto D. (1952) Drama ΨΨΨΨ
Classic Vittorio De Sica film about an indigent old man in Rome who is being evicted and must face the prospects of homelessness and isolation. The old man fails in a suicide attempt and finds a reason for living in his need to continue to care for his dog.

Vincent (1987) Biography/Documentary ΨΨΨ
An interesting examination of the life of Vincent van Gogh. The focus is on the artist's work rather than his mental illness.

Vincent & Theo (1990) Biography ΨΨΨ
The Robert Altman film deals sensitively with van Gogh's troubled relationships with Gauguin and Theo, the incident with the prostitute and the ear, van Gogh's hospitalization, and finally his suicide.

Woman Under the Influence, A (1974) Drama ΨΨΨ
A John Cassavetes film in which Gena Rowlands plays a housewife who has to be hospitalized because of a mental illness that appears to be bipolar disorder. Peter Falk plays her sympathetic but mystified husband.

Wrong Man, The (1956) Crime ΨΨ
Hitchcock film in which a man and his wife (Henry Fonda and Vera Miles) become depressed in response to an unjust accusation of murder.

PERSONALITY DISORDERS
Accidental Tourist, The (1988) Comedy ΨΨΨ
William Hurt plays a withdrawn, unemotional writer whose isolation is compounded when his 12-year-son is senselessly murdered in a fast-food restaurant.

Aguirre: The Wrath of God (1972) Historical/Drama ΨΨΨΨ
Klaus Kinski stars in this Werner Herzog film about the growing delusion of a grandiose Spanish conquistador obsessed with finding the lost cities of gold in the South American Amazon.

Anatomy of a Murder (1959) Drama ΨΨΨΨ
Jimmy Stewart as an attorney defending a man accused of murder. His case rests on the contention that the defendant could not help behaving as he did because the man he murdered had allegedly raped his wife. The film raises interesting questions about the irresistible impulse defense.

Arsenic and Old Lace (1944) Comedy ΨΨ
Frank Capra film about Cary Grant's two aunts who practice mercy killing by giving their gentlemen guests poisoned elderberry wine. Grant worries about the fact that mental illness not only runs in his family, it gallops!

Bad Seed, The (1956) Drama Ψ
Interesting examination of whether or not evil is congenital.

Butley (1974) Drama ΨΨΨΨ
Alan Bates in a Harold Pinter film adaptation of a London play about the life of a British university professor. Bates' wife and lover are both leaving him, and his colleagues are estranged. Bates seems to fail in every interpersonal encounter.

Caine Mutiny, The (1954) Drama ΨΨΨ
Humphrey Bogart is the ship's paranoid captain, who decompensates under the pressure of testimony when he is called to the witness stand. Humphrey Bogart plays the role of Captain Queeg.

> "Captain, I'm sorry, but you're a sick man. I'm relieving you as Captain of this ship under article 184."
> Lt. Maryk relieving Capt. Queeg of Command in *The Caine Mutiny* (1954)

California Split (1974) Comedy ΨΨ
Robert Altman movie starring George Segal and Elliott Gould as two compulsive gamblers. Not as strong a film as *The Gambler*.

PERSONALITY DISORDERS

Come Back to the Five and Dime, Jimmy Dean, Jimmy Dean (1982) Drama ΨΨ
A Robert Altman film in which Sandy Dennis plays a local woman in a small Texas town who is convinced she bore a son by James Dean when he was in town filming *Giant*.

Conversation, The (1974) Drama ΨΨΨ
A Francis Ford Coppola film in which Gene Hackman plays a surveillance expert with a paranoid personality.

Dementia 13 (1963) Horror Ψ
Third rate film about an ax murderer; interesting primarily because it is Francis Ford Coppola's first "serious" film.

Dream Lover (1994) Drama Ψ
Sociopathic woman plots to marry a man and then have him committed to an insane asylum.

Fatal Attraction (1987) Thriller/Romance ΨΨΨ
Glenn Close displays classic characteristics of borderline personality disorder, including fears of abandonment, unstable interpersonal relationships, impulsivity, suicidal gestures, inappropriate and intense anger, and affective instability. This remarkable film is flawed by a contrived and artificial ending.

Five Easy Pieces (1970) Drama ΨΨΨ
Jack Nicholson, raised in an upper-class and gifted family, is a talented pianist who left his affluent life to work in the oil fields. The plot is thin, but the character Nicholson plays is complex and fascinating.

> "Now all you have to do is hold the chicken, bring me the toast, give me a check for the chicken salad sandwich, and you haven't broken any rules."
> Jack Nicholson dealing with an obtuse waitress in *Five Easy Pieces* (1970)

Freaks (1932) Horror ΨΨΨΨ
Fascinating film about a "normal" trapeze artist who marries a midget and then tries to poison him. When his friends find out, they kill her strong-man lover and turn her into one of them.

From the Life of the Marionettes (1980) Drama ΨΨΨ
Bergman film in which a businessman rapes and kills a prostitute.

Gambler, The (1974) Drama ΨΨΨΨ
James Caan plays a university professor of literature who can't control his compulsive gambling. One of the best film portrayals of pathological gambling.

Grifters, The (1990) Crime ΨΨΨΨ
Anjelica Huston stars in this fascinating introduction to the world of the con. Contrast this film with a movie almost as good, David Mamet's *House of Games* (see Treatment section).

PERSONALITY DISORDERS

Knife in the Water (1962) Drama ΨΨΨΨ
One of Roman Polanski's earliest films. A man and his wife on a sailing holiday pick up a hitchhiker. There is mounting sexual tension between the older man and his younger rival. The younger man eventually makes love to the wife after a complex turn of events that occur when the couple become convinced the young man has drowned.

La Cage aux Folles (1978) Comedy ΨΨΨ
Zaza (Albin), the transvestite nightclub performer, is a wonderful example of a histrionic personality. He is dramatic and flamboyant and threatens suicide when things don't go his way.

Le Boucher (1969) Thriller ΨΨΨ
Claude Chabrol film in which a butcher who is also a murderer commits suicide when the woman he loves realizes he is a criminal.

Leave Her to Heaven (1945) Romance/Crime ΨΨ
Protagonist commits multiple murders, watches her brother-in-law drown, and terminates her pregnancy by throwing herself down a flight of stairs with no sense of shame or remorse. Dated but interesting portrayal of an antisocial personality.

Marnie (1964) Thriller/Romance ΨΨ
Hitchcock film about a sexually, frigid kleptomaniac who dominates her new husband. As in other Hitchcock films, the protagonist's problems are found to be rooted in childhood trauma. Watch for the use of a word-association test.

Marriage of Maria Braun, The (1978) Drama/War ΨΨΨ
This Fassbinder film, an allegory about postwar Germany, portrays the dehumanizing effects of war and its aftermath as we watch the commercial success and personal failures of Maria Braun. There is an explosive finale.

Odd Couple, The (1968) Comedy ΨΨΨ
Jack Lemmon is magnificent as the obsessive-compulsive Felix Unger, who uses air freshener and leaves notes on the pillow of housemate Walter Matthau.

Paper Moon (1973) Comedy/Drama ΨΨ
Fun Peter Bogdanovich film, with Ryan O'Neal and daughter Tatum working together as a pair of con artists in the early 1930s.

Pumpkin Eater, The (1964) Drama ΨΨ
Most memorable for the scene in which Anne Bancroft, responding to the stress of eight children and an unfaithful husband, breaks down in Harrods.

Rampage (1992) Drama/Thriller ΨΨΨ
A film that explores the insanity defense, sociopathy, and mass murder. Directed by William Friedkin, who was also the director for *The Exorcist*.

PERSONALITY DISORDERS

Remains of the Day (1994) Romance/Drama ΨΨΨΨ
Anthony Hopkins plays a butler whose rigid personality will not allow him to experience intimacy or genuine love. Few films have been more effective in presenting this reserved, over-controlled, and limiting personality type.

Seance on a Wet Afternoon (1964) Crime ΨΨΨΨ
A British film in which Kim Stanley plays a medium who persuades her husband (Richard Attenborough) to kidnap a child so they can then use her power of clairvoyance to "find" the missing child.

Servant, The (1963) Drama ΨΨΨ
Joseph Losey film in which a wealthy British gentleman and his manservant wind up switching roles. There are strong homosexual overtones in the relationship between the two men, and a complex relationship develops with two women. The film is an interesting examination of dominance and submission.

Silence of the Lambs (1991) Personality Disorders ΨΨΨ
Sir Anthony Hopkins plays one of film history's greatest antisocial personalities, psychiatrist and cannibal Hannibal Lector. Jodi Foster is the FBI agent.

> "A census taker once tried to test me. I ate his liver with some fava beans and a nice Chianti."
> *The Silence of the Lambs* (1991)

Sleeping with the Enemy (1991) Suspense ΨΨ
Julia Roberts plays the battered wife of a possessive and sadistic husband played by Patrick Bergin. Roberts fakes her death and assumes a new identity in a desperate attempt to escape.

Speed (1994) Drama ΨΨ
Dennis Hopper plays a deranged sociopath who programs a bomb to explode if a city bus slows to less than 50 miles per hour.

Stagecoach (1939) Western ΨΨΨ
Classic John Ford movie, with Thomas Mitchell playing a drunken physician. Mitchell won an Academy Award for Best Supporting Actor for his role.

Strangers on a Train (1951) Thriller ΨΨΨΨ
Classic Hitchcock film in which Farley Granger is unable to extricate himself from his involvement with sociopath Robert Walker.

PERSONALITY DISORDERS

Streetcar Named Desire, A (1951) Drama ΨΨΨΨ
Elia Kazan film starring Marlon Brando and Vivian Leigh. Blanche DuBois offers a striking example of a histrionic personality. Brando is unforgettable in the role of Stanley Kowalski.

Sunset Blvd. (1950) Drama ΨΨΨΨ
Billy Wilder film in which a narcissistic, histrionic, and delusional Gloria Swanson clings to the memories of her former greatness as a silent screen star. William Holden plays a young man who exchanges attention and sexual favors for security.

> "They're dead, they're finished! There was a time in this business when they had the eyes of the whole wide world. But that wasn't good enough for them. Oh, no. They had to have the ears of the world, too. So they opened their big mouths, and out came talk. Talk! Talk!"
> *Sunset Blvd.* (1950)

Taxi Driver (1976) Drama ΨΨΨΨ
The premorbid personality of Travis Bickle illustrates delusional paranoid thinking. Bickle would probably meet the criteria for a diagnosis of schizotypal personality disorder.

> "You talkin' to me? [slower] You talking to me? You talking to me? Well, then, who the hell else are you talking — you talking to me? Well, I'm the only one here."
> Travis Bickle rehearsing in *Taxi Driver* (1976)

Thin Blue Line, The (1988) Documentary ΨΨΨ
Gripping documentary examining the unjust incarceration of a man accused of the murder of a Texas policeman.

Toto le Heros (1991) Drama/Comedy ΨΨΨ
An old man in a nursing home reviews his life and his lifelong hatred for his next door neighbor, who appeared to have every advantage. Wonderful example of a paranoid personality disorder.

Violette Noziere (1978) Biography/Crime ΨΨ
Claude Chabrol film based on the true story about a teenage girl who poisoned her parents, eventually killing her father, whom she claimed had raped and abused her.

Wannsee Conference, The (1984) Historical/War ΨΨΨ
Recreation of the Berlin meeting in which Nazi officers first outlined the "final solution" for dealing with the "Jewish problem."

Whisperers, The (1966) Drama Ψ
Dame Edith Evans stars as a lonely old woman, divorced from her husband and estranged from her son, who devotes her days to worry and paranoid ramblings.

Wild at Heart (1990) Comedy/Drama/Romance ΨΨΨ
David Lynch film with excon Nicolas Cage and his lover, Laura Dern, as two antisocial personalities (despite their apparent commitment to each other). Won the Palme d'Ore at Cannes, but not all critics were impressed. Too violent for some tastes.

Wise Blood (1979) Drama ΨΨΨ
John Huston's adaptation of Flannery O'Connor's gothic Southern novel about an obsessed preacher.

ALCOHOLISM

Arthur (1981) Comedy ΨΨ
Dudley Moore as a drunken millionaire who falls in love with Liza Minnelli. A genuinely funny film, but upsetting in its cavalier approach to alcoholism and drunken driving.

Barfly (1987) Comedy/Romance/Drama ΨΨΨΨ
Faye Dunaway and Mickey Rourke play two alcoholics whose lives briefly touch. Good examination of skid row alcoholism; based on a story by cult poet Charles Bukowski.

Beloved Infidel (1959) Biography Ψ
Gregory Peck plays F. Scott Fitzgerald and Deborah Kerr is columnist Sheilah Graham, who tries to save Fitzgerald from his alcoholism.

Born on the Fourth of July (1989) Drama/War/Biography ΨΨΨ
Tom Cruise plays paralyzed and alcoholic Vietnam veteran Ron Kovic in Oliver Stone's film. Stone won an Oscar as best director for this film.

Cat Ballou (1965) Comedy/Western Ψ
Light-hearted film, with Jane Fonda playing a schoolteacher turned outlaw. Lee Marvin got an Oscar for his role as an alcoholic gunman. The film perpetuates the myth of the down-and-out drunk whose shooting skills return after he has had a few drinks. Marvin won an Oscar as Best Actor for his role in this film.

Cat on a Hot Tin Roof (1958) Drama ΨΨΨ
Paul Newman, Elizabeth Taylor, and Burl Ives in a subdued adaptation of Tennessee Williams' play about "mendacity." Alcohol plays a prominent role in the life of almost all the character's lives.

> Big Daddy! Now what makes him so big? His big heart? His big belly? Or his big money?
> *Cat on a Hot Tin Roof* (1958)

Come Back, Little Sheba (1952) Drama ΨΨΨ
Burt Lancaster and Shirley Booth in a film about alcoholism and marriage. Booth won an Academy Award for Best Actress for her role.

Come Fill the Cup (1951) Drama ΨΨ
James Cagney; Jackie Gleason; serious examination of the problems of alcoholism in an ex-newspaperman.

Dark Obsession (1989) Drama/Mystery ΨΨ
Five drunken British military officers are involved in a hit-and-run accident in which the victim dies. The five men take a vow of silence; one is troubled by the decision. Interesting analysis of responsibility for one's behavior while intoxicated.

ALCOHOLISM

Days of Wine and Roses (1962) Drama ΨΨΨ
Blake Edwards film starring Jack Lemmon and Lee Remick. Lemmon teaches Remick how to drink. Lemmon is saved by AA; Remick is unable to stop drinking, despite the consequences.

Drunks (1997) Drama ΨΨΨΨ
This film is the best available introduction to Alcoholics Anonymous. It is highly recommended for any student who will be working with substance abuse issues.

Educating Rita (1983) Drama ΨΨ
Michael Caine as an alcoholic college professor who takes on the task of educating a working-class woman.

Fire Within, The (1963) Drama ΨΨΨΨ
French filmmaker Louis Malle's remarkable account of alcoholism, suicide, and the existential choices that confront us all.

Gervaise (1956) Drama ΨΨΨ
French film based on Emile Zola's story about a young Parisian woman with an alcoholic husband.

Graduate, The (1967) Drama/Comedy ΨΨΨ
A telling indictment of the shallow values of the time (e.g., "plastics"). Mrs. Robinson's alcoholism impairs her judgment and ruins her life.

> "Mrs. Robinson, you're trying to seduce me. Aren't you?"
> *The Graduate* (1967)

Great Man Votes, The (1939) Drama ΨΨ
John Barrymore plays an alcoholic college professor fighting to maintain custody of his children.

Harvey (1950) Comedy ΨΨ
Jimmy Stewart is a happy drunk who goes drinking with Harvey, an invisible six-foot rabbit. When hospitalized, Stewart frequently switches places and counsels his psychiatrist, Dr. Chumley.

Iceman Cometh, The (1973) Drama ΨΨ
Lee Marvin in an adaptation of Eugene O'Neill's play about alcoholism and the pathos of dreams unfulfilled.

I'll Cry Tomorrow (1955) Biography ΨΨΨ
Singer Lillian Roth (Susan Hayward) attempts suicide as a way of coping with her alcoholism before AA support helps her find her way.

Ironweed (1987) Drama ΨΨΨ
Jack Nicholson and Meryl Streep in compelling roles as homeless alcoholics. The film, a very realistic portrayal of life on skid row, should be contrasted with another excellent film made the same year, *Barfly*.

Key Largo (1948) Crime ΨΨΨ
Claire Trevor won Best Supporting Actress for her role as an alcoholic singer forced to beg gangster Edward G. Robinson for a drink during a hurricane in Key West.

Last Night at the Alamo (1983) Drama ΨΨΨ
Fascinating examination of bar culture in a small Texas town. Unforgettable characters, most of whom are coping with alcoholism and adultery.

Lonely Passion of Judith Hearne, The (1987) Romance ΨΨ
Maggie Smith plays a lonely alcoholic who mistakenly believes she has a last chance to find love and meaning in her life.

Long Day's Journey into Night (1962) Drama ΨΨΨΨ
Alcohol is a part of daily life for this deeply troubled family. Numerous examples of family pathology, conflict between father and sons, and denial.

Lost Weekend, The (1945) Drama ΨΨΨΨ
Billy Wilder classic starring Ray Milland as a writer struggling to overcome his alcoholism. Some scenes were filmed at Bellevue, and the examples of delirium tremens are very convincing. Polanski borrowed scenes from *The Lost Weekend* as models for his film *Repulsion*.

> "One's too many and a hundred's not enough."
> A bartender chides Don Birnam in Billy Wilder's *The Lost Weekend* (1945)

My Favorite Year (1982) Comedy ΨΨΨ
A great actor (modeled after John Barrymore and Errol Flynn) who has become a pathetic drunk must confront one of the greatest challenges of his career—a live television performance.

My Name Is Bill W. (1989) ΨΨ
Made-for-TV movie about the founding of Alcoholics Anonymous.

National Lampoon's Animal House (1978) Comedy ΨΨ
One of the best of a hundred or so college films that portray fraternity life as a series of beer busts interspersed with an occasional class. At one point, John Belushi, not the brightest of the fraternity brothers, chugs a fifth of Jack Daniels.

Night of the Iguana, The (1964) Drama ΨΨ
Richard Burton and Ava Gardner star in John Huston's adaptation of Tennessee Williams' play. Burton plays a very convincing alcoholic and erstwhile clergyman.

ALCOHOLISM

Proud and the Beautiful, The (1953) Romance ΨΨ
A film about a woman who helps an alcoholic physician overcome his problems and regain some sense of dignity. Filmed in France and Mexico.

Skin Deep (1989) Comedy ΨΨ
A funny Blake Edwards film about an alcoholic writer who continues to deny his alcoholism long after it has become apparent to everyone else.

Smash-Up, the Story of a Woman (1947) Drama ΨΨ
Melodramatic Susan Hayward film about a movie star who must come to grips with her alcoholism.

Streamers (1983) Drama ΨΨΨ
Robert Altman film about three soldiers waiting to go to Vietnam. The film deals with themes of homosexuality, violence, and racism but also illustrates the alcohol abuse that is pervasive in military life.

Sweet Bird of Youth (1962) Drama ΨΨ
Paul Newman in an adaptation of Tennessee Williams' play about a has-been actress (played by Geraldine Page) addicted to alcohol and drugs who takes up with a young, vital Newman.

Taxi Blues (1990) Drama ΨΨΨ
Alcoholic jazz musician becomes friends with an anti-Semitic taxi driver. This Russian film won the prize for Best Director at Cannes. Fascinating examination of the role of alcohol in the daily lives of the protagonists in Moscow society.

Tender Mercies (1983) Drama ΨΨΨΨ
Sensitive and optimistic film in which Robert Duvall plays a successfully recovering alcoholic songwriter. Duvall won an Oscar for this almost perfect performance.

Trees Lounge (1996) Comedy ΨΨΨΨ
Steve Buscemi wrote and directed this compelling film; and he plays the lead character, a 31-year-old unemployed auto mechanic. Few contemporary films present a more vivid picture of the problems associated with alcoholism.

Under Capricorn (1949) Drama Ψ
A little-known Hitchcock film starring Joseph Cotton and Ingrid Bergman. Bergman is a wealthy socialite whose life is ruined by her alcoholism.

Under the Volcano (1984) Drama ΨΨΨΨ
John Huston directing Albert Finney; excellent portrayal of chronic alcoholism.

Verdict, The (1982) Drama ΨΨΨΨ
Paul Newman in a wonderful role as a disillusioned alcoholic lawyer who becomes genuinely involved with a brain-injured client who is the victim of medical malpractice. He wins the case but continues to drink. Interesting analysis of codependency.

Vital Signs (1986) Drama ΨΨ
Ed Asner in a surpassingly good made-for-TV movie about a father and son, both surgeons, fighting the twin problems of alcoholism and drug abuse.

What Price Hollywood? (1932) Drama ΨΨ
Alcoholic director helps Hollywood waitress become a star. The figure of the alcoholic director may have been modeled after John Barrymore.

When a Man Loves a Woman (1994) Drama ΨΨ
Meg Ryan as a middle-class alcoholic. Melodramatic and somewhat predictable film but an interesting introduction to AA and Al-Anon. The film explores the role of codependency and a husband's role in his wife's alcoholism.

DRUG ABUSE
Bad Lieutenant (1992) Drama ΨΨΨ
Harvey Keitel stars in one of his most powerful roles as a police lieutenant addicted to cocaine, alcohol, and prostitutes. The film illustrates stark abuse of power and the deterioration of family life that accompanies addiction. Keitel's character at one point has a hallucination in which Jesus Christ comes to him.

Bird (1988) Biography ΨΨ
Clint Eastwood directed this biographical film of the life of jazz great and drug addict Charlie "Bird" Parker. Parker was an addict for all of his adult life, and his addiction killed him at the age of 34.

Born on the Fourth of July (1989) Drama/War/Biography ΨΨΨΨ
Antiwar film by Oliver Stone starring Tom Cruise as Ron Kovic, who uses alcohol and drugs to cope with the frustration of paralysis. One of the best of its genre.

Chappaqua (1966) Drama Ψ
Heroin addict checks in for treatment. The film is most notable for short roles by William Burroughs, Ravi Shankar, and Allen Ginsburg.

Christiane F. (1981) Drama ΨΨΨΨ
Powerful and frightening examination of the life of a teenage drug addict in West Berlin. Based on a true story, the film is still gripping almost two decades after it was made.

Clean and Sober (1988) Drama ΨΨΨΨ
Good portrayal of AA, cocaine addiction, and alcoholism.

Cocaine Fiends, The (1936) Drama Ψ
Another "word of warning" film that portrays the dangers of cocaine. Made in the same year as *Reefer Madness*. The message in this film is exaggerated and histrionic but somewhat more realistic in its estimate of the dangers of the drug.

DRUG ABUSE

Connection, The (1961) Drama ΨΨΨ
Heroin addicts in New York wait for their pusher.

Drugstore Cowboy (1989) Drama ΨΨΨΨ
Matt Dillon leads a group of junkies who rob pharmacies to support their habit. William Burroughs plays a junkie priest.

Easy Rider (1969) Drama ΨΨΨ
Classic film of the late 1960s with Jack Nicholson as an alcoholic lawyer and Peter Fonda and Dennis Hopper as marijuana-smoking, LSD-using free spirits. The film is dated but still worth seeing.

Fear and Loathing (1998) Fantasy ΨΨ
Terry Gilliam's adaptation of Hunter S. Thompson's Gonzo journalism classic. The book is better than the film; although the movie does not glorify drug use, it clearly models the behavior and tacitly condones the practice of driving while intoxicated.

Hatful of Rain, A (1957) Drama ΨΨ
Melodramatic film about the life and problems of a drug addict. This was one of the earliest films to honestly examine the problem of drug addiction.

I Don't Buy Kisses Anymore (1992) Comedy/Romance Ψ
Lightweight but entertaining film about an obese male who falls in love with a woman using him as a subject for her master's thesis.

I'm Dancing as Fast as I Can (1982) Drama ΨΨ
Jill Clayburgh plays the role of a high-powered documentary filmmaker who becomes addicted to Valium and requires hospitalization in a special program for addicts. Based on a true story.

Jungle Fever (1991) Drama/Romance ΨΨΨ
Interesting film about race relations and sexual stereotypes, with a subplot involving Gator, the crackhead brother of the protagonist, who is destroying his middle-class family.

La Femme Nikita (1990) Action/Drama ΨΨ
Sociopathic and drug-addicted woman is sentenced to die for murder and then is transformed into a government agent. Most memorable for the drugstore robbery that opens the film.

Lady Sings the Blues (1972) Biography/Musical ΨΨ
Diana Ross plays heroin addict Billie Holiday.

Long Day's Journey into Night (1962) Drama ΨΨΨΨ
Katharine Hepburn plays a morphine-addicted, histrionic mother with an alcoholic son (Jason Robards). One of O'Neill's greatest plays; one of Hepburn's greatest roles. Hepburn's character is a good illustration of a histrionic personality disorder.

Luna (1979) Drama Ψ
Disappointing Bertolucci film, with Jill Clayburgh playing the mother of a drug addict son. The film hints at an incestuous relationship between mother and son.

Man with the Golden Arm, The (1955) Drama ΨΨ
Frank Sinatra and Kim Novak in a dated but interesting portrayal of drug addiction. Good example of the challenge of "cold turkey" withdrawal.

Mask (1985) Biography ΨΨΨ
Bogdanovich film with Cher as the mother of deformed but spunky teenager Rocky Dennis. Sympathetic portrayal of motorcycle gangs. Cher struggles with her angry father and her compulsive use of alcohol and drugs as she works hard to be a good mother.

Naked Lunch (1991) Science Fiction/Fantasy/Drama ΨΨ
This film is based on the novel by William Burroughs and deals with drug abuse, paranoia, and homicide.

New Jack City (1991) Action/Crime ΨΨ
Wesley Snipes and Ice-T in a realistic movie about the business of drugs. Good introduction to cocaine addiction and Narcotics Anonymous.

People vs. Larry Flynt, The (1996) Biography/Drama ΨΨΨ
A good movie about a controversial figure, the film forces the viewer to examine his or her views on pornography and free speech. The film is included in this section because of the effects of drugs on the lives of Flynt and his wife, Althea (Courtney Love), after he is shot and becomes addicted to narcotics.

Platoon (1986) War ΨΨΨΨ
Vietnam veteran Oliver Stone directed *Platoon,* one of the most realistic of dozens of war movies. There is an interesting juxtaposition of "boozers" (those who use alcohol to escape) and "heads" (those who take refuge in marijuana and other illegal drugs).

Postcards from the Edge (1990) Comedy/Drama ΨΨΨ
Mike Nichols' adaptation of a Carrie Fisher story about life as the daughter of a famous actress. The mother is alcoholic; the daughter abuses multiple drugs, including cocaine and sedatives. There are brief scenes of therapy and a terrific cast.

Pulp Fiction (1994) Drama ΨΨΨΨ
Quentin Tarantino film about drugs, crime, depravity, the underworld, and life in urban America. One especially memorable scene involves John Travolta smashing an adrenaline-filled needle into Uma Thurman's chest to revive her after she inadvertently overdoses on heroin.

Reefer Madness (1936) Drama Ψ
Camp film depicting the dangers of marijuana. Ironically, several thousand college students have gone to see this film high on the very drug the film condemns.

DRUG ABUSE

Rose, The (1979) Musical ΨΨ
Bette Midler portrays Janis Joplin and her problems with Southern Comfort and drugs.

Rush (1991) Crime/Drama ΨΨΨ
Two undercover narcotics agents find addiction to be an occupational hazard.

Scarface (1983) Crime ΨΨΨ
Brian De Palma movie starring Al Pacino as a Cuban immigrant mobster who becomes addicted to the cocaine he is marketing. This long film, which tends to be loved or hated, is based on a 1932 Howard Hawks classic with the same name.

Seven Percent Solution, The (1976) Mystery ΨΨ
Sigmund Freud treats Sherlock Holmes' cocaine addiction. Creative idea and historically accurate in documenting Freud's early enthusiasm for cocaine.

Sid and Nancy (1986) Biography ΨΨΨ
Compelling biography of Sid Vicious of the Sex Pistols; offers insight into the worlds of drugs and rock and roll.

Stardust (1975) Drama Ψ
British film about a rock star whose success is tarnished by drug addiction and mental illness.

Sweet Nothing (1996) Drama ΨΨΨ
An effective examination of the futility, desperation, and violence associated with crack addiction. This is a true story based on diaries found in a Bronx apartment in March of 1991.

Synanon (1965) Drama ΨΨ
Interesting only insofar as the film documents the treatment methods practiced in this highly praised treatment program.

Trainspotting (1996) Drama/Comedy ΨΨΨ
A realistic and disturbing film about the heroin scene in Edinburgh. The film presents accurate depictions of cold turkey withdrawal. There is one memorable scene in which a young mother's baby dies while she is high, and she immediately needs a fix to cope with her grief. Several scatological scenes seem gratuitous and unnecessary.

> "I've been known to sniff it, smoke it, swallow it, stick it up my arse and inject it into my veins. I've been trying to combat this addiction, but unless you count social security scams and shoplifting, I haven't had a regular job in years."
> *Trainspotting* (1996)

Veronika Voss (1982) Drama ΨΨ
Rainer Werner Fassbinder film about a German movie star who becomes addicted to morphine. Fassbinder himself died from abuse of alcohol and heroin.

What's Love Got to Do with It? (1993) Musical/Biography ΨΨ
Excellent film biography of singer Tina Turner includes some memorable scenes of husband Ike strung out on cocaine.

Who'll Stop the Rain? (1978) Crime/Drama ΨΨ
Also known as *Dog Soldiers,* this film explores the world of drug smuggling and addiction.

SEXUAL AND GENDER IDENTITY DISORDERS
Adjuster, The (1991) Drama ΨΨΨ
This interesting Canadian film explores voyeurism and exhibitionism.

Adventures of Priscilla, Queen of the Desert (1994) Comedy ΨΨ
Terence Stamp plays an aging transsexual who joins with two friends to travel from Sidney to Alice Springs in the Australian outback to perform a lip-synching routine. Much of the film revolves around the prejudice the three transsexuals encounter.

Angels and Insects (1995) Drama ΨΨΨ
Complex drama about social class, passion, and hidden sexual secrets in a wealthy Victorian household.

Another Time, Another Place (1983) Drama ΨΨΨ
Sensitive film in which a Scottish woman in an unhappy marriage has a brief affair with an Italian prisoner of war working as a laborer on the farm. The man is accused of a rape he did not commit; his lover can save him, but only at the cost of revealing her adultery.

Bad Timing: A Sensual Obsession (1980) Drama ΨΨ
Art Garfunkel, Harvey Keitel, and Theresa Russell in a provocative and explicit film about a psychiatrist who becomes sexually obsessed with a young woman.

Beginner's Luck (1983) Comedy ΨΨ
Lightweight comedy about a law student who becomes involved in a *ménage à trois.*

Belle de Jour (1967) Drama ΨΨΨΨ
Luis Buñuel film with Catherine Deneuve playing a bored housewife who amuses herself by working in a brothel from two until five every afternoon, at least until her sexual obsessions begin to complicate her life. Buñuel may be filming what is just an erotic dream.

Birdcage, The (1996) Comedy ΨΨΨ
Mike Nichols and Elaine May's remake of *La Cage aux Folles.* This film is almost as good, thanks to strong performances by Robin Williams and Gene Hackman.

SEXUAL AND GENDER IDENTITY DISORDERS

Blame It on Rio (1984) Comedy ΨΨ
Two men take their teenage daughters to Rio's topless beaches, and one of the men, 43 years old, has an affair with the 15-year-old daughter of the other. The film has a vaguely incestuous theme and is modeled after the French film *One Wild Moment*.

Blue Angel, The (1930) Drama ΨΨΨΨ
Classic film about a phlegmatic professor who loses everything because of his obsession with a cabaret singer.

Breaking the Waves (1996) Drama ΨΨΨ
A Danish film in which a devout Catholic wife submits to sexual degradation to satisfy the voyeuristic demands of her paralyzed husband.

> "Are you sleeping with other men just to feed his sick fantasies?"
> The question put to Bess in *Breaking the Waves* (1996)

Cabaret (1972) Musical/Drama/Dance ΨΨΨ
Liza Minnelli in a film about sadomasochism, bisexuality, and the relationship between sex and power. One scene in the film is as unforgettable as the classic confession of incest in *Chinatown*. This film won Oscars for Best Actor, Best Actress, and Best Director.

Caesar and Rosalie (1972) Comedy/Romance ΨΨ
Lighthearted and amusing examination of a *ménage à trois*.

Carnal Knowledge (1971) Drama ΨΨ
This Mike Nichols film traces the sexual lives of two college roommates, played by Jack Nicholson and Art Garfunkel, as they age and become increasingly disenchanted with sex, love, and the possibilities inherent in relationships.

Cat on a Hot Tin Roof (1958) Drama ΨΨ
Paul Newman, Elizabeth Taylor, and Burl Ives in a wonderful adaptation of Tennessee Williams' play about "mendacity." In the play, Newman's character is presumed to be homosexual, although this is not at all clear from the film.

Chinatown (1974) Mystery ΨΨΨ
A film about power, incest, and the complexity of human relationships. The male lead is played by Jack Nicholson.

> "You see, Mr. Gettes, most people never have to face the fact that, at the right time and in the right place, they are capable of anything."
> *Chinatown* (1974)

Claire's Knee (1971) Drama ΨΨΨ
An intelligent film in which a middle-aged man becomes obsessed with a young girl's knee.

Close My Eyes (1991) Drama ΨΨ
A British film about brother-sister incest.

Collector, The (1965) Drama ΨΨΨ
Terence Stamp stars as a young man who collects butterflies. He becomes obsessed with Samantha Eggar, kidnaps her, and winds up inadvertently killing her.

SEXUAL AND GENDER IDENTITY DISORDERS

Crash (1996) Drama ΨΨΨ
A David Cronenberg film about people who
become sexually aroused by automobile accidents.
The film presents a plausable hypothesis: people
have developed fetishes for stranger things, and
there are erotic overtones to both cars and speed.

> "You couldn't wait for me? You did the
> Jane Mansfield crash without me!"
> One of many strange interactions in the
> very strange David Cronenberg film
> *Crash* (1996)

Cruising (1980) Crime Ψ
Controversial William Friedkin film, with Al Pacino as undercover policeman who infiltrates
gay bars and bathhouses. The film was condemned by gay activists because it perpetuates
stigma and stereotypes.

Crying Game, The (1992) Drama ΨΨΨΨ
Neil Jordan film which explores homosexuality, transsexualism, interracial sexuality, and the
ability of two human beings to love one another deeply in an asexual relationship. Too complex
to simply explain, the film must be seen to be fully appreciated.

Damage (1992) Drama ΨΨΨ
A Louis Malle film starring Jeremy Irons as a man who develops a sexual obsession for his
son's fiancée. Both the father and the son's girlfriend seem powerless to control their erotic
attachment despite its inevitable consequences.

Day in the Country, A (1936) Romance ΨΨΨΨ
Jean Renoir's adaptation of a short story by Guy de Maupassant that describes the seductions
of a man's wife and daughter.

Fellini Satyricon (1970) Historical ΨΨΨΨ
Controversial Fellini film about the decadence of ancient Rome. The film is visually stunning
and explores human vices ranging from homosexual pedophilia to cannibalism. The film can be
a springboard for a discussion of hedonism gone amuck.

Female Perversions (1996) Drama ΨΨΨ
Confused and often confusing examination of the relationship between women, power,
sexuality, and psychopathology. Based on a scholarly book with the same title by
psychoanalyst Louise J. Kaplan.

Fetishes (1996) Documentary ΨΨΨ
True examination of the clients of Pandora's Box, an elite club catering to the sexual fetishes of
New York City.

Fist in His Pocket (1966) Drama ΨΨΨ
Italian film about a dysfunctional family with multiple examples of psychopathology including
epilepsy, murder, and incest.

SEXUAL AND GENDER IDENTITY DISORDERS

Fried Green Tomatoes (1991) Comedy/Drama ΨΨΨ
Presents a positive, healthy, loving view of an (apparent) lesbian relationship. We are quickly caught up in the complex and intertwined story of these two women.

God's Little Acre (1958) Drama Ψ
Buddy Hackett and Michael Landon star in this adaptation of Erskine Caldwell's tale of depravity and Georgia farm life.

Good Mother, The (1988) Drama ΨΨΨ
A provocative film in which Diane Keaton plays the divorced mother of a six-year-old daughter. Keaton falls in love with an iconoclastic artist, who allows the daughter to touch his penis when she sees him in the bath and expresses normal childhood curiosity. Keaton is eventually forced to denounce her new lover in order to maintain a relationship with her daughter.

Harold and Maude (1972) Comedy ΨΨΨ
A cult film that examines sexual and romantic attraction across generations, and a movie that will force you to reexamine your feelings about age and death.

Henry & June (1990) Drama ΨΨ
Adaptation of Anais Nin diary detailing her *ménage à trois* with novelist Henry Miller and his wife June.

Ju Dou (1989) Drama/Historical/Romance ΨΨΨΨ
Wonderful, visually stunning film examining the complex links that bind a husband, his wife, her lover, and the son of the illicit union. Good illustrations of sexual passion and sexual torment.

Jules and Jim (1961) Drama ΨΨΨΨ
Beautiful and engaging Truffaut film about a complex *ménage à trois* and an ultimate suicide. The film deals with far more than sexuality; it explores fundamental dimensions of human relationships and the boundaries of friendship and love.

Kiss of the Spider Woman (1985) Prison ΨΨΨΨ
A homosexual and a political activist share a prison cell and grow to understand and appreciate each other. William Hurt won an Academy Award for his performance.

La Cage aux Folles (1978) Comedy ΨΨΨ
A gay man and his transvestite lover manage a popular St. Tropez nightclub. Much of the humor revolves around sex roles and the folly of trying very hard to be something you're not.

> "I told them my father was a Cultural attaché. What will they think when they find out he lives with a drag queen?"
> Renato's son in *La Cage aux Folles* (1978)

SEXUAL AND GENDER IDENTITY DISORDERS

Last Exit to Brooklyn (1989) Drama ΨΨ
A film based on the controversial book about life in a sordid Brooklyn neighborhood. The film deals with rape, prostitution, homosexuality, and transvestism, but mostly with the sad and bleak reality of its characters.

Last Tango in Paris (1973) Drama ΨΨΨΨ
Marlon Brando stars in a classic Bernardo Bertolucci film about a man who begins a casual sexual liaison on the day his wife commits suicide. The two lovers never exchange names. The film includes themes of depression, sexuality, loneliness, and cynicism.

Lianna (1983) Drama ΨΨΨ
Sensitive film portraying the emotional life of a woman who leaves her husband and two children after she becomes romantically involved with a lesbian professor teaching her night course in child psychology.

Lolita (1962) Drama ΨΨ
James Mason and Sue Lyons star in a loose adaptation of Vladimir Nabokov's novel about pedophilia and murder. Directed by Stanley Kubrick.

> "What drives me insane is the twofold nature of this nymphet . . . this mixture in my Lolita of tender, dreamy childishness and a kind of eerie vulgarity.
> I know it is madness to keep this journal, but it gives me a strange thrill to do so."
> Humbert Humbert in *Lolita* (1962)

Luna (1979) Drama ΨΨ
A Bertolucci film that explores mother-son incest and addiction. The film is not Bertolucci's best effort.

Manhattan (1979) Comedy/Romance ΨΨΨΨ
Classic Woody Allen film in which his former wife, played by Meryl Streep, has taken a lover, found happiness, and written a book to tell the world about Allen's kinky habits. Allen is consumed with guilt over the fact that he is living with a teenage girl.

Mark, The (1961) Drama ΨΨΨΨ
A British film about a pedophile who serves his sentence and is released, supposedly cured. However, his rehabilitation is hampered by a journalist who reveals the man's past. Interesting film in light of recent court decisions in the U.S. such as *Kansas vs. Hendricks.*

Matador (1986) Comedy/Drama ΨΨ
Almodovar film about a bullfighter who acts in snuff films.

Menage (1986) Comedy ΨΨ
A French film that examines sex roles, sexual stereotypes, and the need for novelty and excitement in sexual relationships.

SEXUAL AND GENDER IDENTITY DISORDERS

Midnight Cowboy (1969) Drama ΨΨΨΨ
Jon Voight leaves Texas to make his fortune in
New York City working as a stud; instead, he
winds up hanging out with Ratso Rizzo, who dies

> "Well, I'll tell you the truth now. I ain't a
> real cowboy, but I am one helluva stud."
> *Midnight Cowboy* (1969)

before the two can escape to Florida. Fascinating and complex character study.

Mona Lisa (1986) Crime ΨΨΨ
Interesting Neil Jordan film about prostitution, exploitation, drug addiction, and love. Filmed in
Soho, the film gives some insight into the two different worlds of prostitution: that of the call
girl and that of the streetwalker.

Montenegro (1981) Drama ΨΨ
A Makavejev film about a bored housewife slowly becoming psychotic. She becomes sexually
liberated and then murders her lover. Despite its psychopathological theme, the film is really
about politics and social class.

Mrs. Doubtfire (1994) Comedy ΨΨ
Robin Williams cross-dresses as an English nanny to have time with his children.

Murmur of the Heart (1971) Comedy ΨΨ
A sensitive, intelligent, and funny French film about an incestuous relationship between a
young mother and her adolescent son.

My Beautiful Laundrette (1985) Drama ΨΨ
The two lead characters are homosexuals, although this fact is almost incidental to the story
about alcoholism, street gangs, race relations, and social class.

My Favorite Season (1993) Drama ΨΨΨ
A French film dealing with adolescent sexuality, family dynamics, and love between a brother
and sister.

My Life to Live/Vivre sa Vie (1963) ΨΨΨ
Jean-Luc Godard's 12-part examination of the life of a prostitute, starring Anna Karina.

My Own Private Idaho (1991) Drama ΨΨ
River Phoenix, who subsequently died of a drug overdose, plays a homosexual prostitute.

Mystery of Alexina, The (1985) Drama ΨΨ
A story about the psychological sequelae of the decision to raise a male child as a female.

Nos Amours, A (1984) Drama ΨΨΨ
A French film exploring the sexuality of a 15-year-old girl and the way it affects her family.

SEXUAL AND GENDER IDENTITY DISORDERS

Of Human Bondage (1934) Drama ΨΨ
Bette Davis stars in this film about the sexual obsession of a club-footed physician for a cruel, vulgar, and manipulative waitress. Based on a novel by Somerset Maugham. This film is far superior to the two adaptations that followed it.

> "You dirty swine! I never cared for you. . . . It made me sick when you kissed me. I only did it because you drove me crazy. And after you kissed me I always used to wipe my mouth – wipe my mouth!"
> Bette Davis berates Leslie Howard in *Of Human Bondage* (1934)

Oscar Wilde (1960) Biography Ψ
Robert Morley plays Oscar Wilde, the wit and playwright who was convicted of sodomy.

Peeping Tom (1960) Thriller ΨΨΨ
Controversial film about a sexual psychopath who photographs his victims as they are dying. Look for the full-length version of the film, which was released in 1979.

Personal Best (1982) Sports ΨΨΨ
Fascinating film that explores the sexual relationship that develops between two women competing for a position on an Olympic team.

Pretty Baby (1978) Drama ΨΨ
This Louis Malle film about pedophilia introduces Brooke Shields as a 12-year-old New Orleans prostitute.

Pulp Fiction (1994) Drama ΨΨΨΨ
Quentin Tarantino film depicts an underworld sadomasochistic den of iniquity run by two sexual sadists in the basement of an Army surplus store. A masochistic slave dressed totally in leather lives in a box in the back of the room.

> "Look, maybe your method of massage differs from mine, but touchin' his lady's feet, and stickin' your tongue in her holiest of holies, ain't the same ballpark, ain't the same league, ain't even the same fuckin' sport. Foot massages don't mean shit."
> Jules and Vincent discuss foot massage in *Pulp Fiction* (1994)

Reflections in a Golden Eye (1967) Drama ΨΨ
A John Huston film in which Richard Burton plays the role of a repressed homosexual Army officer serving on a small Georgia military base. Elizabeth Taylor is his sadistic and sexually liberated wife. The film was banned by the Catholic Film Board.

Rita, Sue and Bob Too (1986) Comedy ΨΨΨ
British film about a married man who winds up in a sexual relationship with the two working-class teenage girls who baby-sit for his children. Interesting examination of the appropriate age of consent and issues of sexual exploitation.

Rocky Horror Picture Show, The (1975) Comedy/Horror/Musical/Dance Ψ
A fun film about a Translyvanian transsexual. From a psychological perspective, the film is not as interesting as those fans who have turned it into a cult classic.

Sailor Who Fell from Grace with the Sea, The (1976) Drama ΨΨΨ
Interesting story of adult romance and child psychopathology; based on a Mishima novel.

SEXUAL AND GENDER IDENTITY DISORDERS

Salo, or the 120 Days of Sodom (1975) Horror Ψ
Pasolini's adaptation of de Sade's famous novel. Set in the fascist Italy of World War II, this violent film is an interesting introduction to the practice of sadism.

Sergeant, The (1968) Drama ΨΨ
Rod Steiger plays an Army sergeant sexually obsessed with a young private in his outfit. Filmed in France.

sex, lies, and videotape (1989) Drama ΨΨΨ
The film revolves around an impotent young man who can achieve orgasm only by masturbating while watching videotapes of women whom he has persuaded to share the most intimate details of their sexual lives. This film won the top film award at the Cannes Film Festival.

Short Cuts (1993) Drama ΨΨ
Most memorable for a scene in which a bored woman talks dirty on the phone to earn a few dollars while she changes her baby's diapers. Her husband wonders why she never talks to *him* like that.

Short Eyes (1977) Prison ΨΨΨΨ
A powerful film about life in "The Tombs," New York City's Men's House of Detention. Short Eyes is prison slang for a child molester.

Some Like It Hot (1959) Crime/Comedy ΨΨ
Tony Curtis and Jack Lemmon pass for women musicians to avoid detection by the mob.

Something About Amelia (1984) Drama ΨΨ
Popular made-for-TV movie about father-daughter incest.

Strange One, The (1957) Drama ΨΨ
Ben Gazzara stars in this film about homosexuality and sadism in a Southern military academy.

Swept Away (1975) Drama/Comedy ΨΨΨ
Lina Wertmuller's examination of sex roles. A rich woman and a poor deckhand are marooned on an island and find sexual excitement and satisfaction in the new roles each assumes.

That Obscure Object of Desire (1977) Drama ΨΨΨΨ
Surrealistic film by Luis Buñuel about violence, love, and sexual obsession in a middle-aged man. The film is complex, intriguing, and full of symbolism.

This World, Then the Fireworks (1997) Drama ΨΨ
This film traces the development of incestuous twins who eventually become con artists.

SEXUAL AND GENDER IDENTITY DISORDERS

Tie Me Up! Tie Me Down! (1990) Comedy/Romance ΨΨΨ
A Pedro Almodovar film about a former mental patient, kidnapping, masochism, and sex roles. Some critics have maintained that the film trivializes the problem of sexual violence and denigrates women.

Tootsie (1982) Comedy/Romance ΨΨΨΨ
Funny Dustin Hoffman film in which an unsuccessful actor finds success when he impersonates a woman. He learns from the process, and the audience learns some important lessons about gender, sex roles, and human relationships.

Torch Song Trilogy (1988) Drama ΨΨΨ
Anne Bancroft and Matthew Broderick in a film adaptation of Harvey Fierstein's play about a homosexual drag queen and his lovers, enemies, and mother.

Two Women (1961) Drama/War ΨΨΨ
Classic Vittorio De Sica film starring Sophia Loren. The film is about love, war, rape, and a mother's love for her teenage daughter.

Unbearable Lightness of Being (1988) Romance ΨΨΨ
A highly sensual film about a Prague neurosurgeon and his inability to separate sex and love. The film is based on the novel of the same name by Milan Kundera.

Victor/Victoria (1982) Musical/Comedy ΨΨ
Blake Edwards film with Julie Andrews as a down-on-her-luck singer who becomes a sensation when she pretends to be a male-female impersonator.

Viridiana (1961) Drama ΨΨΨΨ
This complex Luis Buñuel film tells the story of a young woman who returns home to visit her uncle just before taking vows as a nun. She resembles her dead aunt, and her uncle drugs her while she is wearing her aunt's wedding dress. He plans to rape her but is unable to commit the act. He commits suicide; she inherits his estate and devotes her life to serving the poor.

Visiting Desire (1996) Documentary ΨΨ
Twelve strangers are brought together to act out their sexual fantasies.

Wild Orchid 2: Two Shades of Blue (1991) Drama Ψ
Disappointing film about the daughter of a heroin addict who becomes a prostitute to support her father's habit but who manages to maintain her double identity.

World According to Garp, The (1982) Comedy/Drama ΨΨ
John Lithgow plays transsexual Roberta Muldoon in a film in which troubled sexuality is commonplace.

SCHIZOPHRENIA AND OTHER PSYCHOTIC DISORDERS

Yentl (1983) Musical ΨΨ
Barbra Streisand directed and produced this film, and she has the lead role as a young woman in Eastern Europe who has to pass herself off as a man in order to get an education. Interesting examination of sex roles; terrific performance by Streisand.

SCHIZOPHRENIA AND OTHER PSYCHOTIC DISORDERS

Alone in the Dark (1982) Suspense Ψ
A psychiatrist's family is besieged by a psychotic patient during a citywide blackout.

Amadeus (1984) Biography/Musical ΨΨΨ
The film opens with the court composer Salieri, now old, mad, and suicidal, wondering if he murdered Mozart. Salieri is obsessed with the genius of Mozart and can never forgive his rival for his talent or himself for his mediocrity

Angel at My Table, An (1990) Biography/Drama ΨΨΨΨ
Jean Campion's biography of New Zealand novelist Janet Frame, who was misdiagnosed as schizophrenic and mistreated with electroconvulsive therapy.

Angel Baby (1995) Drama ΨΨΨ
Australian film about two mentally ill people who meet in an outpatient clinic, fall in love, and try to face life together. Unfortunately, their lives fall apart as a consequence of an ill-fated decision to mutually discontinue their medication.

Angel in Red (1991) Suspense Ψ
A psychotic pimp goes gunning for his former employee after she turns to a rival pimp for protection.

Bennie & Joon (1993) Comedy ΨΨΨ
A generally sympathetic portrayal of schizophrenia, with a vivid example of decompensation on a city bus; the film trivializes the problem of schizophrenia by suggesting love alone is enough to conquer the problem.

Berlin Alexanderplatz (1980) Drama ΨΨΨΨ
This film, a 15-hour Fassbinder masterpiece, traces the gradual moral and mental disintegration of a man who leaves prison resolved to live a good life. The film explores exploitation of women, violence, homosexuality, and mental illness.

Betrayed (1988) Political/Thriller Ψ
Debra Winger plays an undercover agent who falls in love with a seemingly simple farmer, actually a right-wing, paranoid fanatic.

Bill of Divorcement, A (1932) Comedy ΨΨ
A mentally ill man is discharged from a psychiatric hospital and returns home to his wife and daughter. Katharine Hepburn's debut as a film actress.

SCHIZOPHRENIA AND OTHER PSYCHOTIC DISORDERS

Birdy (1984) Drama/War ΨΨΨ
Nicolas Cage tries to help his friend, Matthew Modine, who is a catatonic inpatient in a military hospital. Both men are Vietnam veterans, but Modine's problems seem to predate the war.

Camille Claudel (1988) Biography ΨΨΨ
Biographical film of the mistress of Rodin, who spent the last 30 years of her life in an asylum.

David and Lisa (1963) Drama ΨΨΨ
Story of two institutionalized teenagers who become romantically involved. Based on a story by psychiatrist Theodore Isaac Rubin.

Dead of Night (1945) Horror ΨΨΨΨ
Five short episodes loosely linked together. The last of these, "The Ventriloquist's Dummy," stars Michael Redgrave, who has to be hospitalized after he becomes convinced that he and his dummy are exchanging personalities (and, in fact, they are).

Delusions of Grandeur (1973) Comedy Ψ
In seventeenth-century Spain, a wily servant saves his king from the intrigues of a tax collector.

Dressed to Kill (1980) Thriller Ψ
Popular film in which Michael Caine plays Angie Dickinson's psychiatrist. The film confuses transsexuality and schizophrenia, but it is exciting, if not always accurate.

Entertainer, The (1960) Drama Ψ
This film, starring Laurence Olivier and Albert Finney, portrays Olivier as a third-rate vaudevillian whose delusions of grandeur alienate people around him.

Fan, The (1982) Horror Ψ
A Broadway star played by Lauren Bacall is terrorized by an embittered fan.

Fan, The (1996) Drama Ψ
Robert De Niro and Wesley Snipes are wasted in this tired film about a baseball fan who is obsessed with a Giants center fielder.

Fisher King, The (1991) Drama/Fantasy/Comedy ΨΨΨ
Terry Gilliam film in which Robin Williams plays a homeless, mentally ill man who is befriended by a disillusioned former disc jockey. The movie is funny but confusing, and it misleads the public with its suggestion of a traumatic etiology for schizophrenia.

Housekeeping (1987) Drama ΨΨΨΨ
An eccentric aunt comes to care for two sisters in the Pacific Northwest after the suicide of their mother. The girls can't decide if their aunt is simply odd or seriously mentally ill. The viewer confronts a similar dilemma.

SCHIZOPHRENIA AND OTHER PSYCHOTIC DISORDERS

I Never Promised You a Rose Garden (1977) Drama ΨΨΨΨ
Accurate rendition of the popular book by the same name. The patient has command
hallucinations that tell her to kill herself. There is a sympathetic portrayal of psychiatry and
treatment; a breakthrough occurs when the protagonist first realizes she is able to feel pain.

Images (1972) Drama ΨΨΨ
Robert Altman's examination of the confused life of a schizophrenic woman. A difficult film,
but interesting, with a heuristic presentation of hallucinations.

La Dolce Vita (1960) Drama ΨΨΨ
Vintage Fellini film with an interesting vignette in which hundreds of Roman citizens develop
a mass delusion following reports of a sighting of the Virgin Mary.

Lunatics: A Love Story (1992) Comedy ΨΨΨ
A former mental patient spends six months hidden away in his apartment. The lead character
has been described in reviews as agoraphobic, but a more serious diagnosis seems appropriate,
especially in light of the patient's delusions and hallucinations.

Lust for Life (1956) Biography ΨΨΨΨ
Kirk Douglas as Vincent van Gogh and Anthony Quinn as Paul Gauguin. The film portrays the
stormy relationship of the two men and van Gogh's hospitalization and eventual suicide.
Contrast with *Vincent* (1987) and Robert Altman's *Vincent and Theo* (1990).

Madness of King George, The (1994) Historical
Biography ΨΨΨ
Nigel Hawthorne as King George III in an
adaptation of a stage play examining the
reactions of the court and family as the king
becomes increasingly demented (due to
porphyria, a genetic metabolic disorder).

> "One may produce a copious, regular
> evacuation every day of the week and still
> be a stranger to reason."
> An observation by a court doctor in *The
> Madness of King George* (1994)

Magic (1978) Thriller Ψ
Anthony Hopkins' talents are largely wasted in this Richard Attenborough film about a
ventriloquist obsessed with his dummy. Not nearly as good a film as the 1945 movie *Dead of
Night*.

Misery (1990) Horror ΨΨ
Kathy Bates plays an apparently delusional woman who becomes convinced she is justified in
capturing a novelist and forcing him to rewrite his latest novel to meet her tastes. The movie,
like Wagner's music, is better than it sounds.

Outrageous! (1977) Comedy ΨΨ
Canadian film about a gay hairdresser and a woman who is both pregnant and schizophrenic.

SCHIZOPHRENIA AND OTHER PSYCHOTIC DISORDERS

Possessed (1947) Drama ΨΨΨ
Joan Crawford stars in a suspenseful film depicting catatonic schizophrenia with examples of waxy flexibility and numerous other symptoms of severe mental illness.

Promise (1986) Drama ΨΨ
A made-for-TV movie, starring James Garner, about a man who honors a commitment made to his mother to care for his schizophrenic brother. Excellent illustrations of the symptoms of schizophrenia.

Repulsion (1965) Horror ΨΨΨΨΨ
Powerful, unforgettable film about sexual repression and psychotic decompensation. Memorable examples of hallucinations (e.g., arms reaching out from walls); the film culminates in an unforgettable murder scene. This was Roman Polanski's first English language film.

Ruling Class, The (1972) Comedy ΨΨΨ
Brilliant British black comedy in which a member of the House of Lords inadvertently commits suicide and leaves his fortune and title to his delusional, schizophrenic son (Peter O'Toole), who believes he is Jesus (at first) and later Jack the Ripper.

Saint of Fort Washington, The (1993) Drama ΨΨΨ
Schizophrenic man evicted from his home winds up in a shelter, where he is befriended by a street-wise black Vietnam veteran. Good portrayal of the life of people who are both mentally ill and homeless.

Santa Sangre (1989) Horror/Thriller ΨΨΨΨ
A disturbing film about a young man forced to witness the mutilation of his mother and the suicide of his father. We never know if these events are real or simply delusions of a patient. The film is complex and visually stunning.

Scissors (1991) Suspense Ψ
The paranoid delusions of a traumatized young woman take on a frightening reality when she finds her assailant dead.

Shine (1996) Biography/Drama ΨΨΨΨ
True story of David Helfgott, an Australian prodigy whose brilliant career is interrupted by the development of an unspecified mental illness that is probably schizophrenia. The film not so subtly suggests that David's domineering father was directly responsible for his mental illness and conveys the misleading but endearing message that love and hope can conquer mental illness.

> "David, if you go you will never come back to this house again. You will never be anybody's son. The girls will lose their brother. Is that what you want? . . . . You want to destroy the family . . . if you love me you will stop this nonsense."
> David Helfgott's father admonishes him about leaving for New York in *Shine* (1996)

SCHIZOPHRENIA AND OTHER PSYCHOTIC DISORDERS

Shock Corridor (1963) Drama ΨΨ
Journalist feigns insanity in order to get a story from a man admitted to a psychiatric hospital;
later the journalist begins to lose touch with reality.

Snake Pit, The (1948) Drama ΨΨΨ
One of the first films to document the treatment of patients in a mental hospital.

Sophie's Choice (1982) Drama ΨΨΨ
Meryl Streep won an Academy Award for her portrayal of a concentration camp survivor
infatuated with Nathan, who is described as paranoid schizophrenic but who may suffer from a
bipolar disorder. Based on William Styron's novel.

Story of Adèle H, The (1975) Biography ΨΨ
François Truffaut story about the sexual obsession of the daughter of Victor Hugo for a young
soldier she can never marry.

Stroszek (1977) Comedy ΨΨ
Offbeat Werner Herzog comedy about three Germans who come to America in search of the
American dream. They fail to find it in Railroad Flats, Wisconsin. One of the three is
schizophrenic.

Sweetie (1989) Comedy ΨΨΨΨ
Director Jane Campion paints a memorable and realistic picture of a schizophrenic woman and
the difficulties her illness presents for her and her family.

Taxi Driver (1976) Drama ΨΨΨΨΨ
Robert De Niro becomes obsessed with Jodi
Foster and determines to rescue her from
prostitution.

> "Someday a real rain will come and wash all
> the scum off the streets."
> *Taxi Driver* (1976)

Tenant, The (1976) Horror ΨΨΨ
Roman Polanski film about an ordinary clerk who moves into an apartment in which the
previous owner committed suicide. The new owner assumes the personality of the old owner,
becomes paranoid, and commits suicide in the same way as the previous owner.

Through a Glass, Darkly (1962) Drama ΨΨΨΨ
Powerful and memorable Bergman film about a recently released mental patient who spends
the summer on an island with her husband, father, and younger brother.

Who's Afraid of Virginia Woolf? (1966)
Drama ΨΨΨΨ
A Mike Nichols film, with Elizabeth Taylor and
Richard Burton, who appear to have a shared
psychotic disorder involving a son who never

> "Now that we're through with Humiliate the
> Host . . . and we don't want to play Hump
> the Hostess yet . . . how about a little round
> of Get the Guests?"
> *Who's Afraid of Virginia Woolf?* (1966)

really existed; the film also portrays alcoholism and interpersonal cruelty. Elizabeth Taylor and
Sandy Dennis both won Academy Awards for their performances in this film.

NEUROPSYCHOLOGICAL DISORDERS

Awakenings (1990) Drama ΨΨΨ
Robin Williams as neurologist Oliver Sacks treating patient Robert De Niro in a Bronx hospital. The film documents the use of L-Dopa in the treatment of patients with advanced Parkinson's disease. Good portrayal of the daily life of a mental hospital.

Dark Victory (1939) Drama ΨΨΨ
Bette Davis, George Brent, and Humphrey Bogart star; but watch for Ronald Reagan. Davis has a fatal brain tumor. She spends what little time she has left with her brain surgeon husband. The "dark victory" refers to living life well, even when facing death. Remade (not very effectively) with Susan Hayward in *Stolen Hours* (1963).

Death Be Not Proud (1975) Biography ΨΨ
A made-for-TV film based on John Gunthur's moving account of his son's struggle with a brain tumor, which killed the boy at the age of 17. The book provides considerable insight into the neurology of brain lesions.

Do You Remember Love? (1985) Drama ΨΨ
Joanne Woodward won an Emmy for her portrayal of a middle-aged college professor who develops Alzheimer's disease.

Lorenzo's Oil (1992) Drama ΨΨΨ
True story of the Odone family and their desperate struggle to save their son's life. The boy has a rare neurological disease that they are told is ultimately fatal. Good illustration of the effects of chronic illness on family functioning.

Memories of Me (1988) Comedy ΨΨ
Henry Winkler directs Billy Crystal, a high-powered surgeon who has just had a heart attack, and Alan King, his actor father who may have Alzheimer's. It turns out that an aneurysm is present, and father and son eventually learn to care for one another.

Mercy or Murder? (1987) Drama ΨΨ
Made-for-TV movie about a Florida man who went to prison after killing his wife because she had advanced Alzheimer's disease. The film raises interesting questions that society will increasingly be forced to confront.

My Girl (1991) Comedy ΨΨ
Eleven-year-old girl is a hypochondriac with a mortician for a father and a grandmother with Alzheimer's disease.

My Own Private Idaho (1991) Drama ΨΨ
River Phoenix stars as a young male prostitute who has narcolepsy. He is befriended by Keanu Reeves, and the two leave Portland and travel together. Interesting presentations of dreams that occur during narcoleptic episodes.

DISORDERS OF CHILDHOOD AND ADOLESCENCE

On the Waterfront (1954) Drama ΨΨΨΨ
Classic Elia Kazan film starring Marlon Brando
as Terry Malloy, a prizefighter of limited
intelligence who is exploited by almost
everyone around him. Brando won an Oscar as
Best Actor for his performance as Terry
Malloy, who took a dive and spent the rest of his life regretting it.

> "You was my brother, Charley, you
> should've looked out for me just a little bit
> so I wouldn't have to take them dives for the
> short-end money."
> *On the Waterfront* (1954)

Pride of the Yankees (1942) Biography ΨΨΨ
Gary Cooper stars in this Samuel Goldwyn film
about legendary Yankees' first baseman Lou
Gehrig, who had to give up baseball due to
amyotrophic lateral sclerosis, which came to be
known more widely by the eponym "Lou Gehrig's disease."

> "Some people say I've had a bad break, but I
> consider myself to be the luckiest man on the
> face of the earth."
> Lou Gehrig giving up baseball in *Pride of the
> Yankees* (1942)

Private Matter, A (1992) Biography ΨΨ
Provocative made-for-TV movie starring Sissy Spacek as a TV personality who gets national
attention after her decision to abort a child likely to be affected by the drug thalidomide.

Raging Bull (1980) Biography/Sports ΨΨΨΨ
Powerful film depicting the psychological, moral, and mental decline of a prizefighter. Robert
De Niro won an Oscar for his portrayal of Jake LaMotta.

Regarding Henry (1993) DramaΨΨ
Attorney has his life permanently altered following a head injury; his values change as well as
his personality.

The Harder They Fall (1956) Sports ΨΨΨΨ
Humphrey Bogart in his last film, made the year before his death. The movie is very critical of
the sport of boxing and exploitation of fighters by promoters. A slow-witted boxer has a brain
clot and is almost killed in his last fight.

DISORDERS OF CHILDHOOD AND ADOLESCENCE
Best Little Girl in the World, The (1981) Drama ΨΨ
Good made-for-TV movie in which a psychiatrist treats a girl who is suffering from anorexia
nervosa.

Carrie (1976) Horror ΨΨ
This Brian De Palma film is based on a Stephen King novel and depicts the cruelty of
adolescents and some of the stresses associated with caring for a mentally ill mother. Sissy
Spacek's performance is remarkable.

DISORDERS OF CHILDHOOD AND ADOLESCENCE

Equus (1977) Drama ΨΨΨ
Richard Burton examines the meaning and purpose of his own life as he attempts to unravel the psychosexual roots that led an adolescent to blind six horses. Wonderful soliloquies by Burton.

Every Man for Himself and God Against All (1975) Biography ΨΨΨΨ
Werner Herzog film based on a true story about a man who spent an isolated childhood virtually devoid of stimulation. This movie should be contrasted with Truffaut's film *The Wild Child* and the more recent film *Nell.*

Face to Face (1976) Drama ΨΨ
Bergman film in which Liv Ullmann plays a suicidal psychiatrist estranged from her husband and 14-year-old daughter. During a coma that results from an overdose of sleeping pills, Ullmann dreams about a childhood experience in which she was punished by being locked in a closet.

Fanny and Alexander (1983) Drama ΨΨΨΨ
Bergman film about two young children and the ways in which their lives change when their father dies and their mother remarries. The film is sensitive, tender, and haunting and shows how the world looks through the eyes of a 10-year-old.

> "Therefore, let us be happy, let us be kind, generous, affectionate, and good. Therefore, it is necessary, and not in the least shameful, to take pleasures in the little world, good food, gentle smiles, fruit-trees in bloom, and waltzes."
> *Fanny and Alexander* (1983)

Forbidden Games (1951) War/Drama ΨΨΨΨ
Two children create and share a private fantasy world. Beautiful French film that juxtaposes the innocence of childhood with the horror of war.

Four Hundred Blows, The (1959) Drama ΨΨΨΨ
Semiautobiographical film by François Truffaut about a 13-year-old boy who gets caught up in a life of truancy and petty crime. His mother sleeps around; his father is preoccupied and distant. This movie is reported to be Truffaut's favorite film.

Innocents, The (1961) Horror ΨΨΨ
Deborah Kerr plays a governess hired to care for two precocious children. Is she hallucinating or delusional, or are there ghosts in the house? Interesting sexual tension between Kerr and the boy. Based on the Henry James novella *Turn of the Screw.*

Kids (1995) Drama ΨΨΨ
Gritty and disturbing film about sex, drugs, and violence. The main character is a teenager with AIDS who preys on young adolescent girls, taking particular pride in seducing virgins.

Leolo (1992) Comedy ΨΨΨΨ
Leo, an adolescent boy growing up in a very dysfunctional family in Montreal, is unable to accept the reality of his genetic heritage and concocts a fantasy in which he was accidentally conceived by sperm that crossed the Atlantic in a Sicilian tomato.

DISORDERS OF CHILDHOOD AND ADOLESCENCE

Little Man Tate (1991) Drama ΨΨΨ
Jodi Foster directed this film about a child prodigy and the tensions that arise between his mother and the psychologist to whom the child's education is entrusted. Foster acknowledged that the film is partly a retelling of her own experiences.

Lord of the Flies (1963) Drama ΨΨ
Film adaptation of William Goldman's novel about a group of school children who quickly shed the thin veneer of civilization and become savages. Both the film and book raise interesting questions about nature and nurture. Remade in 1990.

Los Olvidados/The Young and the Damned (1950) Drama ΨΨ
Luis Buñuel film about juvenile delinquency in the squalid slums of Mexico City.

Mommie Dearest (1981) Biography ΨΨ
A film about the pathological relationship between Joan Crawford and her adopted daughter. The movie suggests that Crawford suffered from bipolar disorder.

Nell (1994) Drama ΨΨΨ
Jodi Foster plays a feral child raised in isolation in the North Carolina woods. She is terrified of the doctor who discovers her and speaks her own odd language. The doctor consults an expert on child psychology. Interesting examination of Rousseau's "natural savage."

Pelle the Conqueror (1986) Drama ΨΨΨΨ
Incredibly moving film about lust, passion, dreams, aging, hope, pragmatic romance, and, most of all, the love between a father and his son. The film won the Grand Prix at the Cannes Film Festival and an Academy Award as Best Foreign Film.

Pixote (1981) Drama ΨΨΨΨ
Moving film about the squalid, depressing lives of street children in Sao Paulo. In the film, the child, Pixote, commits his first murder at the age of 10. Ironically, the child star actually was shot and killed by the police five years after the film was released.

Rebel Without a Cause (1955) Drama ΨΨΨ
Dated but still interesting examination of teenage alienation, violence, and family pathology. James Dean is the rebellious protagonist. All three stars (Dean, Natalie Wood, and Sal Mineo) met violent deaths (a car wreck, a drowning, and a murder).

> "Boy, if, if I had one day when I didn't have to be all confused, and didn't have to feel that I was ashamed of everything . . . ."
> *Rebel Without a Cause* (1955)

Salaam Bombay! (1988) Drama ΨΨΨ
Remarkable story about the way indigent children manage to survive to adulthood on the mean streets of Bombay.

Splendor in the Grass (1961) Drama ΨΨ
A teenage girl unable to come to grips with adolescent sexuality winds up in a psychiatric hospital.

Tin Drum, The (1979) Drama/War ΨΨΨ
Political allegory about a child who decides to stop growing. Based on a Gunter Grass novel, the film won an Academy Award as Best Foreign Film. The film recently received considerable attention because a scene in which the child has oral sex with an adult was judged to be obscene under Oklahoma law.

To Kill a Mockingbird (1962) Drama ΨΨ
Robert Duvall makes his film debut as Boo Radley, a retarded man who kills another man in order to protect two children.

Tree Grows in Brooklyn, A (1945) Drama ΨΨΨ
Elia Kazan film about a poor Irish family living in Brooklyn at the turn of the century. The family's problems are complicated by the father's alcoholism.

Welcome to the Dollhouse (1996) Comedy ΨΨΨ
Interesting examination of families, emerging sexuality, and the cruelty of adolescents.

Wild Child, The (1969) Drama ΨΨΨΨ
François Truffaut's engaging film about the life of a feral child, the "Wild Boy of Aveyron." Based on a true story and the journal of Jean Itard, the doctor who set out to educate the child. Truffaut himself plays the role of Itard.

Wish You Were Here (1987) Drama ΨΨ
A teenage girl coming of age in Great Britain in the early 1950s must come to grips with her emerging sexuality.

MENTAL RETARDATION AND AUTISM

Being There (1979) Comedy ΨΨ
Peter Sellers plays the role of a mildly mentally retarded gardener who finds himself caught up in a comedy of errors in which his simple platitudes are mistaken for wisdom. This film is a precursor to *Forrest Gump*.

Best Boy (1979) Documentary ΨΨΨΨ
Ira Wohl's moving tribute to his mentally retarded cousin examines the options facing the young man when his father dies and his aging mother is no longer able to care for him. This film won an Academy Award as Best Documentary film.

Bill (1981) Biography ΨΨ
Mickey Rooney won an Emmy for playing a mentally retarded man forced to leave an institution after 46 years in this made-for-TV movie.

MENTAL RETARDATION AND AUTISM

Boy Who Could Fly, The (1986) Fantasy ΨΨ
Love story about the affection that develops between a teenage girl whose father has just committed suicide and a new neighbor who is autistic.

Charly (1968) Drama ΨΨ
Cliff Robertson won an Oscar for his role as a mentally retarded man who is transformed into a genius, only to find himself reverting back to a state of retardation.

Child Is Waiting, A (1963) Drama ΨΨ
Burt Lancaster and Judy Garland star in this film about the treatment of children with mental retardation living in institutions.

Dangerous Woman, A (1993) Drama ΨΨ
Debra Winger plays a mildly retarded woman who becomes involved with an itinerant alcoholic.

Day in the Life of Joe Egg, A (1972) Comedy ΨΨ
British black comedy that examines the issue of mercy killing.

Dodes'ka-den (1970) Drama ΨΨΨ
Akira Kurosawa film about a mentally retarded boy living in the slums of Tokyo.

Dominick and Eugene (1988) Drama ΨΨΨ
A mildly mentally retarded man works picking up garbage so he can send his brother to medical school. The story revolves around the relationship between the two brothers and provides good insight into the quality of life possible for someone who is mildly mentally retarded.

Forrest Gump (1994) Fantasy ΨΨΨ
Traces the life of Forrest Gump, who triumphs in life despite an IQ of 75 and a deformed spine. The film will make you examine your own stereotypes about retardation.

House of Cards (1993) Drama Ψ
Tommy Lee Jones is wasted in an insipid movie about a young girl who becomes autistic and withdrawn.

Larry (1974) Biography ΨΨ
Dated but still interesting film about a man discharged from a psychiatric hospital and forced to cope with the outside world. The film suggests the patient himself isn't really ill but still acts strange because he has grown up in a world where everyone acts a little odd.

Of Mice and Men (1992) Drama ΨΨΨ
John Malkovich as Lenny, a mentally retarded farmhand. This is a wonderful film, but see the 1939 original as well.

VIOLENCE, ABUSE, AND ANTISOCIAL BEHAVIOR

Rain Man (1993) Human Interest ΨΨΨ
Dustin Hoffman plays an autistic man who is
also a savant, initially exploited by an older
brother. Dustin Hoffman read widely about
autism and worked with autistic people when preparing for this role.

> "I know you're in there somewhere."
> Charlie Babbitt responds to his brother
> Raymond, *The Rain Man* (1993)

Sling Blade (1996) Drama ΨΨΨΨ
Billy Bob Thornton wrote the screenplay,
directed the film, and played the lead in this
remarkable film, which examines the life of a 37-year-old retarded man who has been
incarcerated in a mental hospital for the past 25 years after killing his mother and her lover.
The fact that Childers winds up committing a third murder after being released perpetuates the
myth that people who are retarded are potentially dangerous.

> "I reckon I got no reason to kill no one. Uh,
> huh."
> Carl Childers in *Sling Blade* (1996)

Tim (1979) Drama ΨΨ
An older woman has an affair with a mildly retarded man.

Unforgotten: 25 Years After Willowbrook (1996) Documentary ΨΨΨΨ
Geraldo Rivera follows up on the original Willowbrook State School expose and contrasts the
grim reality of institutional life with the current success of some survivors, including Bernard
Carabello, a man abandoned by his parents at age three because he had cerebral palsy, who
spent 18 years at Willowbrook.

What's Eating Gilbert Grape (1993) Drama ΨΨΨ
Johnny Depp stars in this interesting portrayal of the dynamics of a rural Iowa family and small
town America. Depp's life revolves around the care of his retarded brother and his morbidly
obese mother.

VIOLENCE, ABUSE, AND ANTISOCIAL BEHAVIOR

Accused, The (1988) Drama ΨΨΨΨ
Jodi Foster won an Academy Award for Best Actress for her role as a woman who is gang
raped in a bar. Her character chooses to prosecute for rape rather than aggravated assault; and
the film examines the legal relevance of lifestyle (alcohol, drugs, and promiscuity) to the event
and the complicity of bystanders. Based on a true story.

Anatomy of a Murder (1959) Drama ΨΨΨΨ
Classic courtroom drama in which Jimmy Stewart
plays a prosecuting attorney in a case involving
rape and promiscuity. The film presents an
interesting analysis of the "irresistible impulse"
defense.

> "You can't have my hand, but you can have
> the rest."
> Antonia rejects marriage but agrees to sex
> with her farmer suitor in *Antonia's Line*
> (1995)

VIOLENCE, ABUSE, AND ANTISOCIAL BEHAVIOR

Antonia's Line (1995) Comedy ΨΨΨ
Remarkable film about the resiliency of the human spirit, the power of love, and the importance of families. It is included here because of its treatment of a rapist, but also because of its treatment of people with mental retardation, the suicide of a major character, the film's open acceptance of sexual differences, and its healthy attitudes about aging and death.

Apocalypse Now (1979) War ΨΨΨΨ
Francis Ford Coppola produced and directed this classic war film, which stars Marlon Brando, Robert Duvall, and Martin Sheen. The film is loosely based on Joseph Conrad's *Heart of Darkness* and was designed to drive home the madness of war, as well as its folly. Perhaps the best-known line in the film is "I love the smell of Napalm in the morning."

> "Every man has got a breaking point. You and I have. Walter Kurtz has reached his. And, very obviously, he has gone insane." An Army general tries to describe the aberrant behavior of Colonel Kurtz in *Apocalypse Now* (1979)

Bad Lieutenant (1992) Drama ΨΨΨ
Cocaine-addicted, alcoholic police officer who abuses his position and his family reexamines his life and values after investigating the case of a nun who refuses to identify the man who has raped her.

Badlands (1973) Crime/Drama ΨΨΨ
Film based on a true story about a sociopathic young man who takes up with a 15-year-old girl and goes on a killing spree. The film effectively portrays the lack of guilt and remorse that in part defines the antisocial personality.

Blue Velvet (1986) Mystery ΨΨΨΨ
A powerful and engrossing film about drugs, sexual violence, and sadomasochism. Dennis Hopper plays Frank Booth, a sociopathic and sadistic drug addict who appears to be evil personified.

> "He kidnapped them to control her, to make her do things. Then she wanted to commit suicide so he started cutting off ears as a warning to her to stay alive. I'm not kidding. Frank loved blue. Blue velvet." *Blue Velvet* (1986)

Bonnie and Clyde (1967) Crime ΨΨΨ
Perhaps the best of its genre, this landmark film examines the lives of five of the most fascinating characters in the history of crime.

> "I ain't much of a lover boy. But that don't mean nothin' personal about you. I never saw no percentage in it. Ain't nothin' wrong with me. I don't like boys. . . ." Clyde Barrow to Bonnie Parker in *Bonnie and Clyde* (1967)

Boston Strangler, The (1968) Crime ΨΨ
Tony Curtis, George Kennedy, and Henry Fonda in a film that attempts to portray the inner life of a serial killer.

Boxing Helena (1994) Drama Ψ
Eminent surgeon is rebuffed by beautiful woman. She is injured while trying to escape from him, and he eventually amputates her arms and legs. Directed by the daughter of David Lynch.

VIOLENCE, ABUSE, AND ANTISOCIAL BEHAVIOR

Bridge on the River Kwai, The (1957) Drama ΨΨΨΨ

Alec Guiness plays an Academy Award-winning role as a British colonel who becomes so obsessed with building a bridge that he loses sight of his loyalty and allegiance to the allied forces.

> "Do not speak to me of rules. This is war. This is not a game of cricket. He's mad, your Colonel. Quite mad."
> *The Bridge on the River Kwai* (1957)

Cape Fear (1991) Thriller ΨΨΨΨ

Interesting Scorsese remake of a 1962 classic. This version includes Nick Nolte playing a sleazy attorney and Robert De Niro is a sociopathic ex-con out to get revenge by hurting Nolte and his family and seducing his teenage daughter.

Casualties of War (1989) Drama ΨΨΨ

Sean Penn leads a group of five soldiers who kidnap and rape a Vietnamese girl and subsequently kill her. Michael J. Fox subsequently shows the moral courage to confront the four rapists and murders. Based on a true story.

Compulsion (1959) Crime ΨΨΨ

Two homosexual law students kidnap and kill a young boy. Based on the Leopold-Loeb case, the film examines the morality of capital punishment and features Orson Wells in the role played by Clarence Darrow in the actual case.

Cook, the Thief, His Wife & Her Lover, The (1989) Drama ΨΨΨΨ

Peter Greenaway film far too complex to capture in a sentence or two. Full of psychopathology, the film deals with passion, deceit, gluttony, murder, cannibalism, and man's inhumanity to man. It is a film you won't soon forget.

Copycat (1995) Drama ΨΨΨ

Sigourney Weaver plays a forensic psychologist trying to understand the psyche of a serial killer who models his murders after those committed by infamous murderers, such as Son of Sam and the Boston Strangler.

Dead Man Walking (1995) Drama ΨΨΨΨ

Susan Sarandon and Sean Penn star in this dramatic examination of a nun's need to understand and help a man sentenced to die for the

> "They got me on a greased rail to the Death House here."
> Sean Penn in *Dead Man Walking* (1995)

rape and murder of two teenagers. The film skillfully examines the death penalty, family dynamics, themes of redemption, and the mitigating role of drugs without ever providing easy answers. Sarandon won an Academy Award for her performance in this film.

Deliberate Stranger, The (1986) Drama Ψ

Made-for-TV movie about serial killer Ted Bundy.

VIOLENCE, ABUSE, AND ANTISOCIAL BEHAVIOR

Deliverance (1972) Adventure ΨΨΨ
Jon Voight, Ned Beatty, and Burt Reynolds on a white water rafting trip in Appalachia. Beatty winds up being sodomized; Reynolds kills the

> "Lewis, don't play games with these people."
> *Deliverance* (1972)

rapist, using a bow and arrow. Based on a James Dickey novel, the film raises interesting questions about personal responsibility and social justice.

Disclosure (1994) Drama ΨΨ
A less-than-illuminating film about reverse sexual discrimination. Stars include Demi Moore and Michael Douglas; based on a novel by Michael Crichton.

Dog Day Afternoon (1975) Crime ΨΨΨ
Al Pacino holds up a bank to get enough money to fund a sex-change operation for his homosexual lover. Good illustration of a basically good person caught up in an intolerably stressful situation.

Down and Dirty (1976) Drama ΨΨ
An interesting examination of the effects of poverty, squalor, and alcoholism on an Italian family.

Dressed to Kill (1980) Thriller Ψ
The film confuses transsexualism and schizophrenia but offers good suspense. Mimics Hitchcock.

Executioner's Song, The (1982) Made for TV Drama ΨΨ
Tommy Lee Jones plays serial killer Gary Gilmore. Based on a story by Norman Mailer.

Extremities (1986) Drama Ψ
Farrah Fawcett plays a victimized woman who gets revenge on the man who rapes her.

Godfather, The (1972), **The Godfather, Part II** (1974), and **The Godfather, Part III** (1990) Drama ΨΨΨ
The three-part gangster trilogy, directed by Francis Ford Coppola, examines violence, corruption, and crime in America.

> "We'll make him an offer he can't refuse."
> *The Godfather* (1972)

Halloween I-V (1978, 1981, 1982, 1988, 1989, 1998) Horror Ψ
Infamous mass murderer depicted as an escaped mental patient and a deranged toy maker. These films have contributed significantly to the negative stereotypes of mental illness.

Hand That Rocks the Cradle, The (1992) Thriller/Drama Ψ
Sociopathic woman seeks revenge for the suicide of her husband by moving in and taking over the family of the woman she holds responsible for her husband's death. Predictable performances, but still an engrossing film.

Heavenly Creatures (1994) Drama ΨΨΨ
A New Zealand film directed by Peter Jackson and based on the true story of two adolescent girls who grow up sharing a fantasy world. When the mother of one of the girls decides to separate the children, they murder her. One of the girls, Ann Perry, now lives in England and writes mystery novels.

Henry: Portrait of a Serial Killer (1990) Crime/Horror ΨΨΨ
A violent, controversial film about mass murderer and sociopath Henry Lee Lucas. A scene in which Lucas and his roommate videotape one of their murders is especially unnerving.

> "She'd make me watch it . . . . She'd beat me when I wouldn't watch her . . . . She'd make me wear a dress and they would laugh."
> Henry Lee Lucas describing abuse by his prostitute mother. Lucas bragged that he killed when he was 14, in *Henry: Portrait of a Serial Killer* (1990)

Honeymoon Killers, The (1970) Crime Ψ
A very realistic black-and-white film based on the true story of a couple who lured, exploited, and then killed lonely women. Both the man and the woman were executed at Sing-Sing Prison.

I Spit on Your Grave (1980) Horror Ψ
A terrible film in which a woman systematically gets revenge on the four men who raped her.

In Cold Blood (1967) Biography/Crime ΨΨ
This film is based on a Truman Capote biographical novel about two sociopaths who kill a Kansas family. The film explores the family dynamics that in part lead to the senseless murders.

> "They all felt physically inferior or sexually inadequate. Their childhood was violent. . . They couldn't distinguish between fantasy and reality. They didn't hate their victims, they didn't even know them."
> A doctor describes serial killers in *In Cold Blood* (1967)

Killing Fields, The (1984) Drama ΨΨΨ
Gripping film about the horrors of war and the particularly gruesome and cruel practices of the Khmer Rouge in Cambodia following the evacuation of American soldiers from Vietnam in 1975.

Looking for Mr. Goodbar (1977) Drama ΨΨ
Diane Keaton plays a special education teacher with a compulsive need to pick up men in bars and engage in sadomasochistic sex. There are numerous examples of family pathology in the film, and it is interesting to remember how casual sexuality was in a time before AIDS.

M (1931) Crime/Drama/Horror ΨΨΨΨ
A must-see Fritz Lang film (his first "talkie") starring Peter Lorre as a sexual psychopath who molests and murders little girls. When tried by a vigilante jury, he pleads irresistible impulse, but the jury is not impressed.

Midnight Express (1978) Biography ΨΨΨ
True story about an American college student who is busted for trying to smuggle two kilograms of hashish out of Turkey and is treated brutally in Turkish prisons before eventually escaping.

VIOLENCE, ABUSE, AND ANTISOCIAL BEHAVIOR

Murder in the First (1995) Drama ΨΨ
A man imprisoned in Alcatraz for petty theft in the 1930s is put in solitary confinement for three years, becomes deranged, and then kills a guard. The film suggests the system is to blame for the crime. Based on a true story.

Natural Born Killers (1994) Crime/Drama ΨΨΨ
A violent Oliver Stone film written by Quentin Tarantino and starring Woody Harrelson and Tommy Lee Jones. The film depicts a couple who celebrate their roles as mass murderers and find their new status as cult figures a welcome reprieve from the dreariness of the life they left behind.

> "Insane, no. Psychotic, yes. A menace to living creatures, yes. But to suggest that they're insane gives the impression that they don't know right from wrong. Mickey and Mallory know the difference between right and wrong. They just don't give a damn."
> A psychiatric opinion in *Natural Born Killers* (1994)

Night Porter, The (1974) Drama/War ΨΨ
A former Nazi officer who sexually abused a 14-year-old girl in a concentration camp has the tables turned on him when she shows up at the hotel in which he works. This is one of several films linking Nazi practices with sadomasochistic sex.

Once Were Warriors (1994) Drama ΨΨΨΨ
Important New Zealand film about substance abuse and domestic violence among urban Maori tribespeople. The film will help you understand a different culture, as well as the ways in which alcoholism interacts with spousal and child abuse in almost every society.

> "It's the same old story. I've got to learn to keep my mouth shut."
> Beth blaming herself for the beating she has received from her husband in *Once Were Warriors* (1994)

Peeping Tom (1960) Thriller ΨΨΨ
Controversial film about a psychopathic murderer who photographs his vicims as they die.

Play Misty for Me (1971) Thriller ΨΨΨ
The first film directed by Clint Eastwood. A California disc jockey becomes involved with a listener who is clinging, dependent, fanatical, and ultimately homicidal. Interesting portrayal of sexual obsession.

Prick Up Your Ears (1987) Biography ΨΨΨΨ
A film showing the homosexual relationship and eventual murder/suicide of playwright Joe Orton and his lover.

Rampage (1992) Thriller ΨΨΨ
This movie, directed by William Friedkin, challenges many of the assumptions educated people are likely to hold about the insanity defense.

Rashomon (1950) Drama ΨΨΨΨ
Classic Akira Kurosawa film in which a rape-murder is described from four different perspectives by the four people involved. The film makes the point that reality is subjective and that truth, like beauty, is truly in the eye of the beholder.

VIOLENCE, ABUSE, AND ANTISOCIAL BEHAVIOR

Reservoir Dogs (1992) Drama ΨΨΨ
Extremely violent but powerful Tarantino film with a graphic and realistic torture scene in which a sociopathic sadist derives great pleasure from using a razor to slowly torment a bound and gagged undercover policeman.

> "Now I'm not gonna bullshit you. I don't really care about what you know or don't know. I'm gonna torture you for awhile regardless. Not to get information, but because torturing a cop amuses me. There's nothing you can say, there's nothing you can do. Except pray for death."
> The sadistic Mr. Blonde in *Reservoir Dogs* (1992)

River's Edge (1986) Drama ΨΨΨΨ
A riveting film based on a true-life incident in which a young man kills his girlfriend and then shows the decomposing body to a series of friends. It takes days before one of his friends finally notifies authorities about the murder.

Rope (1948) ΨΨ
Experimental Hitchcock film about two young homosexual men who kill a friend for sport and then hide the body in a room in which they are hosting a cocktail party. Based on the Leopold-Loeb case.

Santa Sangre (1989) Horror ΨΨΨΨ
A controversial but unquestionably powerful Jodorowsky film about a boy growing up in bizarre circumstances. There are strong themes of violence and incest. Roger Ebert called this film "a collision between Freud and Fellini."

Seven (1995) Drama ΨΨΨ
Morgan Freeman and Brad Pitt star in this engrossing film about a serial killer who is obsessed with the seven deadly sins (pride, envy, gluttony, lust, anger, covetousness, and sloth) and who kills his victims accordingly (e.g., a man who is gluttonous is forced to eat until he dies from overeating).

Seven Beauties (1976) Comedy/Drama
Lina Wertmuller film in which the protagonist (the brother of the seven sisters alluded to in the title) must perform degrading sexual acts for the female commandant of a German prison camp to survive the war.

Stone Boy, The (1984) Drama ΨΨ
Robert Duvall and Glenn Close star in this slow-moving but intelligent film about a young man who accidentally shoots his brother and the effect the shooting has on the entire family.

Straw Dogs (1971) Crime ΨΨΨ
Provocative and violent Sam Peckinpah film, with Dustin Hoffman as a peace-loving mathematician who resorts to violence after his wife is raped.

Tattoo (1981) Drama Ψ
Mentally ill tattoo artist kidnaps a model and uses her body as a canvas for his art. This is the type of movie that perpetuates stigma and prejudice.

TREATMENT

Thelma and Louise (1991) Drama/Comedy ΨΨΨ
Two women friends on the road for a weekend lark wind up fleeing from the law and end their lives in a defiant suicidal act. Powerful feminist film.

Time to Kill, A (1996) Drama ΨΨΨ
Samuel Jackson plays an angry father who murders two white men who have raped his daughter. The film explores themes of racial and social justice, temporary insanity, and justifiable homicide.

Treasure of the Sierra Madre, The (1948) Drama ΨΨΨΨ
Tremendous John Huston film starring Humphrey Bogart. The movie explores obsessive greed, the folly of avarice, and the ways in which love of money can come to be the dominant force in one's life. Bogart's character is an example of a paranoid personality disorder.

> "Badges? We ain't got no badges! We don't need no badges. I don't have to show you any stinkin' badges!"
> *The Treasure of the Sierra Madre* (1984)

Triumph of the Spirit (1989) Biography ΨΨΨ
Story of Auschwitz concentration camp during World War II. Good introduction to the horrors and stress of concentration camp life.

Two Women (1961) War/Drama Ψ
This Vittorio de Sica film starring Sophia Loren examines war, rape, coming of age, and mother-daughter relations. Loren won an Academy Award as Best Actress for this film.

Virgin Spring, The (1959) Drama ΨΨΨ
An Ingmar Bergman film examining the rape and murder of a young girl by three bandits.

TREATMENT
Article 99 (1992) Comedy Ψ
Unsuccessful M*A*S*H*-like attempt to ridicule the quality of care provided in Veterans Administration medical centers.

Bad Timing: A Sensual Obsession (1980) Drama ΨΨ
Interesting and provocative film in which a psychiatrist becomes sexually involved with a troubled and self-destructive woman.

Badlands (1973) Crime/Drama ΨΨΨ
Film based on a true story about a sociopathic young man who takes up with a 15-year-old girl and goes on a killing spree. The film effectively portrays the lack of guilt and remorse that in part defines the antisocial personality.

Beautiful Dreamers (1992) Drama/Biography ΨΨΨΨ
True story about poet Walt Whitman's visit to an asylum in London, Ontario. Whitman is shocked by what he sees and persuades the hospital director to offer humane treatment. Eventually, the patients wind up playing the townspeople in a game of cricket.

Beyond Therapy (1987) Comedy Ψ
Disappointing Robert Altman film about New York yuppies and their psychiatrists.

Butcher's Wife, The (1991) Romance/Fantasy ΨΨ
Greenwich Village psychiatrist Jeff Daniels finds Demi Moore, the butcher's wife, is giving advice at least as good as his own.

Cabinet of Dr. Caligari, The (1919) Horror ΨΨΨΨ
German expressionistic film about hypnosis and the power of a hypnotist to induce others to do his bidding. One of the earliest presentations of the madman who runs a psychiatric hospital.

Captain Newman, M.D. (1963) Comedy/Drama ΨΨΨ
Sympathetic story about an Army psychiatrist (Gregory Peck) taking on the military bureaucracy to provide effective treatment for Bobby Darin. Darin is clearly manic and ultimately commits suicide.

Carefree (1938) Musical/Dance ΨΨ
Fred Astaire is a psychiatrist who was talked out of being a dancer. Ginger Rogers is referred to him for treatment (hypnosis) so she can learn to love one of Astair's friends; he complies with her request but predictably falls in love with her himself.

Caretakers, The (1963) Drama Ψ
Second-rate film that documents life in a West Coast psychiatric hospital and portrays some of the problems associated with introducing innovations in hospital settings.

Chattahoochee (1990) Drama ΨΨΨ
Korean War veteran with a post-traumatic stress disorder is hospitalized and treated. Dennis Hopper has a major role as a fellow patient.

Clockwork Orange, A (1971) Science Fiction ΨΨΨΨΨ
Fascinating interpretation of Anthony Burgess' novel. The portrayal of aversion therapy is somewhat heavy-handed but raises legitimate questions about the appropriate limits of behavior modification.

> "There was me, that is Alex, and my three droogs, that is Pete, Georgie, and Dim. . . and we sat in the Korova Milkbar trying to make up our rassoodocks what to do with the evening."
> Alex in *A Clockwork Orange* (1971)

TREATMENT

Color of Night (1994) Drama Ψ
Bruce Willis plays a disillusioned psychologist who gives up his practice after a patient commits suicide and Willis discovers he is no longer able to perceive the color red. Much of the plot revolves around a patient with multiple personalities who is simultaneously a group therapy patient (as a male) and, unknown to Willis, his lover (in a core personality named Rose).

Couch Trip, The (1988) Comedy Ψ
Dan Akyroyd plays the role of a psychiatric patient who escapes from an institution and then passes himself off as a Beverly Hills psychiatrist. The film reinforces the notion that psychiatry is mainly pretentious language and social manipulation.

Dark Past, The (1948) Crime ΨΨΨ
A psychologist is taken prisoner and tries to use his training to help his captor. Remake of the film *Blind Alley*.

Dead Man Out (1989) Drama ΨΨ
Superior and timely made-for-TV movie about a psychiatrist treating a convict so the man will be sane enough to be executed. The film raises meaningful questions about ethical issues and the appropriate limits of professional practice.

Dream Team, The (1989) Comedy ΨΨ
Four psychiatric patients are being taken to a game in Yankee Stadium when their doctor/escort is knocked unconscious and hospitalized. The entire film appears to be based on the well-known (and better done) shipboard outing by Jack Nicholson and his friends in *One Flew over the Cuckoo's Nest*.

Face to Face (1976) Drama ΨΨΨ
Liv Ullmann plays a psychiatrist whose life is falling apart. She attempts suicide by taking an overdose of pills and winds up in a coma. Interesting dream sequences with Bergman's usual presumption of childhood trauma as the trigger for adult unhappiness.

Fear Strikes Out (1957) Biography/Sports ΨΨΨ
Anthony Perkins as baseball player Jimmy Piersall, who suffers a mental breakdown as a result of his inability to please a domineering, demanding father. Piersall was successfully treated with psychotherapy and ECT and eventually staged a comeback.

Final Analysis (1992) Thriller/Drama ΨΨ
A complex film that pays homage to Hitchcock; interesting issues of childhood sexual abuse, repressed memories, professional responsibility, and the doctor-patient relationship.

Fine Madness, A (1966) Drama ΨΨΨ
Sean Connery plays Samson Shillito, an eccentric and unconventional poet who is hospitalized and lobotomized because of his sexual peccadilloes and the fact that he can't conform to societal expectations. The film was ahead of its time in raising important issues about the rights of people with mental illness.

Flame Within, The (1935) Drama Ψ
Dated and somewhat insipid film about a psychiatrist who falls in love with a patient.

Frances (1982) Biography ΨΨΨΨ
A vivid portrayal of the life of actress Frances Farmer, including her institutionalization, lobotomy, and alcoholism.

Good Will Hunting (1997) Drama ΨΨΨ
Robin Williams won an Academy Award as Best Supporting Actor for his role as a counseling psychologist teaching at a community college and treating a troubled young man who is extraordinarily gifted mathematically.

High Anxiety (1977) Comedy ΨΨ
Mel Brooks spoofs Hitchcock films and introduces the Institute for the Very, Very Nervous.

Home of the Brave (1949) Drama/War ΨΨΨ
Black soldier suffers a mental breakdown and is treated by a sympathetic psychiatrist. One of the first films to deal honestly with racism and bigotry.

House of Games (1987) Crime ΨΨ
A psychiatrist specializes in the treatment of gambling addiction. Fascinating introduction to the world of the con.

Inside/Out (1997) Drama ΨΨΨ
A Rob Tregenza film about life in a psychiatric hospital that was well received at the 1998 Sundance Film Festival. The film documents that both the patients and the staff had to cope with the difficult demands of life.

King of Hearts (1966) Comedy/Drama/War ΨΨΨ
A Scotsman separated from his unit wanders into town, abandoned by all except the inmates of the local insane asylum. Must-see film for those interested in attitudes about mental illness.

Ladybird, Ladybird (1993) Drama ΨΨΨ
Dramatic presentation of the clash between the rights of a parent and society's need to protect children.

Lilith (1964) Drama ΨΨ
Strong cast (Peter Fonda, Gene Hackman, Warren Beatty, and Kim Hunter) supports a weak script about a psychiatric inpatient who seduces a neophyte therapist.

TREATMENT

Lost Angels (1989) Drama ΨΨ
Donald Sutherland plays a psychiatrist treating a Los Angeles adolescent who is angry and troubled but probably not mentally ill.

> "When insurance paid for a year in a place like this, we said it took a year to help a kid. Now insurance pays for three months, and, presto, it takes three months to turn a kid around."
> Donald Sutherland complaining about the system in *Lost Angels* (1989)

Ludwig (1973) Biography Ψ
Long and somewhat tedious film about the mad king Ludwig of Bavaria. Good costumes and scenery, but the film teaches us little about mental illness or Ludwig himself.

Macbeth (1971) Drama ΨΨΨ
Powerful Roman Polanski adaptation of Shakespeare's play. It is interesting to speculate about the obsessions of Lady Macbeth and to compare Polanski's version with the earlier Orson Wells adaptation.

Man Facing Southeast (1986) Drama ΨΨΨΨ
Fascinating Argentine film about a man without identity who shows up at a psychiatric hospital claiming to be from another planet. It seems that this is not just another patient, and neither the hospital staff nor the film's audience ever figure out exactly what is happening.

Man Who Loved Women, The (1983) Comedy Ψ
A remake of the François Truffaut film of the same name. This film involves long sequences in which Burt Reynolds unburdens himself to his psychiatrist.

Marat/Sade (1966) Drama ΨΨΨΨ
In the early 1800s, the inmates of a French asylum put on a play directed by the Marquis de Sade (a patient) and based on the bathtub assassination of Jean-Paul Marat. The play incites the patients to riot.

Mine Own Executioner (1947) Drama ΨΨ
Confused and troubled psychoanalyst tries to help out a schizophrenic veteran.

Mr. Deeds Goes to Town (1936) Comedy ΨΨΨ
Frank Capra film in which Gary Cooper inherits $20 million and is judged insane when he decides to give it all away to needy farmers.

No Time for Sergeants (1958) Comedy Ψ
Andy Griffith stars; Don Knotts plays an Army psychiatrist.

No Way Out (1950) Drama ΨΨΨ
This was Sidney Poitier's first film. Poitier plays a black physician treating two racist hoodlums. When one dies, his brother (Richard Widmark) incites a race riot. The film was one of the earliest serious examinations of racism in postwar America.

Nobody's Child (1986) Biography ΨΨ
Marlo Thomas won an Emmy for her role as a woman who experiences tremendous personal and professional success when she is released after spending 20 years in a mental hospital.

Now, Voyager (1942) Drama ΨΨΨ
Her psychiatrist and inpatient treatment help sexually repressed Bette Davis find meaning and purpose in her life by serving as a surrogate mother for the daughter of a man she loves. The title comes from Walt Whitman's *Leaves of Grass*.

Nuts (1987) Drama ΨΨΨ
Barbra Streisand plays a prostitute who has killed a patron. She is resisting an insanity defense, and through flashbacks we learn that she was sexually abused as a child. Interesting examination of civil liberties and forensic psychiatry.

One Flew over the Cuckoo's Nest (1975)
Drama ΨΨΨΨ
Classic film with Jack Nicholson as Randle P. McMurphy, who takes on Nurse Ratched and the psychiatric establishment. The film offers good insight into life on an inpatient ward, although

> "Now tell me, do you think there is anything wrong with your mind?" "Not a thing, Doc. I'm a marvel of modern science."
> *One Flew over the Cuckoo's Nest* (1975)

the portrayal of ECT is stereotyped and inaccurate; in addition the suicide of Billy seems to be simplistically linked to his domineering mother. This film took all five of the top Oscars in 1975: Best Picture, Best Actor, Best Actress, Best Director, and Best Screenplay.

Passion of Joan of Arc, The (1928) Historical ΨΨΨ
Historically important silent film that portrays the burning of Joan of Arc as a heretic. The mental status of Joan of Arc remains a controversial subject for historians interested in psychopathology.

President's Analyst, The (1967) Spy/Comedy ΨΨ
James Coburn plays a psychoanalyst working for the President of the United States.

Pressure Point (1962) Drama ΨΨΨ
A black psychiatrist (Sidney Poitier) treats a racist patient (Bobby Darin). Based on a case from Linder's *The Fifty-Minute Hour*.

Prince of Tides, The (1991) Drama/Romance ΨΨΨ
Barbra Streisand plays a psychiatrist who becomes sexually involved with the brother of one of her patients (Nick Nolte). The film raises interesting questions about the proper limits of the doctor-patient relationship.

Rampage (1992) Drama/Thriller ΨΨΨ
William Friedkin film about an apparent sociopath who is arrested and tried for murder. The film raises important questions about capital punishment, the not guilty by reason of insanity (NGRI) plea, and the role of the expert witness in the courtroom.

TREATMENT

See You in the Morning (1989) Drama ΨΨ
A film about a Manhattan psychiatrist with multiple problems, including a failed first marriage. Interesting group therapy sequences, and lots of speculation about motivation and purpose.

Shock Corridor (1963) Drama ΨΨ
Samuel Fuller film in which a journalist has himself admitted to an insane asylum in order to get an inside story on a murder but soon becomes psychotic himself. The film is better than it sounds.

Spellbound (1945) Thriller ΨΨΨ
Ingrid Bergman plays a psychiatrist treating Gregory Peck's amnesia.

Still of the Night (1982) Thriller Ψ
A psychiatrist becomes romantically involved with a woman who may have murdered one of the psychiatrist's patients.

Teresa (1951) Drama Ψ
Notable only because it stars Rod Steiger in his first role. Steiger plays a psychiatrist in the film.

Through a Glass, Darkly (1962) Drama ΨΨΨΨ
Classic Bergman film that follows the life of a mentally ill woman after she is treated with ECT and released from a mental hospital.

Touched (1983) Romance Ψ
Two patients on a psychiatric ward fall in love and try to set up a life together after they escape.

Whispers in the Dark (1992) Thriller/Drama ΨΨ
This murder mystery revolves around a psychiatrist who becomes overly involved in the lives of her patients. Mainly useful as a vehicle for discussion of professional issues and lessons on how *not* to behave in therapy.

APPENDIX C

The American Film Institute's *100 Best of 100 Years*

1. *Citizen Kane (1941)*
2. *Casablanca (1942)*
3. *Godfather, The (1972)*
4. *Gone With the Wind (1939)*
5. *Lawrence of Arabia (1962)*
6. *Wizard of Oz, The (1939)*
7. *Graduate, The (1967)*
8. *On the Waterfront (1954)*
9. *Schindler's List (1993)*
10. *Singin' In the Rain (1952)*
11. *It's A Wonderful Life (1946)*
12. *Sunset Boulevard (1950)*
13. *Bridge On the River Kwai, The (1957)*
14. *Some Like It Hot (1959)*
15. *Star Wars (1977)*
16. *All About Eve (1950)*
17. *African Queen, The (1951)*
18. *Psycho (1960)*
19. *Chinatown (1974)*
20. *One Flew Over the Cuckoo's Nest (1975)*
21. *Grapes of Wrath, The (1940)*
22. *2001: A Space Odyssey (1968)*
23. *Maltese Falcon, The (1941)*
24. *Raging Bull (1980)*
25. *E.T. the Extra-Terrestrial (1982)*
26. *Dr. Strangelove (1964)*
27. *Bonnie & Clyde (1967)*
28. *Apocalypse Now (1979)*
29. *Mr. Smith Goes To Washington (1939)*
30. *Treasure of the Sierra Madre (1948)*
31. *Annie Hall (1977)*
32. *Godfather Part II, The (1974)*
33. *High Noon (1952)*
34. *To Kill A Mockingbird (1962)*
35. *It Happened One Night (1934)*

36.	*Midnight Cowboy (1969)*
37.	*Best Years of Our Lives, The (1946)*
38.	*Double Indemnity (1944)*
39.	*Doctor Zhivago (1965)*
40.	*North By Northwest (1959)*
41.	*West Side Story (1961)*
42.	*Rear Window (1954)*
43.	*King Kong (1933)*
44.	*Birth of A Nation, The (1915)*
45.	*Streetcar Named Desire, A (1951)*
46.	*Clockwork Orange, A (1971)*
47.	*Taxi Driver (1976)*
48.	*Jaws (1975)*
49.	*Snow White & the Seven Dwarfs (1937)*
50.	*Butch Cassidy & the Sundance Kid (1969)*
51.	*Philadelphia Story, The (1940)*
52.	*From Here To Eternity (1953)*
53.	*Amadeus (1984)*
54.	*All Quiet On the Western Front (1930)*
55.	*Sound of Music, The (1965)*
56.	*M*A*S*H (1970)*
57.	*Third Man, The (1949)*
58.	*Fantasia (1940)*
59.	*Rebel Without A Cause (1955)*
60.	*Raiders of the Lost Ark (1981)*
61.	*Vertigo (1958)*
62.	*Tootsie (1982)*
63.	*Stagecoach (1939)*
64.	*Close Encounters of the Third Kind (1977)*
65.	*Silence of the Lambs, The (1991)*
66.	*Network (1976)*
67.	*Manchurian Candidate, The (1962)*
68.	*American In Paris, An (1951)*
69.	*Shane (1953)*
70.	*French Connection, The (1971)*
71.	*Forrest Gump (1994)*
72.	*Ben-Hur (1959)*
73.	*Wuthering Heights (1939)*
74.	*Gold Rush, The (1925)*

75.   *Dances With Wolves (1990)*
76.   *City Lights (1931)*
77.   *American Graffiti (1973)*
78.   *Rocky (1976)*
79.   *Deer Hunter, The (1978)*
80.   *Wild Bunch, The (1969)*
81.   *Modern Times (1936)*
82.   *Giant (1956)*
83.   *Platoon (1986)*
84.   *Fargo (1996)*
85.   *Duck Soup (1933)*
86.   *Mutiny On the Bounty (1935)*
87.   *Frankenstein (1931)*
88.   *Easy Rider (1969)*
89.   *Patton (1970)*
90.   *Jazz Singer, The (1927)*
91.   *My Fair Lady (1964)*
92.   *Place In the Sun, A (1951)*
93.   *Apartment, The (1960)*
94.   *Goodfellas (1990)*
95.   *Pulp Fiction (1994)*
96.   *Searchers, The (1956)*
97.   *Bringing Up Baby (1938)*
98.   *Unforgiven (1992)*
99.   *Guess Who's Coming To Dinner (1967)*
100.   *Yankee Doodle Dandy (1942)*

REFERENCES

Abadinsky, H. (1993). *Drug abuse* (2nd ed.). Chicago: Nelson-Hall.

Abel, G. G., Becker, J. V., & Cunningham-Rathner, J. (1984). Complications, consent, and cognitions in sex between children and adults. *International Journal of Law and Psychiatry, 7,* 89–103

Allen, J., & Smith, W. (1993). Diagnosing dissociative disorders. *Bulletin of the Menninger Clinic, 57,* 328–343.

American Psychiatric Association (APA). (1994). *Diagnostic and statistical manual of mental disorders* (4th ed.). Washington, DC: Author.

Andreasen, N., Flaum, M., Swayze, V., Tyrrell, M., & Arndt, S. (1990). *Archives of General Psychiatry, 47,* 615–621.

Armstrong, R. B., & Armstrong, M. W. (1990). *The movie list book: A reference guide to film themes, settings, and series.* Jefferson, NC: McFarland & Company.

Arndt, W. B., Jr. (1991). *Gender disorders and the paraphilias.* Madison, CT: International Universities Press.

Bachman, R. (1993). Predicting the reporting of rape victimizations: Have rape reforms made a difference? *Criminal Justice and Behavior, 20,* 254–270.

Barnard, G.W., Fuller, A.K., Robbins, L., & Shaw, T. (1989). *The child molester: An integrated approach to evaluation and treatment.* New York: Brunner/Mazel, Inc.

Beauchamp, T., & Childress, J. (Eds.). (1989). *Principles of biomedical ethics.* New York: Oxford University Press.

Beck, A., & Emery, G. (1985). *Anxiety disorders and phobias: A cognitive perspective.* New York: Basic Books.

Beck, A., Rush, A. J., Shaw, B., & Emery, G. (Eds.). (1979). *Cognitive therapy of depression.* New York: Guilford Press.

Beck, A., Steer, R., Beck, J., & Newman, C. (1993). Hopelessness, depression, suicidal ideation, and clinical diagnosis of depression. *Suicide and Life–Threatening Behavior, 23,* 139–145.

Bernstein, E., & Putnam, F. (1986). Development, reliability, and validity of a dissociation scale. *The Journal of Nervous and Mental Diseases, 174,* 727–735.

Bianchi, M. D. (1990). Fluoxetine treatment of exhibitionism. *American Journal of Psychiatry, 147,* 1089–1090.

Blanchard, R., & Hucker, S. J. (1991). Age, transvestism, bondage, and concurrent paraphilic activities in 117 fatal cases of autoerotic asphyxia. *British Journal of Psychiatry, 159,* 371–377.

Boon, S., & Draijer, N. (1993). Multiple personality disorder in the Netherlands: A clinical investigation of 71 patients. *American Journal of Psychiatry, 150,* 489–494.

Bourdon, K., Rae, D., Locke, B., Narrow, W., & Regier, D. (1992). Estimating the prevalence of mental disorders in U.S. adults from the epidemiologic catchment area survey. *Public Health Reports, 107,* 663–668.

Briere, J. (1989). University males' sexual interest in children: Predicting potential indices of "pedophilia" in a nonforensic sample. *Child Abuse and Neglect, 13,* 65–75.

Buchbaum, M. S., Haler, R. J., Potkin, S. G., Nuechterlein, K., Stofan Bracha, H., Katz, M., Lohr, J., Wu, J., Lottenberg, S., Jerabeck, P.A., Trenary, M., Tafalla, R., Reynolds, C., & Bunney, W. E., Jr. (1987). Frontostriatal disorder of cerebral metabolism in never–medicated schizophrenics. *Archives of General Psychiatry, 49,* 935–942.

Butler, R., & Braff, D. (1991). Delusions: A review and integration. *Schizophrenia Bulletin, 17,* 633–647.

Canby, V. (1981). Review of *Arthur. New York Times* (July 17, p. 10).

Cantwell, D. (1989). Conduct disorders. In H. Kaplan & B. Sadock (Eds.), *Comprehensive textbook of psychiatry/v.* Baltimore, MD: Williams & Wilkins.

Cardea, E., & Spiegel, D. (1993). Dissociative reactions to the San Francisco Bay Area earthquake of 1989. *American Journal of Psychiatry, 150,* 474–478.

Casson, I. R., Siegel, O., Sham, R., Campbell, E. A., Tarlau, M., & DiDomenico, A. (1984). Brain damage in modern boxers. *The Journal of the American Medical Association, 251,* 2663–2667.

Centerwall, B. S. (1992). Vladimir Nabokov: A case study in pedophilia. *Psychoanalysis and Contemporary Thought, 15,* 199–239.

Chalkey, A. J., & Powell, E. E. (1983). The clinical description of forty–eight cases of sexual fetishism. *British Journal of Psychiatry, 142,* 292–295.

Cinemania 97. Microsoft Corporation (CD–ROM). Seattle, WA: Microsoft.

Classen, C., Koopman, C., & Spiegel, D. (1993). Trauma and dissociation. *Bulletin of the Menninger Clinic, 57,* 178–194.

de Sade, D. A. F. (1957). *The 120 days of Sodom.* Paris: Olympia Press.

Denzin, N. K. (1991). *Hollywood shot by shot: Alcoholism in American cinema.* New York: Aldine De Gruyter.

Dietz, P. E. , & Evans, B. (1982). Pornographic imagery and prevalence of paraphilia. *American Journal of Psychiatry, 139,* 1493–1495.

Dormire, S. (1993). Ethical models: Facilitating clinical practice. *Clinical Issues Perinatal Womens Health Nursing, 4,* 526–533.

Emery, A. E. H., & Mueller, R. F. (1992). *Elements of medical genetics.* New York: Churchill–Livingstone.

Felthous, A. (1993). Substance abuse and the duty to protect. *Bulletin of the American Academy of Psychiatry & the Law, 21,* 419–426.

Folstein, M.F., Folstein, S.E., & McHugh, P.R. (1975). Mini mental state. *Journal of Psychiatric Research, 12,* 196–198.

Ford, C. V. (1983). *The somatizing disorders: Illness as a way of life.* New York: Elsevier Biomedical.

Forsyth, C. (1992). Parade strippers: A note on being naked in public. *Deviant Behavior, 13,* 391–403.

Freund, K., Watson, R., & Dickey, R. (1990). Does sexual abuse in childhood cause pedophilia? An exploratory study. *Archives of Sexual Behavior, 19,* 557–568.

Gay, P. (Ed.). (1989). *The Freud reader.* New York: W. W. Norton & Company.

Geller, J., & Harris, M. (Eds.). (1994*). Women of the asylum: Voices from behind the walls, 1840–1945.* New York: Doubleday.

Goodwin, D.W. (1991). *Alcohol and the writer.* New York: Viking/Penguin.

Haas, L., & Haas, J. (1990). *Understanding sexuality.* St. Louis: Mosby.

Heinrichs, R. (1993). Schizophrenia and the brain. *American Psychologist, 48,* 221–223.

Helminski, F. (1993). Near the conflagration: The wide duty to warn. *Mayo Clinic Proceedings, 68,* 709–710.

Helzer, J. E., Canino, G. J., Yeh, E. K., Lee, C. K., Hwu, H. G., & Newman, S. (1990). Alcoholism — North America and Asia. *Archives of General Psychiatry, 47,* 313–319.

Hermann, D. (1990). Autonomy, self–determination, the right of involuntarily committed persons to refuse treatment, and the use of substituted judgment in medication decisions involving incompetent persons. *International Journal of Law and Psychiatry, 13,* 361–385.

Herold, E. E., Mantle, D., & Zemitis, O. (1979). A study of sexual offenses against females. *Adolescence, 14,* 65–72.

Hill, G. (1992). *Illuminating shadows: The mythic power of film.* Boston, MA: Shambhala Publishers.

Hoffmann, A. (1968). Psychotominetic agents. In A. Burger (Ed.*), Drugs affecting the central nervous system* (Vol. 2). New York: Marcel Dekker.

Holden, T.E., & Sherline, D.M. (1973). Bestiality, with sensitization and anaphylactic reaction. *Obstetrics & Gynecology, 42,* 138–140.

Holmes, R. M. (1991). *Sex crimes.* Newbury Park, CA: Sage.

Hyler, S. E. (1988). DSM–III at the cinema: Madness in the movies. *Comprehensive Psychiatry, 29,* 195–206.

Hyler, S. E., & Bujold, A. E. (1994). Computers and psychiatric education: The "Taxi Driver" mental status examination. *Psychiatric Annals, 24,* 13–19.

Hyler, S. E., Gabbard, G. O., & Schneider, I. (1991). Homicidal maniacs and narcissistic parasites: Stigmatization of mentally ill persons in the movies. *Hospital and Community Psychiatry, 42,* 1044–1048.

Innala, S. M., & Ernulf, K. E. (1992). Understanding male homosexual attraction. *Journal of Social Behavior and Personality, 7,* 503–510.

Jamison, K.R. (1993). *Touched with fire: Manic–depressive illness and the artistic temperament.* New York: The Free Press.

Kanas, N. (1988). Psychoactive substance use disorders: Alcohol. In H. H. Goldman (Ed.), *Review of general psychiatry* (2nd ed.). Norwalk, CT: Appleton & Lange.

Kellner, R. (1991). *Psychosomatic syndromes and somatic symptoms.* Washington, DC: American Psychiatric Press.

Kernberg, O. F. (1988). Clinical dimensions of masochism. *Journal of the American Psychoanalytic Association, 36,* 1005–1029.

Kernberg, O. F. (1994). The erotic in film and in mass psychology. *Bulletin of the Menninger Clinic, 58,* 88–108.

Kessler, R., McGonagle, K., Zhao, S., Nelson, C., Hughes, M., Eshleman, S., Wittchen, H., & Kendler, K. (1994). Lifetime and 12–month prevalence of DSM–III–R psychiatric disorders in the United States. *Archives of General Psychiatry, 51,* 8–19.

Kihlstrom, F., Glisky, M., & Angiulo, M. (1994). Dissociative tendencies and dissociative disorders. *Journal of Abnormal Psychology, 103,* 117–134.

Kluft, R. (1991). Multiple personality disorder. In A. Tasman & S. Goldfinger, (Eds.), *Review of psychiatry, volume 10* (pp. 161–188). Washington, DC: American Psychiatric Press.

Lazarus, J. (1994). Ethics (foreword). In J. Oldham & M. Riba (Eds.), *Review of Psychiatry, volume 13* (pp. 319–320). Washington, DC: American Psychiatric Press.

Lazarus, R., & Folkman, S. (1984). *Stress, appraisal and coping.* New York: Springer.

Lebegue, B. (1991). Paraphilias in the U.S. pornography titles: "Pornography made me do it" (Ted Bundy). *The Bulletin of the American Academy of Psychiatry and the Law, 19,* 43–48.

Lee, K. (in press). Anxiety disorders. In M. A. Boyd & M. A. Nihart (Eds.), *Psychiatric mental health nursing.* New York: J. B. Lippincott.

Li, D., & Spiegel, D. (1992). A neural network model of dissociative disorders. *Psychiatric Annals, 22,* 144–147.

Lowenstein, R. (1991). Psychogenic amnesia and psychogenic fugue: A comprehensive review. In A. Tasman & S. Goldfinger, (Eds.), *Review of Psychiatry, volume 10* (pp. 189–222). Washington, DC: American Psychiatric Press.

Lowenstein, R. (1993). Dissociation, development and the psychobiology of trauma. *Journal of the American Academy of Psychoanalysis, 21,* 581–603.

Maltin, L. (Ed.). (1994). *Leonard Maltin's movie and video guide.* New York: Penguin Books.

Manschreck, T. (1989) Delusional (paranoid) disorders. In H. Kaplan & B. Sadock (Eds.), *Comprehensive textbook of psychiatry/v* (816–829). Baltimore, MD: Williams & Wilkins.

Markway, B. G., Carmin, C. N., Pollard, C. A., & Flynn, T. (1992). *Dying of embarrassment: Help for social anxiety and phobia.* Oakland, CA: New Harbinger.

Miller, N., & Gold, M. S. (1990). Benzodiazepines reconsidered. *Advances in Alcohol and Substance Abuse, 8,* 67–81.

Monahan, J., & Shah, S. A. (1989). Dangerousness and commitment of the mentally disordered in the United States. *Schizophrenia Bulletin, 15,* 541–553.

North, C., & Smith, E. (1992). Posttraumatic stress disorder among homeless men and women. *Hospital and Community Psychiatry, 43,* 1010–1016.

O'Connor, N. (1989). The performance of the "idiot–savant:" Implicit and explicit. *British Journal of Disorders of Communication, 24,* 1–20.

Omnibus Budget Reconciliation Act of 1990. Public Law No. 101–158 Paragraph 4206, 4751.

Paniagua, C., & DeFazio, A. (1989). Psychodynamics of the mildly retarded and borderline–intelligence adult. In R. J. Fletcher & F. J. Menolascino (Eds.), *Mental retardation and mental illness.* Lexington, MA: Lexington Books.

Perilstein, R. D., Lipper, S., & Friedman, L. J. (1991). Three cases of paraphilias responsive to fluoxetine treatment. *Journal of Clinical Psychiatry, 52,* 169–170.

Pettis, R. (1992). Tarasoff and the dangerous driver: A look at the driving cases. *The Bulletin of the American Academy of Psychiatry and the Law, 20,* 427–437.

Pettis, R., & Gutheil, T. (1993). Misapplication of the *Tarasoff* duty to driving cases: A call for a reframing of theory. *The Bulletin of the American Academy of Psychiatry and the Law, 21,* 263–275.

Putnam, F. (1985). Multiple personality disorder. *Medical Aspects of Human Sexuality, 19,* 59–74.

Putnam, F. (1991). Dissociative phenomena. In A. Tasman & S. Goldfinger, (Eds.), *Review of psychiatry, volume 10* (pp. 145–160). Washington, DC: American Psychiatric Press.

Rabkin, L. Y. (1977). *The celluloid couch: Psychiatrists in American films.* Annual meeting, American Psychological Association, San Francisco.

Rappaport, E. A. (1968). Zoophily and zoerasty. *Psychoanalytic Quarterly, 37,* 565–587.

Rebal, R. F., Faguet, R. A., & Woods, S. M. (1982). Unusual sexual syndromes. In C. T. H. Friedmann & R. A. Faguet (Eds.), *Extraordinary disorders of human behavior* (pp. 121–54). New York: Plenum.

Regier, D., Narrow, W., & Rae, D. (1990). The epidemiology of anxiety disorders: The epidemiologic catchment area (ECA) experience. *Journal of Psychiatric Research, 24,* 3–14.

Ressler, R. (1986). Murderers who rape and mutilate. *Journal of Interpersonal Violence, 1,* 273–287.

Russell, D. E. H. (1983). The incidence and prevalence of intrafamilial and extrafamilial sexual abuse of female children. *Child Abuse and Neglect, 7,* 133–146.

Russell, D. E. H. (1984). The prevalence and seriousness of incestuous abuse: Stepfathers vs. biological fathers. *Child Abuse and Neglect, 8,* 15–22.

Sabatino, C. (1993). Surely the wizard will help us, Toto? Implementing the patient self–determination act. *Hastings Center Report, 23,* 12–16.

Sacks, O. (1985). *The man who mistook his wife for a hat and other clinical tales.* New York: Summit Books.

Saxe, G., van der Kolk, B.A., Berkowitz, R., Chinman, G., Hall, K., Lieberg, G., & Schwartz, J. (1993). Dissociative disorders in psychiatric inpatients. *American Journal of Psychiatry, 150,* 1037–1042.

Schreiber, R. (1973). *Sybil.* Chicago: Henry Regnery.

Schulz, S., & Tamming, C. (Eds). (1989). *Schizophrenia: Scientific progress.* New York: Oxford University Press.

Shabecoff, P. (1987). Stress and the lure of harmful remedies. *New York Times,* October 14, 12.

Shaffer, D. (1989). Child psychiatry. In H. Kaplan & B. Sadock (Eds.), *Comprehensive textbook of psychiatry/v.* Baltimore, MD: Williams & Wilkins.

Smith, G. R., Jr. (1990). *Somatization disorder in the medical setting.* DHHS Pub. No. (ADM)90–1631. Washington, DC: U.S. Govt. Printing Office.

Steinberg, M. (1991). The spectrum of depersonalization: Assessment and treatment. In A. Tasman & S. Goldfinger (Eds.), *Review of psychiatry, volume 10* (pp. 223–247). Washington, DC: American Psychiatric Press.

Strasburger, V.C., & Willis, E. (1998). Media violence. *Pediatric Clinics of North America, 45,* 319–331.

Sullivan, H. (1953). *The interpersonal theory of psychiatry.* New York: W.W. Norton.

Swift, W. J., & Wonderlich, S. (1993). House of Games: A cinematic study of countertransference. *American Journal of Psychotherapy, 47,* 38–57.

Szymanski, L.S., & Crocker, A.C. (1989). In B.J. Sadock (Ed.), *Comprehensive textbook of psychiatry* (5th ed.). Baltimore, MD: Williams & Wilkins.

Trachtenberg, R. (1986). Destigmatizing mental illness. *The Psychiatric Hospital, 17,* 111–114.

Uhde, T., Tancer, M., Black, B., & Brown, T. (1991). Phenomenology and neurobiology of social phobia: Comparison with panic disorder. *Journal of Clinical Psychiatry, 52,* 31–40.

Veitia, M. C., & McGahee, L. (1995). Ordinary addictions: Tobacco and alcohol. In D. Wedding (Ed.), *Behavior and medicine* (2nd ed.). St. Louis: Mosby–Yearbook.

Weaver, J. B., Brosius, H., & Mundorf, N. (1993). Personality and movie preferences: A comparison of American and German audiences. *Personality and Individual Differences, 14,* 307–315.

Wedding, D., & Corsini, R. (1995*). Current psychotherapies.* Itasca, IL: Peacock.

Wettstein, R. (1994). Confidentiality. In J. Oldham and M. Riba (Eds.). *Review of psychiatry, volume 13.* Washington, DC: American Psychiatric Press.:

Woodward, B. (1985). *Wired: The short life and fast times of John Belushi*. New York: Pocket Books.

Young, F., Newcorn, J., & Leven, L. (1989). Pervasive developmental disorders. In H. Kaplan & B. Sadock (Eds.), *Comprehensive textbook of psychiatry/v*. Baltimore, MD: Williams & Wilkins.

Zellman, G. (1992). The impact of case characteristics on child abuse reporting decisions. *Child Abuse and Neglect, 16,* 57–74.

INDEX